C'MON THE FERRY

A HISTORY OF BRITON FERRY RFC 1888–2014

"For the Ferry team are a grand old team"

Martyn Bate

First published 2020 by Shakspeare Editorial for BFRFC

Typesetting and design: www.shakspeareeditorial.org

With thanks to Media Wales for permission to use extracts from local papers

This book is dedicated to the Ferry's own 'Stadler and Waldorf'

Leighton Bate **and** Haydn Best

**My late father and father-in-law never missed a
match between them, home or away**

I hope they are looking down with satisfaction, pleasure and pride

CONTENTS

ILLUSTRATIONS

ACKNOWLEDGEMENTS

With thanks to all of the following for their stories, pictures and memorabilia, without which my job would have been even more difficult:

Roger Amphlett*
Kevin Bowring
Heather Broom
Chris Chappell
Keith Davies
Jonathan Davies
Malcolm Edwards
John Evans
Brian Evans
Mrs Griffiths-Phil
Ken Harris
Allan Hopkins*
Spike Hughes, Barnstaple RFC
Jim Jones
Howard Jones, Glamorgan County RFC
Meiner Keefe
Tony Lewis Pyle
Ron Lilley
National Library of Wales
Neath Courier
Neath Guardian
Neath Library
Barrie Nicholls*
David Parker, for 1955 tour to Ireland photos and report
Keith Phillips
Gwyn Prescott, for his book Call Them to Remembrance
Mike Price, Neath RFC
Cyril Roberts*
Jonathan Skidmore
South Wales Daily Post
South Wales Echo
South Wales Evening Post
Keith Standing*
Swansea Library
Brian Tobin
Frank Williams
Billy Williams*
Myra Woodlands

* deceased

And for much needed funding, my thanks to:

Mrs. J.C. Phillips
Mr. S. Lewis
Mr. D. Whitelock
Mr R. Lilley
BFRFC Supporters
BFRFC
Mr N. Lovering
Mr J. Hicks
Mr M. Moran
Briton Ferry Town Council

And a massive thanks to my wife Jillian and to my family for being so patient with me in my quest

FOREWORD

Well, they said it would never be completed. It has been a labour of love for over 15 years, and at times very stressful, but I hope that you will find some enjoyment in this book. Whether you are a former or current player, a coach, a committeeman, a supporter or a family member, if you are looking for memories, I hope you find them within!

A substantial amount of club history has been destroyed, mostly by fire. The first time was when the club was based in the Harp Hotel, and a blaze destroyed all the pre-1914 records. The second was when a member's son decided to help the war effort, after a 1940 appeal for waste paper, by giving all the club records to this great cause! Then, in 1957, a fire in the Grandison base destroyed all the old photos, four sets of jerseys, five balls, track suits, boots and souvenirs of post-war tours – then valued at about £200!

So, with the best will in the world, the contents had to rely on snippets in the press,* word of mouth and, in some cases, family memorabilia. This means they are necessarily incomplete and may not be wholly accurate. If, after reading this volume, you think you have something to add, or have any extra information at all, the author would be glad to hear from you via BFRC, and is happy to make amendments.

Martyn Bate

* such as regular reports in the *Neath Gazette* made by a writer known as "old un"

When the records talk about a minor, I believe this was when a player touched down behind his own try line, a bit like an own goal, which resulted in a point for the opposition

THE FERRY SONG

*In the evening by the moonlight
you can hear those banjos playing
In the evening by the moonlight
you can see those singers swaying.*

*And the old folks they enjoy it
as they sit around and listen,
to the music of the banjos in the moonlight.*

*Moonlight, moonlight, jolly fine moonlight
moonlight, moonlight night*

*Moonlight, moonlight, jolly fine moonlight
moonlight, moonlight night*

*Farewell ladies, farewell ladies, farewell ladies,
we're going to leave you now
Merrily we roll along, roll along, roll along,
merrily we roll along o'er the deep blue sea*

*For the Ferry team are a grand old team
whenever we're on tour
We don't shout, we throw the ball about
and that's how we get the score*

*We have two old stalwarts in Roy and Sam,
they always tell you to take your man
So we're going on a tour to the Isle of Man,
look out here we come.*

*Sherovoldi, Sherovoldi Shiva,
Sherovoldi, Sherovoldi Shiva,
Sherovoldi, Sherovoldi Shiva,
Lah de dido stitch, stich stitch*

*Beto, Beto, Beto Beto, lah di di di dido
Beto, Beto, Beto Beto, lah di di di dido
Beto, Beto, Beto Beto, lah di di di dido*

*Lah de dido stitch, stich stitch
F E Double R Y –
FERRY*

INTRODUCTION

There were a number of rugby teams in the Briton Ferry area prior to 1888, such as The Crusaders, Melbourne, W.H.P. Jenkins XV, Briton Ferry Athletic, Briton Ferry All Whites, BF. Excels, Grandos, Village Boys and Giant's Grave. Steelworkers were always the backbone of the Ferry teams, which were later strengthened by the arrival of players from close neighbours the Melyn Barbarians club.

The formation of Briton Ferry RFC in 1888 created a great deal of interest within the local community and in the early years, the club flourished out of its headquarters in a local pub, The Grandison. The local estate agent, Mr W.H.P. Jenkins was virtually the father of the club and was instrumental in getting a lease on the ground in the early 1900s. He donated a set of jerseys, in royal blue with gold and white hoops, on behalf of the Earl of Jersey (his brother in law). The Earl's racing colours gave the club an identity that survives to this day (although around 1925/26 the jersey colours went black and amber until they reverted back to blue and gold in 1949/50).

The name Briton Ferry has been touted as coming from very early times. When Geraldus Cambrensis crossed the river Neath at this point in 1188 with Archbishop Baldwin, he crossed in a boat, so the town of the bridge became the town of the ferry: Bridgetown Ferry or Brigeton Ferry or Briton Ferry.

There were early signs that the Ferry would influence Welsh rugby. The first secretary of the reconstituted South Wales Football Union in 1879 was a Briton Ferry man, Maurice Ivor Morris, who had been educated at

Cheltenham College. He apparently played cricket better than he did rugby, and made many influential rugby contacts through playing for South Wales Cricket Club.

> Local doctor, E.V. PEGGE, was capped at forward against England. He was a Neath player at the time, a club that was considered to be well off. Pegge proved it to be so when he missed the departure of the team for their tour of Devon in 1887. So he chartered a special train to catch up with the them! He was also voted on to the Welsh Union committee in 1892, along with Gavin Henry of Llanelli, as representative for the West Wales region.

I.1 Doctor Pegge

The Ynysymaerdy ground was originally acquired from the Earl of Jersey as a permanent home for cricket in 1887. He was a generous benefactor: providing facilities free of rent; fencing the ground; taking steps to improve the wicket; ensuring that a number of former county players were hired as professionals or groundsmen. All of which made the Briton Ferry Town C.C. one of the top sides in the area.

> The EARL OF JERSEY was president of the WFU from September 1881 to 1885, which was seen as a drive for respectability by the union, as he was a top peer of the realm. Victor Albert George Child-Villiers, 7th Earl of Jersey (1845–1915), was educated at Eton and Balliol, he was a grandson of Robert Peel, and a descendant of Henry VII. The founder of his line, the first Earl, had distinguished himself in the civil war during the seventeenth century – probably on the side of Oliver Cromwell! He owned 19,400 acres, half of which were in Glamorgan. His estates provided him with annual income of £18,000 but, as a generous benefactor of both the Briton Ferry and St Thomas areas, he spent £60,000 on a variety of public amenities, from roads to libraries and sports facilities (his favourite sport was amateur athletics). He was paymaster-general of the Salisbury Conservative government in 1889 and governor-general of New South Wales (1890–1893).

PART 1: 1888–1900

1.1 Briton Ferry Excelsiors Football Team 1899/1900

1888/89–1889/90

The first captain of the side was G. Phillips, who also went on to captain the 1889/91 season. The first club secretary was Mr Brinley Aubrey. The earliest report of a game was that played against Morriston Second XV, in October at Morriston. Briton Ferry lost by 1 try and 6 minors to 3 minors. The *Neath Gazette* said it was an 'evenly contested game'.

Later in October they played at home to Neath Second XV and were again defeated by 2 minors to 1.

Other local teams reported at the time were Melyn Rovers, Llansamlet Harriers, Melbourne and Brynymor from Swansea.

The Ferry Second XV were next reported in November in a local derby match against Vernon Excelsiors. The Excelsiors won by 1 try and 3 minors to 2 minors. The secretary of the Excelsiors was Mr J.G. Burns of Ritson Street, who requested that if any junior team (aged from 15–17 years) within 12 miles would like to play them to contact him. The First XV were short of players in the next match at the Ferry against Morriston. They were joined by some of the Second XV and managed to eke out a victory by 1 try and 2 minors to one penalty.

The Excelsiors were reported to have played the Village Boys from the Swansea area in January of 1891. They lost by 1 goal, 5 tries, and 6 minors to 0!

A report in December stated that an away game at Swansea Harlequins was delayed by the late arrival of the Ferry team, who then had to cajole the Swansea side to eventually play the game. The second half was played in

Captain
G. Phillips

5

total darkness. The scores were Harlequins 1 try and 2 minors to the Ferry's 2 minors.

The final reported game in December was an away game at Stradey Park against Llanelli A, where they went down to a heavy defeat by 1 goal and 4 tries to 0.

Then in the New Year, on 19 January, the club played against a team from GWR locos (Neath), defeating them by 1 try and 4 minors to 0.

F. O. Hutchinson
Briton Ferry - Neath Wales
1894 - 1896

1.2 F.O. Hutchinson

FRED HUTCHINSON played three times for Wales, and also represented Glamorgan County RFC in their first game at Lancashire in October 1892 while playing for Neath RFC.

1890/91

The papers reported that Ferry played at home to Llansamlet Harriers. A very close game ended in a draw in favour of the Harriers, 5 minors to 3.

A report of a match at home, Briton Ferry Harlequins v. Neath Abbey, states the Ferry won by 2 tries and 3 minors to 3 minors. D. Steer and T. Harris were the try scorers, T. Davies kicked a goal.

On tour

There was a report that the club had travelled by boat to play Jersey Marine.

Captain
G.L. Pegge

1891/92

As the club's profile was rising, there were several match reports in local papers.

They played at Morriston Second XV in September and lost by 1 try and 5 minors to 3 minors.

On a very rainy 10 October they hosted Neath RFC Second XV on a wet, slippery pitch, refereed by Mr W.H. Thomas of Morriston Rugby Club. The Ferry kicked off through Hopkin Thomas after winning the toss, but Neath's rushes were fast and furious in the first half. The Ferry had the better of the play in the second half. The score was 2 minors to 1 to Neath.

On 7 November they played host to Glynneath. Apparently, the referee gave a free kick to the Ferry which Glynneath disputed to such an extent that they left the ground – and lost by 2 minors to 1 drop goal.

Captain
H. Hutchinson

On Saturday 21 November there was a report of a match between the Ferry and Morriston. The Ferry were shorn of eight of their first team for this game and had to use players from their second team, but they gave a good account of themselves and had the best of the game throughout. The visitors were lucky to score a penalty goal against the Ferry's score of 1 try and 2 minors.

It seems that the missing players, en-bloc and without notice, had travelled to see Swansea v. Newport instead of playing in their own match. This was disappointing as Morriston were one of the top sides in the area and a full-strength side could have given the Ferry a famous victory.

In December, the Ferry arrived late for the kick-off against Swansea Harlequins, which caused much confusion (a repetition of their visit in the 1888/89 season).

Instead of 3 p.m it ended up starting at 4.45 p.m and lasted only a quarter of an hour each way. Once again it ended in complete darkness, with a similar score line of 1 try and 1 minor for Harlequins to the Ferry's 2 minors. Most of the Swansea team had drifted away long before the kick-off to watch the Swansea and Cardiff Second XV match.

The Ferry were also in the Llanelli A Team fixture list for the season and played them away in December and at home in January.

1892/93

A game against the Harriers at Llansamlet was played out in bad weather in front of a very small crowd. The Ferry were reported as having the heavier side, but the home team were a little smarter in the open. Final score was 2 tries and 3 minors to 0 in favour of the home side.

Captain
H. Hutchinson

Match results place BFRFC scores first

1893/94

The change in scoring values lasted until 1904/05.

Captain

Sid May

Score values

Try became 3 points
Conversion 2 points

11

1894/95

Mr J.R. Davies became club secretary.

A practice game under Rugby rules was played at Baglan ground and it was reported that the Ferryites would become a formidable crowd to encounter.

On 13 October they played Aberavon Excelsiors on the Baglan ground and were 1 try and 1 minor down at half-time. After some stout defence from Johnson and some good back play from the half-backs (Reverends Davies and Williams), they managed to convert a Davies try to win the game.

> By coincidence, the first association football match played in Briton Ferry was at the cricket field on Saturday 11 November 1894 against Neath, which the Ferry won 1–0, scored by Arthur Williams.

Captain
T.G. Myers

The 'Baglan rugby team' then beat Aberavon Excelsiors in a return match by 3 tries to 0, Tom, Jack and Evan Davies were the scorers. This meant that they had gone unbeaten for six matches on the trot.

They were due to play Tondu at home on 9 March 1895, but Tondu didn't turn up. So Ferry hastily arranged a game against Skewen, which didn't kick off until 5 p.m, by which time some Ferry players had gone missing, so they fielded a weakened side. Hopkin Thomas kicked off for the home side, but they soon found themselves in trouble at half-time and were down by 5 minors to 0. They rallied in the second half and ended the game victorious by 1 goal and one try to 5 minors – Poley and Dan Morgan scored tries, and D. Davies the goal. Prominent players for the Ferry were half-backs Evan Davies and Morgan, Poley in the centre and Davey at fullback. A newspaper article

Match results place BFRFC scores first

mentions that a photograph of the team was on display in the window of Mr Perrett, tobacconist, and that the team had come on well and were an ideal football club who had won every match played thus far this year.

Annual supper

On 4 May 1895, the club held it's first Annual Supper at the Dock Hotel. Members of the 'Baglan Football Club' and a few friends sat down to an excellent supper prepared by the hostess Mrs. Norman. The president, Mr W.H.P. Jenkins JP, presided over the entertainment, assisted by M.H. Hunter and Fred Hutchinson. This comprised:

- an overture played by Mr W. Hughes (Cymmer), accompanist for the evening
- the chairman's toast to the Queen and the Prince and Princess of Wales, drunk with musical honours
- a song from Mr R. Phillips
- a club report read by Mr Daniel Prosser, which showed that the club had played fifteen matches, won ten, drawn one and only lost four
- the financial statement, which showed a small deficiency that was very kindly put right by the president
- a duet sung by Messrs S.R. Poley and J. Perrett
- Mr T. Thomas proposed a toast to the President, Lord Jersey, Lord Villiers, Mr R.W. Llewelyn and Mrs Llewelyn. He spoke of their past generosity and that he hoped they would find them a field for next season
- a few more songs from Messrs Matt Hughes, F. Hutchinson and Dan Morgan
- Mr W.H.P. Jenkins responded to the toast by thanking Mrs Llewelyn for giving them a field last season, and stating that he would do his best to find one for them next season, he also complimented the team on their past success and hoped that further success would follow
- Mr H. Perrett and Mr T. Thomas sung some Welsh songs
- Mr M.H. Hunter proposed a toast to the club, followed by responses from Mr J.R. Davies (captain), Mr Daniel Prosser (secretary) and Mr Reginald Poley on behalf of the committee
- Some comic songs then followed from Mr M. Pughes and Hopkin Thomas

- Mr Lewis Jenkins, who joined the party during the toasts, stated that he would be pleased to give an annual subscription to the club
- The chairman then proposed a toast to the hostess for excellent catering and a fine evening.

1895/96

On 21 September 1895, Mr Leyshon Williams of Hunter Street formed a new team, the Briton Ferry Thursdays. Several junior teams were sprouting up, which helped to strengthen the senior club. They were all looking forward to a good season with a good fixture list made up by Mr Dan Prosser the energetic secretary.

> The club was now playing on a new field on the Old Road, the 74-year lease to which was kindly acquired and donated by Mr W.H.P. Jenkins, club president and brother-in-law to the Earl of Jersey. Somebody quipped that if the club continued the success of the previous season they might be able to erect some changing rooms, and may also need to build a press box!

The season started with a win over a District XV by 1 goal and 1 try to 0. They played with a two three-quarter formation, the other two going forward! Halves Jack Jones and Evan Davies and threes Tom Davies, Poley, Fred Gwynne and Gwyn Thomas, all played well.

Captain
T.G. Myers

On 12 October, a reporter from the *Neath and Mid Glamorgan Gazette* stated that he'd approached the Old Road ground to attend a match against Neath YMCA and was astounded to find that the ground was guarded all around by canvas, which made him think that he was entering a first-class ground. The game ended in a 0–0 draw, which was a little disappointing. Meanwhile, the second team were playing away at Clydach and won with 2 goals (1 drop goal) and 1 try to 0.

A 0–0 draw at home followed, against local rivals Melyn Quins, who were playing in the Swansea and District Football league. Ferry lost the return match in Neath at the end of October, by 2 tries and 2 minors to 2 minors.

November got off to a great start when both the senior and Second XV teams produced victories over Aberavon A (who had previously been unbeaten, hence their nickname, Giant's Grave) in Aberavon. The First XV scored 2 tries to 1 drop goal; the Second XV beat them at home by 2 tries to 0.

The First XV followed this up with another away victory, 2 tries to 0, at Swansea East Side Stars. The team selected was: back Dan Morgan; three-quarters T. Davies (captain), G. Poley, A. Davey and G. Williams; half-backs Evan Davies and Jack Jones; forwards R. Davies, T. Harry, Brown, C. Thomas, H. Richards, Fay, H. Lewis and J. Davies.

In the next game, Llwynpia Second XV at home, two changes were made to the Ferry team, D. Evans and J. Phillips up front for Fay and J. Davies.

In the December return game against Aberavon A, the Ferry were victors once again, this time by 2 goals and 1 try to 0 (with Evan Davies dropping two goals and T. Parry scoring the try). Baglan resident Mr W.H.P. Jenkins, JP, kicked off the match!

In the return match at home to the East Side Stars the Ferry was once again victorious by 2 tries to 0, which brought the year to an end.

1896/97–1899/1900

Sid Lewis took over as captain for the 1896/97 season, followed by W. John and then Jack Williams, before the century was seen out by Phil Martin.

In October 1898 the Ferry, then known as the Athletic, took on the Neath Excelsiors and beat them by 3 tries to 1. The papers noted that the team was a good one and that they should stick together and go on to have a good season.

On 29 April 1899, there were reports of a match against Glynneath in the final of a local cup competition, defeating them by 1 minor (11 points to 0) this was probably the first trophy win for the club.

Around this time the club was based in the old Jersey Hotel and was playing on the Gould field (behind the police station).

In January 1900 the *Neath Gazette* reported that only the Dingle (Skewen) had managed a win on the Ferry ground so far this season, where they were due to play Swansea Second XV the following week. In their first meeting earlier that season, Ferry had been heavily defeated by 7 goals and unfortunately, once again, they were defeated by 4 goals and 2 tries to 0. Half-backs Rogers and Evan Thomas and S. John and Arthur Davey were the pick of the Ferry team that had drawn 0–0 away at Llansamlet the previous week. The team consisted of: fullback D.J. Parker; three-quarters E. Thomas, H. Rogers, D.J. Howells and A. Llewelyn; half-backs T. Wilson and P. Martin; forwards J. Evans, A. Davey, A. Lewis, S. John, G. Smart, D. Smart, R. Richards and T. Mills.

Captains

Sid Lewis 1896/97
W. John 1897/98
Jack Williams 1898/99
Phil Martin 1899/1900

PART 2: 1900-1910

2.1 Briton Ferry Rugby Team 1900/01 outside the Grandison (donated by Jeff Hawes)

1900/01

In this season the club was admitted to the WRU as a full member.

In October 1900 it was reported that the team had become defunct and that the playing field was to be taken over by a young team called the Excelsiors, but the side was back up and running in November. However, Neath Excelsiors beat them by 2 tries. The game report stated that the Ferry players let their tempers get the better of them.

AGM

The end of season AGM was held at the Harp Hotel. The officers elected for the following season were: captain, Mr George Llewelyn; vice captain, Mr Harry Rogers; treasurer, Mr J. Mainwaring; and secretary, Mr W.J. Donovan of Hunter Street.

Youth rugby

Other junior teams were popping up, such as the Mansel Excelsiors, who lost 3–5 to St Catherine's in January 1901 – Nash Davey was the try scorer.

Captain
Arthur Davy

1901/02

This season had a lively fixture list.

The side defeated Sketty by 23–0 in October. The game was reported to have been played with a fine spirit and in front of a large crowd – even some of the club's vice presidents turned up for the game.

> The *Neath Gazette* reported that in previous weeks people had been seen 'skulking around' on the outside road in order to view the game without paying!

This was followed by a visit to play the unbeaten Swansea Excelsiors. The side selected was: fullback D. Poley; threes Humphreys, Rogers, Thomas and Evans; halves new lad Crocker and D. Williams; forwards White, Dean, Campbell, G. Phillips, A. Davey, D. Phillips, T. Davies and Ben Phillips.

Captain
George Phillips

The following week they were away at St Helens to play Swansea Second XV, and were defeated by 3–10. Wing Humphreys scored the Ferry's try. The Reds, as they were called then, played well but were outdone by a heavier pack.

Treorchy reserves were the visitors for the next game and, once again, the Ferry fell to a narrow last-minute defeat by 1 try to 0. Half-back Will Davies had transferred to Aberavon, so Phil Martin had been asked to turn out. The practice was for the away team to bring their own referee and, unfortunately, there was a disallowed try by Humphreys.

The Swansea Excelsiors failed to keep the next engagement, so they faced a District XV. They were beaten in a fast game and the Second XV gave a good

Match results place BFRFC scores first

account of themselves before succumbing to a stronger Ferry XV by 3 goals and 4 tries to 1 goal (27–5).

Once again fate was against Ferry as the next planned fixture was cancelled and a game was hastily arranged against previously unbeaten Neath Excelsiors. Ferry lost to a last-minute field goal. They were well beaten up front, but in the loose and in the back division they were far superior, especially wing Harry Humphries, half-back Phil Martin and fullback Poley. It was also reported that if they trained then they'd win more matches, and that they must learn to heel out cleanly so as to give their backs (a really smart lot!) a chance to handle and get tries, which they were more than capable of doing.

The next opponents were Skewen, whose side included ex-Neath players Harry Hanford, Charlie Morris and J. Evans, and brothers Curtis and Beynon of Maesteg. A record gate was expected in the Ferry. The crowd was not disappointed as the game was a cracker, despite losing Davey after just ten minutes, and then having to play a forward at outside-half. The Ferry won by 1 try to 0. The Second XV were also playing, with: fullback Daniels; threes Bennett, D. Phillips, Sam Morgan and R. White; halves D. Davies and W. Powell; and forwards W. Phillips, D. Jones, J. Bowen, J. Edwards, W. Morris, C. Thomas, Evan Griffiths, C. Callen, R. Phillips and D. Price.

Further fixtures up to Christmas were against Bryncethin, Britannia and Ogmore Vale at home.

On Christmas Day they lost at home to Swansea Excelsiors by 1 try to 0 in a complacent display.

The first game of the new year was against Swansea A at home. Unfortunately, they were a little under strength without Humphries, Crocker, Johnson or the captain, Llewelyn. They succumbed by a score of 4 goals and 2 tries to 0. The crowd was a reasonable size, despite the poor conditions.

A dour home draw with Gilfach followed, in which the home fullback, Evan J. Davies, was the pick of the team, along with Rogers and Howell Jones. Once again, the visiting side's referee proved a little tetchy and disallowed a perfectly good score – as far as the home side were concerned!

The next game came at the end of January, against a strong Llangennech side, followed with a visit to Glyncorrwg on a cold and windy day. Ferry came away with an 11–0 victory. Tries from Rogers, Howell Jones and Humphries and the game was refereed by Evan J. Davies!

Some changes were made for the next game against Britannia of Swansea; in came Noah on the wing, Southwood Thomas at half-back and forwards George Llewelyn, B. Allen, Dean, Matthews and Tom Davies. Once again, they were let down by a side who didn't turn out for the game.

A visit to Llangennech was next, but without such key players as Poley, Thomas, Phillips, Matthews and Mills. They put up a good fight but lost by 1 goal to 0 (0–5)

The next opponents were Crynant. Ferry were without Harry Rogers for the first time this season, and they also made a change up front, picking P.C. Newton for a trial match.

Gilfach away was the next challenge and they came away with a good victory of 1 goal and 2 tries to 0 (11–0, wing Humphries scored 2 tries).

In a midweek match against the Neath Crusaders, at Neath, Ferry totally overran their opponents, outscoring them by 3 goals and 4 tries to 0. Humphreys bagged a hat trick and Newton, Matthews and Phillips were the try scorers.

They were back on their travels the following Saturday, this time to Bryncethin. Not only were they playing against the home team, but also against players from Bridgend, Tondu and Maesteg. They came out victorious by 11–8 (Allen, W. Phillips and Rogers were the try scorers).

Ferry finished the season with games against Neath Excelsiors, Neath Thursdays (on Good Friday in the Ferry), Ogmore Vale (away), Ton Pentre (home) and Maesteg (away).

Tour

On Boxing Day morning Ferry set off on their first ever tour, to Tenby, an unbeaten home side. Ferry took their home record with 1 drop goal to 0 (from half-back S. Thomas). They were reported to have had a grand time and returned home on the evening of Friday 27 December.

Other news

It was also reported that the Ferry soccer side used the rugby field for a game against Swansea Teachers, as the cricket field was having a new square laid. Incidentally, the Whites (as the soccer team were called) won by 1–0.

1902/03

The season opened with a practice game and some new players, such as H. Jones at fullback, M. Powell at three-quarter, Walter Jenkins at half-back and P.C. Lisk up front.

Their first game was at Bryncethin, which they lost 0–11.

The Second XV were due to play away to Aberavon All Whites, but the opposition cancelled the game. It was reported that the First XV were to travel to the game on the 1.30 p.m. GWR.

> As the Ferry were now full WRU members the fixtures were stepping up a level. This also meant that the Union supplied referees for the games, which was reported to have raised the standards of both players and supporters!

Taibach were defeated at their home ground, 10–5. Walter Jenkins scored a fine try and Howell Jones and T. Nicholls were prominent. It was reported that the Taibach supporters were "greatly interested in the football, as the referee can testify" – no change there then!

Captain
George Phillips

> The papers noted that the club had the strongest fixture list so far in their history (included in which were the Newport Second XV) and that they had plenty of players, a good captain, an energetic secretary and a hard-working set of committee men – no change there either.

The might of the Newport Second XV were next, at home. Despite a brave performance Ferry lost 3–11, the only score was a fine try by Allen.

A visit to Treherbert gave Ferry another win, this time by 3–0 with Harry Rogers scoring the only try. Ferry went to this match four or five senior players short and so did well to come away with the win. It was reportedly a very rough game in which the home side had a predisposition to "have the man" after the ball had gone. The report also said that the "chesty ones who only played at home should not be selected at all."

Meanwhile the Second XV played out a home draw with Kenfig Hill.

The First XV's next opponents were Aberavon All Whites. The team consisted of: fullback S. Daniels; three-quarters Aubrey, Rees Phillips, Morgan and Young; halves W. Reynolds and T. Hiley; and forwards J. Thomas (captain), J. Lewis, W. Powells, W. P. Morgan, D. Ball, White, William Morris and Bowen; with E. Williams as reserve.

They followed this up with a trip to Bryncoch, when they lost heavily, and then a local derby with the Grandison XV, which they won by 3 tries to 0 (Poley, White and Hiley the scorers). Skewen Valve were the next opponents and they lost by 1 try to 0.

The First XV's next opponents were Taibach, this time at home. It was another rough match in which it was reported that the referee (not an independent) paid little heed to anything that was going on. The game ended in a 12–9 win for the Ferry, with Poley and P.C. Lisk scoring tries and Mansel Jones kicking the goals.

A disappointing away draw with the Seaside Star followed. Other players who were prominent during these games were wing Fetchitt, centre Leyshon Thomas, half-back Gillespie and, up front, E. Emmanuel for the First XV and forward Notcher, and backs Evan White and E. Williams for the Second XV.

They then failed to visit Treorchy, because they couldn't get an answer from Treorchy's secretary.

Neath Second XV were the next senior opponents. It was a disappointing game, although the Ferry were victors by 1 try to 0, scored by Poley.

The next opponents, Cynon Stars, were formidable indeed, as they were the reigning South Wales Challenge Cup holders. Ferry narrowly lost the game in an exciting match. On the same day, the Second XV defeated the Vernon Crusaders by 1 goal and 3 tries to 0 – and then played Kenfig Hill away in their next match.

The First XV narrowly lost their next game at St. Helens against Swansea Second XV, 9–12. George Williams and new boy Chris Hendra were the try scorers.

A 3–3 draw at home to Bryncethin followed. Leyshon Thomas was the try scorer.

Match results place BFRFC scores first

The next opponents were Pontypridd away for the First XV, and Grandison at home for the Second XV. Then the Llanelli Starlights cancelled their game against the First XV, but the Second XV gave Cwmavon a heavy hiding by 1 goal and 6 tries to 0, Lisk and Poley were the chief contributors. The First IX then paid a visit to Llanelli to play Morfa Rangers, while the Second XV played the Aberavon All Whites.

On Christmas Day morning the First XV played at home to the Seaside Stars and beat them 10–9. In the afternoon the Second XV took on the Grandison.

Neath Second XV were to pay a visit on Boxing Day morning, and it was reported that the whole squad would need to train well for these upcoming games – it appears that the Second XV were leading the way on the training field. The result was 8–3 to the Ferry.

In the last game of the year Ferry were defeated at home by Pontardulais, 3–13.

The first game of the new year was a tough start away to Newport Second XV, while the Ferry Second XV were to play Kenfig Hill. Lovett was drafted in on the wing for the firsts and into the Second XV came Evan and David White in the second row. The Newport game resulted in a fine win by the Ferry, 4–0, with Southwood Thomas dropping a fine goal. It was reported that the Newport papers showed very bad taste and a lack of grace over the defeat of their local team and that the 'Tanner's' supporters were very kind with their remarks, hootings and jeers!

The next opponents were to be Bridgend away, but the match was cancelled due to a frozen pitch. Meanwhile, the Second XV defeated Neath Abbey by 2 goals and 4 tries to 0.

The following Saturday the First XV game against Seaside Stars was cancelled by mutual consent. Most of the senior XV went to watch Neath play Swansea as two of their number, Matthews and Emmanuel, had been selected to play for Neath. It was reported that both had decent games, but that if the other six forwards been in the same condition as the Ferry pair then they would not have been up against it in the last twenty minutes.

Meanwhile, the Second XV failed to raise a side for a home game against the Aberavon All Whites, which upset both the opposition and the home committee. The away side turned up to find only half the Ferry players present.

A February visit to Cynon Stars was against a good side. Ferry had a scratch side, with four backs and three forwards missing. This proved too much in the end, although the final score of 0–19 was not a true reflection of the game. Meanwhile the Second XV drew at home against the Skewen Valve boys.

The next game was at home to Treherbert Second XV. Once again changes had to be made due to the unavailability of George Phillips, Lovett, Emmanuel and A. Davey. In came the young wing Edgar Poley, who scored the only try. He was the younger brother of the more senior Poleys in the first team. They lost a tough encounter by 3–6 – and also lost fullback T.R. Nicholls with a dislocated shoulder after a late charge by the opposing winger.

The club held a successful smoker on Saturday 7 February at their headquarters, the Harp Hotel. A strong muster of players and other members all enjoyed the capital programme provided by Mr Llewelyn Thomas. He'd secured the Neath Amateur Dramatic Society, the most promising of which were Messrs A.B. Edwards, J. Evans, G. Treharne and W. Skinner (accompanist). A recitation of "The Silver King's Dream" was the highlight of the night, with some locals joining in with Messrs Lodwick, Ted Humphries, D. Humphries and Llewelyn Thomas. T.R. Nicholls gave an account of the club's welfare. The landlord, Mr Mainwaring (also club treasurer), and the committeemen were heartily thanked for defraying the cost of the refreshments, tobacco, cigarettes and so on. Mr Wild wished the club success and promised to subscribe half a guinea to the club's funds. The good feeling between players and committee was highlighted in a jolly evening, which finished with a rendition of the national anthem.

The next game was at home against a spirited Sketty side, who took the game to the Ferry and won 0–6. It was reported that the Ferry forwards would do better if they stopped talking and knuckled down to playing, as they were up against a heavy lot and the three-quarters hardly had a look in.

An away trip to a strong Pontardulais side was the next challenge and into the side came fullback J. Dixon and half-back H. Price. The Second XV played Neath Castle Stars at home on the same day.

On the following Saturday, a Treorchy Stars side did not appear. As the team was already on the field, they prepared for the next week's battle against an unbeaten Swansea Second XV. Strict training was adhered to and the team selection put Wilson in at half-back and N. Moore and Green up front. It was hoped that neither team would resort to unworthy tactics or lose tempers – win or lose Reds, be sports! The game was played at Briton Ferry in fair conditions but with a strong cross wind, which made things a little unpleasant at times. The largest crowd of the season turned up to watch a fine, hard-fought game. The lighter Ferry forwards gave their all and fullback Poley was outstanding in defence. A first half try for Swansea was the only score. According to the home supporters, the scorer, Coad, crossed five yards into touch outside the goal line, but the score was given, the conversion was missed, and their record stood unbroken.

There was no game for the First XV the following Saturday but the Second XV played at Cwmavon.

Back on the field of play the Ferry XV were run narrowly close by the Grandison XV, but won 6–5. Incidentally, the Grandison side had won the Dewar shield (offered by the Neath Rugby Club) for the third year on the trot and were presented with five guineas by the Neath chairman, District Councillor Edmund Law. Grandison were also the only side to beat the Swansea league champions Danygraig; they finished the season with a record of played 28, won 18, drew 5, lost 5, for 178 points against 62. Their top try scorer was the excellent centre Chris Hendra, with 12 tries.

The next challenge for the Ferry was a return match with Sketty, at the away venue. This time the lighter forwards prevailed, and Neville Moore got the only score. By all accounts they had a lot more of the game than the unrevealed score indicated.

A trip was organised to play Tenby on Good Friday, but as the club were offered no guarantees there was to be no Saturday game, as it was not certain that their costs could be covered. They lost the match after a brave first half display to an excellent Tenby XV.

The finale of the season was a match against Gordon's Swansea XV at home, a big task for the Ferry side. Aberavon offered to lend them their crack centre and winger – brothers Lewis and Willie Thomas – which was much appreciated by the home team and their supporters. Also, the Swansea side must be praised for paying this visit at the end of a tough season, which hopefully benefited the whole sporting fraternity of the Ferry. The game was refereed by Dr E.V. Pegge.

AGM

The club's annual meeting was held at the Harp Hotel on 15 August and was very well attended. The officers elected for the coming season were: captain, Ben Phillips; vice captain, Harry Rogers; Second XV captain, William Howells; honourable secretary, Brinley Aubrey (his second season); honourable treasurer, Ed Williams; committee, Messrs E. Pumphreys, T. Rees, Ll. Thomas, J. Phillips, T. Newton, Evan Davies, A. Davey, Arthur Williams, Tom Mills, J. Davies, and J. Stuart.

A beautiful gold medal was suitably inscribed and presented by the members to the captain for his efforts over the past three seasons. A silver medal was presented to the player who put in the most training during the season, Mr W.J. Morgan. A capital photograph of the club had been taken by Mr Howells, photographer of Neath Road, meant for presentation to the late Mr John Mainwaring, treasurer and landlord of the club's headquarters. It was presented to Mrs Mainwaring, in recognition of what a big loss he was to the club and of everything he'd done to help the club along.

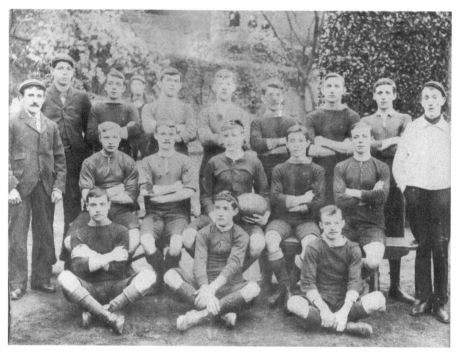

2.2 1902/03

Other news

The town's cricket XI played a game in September against W.J. Bancroft's XI (a Welsh Rugby international) and won by 23 runs!

1903/04

In a trial match between the probables and the possibles some new names emerged, such as: backs D. Gabe, R. Richards and Tom Hughes; forwards Tom Jones, J. Glendenning, Ben Davies, J. Bowen and Evan Griffiths; and reserves T. Vaughan, Jeff Lewis, W. Rourke and W.H. Morgan. The game was played on the cricket pitch, after a soccer game. It ended with a 6–3 win for the probables. As both selected fullbacks were unavailable, the veterans Daniels and John Evans manfully filled in for both sides in a no holds barred match.

This was followed a week later, at the same venue, by a First XV v. Second XV match. Both sides were short of their regular players, but it still showed a good benefit for the club's future.

While the Second XV entertained Kenfig Hill at home for the first fixture of the season, the First XV were away at Neath Excelsiors. Will Phillips had transferred to Aberavon and the club wished him well on his new venture, but he did turn out for this first fixture, which ended in a 3–3 draw, despite the Neath side's questionable tactics. Even before the game they turned up in pairs an hour late for kick-off. The Ferry side looked the best, both in style and turn out in their smart new kit, and in their general play.

Captain
Ben Phillips

The next match was Swansea Excelsiors at home. The first half started with the much heavier Swansea pack trying to take full advantage of the slope and at the half-time whistle the score was 3–5 to the Excelsiors. W. Phillips was the Ferry's try scorer. In the second half the

Ferry stepped up a gear and ran in tries through centre Tom Wilson and a forward rush from Rees to win the game 9–5.

A large band of supporters travelled with the side to the next fixture against Swansea Second XV at St. Helens, where an unusually large crowd awaited them (especially since it was a Second XV side). The papers said that the Ferry had earned the respect, if not the fear, of the Swansea side during their outings the previous season and an excellent game was anticipated. The crowd were not disappointed and, although the game ended in a big defeat for the Ferry, they were not too disheartened in losing to a bigger better team, by 3–24. George Williams scored the only try.

A trip to Carmarthen was next on the agenda and the team were to leave on the GWR at 1.20 p.m. They had a front row of Phillips, namely Rees, George and William, and Jno. Phillips at scrum-half. The Carmarthen team were strengthened by the inclusion of Alby Davies of Llanelli and Will Thomas of Aberavon, who were both at the local college. The game ended in a 0–0 draw. Despite the fact that the Ferry forwards were outweighed by stones up front, they battled on manfully. The Second XV team included some new names for their game with Neath Junior Excelsiors at home – David Wedlake, E. Barrett and Tom Ireland up front.

At the beginning of November, forward William Phillips left for America. As there had been no advance indication of this happening the club were unable to make any formal presentation before his departure.

A home game against Bryncethin was the next fixture, which ended in a 3–3 draw. Jack Phillips was the try scorer. Due to both injury and unavailability the side was missing some key players, such as backs D. Poley and H. Rogers, and up front A. Lewis and Emanuel and A. Davies. But, once again, the forwards especially stood up to larger opponents – in particular the two second team lads, Ben Davies and J. Bowen.

Other sides played at Briton Ferry, such as the Crusaders and the Giant's Grave. When these two met in November the game ended in a 0–3 win for the Crusaders. J. Davies was the try scorer. They followed this up with an away win at Talbot Athletic, 3 tries to 1. The Crusaders were then defeated by St. Joseph's, 2 tries to 0, before winning 11–0 against Glyncorrwg. Among their players were: fullback D. Davies; threes S. Bailly, J.Y. Richards, E. Thomas and H. Price; halves M. Samuel and Ned Thomas; and forwards R. Thomas, D. Thomas, W. Thomas, J. Davies, L. Williams, J. Woolacot, A. Evans, and D. Petherick; also R. Williams, D. Evans and J. Watkins.

November continued for the Ferry with another 0–0 draw with Neath Excelsiors at home. It was another plucky, hard fought match, and once again changes had to be made before the next challenge, league side Treorchy with their huge ex-international forwards Ramsey and Bob Jones. George Llewelyn returned to the side as captain, David Thomas at fullback, Poley and T.C. Davies into the three-quarters, and George John and Will Carney up front. Due to the late arrival of the away side the game was only played for twenty-five minutes each way. The Ferry was two players short, and against the heaviest pack they had ever faced, so went down by 3 tries to 0. The players who failed to show were T.C. Davies and Carney. A knock-on effect was felt when the Second XV failed to put out a team to visit Skewen, despite the fact that a general meeting had been called the previous week to air any grievances among the players and committee. Sadly, this too was poorly attended!

Unfortunately, the First XV were unable to put things right on the field the following week as their opposition, the Llanelli Starlights, had disbanded.

The Second XV had a game at home to the Bridgend White Stars, which ended in a 3–3 draw. So far in the season the Second XV had won against Kenfig Hill and lost to junior Neath Excelsiors at home as well as playing Skewen United; away from home they had lost 8–10 to Christchurch of Swansea, drawn 0–0 with Aberavon All Whites and played Tonna.

A visit to Cilfynydd is never easy and this proved to be the case for the First XV in their next game, which they lost 0–14.

Mr Aubrey (secretary) called all local teams within ten miles of the Ferry to enter the Briton Ferry Challenge Cup by the end of December.

A home game against Felinfoel was the next challenge and the Ferry came through with flying colours, winning 11–0, with tries from the impressive George John, J. Phillips and skipper George Llewelyn. The game ended in semi-darkness due to the late arrival of the away team.

Ferry were delayed for their next game as the train was late taking them to Bridgend. The team had one change, Sam John of the Workingmen's Club played at forward in place of B. Phillips. The game was well fought and the Bridgend supporters warmed to the occasion in a fine sportsmanlike manner. They had beaten Llanelli the previous week and were looking for a big win. They had all of the play but could not score; two of their 4 tries were stated to be controversial refereeing decisions – it was Ferry 0.

On Christmas morning 1903 the First XV took on the Workingmen's Club at the Ferry with an 11 a.m. kick-off, on a favourable day with a record crowd. Fred Hutchinson, the Welsh international, refereed the game. At half-time, with the Ferry playing up the slope, the score was 0–0, but in the second half tries from George Phillips and Jack "Our Kid" Phillips, who also kicked a conversion, gave Ferry an 8–0 win. The veterans in the Workingmen's side played well, such as Evan Davies, Sam John, Jack and Dai Evans, and A. Hutchinson. In the afternoon the Second XV entertained the Ferry Crusaders who, being the smaller of the two sides were that much nippier and scored the only try of the match through Price. The Crusaders then went on to lose by 1 try to 0 to old Ferry rivals Cefn Cribbwr a week later.

The new year opened with a visit to Ammanford, it took the club 130 minutes to travel the 25 miles to the ground and they finally arrived at 3.10 p.m, and kicked off at 3.30 p.m. They were without three of their best forwards, George John, George Phillips and P. Phillips, so 'Gentle' Arthur Green, committeeman Jack Phillips and Dai 'Trainer' Thomas took their places. The Ferry played far better to the conditions and emerged winners by 2 tries to 0. Evans and Wilson were try scorers. The Second XV also won against Christchurch, with a Mills drop goal against a sole penalty. The Crusaders had an excellent win against Neath Barbarians, 20–0!

The First XV went on to further fine wins that month with a heavy win over Swansea Excelsiors and Carmarthen by more than 20 points. The Second XV also found winning ways by defeating Pyle away from home. They ended the month with an eagerly awaited home fixture against Swansea Second XV, but on a dismal day – rugby and weather wise – a small crowd watched the Reds defeated by 18–0. The highlight of the game was a Jack Bancroft drop goal in the second half from a mark which was both wide out and at long range. The Swansea side had only been beaten once in two years – and that was by Aberdare the previous week.

A few cancelled games due to the weather and visitors failing to turn up made a poor start to February, but a scratch team went down to Pontardulais and gave a good account of themselves, losing narrowly.

Then came the visit of Cilfynydd. A tight match, on a fine day, in front of a small crowd. The Ferry went behind by 1 try to 0, but battled on to equalise through as fine an individual try as you'll see after a jinking angular run by the centre Harry Rogers. The game ended in a 3–3 draw. Merriman played well on the wing and a strong feature was his cross kicking. On the same day, the

Crusaders won up in Glyncorrwg by 4 tries to 0. They had to leave the field ten minutes early due to the bad conduct of the spectators!

A home game against Pontardulais saw a few changes in the Ferry side, with new players such as fullback E. Thomas, centre Saunders and up front J. Hemmings. They were all part of a fine 11–3 win. Merriman, Ike Evans and Saunders were try scorers and Saunders added a conversion.

The semi-finals of the Briton Ferry Challenge cup (George Smart Trophy) were held at the Ferry ground on 12 March in a double header between Tonna and the Crusaders, and the Ferry and the Grandison. A charge of sixpence for the two matches was thought to be one of the reasons for a smallish crowd! Tonna won the first game by 1 try to 0. The second game kicked off at 4.50 p.m, Abraham the Grandison winger was the first try scorer and Davies for the Ferry equalised just before half-time, but Abraham scored an excellent second try to win the game for the Grando, who went on to beat Tonna in the final by 2 tries to 0 after extra time.

The Ferry First XV suffered a heavy defeat up in Treorchy, and finished their season with a home fixture against Ammanford.

AGM

During the AGM in August – again at the Harp Hotel – Mr Tom Rees occupied the chair, secretary Mr Aubrey submitted the accounts, which showed the club to be in an exceptionally sound financial position.

The officers elected for the coming season were: captain, Mr George Llewelyn; vice captain, Harry Rogers; Second XV captain Mr E. Barrett; Second XV vice captain Robert Thomas; secretary and treasurer re-elected. Committee: H. Thomas, J. Williams and William Rogers elected in place of Evan Davies, Newton and Davey.

1904/05

The published Crusaders fixtures included teams such as Melyn White Stars, Ystrad Excelsiors, Landore Excelsiors, Cadoxton, Gendros Juniors, Pontyclun Recreation and St Paul's (Llanelli).

The Ferry started off the season very badly and lost by 11 points at home to Pontardawe.

The following week they fought to a very creditable 3–3 draw against Swansea Second XV at St. Helens – Bob White was the try scorer. After the manner of the defeat the previous week everybody at the Ferry felt they were on a hiding for nothing, but the Ferry forwards had other ideas and ended the match with heads held high.

They followed this with two home wins. The first against Skewen by 5–3, with Rees Phillips the try scorer and Jack Phillips converting. The second was a tight, well-fought game against Danygraig, 8–7, Rogers the try scorer and Saunders converting.

November started well. They entertained Tenby and defeated them by a huge margin – 4 goals and 4 tries to 0. Saunders scored four tries, Rogers one and Merriman two.

Then the inevitable defeat followed, away to Cadoxton. Before they once again produced the goods and beat Danygraig by 8–0 at home – L. Jones and Wilson the try scorers and Saunders converting. Frank Taylor made an appearance for Ferry, who did have the most accomplished player on the field in H.J. Taylor at fullback. On the same day, the Second XV were defeated by the Crusaders 0–3; and, in a preliminary schools' league match before the

Captain
Ben Phillips

First XV game, Briton Ferry and Herbert Road lost to Neath North by 3 tries to 0.

A visit from the Cardiff reserves, especially since the Cardiff First XV had no match, was quite a way to start December.

On Christmas Day the Ferry travelled to Aberavon for their first ever match and came away with a winning score of 8–6. The team that day was: fullback Albert Freethy; threes Merriman, Rogers, Jones and Saunders; halves T. Wilson and J. Phillips; and forwards George Llewelyn (captain), George Phillips, Rees Phillips, Ben Phillips, E. Evans and J. Llewelyn. They scored a try in each half, Merriman in the first half and Rogers in the second which Saunders converted. Reports stated that the difference in the two sides was that the Ferry were 'in the pink' after some keen training sessions with trainer Tom Bright, and that the performance on the day was down to a good team combination playing together.

They followed this up with another outstanding win at home to Swansea Second XV. Although the Reds had the upper hand all the way through the game, up front and in the centre especially, Ferry achieved 3 tries to 0 – try scorers were Ben Phillips (1) and George Phillips (2).

They ended the year with a handsome win at home to Pontycymmer. They had to don mixed jerseys as the visitors were in red, but they went on to win by 26–0 (S. Jones, Harry Rogers, B. Phillips and Jack Phillips (2) were the try scorers).

Treorchy were the First XV's next opponents to visit the Ferry and they lost by 20–0. Fine tries scored by Rogers (2), Saunders and J. Jones were reported as some of the best tries ever seen on the ground!

A story in the local paper said that a full-size portrait of Inspector Roberts, who was deemed to be the 'gut' of Briton Ferry rugby, on display in the window of local photographer Mr Howells, reflected and reminded the public of the readiness and spontaneity of the sporting fraternity to show their appreciation of any services rendered to sport.

In February Ferry beat Pontardulais at home by 12–0, and then completed the double in April by winning 8–5.

In March they defeated Llangennech by 11–0 at the Ferry, but finished the season on Good Friday by losing at the Gnoll to Neath by 0–20.

Youth rugby

There was also joy at school level as five Briton Ferry lads (Brown, Edgar Cooper, D. Thomas, Ball and Harris) were selected to play for Neath Schools against Swansea Schools. All five played well and Cooper was selected to play for West Wales against East Wales later that season.

1905/06

A famous year in Welsh rugby history as the national team inflicted their first defeat on the New Zealand All Blacks.

At the start of the season Ferry lost at Maesteg in September, 3–6. In October they defeated Brynsawel by 24–5 and Bridgend (away) by 5–0, and then inflicted another defeat on Swansea Second XV, this time by 3 tries to 0 (the scorers were Merriman (2) and H. Rogers).

Melbourne lost to the Briton Ferry Whites by 6–0, before defeating the Grandison 21–8 on the same field.

In November, the First XV played an away fixture with Pontardulais, then suffered a narrow 0–6 away defeat to Aberavon, then an away defeat at Skewen, 3–5. Backs D.O. Thomas at centre and half-backs T. Williams and Jack Phillips, and R. Campbell and P.C. Foley up front were all playing well at the time. Ferry finished the month with a home draw against Danygraig of 0–0.

Captain
Evan Davies

They finished the year with a visit to Aberavon. They'd made several changes to the team. In came fullback Fred Rees, backs Bob Thomas and W.J. Sanders, and forwards E. Williams and A. Ball, but they lost 0–16.

In January, the Briton Ferry Crusaders lost at Neath Abbey 0–8, and the Ferry First XV lost at Bridgend 3–5, Merriman was again the try scorer. On 13 January Penarth Second XV were to have played at the Ferry, but they inexplicably failed to turn up. There was also a return fixture with Pontardulais.

In February, the First XV lost at Neath Abbey by 1 drop goal (4 points) to 0. Although they put out a weakened side the game was very tight. They also drew 0–0 at Treorchy, and lost the return match with Danygraig at St. Thomas' Athletic ground by 1 try to 0, with Hughes coming in at fullback.

Ferry lost in the return match with Swansea Second XV by 1 try to 0, in which a certain J. Bancroft figured at fullback and Trew at half-back. The Ferry made one change, at fullback, with J.T.R. Evans coming into the side. The game was played in atrocious conditions, and it was reported that if conditions had been fairer then a far better game would have ensued between two fine young sides.

Tenby visited the Ferry in March and were defeated in a fine game by 5 tries to 0, with Bayley (2), Phillips, Evans and Wilson the try scorers.

They also paid a visit to Penarth during April.

2.3 1905/06 Giants Grave RFC, Briton Ferry

Youth rugby

The junior teams were in action at Llewelyn's field in October.

1906/07

The season started with a practice session in September, followed by a Captain's XV v. Vice Captain's XV.

A strong fixture list opened with a 0–0 draw away at St. Helens against Swansea Second XV, followed by an away fixture with Treorchy and a home fixture against Morriston.

In November, Cardiff's A team defeated Ferry, 0–8. This was followed by a 0–12 home defeat to Roath. But they pulled back with a 12–0 win at Bridgend and a narrow 5–4 home win over Cardiff A.

But there was a run of defeats in December: away to Penarth, 5–17; at home to Danygraig, 0–5; to Newport Second XV, 3–5; and 0–18 away to Aberavon on Boxing Day. On Christmas Day they played at home against Mr Arthur Jones' XV, a mixed team from Swansea.

The Briton Ferry Crusaders drew 3–3 in Resolven in September and lost to Neath Abbey 0–13 and Aberavon Reserves 0–11. In December they suffered a second defeat to Aberavon Reserves, 10–14.

Captain
Fred Perrett

The New Year started with a 0–8 away defeat against Danygraig, but they bounced back a week later when they defeated Glyncorrwg at home by 12–0, another away defeat followed, 5–11 to Ogmore Vale.

In February, the club entertained Cardiff Mackintosh and Cardiff Romilly, whom they defeated 3–0, and they visited Maesteg, where they lost 0–40, and at Tredegar.

The Ferry Crusaders had away fixtures with Hospital Rangers, where they drew 0–0, and with Tonna.

In March, strangely, the Ferry was involved in two 0–0 draws on the trot at home – against the Ferry Crusaders and Treorchy.

The Second XV drew 0–0 at Cwmavon. Prominent players at this time were Pugh, Jack Phillips, Arthur James and outside-half W.J. Jones.

The season closed with defeats at Danygraig, this time 0–17, at Cwmbran 0–5 and at Aberavon 0–3. But at home they defeated Bridgend 5–0 (Wilson scored the try and then converted it).

1907/08

George Llewelyn went on to skipper the side in 1909/10, 1910/11, 1911/12 and 1912/13.

The season started late and not as they wanted, with a 0–6 defeat in the first reported game at Maesteg. Two further defeats followed, on the road at Llywnypia United (0–6) and at Treorchy (0–9).

An excellent 3–0 home win over Swansea Second XV was a good pick me up. This match was refereed by a local man for the first fifteen minutes as the appointed referee was delayed by a problem on the railway line. Thomas the fullback played well, as did J. Brennan and T. Wilson in the three-quarters, but the best player on the field was the Ferry captain, G. Llewelyn. The Swansea fullback was ex-Ferry player Fred Rees.

The Crusaders lost 0–3 up in Pontardawe.

There were more home wins in November. First over Danygraig by 5–0 and 6–3 over Cardiff Romilly. Then 3–0 over Ogmore Vale, in which Wilson the outside-half was outstanding. A home game with Mynyddbach was cancelled.

An away fixture with Aberavon was cancelled in December.

Evan White was outstanding throughout a home match against Danygraig. He charged down a clearance kick straight from the kick-off to score Ferry's only try in a 3–5 defeat. They also lost 0–9 to Neath on 28 December.

In the New Year, return fixtures with both Mynyddbach in January and Aberavon in March were cancelled. Ferry

Captain
George Llewelyn

were defeated at Danygraig (5–8) and at Bridgend (3–5) in January, but won at home against Llywnypia 3–0 that month.

Defeats continued in February, 5–9 at home to Treorchy and 5–7 away at Bridgend.

March at Maesteg was a 0–3 away defeat, followed by an away game at Llywnypia. Then finally a 3–0 home win over Hendy.

In April, Ferry lost to Neath at the Gnoll by 0–41!

2.4 Briton Ferry 1908/09

Match results place BFRFC scores first

1908/09

Once again under the captaincy of Ben Phillips, the side played away games against Bridgend and Swansea Second XV in October, losing 3–22 and 0–11 respectively. They did defeat Pencoed at home by 5–0, before ending the month with another away defeat. This was to Swansea East Side team Danygraig, 0–13, in which a Ferry forward was sent off for "over vigorous" play.

In November they defeated Hendy at home by 3–0 and played out a 0–0 draw at home to Ystalyfera.

Into dark December, and three more away defeats, at Newport Second XV (0–9), at Llywnypia (0–9) and at Neath (0–23).

They were winning the return match at home to Danygraig by 4–0, after a Reggie Davies drop goal, when a Danygraig player headed for the line. The touch judge raised his flag to indicate a foot in touch, then changed his mind, then raised it again when he realised that the player had gone over the try line. The referee disallowed the try, but Danygraig still claimed a 4–5 victory. The game ended in a fiasco as the Danygraig team walked off the field in protest, but the result stood, and the WRU suspended the Danygraig captain for his actions.

Captain
Ben Phillips

New Year games against Hendy and Swansea Second XV were both away. The Swansea game ended in a narrow 0–8 defeat – outstanding players were the captain George Llewelyn up front, H. Harris on the wing and T. Griffiths at inside-half.

In February they had return games against Newport Second XV and Llywnypia at home. They lost both by 0–3 and 5–6 respectively. A home game with Danygraig was called off, as the Swansea team couldn't raise a side.

A 0–9 defeat at Maesteg followed in March, before a crunch meeting with Danygraig at their ground in April. Despite leading at half-time through a George Llewelyn try, Ferry lost 17–3. They faced Neath in the final game of the season and were heavily defeated 4–38 by a much better, pluckier team, with only a drop goal to show for their efforts.

Around the district

There were interesting reports of other games during the season. When the Village Boys played St. Thomas at Penrhiwtyn, Jabez Thomas scored a try, and prominent players were Ray Gower (who broke a leg during the match), D. Evans and winger H. Woodland.

Briton Ferry Melbourne played Neath Juniors and lost 0–13.

Among other changes in the districts, Llanelli Hospital Wanderers was renamed Llanelli Second XV.

2.5 Briton Ferry Melbourne 1908/09

Match results place BFRFC scores first

1909/10

The new season began with a 3–0 win over local combination side Melbourne and District.

October started with a 0–0 home draw with Skewen, and a 13–0 home win over Pencoed, in which the forwards dominated. It was reported that the team was a very strong one time and would take some beating this season!

Ferry then went on to defeat Hendy away from home by 3–0, before suffering a narrow defeat by 0–3 at home to Swansea Second XV, which lost Ferry their unbeaten at home tag. The game was played in torrential rain and the only score came from a Fred Rees penalty.

Two more wins over Glynneath (11–0) and Ystalyfera (3–0) and a defeat at Resolven by 0–3 followed in November.

The last month of the year saw a 6–4 home win over Porthcawl, before defeats by both Neath Second XV (3–11) and Neath themselves (0–31). Ex-Neath outside-half Jack Phillips was the pick of the Ferry team, and Evan Williams on the left wing showed great promise.

Captain
George Llewelyn

Then another game ended with the opposition walking off the field as they were "fed up" with the referee's rulings. This time it was Resolven who abandoned the match.

There were two big games in January, one against Llanelli Second XV, which ended in a draw, and one against Swansea Second XV at St Helens, which they lost 0–29.

February proved to be an uneventful month with defeats by Skewen away (3–6), Resolven at home (0–6) and Bridgend at home (0–3). In the Bridgend game, ex-

Neath forward Rees Phillips turned out for the Ferry in the absence of Bob White. Ferry ended the month with a 0–0 draw at Porthcawl.

Another string of narrow defeats followed in March – away to Glynneath (0–8), Skewen (0–3) and Neath Second XV (0–15) – before Ferry eked out a 3–3 draw with Neath Crusaders. During this Good Friday afternoon match Jack Phillips was outstanding for the Ferry, and many Skewen and Neath Second XV players turned out to assist.

A return match with Llanelli Second XV in the final month of the season ended in a 0–14 defeat. Just to rub salt into the wounds, they'd travelled with just ten players and had to 'borrow' five Llanelli players. They ended the season with a narrow 0–6 defeat away to Skewen.

PART 3: 1910-1920

The First World War Years

3.1 Briton Ferry Steel RFC before 1914

3.2 Briton Ferry Village Boys XV cup winners 1910/11

1910/11

Reports in September said that, due to the efforts of both committee and members, the season had got underway with a large number of players available, including quite a few new ones. As the month progressed the club's heavy obligations had started to lighten, and they were looking forward to a successful run of matches and more funds to run the club.

In October, the first game ended in a home win over Ammanford by 8–3, but they ended the month with a heavy defeat at Maesteg by 24–3.

November's home fixture against Llanelli's Second XV ended in victory, and they continued an unbeaten home record with wins over Hendy and Treherbert. They were defeated at Hendy 0–17, before defeating Ystalyfera at home 8–0.

> A paper reported that both the attractive fixture list and the good rugby being played still couldn't raise home game attendancess, but that football enthusiasts could go further and see worse matches than if they visited the Ferry.

December saw yet another home win, a narrow 3–0 over Maesteg, then a fixture away to Swansea Second XV. The month ended with a last-minute fixture on Boxing Day against Aberavon at the Talbot Athletic Ground – unfortunately the Ferry lost 0–19. Aberavon had been due to play Paris Racing, who had dropped out because of distorted ideas about the dangers of the colliers' strike! The Ferry team was: fullback R. Davies; three-quarters Rees Phillips, Dick Jones, Ernie Williams and Reg Davies; half-backs Jack Phillips and T. Wilson; and forwards R.

Captain
George Llewelyn

Thomas (captain), D. Hoskin, Phil Phillips, Perrett, J. Nash, F. Barrett, Sid Davies and Evan Jones.

Ferry's unbeaten home tag was removed in the new year return fixture against Swansea Second XV. which they lost 3–5. It was a controversial game, as the home crowd took an instant dislike to both the away side and the referee from Llanelli, Mr Jenkins. Complaints were received from both the referee and some of the away players and officials about being struck by objects after the game. These unfortunate scenes threatened to stop future fixtures between the two clubs.

A trip to the Gnoll to play Neath Second XV was the next test and the Ferry lost 0–6 in front of one of the largest crowds at a Second XV match that season. Three-quarters Jack Phillips and Shorney were the pick of the side.

A March return game with Llanelli Second XV at Stradey was refereed by one Albert Freethy (see 1904/05 season team). To complete the season they unfortunately lost four games on the trot to Skewen 0–13–0, Treherbert 0–9, Maesteg 0–12, and to the Welsh champions, Neath, 0–49.

Off the field

However, the club was struggling with off the field funding and ended the season in debt.

1911/12

3.3 Briton Ferry Town Pavilion, 1911

With some extra funding and a good fixture list the season looked promising from the start. Most of the previous season's players were still available and some new recruits gave the club fresh impetus. Some of the newcomers had come down from Monmouthshire to work in the area and were anxious to throw in their lot with the Ferry. Neath Second XV had disbanded due to lack of funds from their gate money.

The season started off with a heavy defeat at Bridgend by 0–29. They then played away fixtures at Danygraig and Mansel, before defeating Treherbert at home by 3–0.

In November, a home draw to Ystalyfera 0–0 and an away draw to Glynneath 3–3, then led to an away draw with Ystalyfera in December, again both sides failed to score. Skewen were their next opponents and Ferry lost this away game by 0–3. They then suffered another away

Captain
George Llewellyn

defeat at Swansea Second XV, 3–11. Outstanding on the day was veteran forward George Llewelyn. Ferry secretary Mr Jones refereed the game.

Christmas Day saw a home fixture against Neath Crusaders, before they ended the year with a 5–3 revenge home win over Bridgend. It was played in front of a record crowd and finished almost in darkness, due to the late arrival of the visitors. A try under the posts after a nippy break by scrum-half E. Thomas, converted by J. Hughes, proved to be the winner. Again, Llewelyn played well and was the pick of the forwards, along with Fred Perrett. Outside-half Dick Davies was not his usual self and had a kick charged down, which almost resulted in a score.

In the New Year there was another revenge home win of 7–0 over Danygraig and then a 3–5 away defeat to Glynneath, followed by two home wins, over Mansel (9–0) and Resolven (6–3).

On 2 March there was a 3–9 away defeat to Skewen, then a 0–3 home defeat to Swansea Second XV, followed by a home draw with Skewen (3–3) and a 9–0 home win over Ystalyfera.

The season ended in April with a 0–19 defeat at Resolven.

AGM

The AGM was held in July at the Globe Hotel in Briton Ferry, with Mr Llewelyn Thomas in the chair. He commented that on the field the club had been very successful but that off-field affairs were not looking so healthy. But there was promise of better things to come, with a number of new signings for the next season, and fixtures with the likes of Pontypridd, Llanharan and Merthyr.

The secretary Mr W.J. Jones stated that the season's expenditure amounted to £69 13s 11d, and receipts came to £62 8s 2½d – leaving the club in the red to the tune of £7 5s 8½d!

It was unanimously voted that Lord Jersey be contacted to become president for the coming season. Mr Jones and Mr T.J. Thomas were re-elected as secretary and treasurer respectively. The committee would consist of Messrs. W. Brown, R. Phillips, P. Phillips, G. Morris, J.H. Jones, E. Emmanuel, E. Humphreys, G. Thomas, G.J. Richards, D. Ireland, C. Callaghan, T. Richards, D. Daniels, and J. Donald. T. Ireland was appointed as trainer and Mr G. F. Llewelyn was elected captain.

1912/13 – 25TH

The first game of the season was a home fixture on 14 September against a District XV, which the Ferry won 22–5. An away defeat at Bridgend (0–15) was followed by an October visit to Llanelli to play their second string. The team was: fullback R. Davies; threes W. Wellington, W. Griffiths, Jabez Thomas and Reggie Thomas; half-backs Tony Thomas and J. Phillips; and forwards from G.F. Llewelyn, R. Jones, J. Brady, R. Thomas, Bob Phillips, A. Edwards, J. Anthony, J. Nash, C. Evans and G. Ball.

An 8–8 away draw with Pontypridd took them into the November return match and a 4–0 home win for the Ferry – with a Jack Phillips drop goal. At the end of the month Albert Freethy refereed a 0–0 draw in Glynneath, with the return match going the way of the opposition by 0–6.

Merthyr visited in December; Anthony, Brady and Bob Phillips were outstanding in defence and Ferry defeated the visitors 3–0. They then ran up the same score at home to Llanharan, J. Phillips was the only scorer, to maintain an unbeaten home record.

Captain
George Llewellyn

> The inclusion of Fred Perrett (a product of the Ferry, a teetotaller and a non-smoker) in the Welsh team, prompted the organisation of a smoker evening in his honour to celebrate him gaining his full cap. The club also sent him a personal letter of congratulations as a memento.

December's fixtures ended with a home match against Bridgend on a rain-sodden field. Tries by G. Llewelyn and Dick Thomas brought in yet another home win for the Ferry.

Ferry could only muster a depleted side for New Year a visit to Ystalyfera, which ended in a draw against a previously unbeaten side! A visit to Pontypool the following week was followed by another draw, this time by 0–0 at home to Skewen. A 5–0 win at home over Llanelli Second XV completed the fixtures for January.

February's first game, against Danygraig at home, was cancelled due to heavy rain. George Llewelyn's men kept up their winning streak with a fine 5–0 away win at Swansea Second XV. A newspaper article remarked that the Ferry had relied on George for many a season and that he was currently in his fourteenth season as captain (when it was actually his fifth!).

In March, ex-Ferry Fred Perrett played his best game for Wales, against Ireland. In May, he was quoted as signing on for Leeds Rugby League club for what was then the biggest fee that year for a Welsh forward.

Ferry lost their home ground record with a 3–11 score in March on Easter Monday. In a torrid, rough game against Treherbert, Jabez Thomas was the try scorer for the Ferry, with Bob Williams playing very well.

To complete the season Ferry suffered another 3–11 defeat in April, away to Llanelli Second XV.

In May, the front pages of the *Mid-Glamorgan Herald* and the *Neath Gazette* announced that, on the occasion of his wedding at the Globe Hotel, Mr Llewelyn Thomas was presented with a massive marble clock, suitably inscribed, and a pair of bronzes. He had long presided over the club's destiny and many people rose to toast his marriage with good wishes.

AGM

The AGM was held in the Globe Hotel in August, with Mr J.H. Jones presiding as chairman. The small attendance reported was probably due to the heatwave. It was also noted that due to inclement weather during the season and to spectators watching games "over the hedge" that the gate money was not worth banking. The club finished up in debt to the tune of £36 8s 3d, which included a lower than expected grant of £5 from the WRU.

It was hoped that the excellent fixture list for the coming season would turn things around. It was also quoted that the club was becoming a nursery for talent that the local first-class clubs were tapping into regularly, and that these players were even progressing to further honours, such as playing for Wales.

Dick Thomas was selected as captain for the following season and Jabez Thomas as his vice captain. With Mr Thomas Thomas running as treasurer and Tom Thomas as secretary, it looked like a total Thomas takeover!

The rest of the committee for the coming season was: Llewelyn Thomas, P. Phillips, D. Ellis, G. Jones, E. Humphreys, J. Bradley, W. Brown, C. Callan, Rees Phillips, T. Ireland, J.M. Bowen and James Thomas. It was also decided that Mr A.T. Williams of Baglan House be approached to become president for the new season.

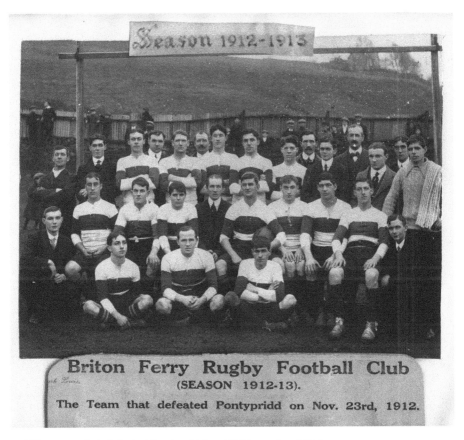

3.4 The team that defeated Pontypridd on 23 November 1912

1913/14

The season started with a narrow 0–6 defeat at Bridgend, it was also Bob Richards first game for the club. They also lost 0–22 that month at Aberavon.

In October they defeated Danygraig twice at home, by 15–3 and 9–3. The team for the home game featured: fullback D. Thomas; three-quarters N. Edwards, E. Treharne, G. James and L. Nicholls;, half-backs Jabez and Tom Thomas; and forwards R. Thomas, G. Ball, J. Nash, J. Anthony, R. Phillips, J. John, A. Edwards, T. Collier and W. Dowse. They also lost at home to Skewen by 11–3, relinquishing their home record early in the season. Dai Thomas scored their only try of the game; Bob Phillips was sent off after a bout of fisticuffs; while Reggie Davies had to leave the field due to an injury. They finished the month with an away defeat at Skewen (0–12).

Ferry began November with an away defeat at Gowerton, this time by 3–12. Treharne was the try scorer.

Two more defeats followed in a miserable November, at Pontardawe (0–29) and Glynneath (0–6), which saw the return of Ivor Morris.

The Cherry and Whites also struggled through December, with further defeats to Pontardawe at home (0–9) and to Swansea Second XV (6–11). The Pontardawe kick-off was delayed due to the late arrival of the away team, and the game had to be curtailed due to the darkness. Forwards Dowse and Bradley were outstanding players.

The new year started with a 0–0 draw at home to Glynneath, then a repeat game against Danygraig. January ended with a 0–16 defeat at Carmarthen Quins.

Captain
Dick Jones

Vice captain
Jabez Thomas

Match results place BFRFC scores first

A February game at home against Gowerton and Bryncethin was lost 3–11 (Billie Nicholls score Ferry's only try), while an away game to Pontardawe was lost, by only 0–5.

In March, Ferry were defeated at home 0–11 by Swansea Second XV. Neath offered to play the Ferry to raise some much-needed funds and interest. It appears that the club didn't take up the offer and failed to put out a team on Thursday 14 March. This was also the month when Fred Perrett transferred from Rugby League Leeds to Hull.

Briton Ferry finished the season with an away game at Glynneath.

Some players that featured during the season were G. Francis, R. Jones, F. Matthews, W. Thomas, D. Jarrett, E. John, E. Harry and F. Barrett.

JACK JONES played his first game for Neath against Llanelli in November, and was quoted as being one of their best forwards.

3.5 Jack Jones

FRED PERRETT was just one of the many who sadly gave his life during the course of the Great War, as did ex-secretary Brinley Aubrey.

Fred Leonard Perrett died of his wounds in Boulogne on 1 December 1918, the last week of the Great War. He had played for Aberavon, Neath and Glamorgan County and had won five caps for Wales. His name was not on the list of rugby internationals who had made the supreme sacrifice, it was believed because he had signed up to go north in 1913. He'd regularly been referred to as one of the best forwards on the field of play. He'd left the Ferry in 1911 to join Aberavon, and had joined Neath a year later, two months later came his debut for Glamorgan County. He was originally selected to play for a Rest of Wales XV in a low-key charity match in 1912 and had a trial for Wales in December 1912. He was selected to play against the Springboks nine days later, at 21 years of age.

Wales lost by only 0–3! Five days later he again faced the 'Boks', this time in Neath colours, (a narrow 3–8 defeat). He initially rejected offers from both Bramley and Hunslet to go north but after playing against Ireland in May 1913, he succumbed to a generous offer from Leeds, as he was out of work at the time. The press claimed it was the largest ever payment to a forward at the time. He made his Leeds debut in September but in 1914 he transferred to Hull, where he worked in a shipyard as a plater's helper.

3.6 Fred Perrett

Perrett enlisted in the Welsh Guards on 20 July 1915 (they had been formed that February). He initially guarded captured German spies in the Tower of London. He went out to France in late February 1916 and fought at the Somme and Ypres. He was promoted to Lance Corporal and was recommended for a commission by his commanding officer. He began officer training around Christmas 1916 and was commissioned on 27 June 1917 in the Royal Welch Fusiliers. He received a slight gunshot wound to his shoulder in April 1918 at the Somme. In the battle of Sambre on 26 October, he bravely led his men into the attack but was severely wounded in the left hand and right thigh, probably by machine gun fire. He died of secondary haemorrhaging two months later and was buried in the Terlincthun British Cemetery, just outside Boulogne.

1914/18 – THE GREAT WAR

In a meeting held between Neath and the District in September 1914 it was decided that all games would be called off for the period of the war. On 4 September, the Welsh Rugby Union met and followed suit by suspending all games involving their member clubs for the duration.

Games started to be played during the 1918/19 season after the Christmas period but most clubs would start in the new 1919/20 season.

There are no records of Briton Ferry playing until this new season, except for a match on 10 May 1919 against a George Llewelyn XV containing the likes of J. Bancroft and T. Parker. Billy Trew refereed the game. Llewelyn went on to play for Ferry and then become club secretary.

Captain 1918/19
Dick Thomas

1919/20

It was a pick-me-up for everyone to get involved in sport after the war years.

> When the team changed in the Dock Hotel, the Ferry Town Silver Band sometimes led the march to the ground, playing what was then the club tune 'My father had a barrow'. The years before that they used the old Jersey Arms as headquarters and played on Gould's field, behind the present police station.

Ferry started off the season at a new ground in Cwrt Sart, with a game against Loughor. The ground had been given to them by Mr J.B. Williams on behalf of Lord Jersey, and it was opened when Mr G. Llewelyn kicked off in place of the president, Mr A.J. Jones. The match was attended by a large crowd and they won a tough encounter (2 converted tries to 1). Tries from Jack Thomas and Dick Thomas were both converted by fullback Lyon Hill, to a try and conversion from the opposition.

Next was an away game at the Gnoll against a formidable Neath team, which was reported on in the local papers by rugby correspondent 'Hotspur'. He'd heard murmurs from Briton Ferryites that their team was going to do to Neath what Glynneath had just failed to do the previous week, he laughed it off at the time and reported that the Ferry were in no way as strong as Neath and that whatever team Neath selected they would put a "goodly score up" against them. The Ferry team that day was: fullback Lyon Hill; threes R. Davies, Evan Davies (of Maesteg), Tom Griffiths and J. Beard; half-backs W. Beynon and D. Handford; and forwards R. Thomas (captain), R. Jones, J. John, C. Bannister, J. Thomas, J. Jones, A. Edwards and L. Edwards. Bannister, Jack

Captain
Dick Thomas

Playing record
P 31
W 17
D 8
L 6

Match results place BFRFC scores first

Thomas and Arthur Edwards were outstanding and the Ferry went on to victory. It appears this rattled Hotspur!

Season 1919-1920

Top Row:- D. Lewis. J. Evans. D. Daymond. S. Daymond. G. Thomas. R. Jones. N.Clarke.J.Bowen.
2nd Row:- G. Llewellyn. T. Bright. S. May. T. Newton. M. Watkins. A. Edwards. J. Anthony.
T. Ireland. W.Jones. R. Phillips.
3rd Row:- P. James. W. Aday. R. Butler. P.G.Jenkins(Sec) R. Thomas(Capt) I. Jones. L. Thomas. (H.Hopkins.
E. Thomas. W. Baker. A. Myersgough. W. Bevan.(V/Capt) D. Hanford. B. Phillips.
J. Watkins. J. Williams.

3.7 1919/20

Two weeks later Swansea found themselves without a game as Pontypool were not able to travel due to a railway strike, and it was thought that the journey was too long to make by charabanc. So the Ferry filled in and duly played their part. They led 3–0 at half-time, following a Jim Jones try, but unfortunately lost 3–18. It was reported that the crowd seemed to be half made up of Ferry supporters, who were a "noisy lot" and indeed it was rare to find such a noisy crowd! There were a few changes in the Ferry side, into the threes came F. Nicholls and D. Trolley, with M. Watkins up front.

A trek up to Glyncorrwg was next up for the Ferry and more changes were made with D.L. Thomas, E. Treharne, Tuan Thomas and W.G. Thomas in the backs and Jack Anthony and G. Barnard up front. They won, as they did a week later at home to Pontypridd United. The forwards were reported to be outstanding that day and were being touted as the best pack in the district.

Some names, such as Bannister, Arthur Edwards, Dick Thomas, Johns, L. Edwards and Dick Jones were even mentioned as possible Welsh trial material!

At the end of October a Neath & District XV visited the Ferry, and the home side were victorious.

The next fixture was a tough visit to Maesteg. They brought in new players, W. Adey in the backs and the formidable centre W.H. Rees. They narrowly lost a tough game by 0–3.

They maintained their home ground record with a 0–0 draw to Ogmore Vale, before bagging a cracking home win against Treorchy by 15–5

A December visit to St. Helens to play Swansea Second XV also ended in a win, this time by 6–0, scoring two tries in the process. Ogmore Vale was the next away fixture, and the last before Christmas. This ended in a 3–3 draw with Davy scoring the only try. Outstanding players were Dick Thomas (the skipper), Leon Rees and fullback T. Griffiths.

On Christmas Day they visited Aberavon, who proved much too strong on the day and won 0–20.

Cardiff Grange visited in the new year and were beaten by the Ferry, who also won at home to Maesteg by 1 try to 0. Reports stated that the forwards were outstanding and that half-back Will Bevan had played his finest game. In a return fixture with Pontypridd they were defeated for only the fourth time that season, but half-back Billie Bevan received a kick to the head and suffered a nasty injury.

Ferry also visited Pontardulais and won. The last game of the month was with Aberavon and their unbeaten home record was on the line. The team selected was: fullback Tom Griffiths; threes Tuan Thomas, W.H. Rees, E. George and W. Adey; half-backs Eddie Watkins and D. Handford; forwards R. Thomas (captain), Jim John, M. Edwards, J. Thomas, J. Anthony, M. Watkins, J. Bannister and A. Edwards. Some last-minute changes disrupted the team significantly when W.H. Rees didn't turn up and Eddie Watkins was injured. Tuan Thomas was moved to half-back and Harry Green (who hadn't played for years) took his place on the wing. Llewelyn Edwards went to the centre and ex-Neath forward Rees Phillips came into the pack. Aberavon had felt that they could be in for a rough ride despite their earlier win over the Ferry. The Ferry Town Silver Band was in attendance, and a record crowd of approximately 5,000 was reported! Aberavon won by 3 goals (2 penalties and 1 from a mark), and 3 tries to 0 (0–18).

JIM JONES appeared for Aberavon (he was later to play for the Ferry), as did record try scoring wing Johnny Ring. Jim Jones became Wales' 291st international in April 1919 against New Zealand Services and went on to play another five times for his country. He was originally from Briton Ferry and played for Treherbert and Swansea before joining Aberavon, where he was skipper in 1914 (the year they won the Challenge cup). His brother Billy Thomas also played for Swansea and was capped by Wales Youth, he then went north to York Rugby League. Jim's career ended early due to a serious injury, when he was left at the side of the pitch. His hands were paralysed and, despite seeking medical help from specialists in London, nothing could be done for him! He helped his grandmother run the Royal Dock Hotel in the Ferry, but sadly died aged just 40 in 1932, leaving a wife, Dorothy, and two children, Jim (James Afon) and Norma.

3.8 Jim Jones: Treherbert, Briton Ferry, Aberavon (Captain), Swansea and Wales 1919 (6 caps)

February's fixtures started with two away games, against old rivals Skewen and Monmouthshire league champions Tredegar. The latter ended in a 0–0 draw, but was reported as being their best display of the season. The home supporters were full of praise for the way they played an entertaining open game with some lovely movements among the backs.

A big home win over Glyncorrwg followed. A drop goal by Dai Hanford and a try by S. Diamond put them 7–0 up at half-time. In the second half two tries from centre Ivor Jones and a try and a huge penalty kick from near the halfway flag ended the scoring at 21–0, in a one-sided match. The month finished with a trip up to Cefn Cribbwr.

March produced a creditable away draw with Pontardulais. On the afternoon of Thursday 11 March Swansea brought a weakened First XV to the Ferry and were defeated by 1 Dymond try to 0. The match was watched by a large crowd as most of the local district works were idle, therefore the 4.45 kick-off. The match was in return for Ferry's visit earlier in the season.

A return visit to Loughor was also made in March with both D. Dymond and S. Dymond selected.

In an Easter visit to local rivals Skewen, Ferry were looking for a double, having defeated then at home earlier that season. The squad was: fullback T. Griffiths; threes Tuan Thomas, Ivor Jones, G. Ireland, W. Adey, A. Flynn, J. Phillips; half-backs Willie Jones, W. Bevan, D. Handford; and forwards R. Thomas (captain), Jim John, M. Watkins, M. Davies, C. Bannister, J. Anthony, T. Dobson, A. Edwards, S. Dymond, D. Dymond, S. May, E. Gill and E. Davies.

Neath also visited the Ferry in April and went away with a 1 try to 0 victory to revenge the Ferry win earlier that season by the same score. This brought the season to an end.

An extra game was played on the 1 May to raise funds for the Ferry Town Silver Band. The opposition was a G.F. Llewelyn XV, which he captained. Ferry won the game 10–5, with tries from Adey and Tuan Thomas, and a drop goal by Hanford to a Dick Jones try, converted by Flynn.

Annual dinner

The annual dinner was at the Royal Dock Hotel in late May. The spread was provided by the host Mr A.J. Jones and a large number of players, committee and supporters attended. Chairman Mr G.F. Llewelyn congratulated the club on the season's playing record. He then presented a team photograph to each member and to the committee. The secretary, Mr Phil G. Jenkins, announced that he would be leaving the district to take over an appointment near Chepstow. He was thanked for his service to the club and presented with an inscribed gold watch by Mr Ben Phillips.

Other news

An athletics competition was held at the BFRFC ground on 28 August. The prize money was: 100 yards open handicap, £15; 300 yards open handicap, £10. Among several other events there was even whippet racing, with a prize of £28.

In May, fullback Tom Griffiths played for Neath against Aberavon. He had played for the Ferry earlier that season, but as a Neath boy he had played for the Melyn Barbarians before the war.

During the 1919/20 season Jack Jones was again selected to play for Neath.

PART 4: 1920–1930

The 1920s were probably the most successful decade in the club's history. Under captain Rawlings the team proved almost invincible, and the newspapers of the day reported that it was not unusual for the whole town to attend home games! Indeed, future Prime Minister Ramsey Macdonald was a visitor to one home game, and did the honours of kicking off.

Fullback Ivor Jones played for Neath after returning from four years with the army in France. He had made his name there playing for the, then unbeaten, 6th Welsh regiment. He then had a short stint with the Ferry before returning to play for Neath in 1920.

1920/21

Forward John Griffiths played for Aberavon in a trial match on 4 September. On the same day fellow forward Moses Davies played for Neath against a District XV. Earlier that week fullback Tom Griffiths played for the District XV against Neath, broke his collar bone and played on.

In trial matches at the Ferry on 11 September the teams were:

A Team – fullback Dai Williams of Swansea; threes W. Adey, Ivor Jones, Tuan Thomas, L. Rees and J. Down; halves D. Handford, L. Thomas, B. Vaughan; and forwards R. Jones (captain), M. Watkins, Moses Davies, S. Dymond, D. Dymond, C. Bannister, A. Edwards, E. Gill, S. May and D. Dobson.

B Team – fullback W. Jones; threes L. Lewis, Leslie Morris, George Williams, L. Phillips, A. Thomas; halves S. Cox, D.L. Thomas, G. Thomas; and forwards Dick Thomas (captain), J. Baker, P. Morgan, M. Davies, R. Davies, A. Huxtable, S. Davies, D. Parr, J. Mort, W. Williams and M. James.

Captain
Morgan Watkins

The press printed an interesting article about the new laws and advice to referees from Mr Gilbert Evans of the Yorkshire RFU Society of Referees:

- Take a commonsense and fair view of matters and do not get bustled.

- Get as much practice as possible, and keep fit.

- Do not blow your whistle, except when you want to stop the game.

- The value of a drop goal is 4 points, a penalty goal and a goal from a mark 3 points, do not mix these values!

How relevant is this advice to today's game?

The club season started with a couple of wins. First, over Swansea Second XV at home (3–0, Mog Walters try). Second, Ogmore Vale away, when backs L. Phillips and J. Down and forward C. Bannister came into the side.

Next up was a home fixture with Tredegar (both games against them had been played away the previous season, which resulted in a draw and a narrow defeat). Ferry were defeated again, 3–11.

October fixtures were against Glynneath (lost 0–3), Resolven and Bryncethin away and Pontypridd in the Ferry. According to match reports this was one of the best games seen at the Ferry for a long while, but while the score line brought a smile to Ferry faces 7–4 (Ivor Jones drop goal and Down with a try), the day was tinged with sadness as outside-half D.L. Thomas suffered a broken leg during the match.

There were also reports that the away game at Pandy Park against Bryncethin was the best game seen there for many a season, in which the home team won 3–8.

In a November Thursday afternoon game against Gendros, the Ferry won 15–6, with 1 converted goal, 1 drop goal and 2 tries. In the following game against Ogmore Vale away, Ferry were defeated 0–6.

The next challenge was a tough one as the visitors were Vale of Neath champions Glynneath, who came with an unbeaten record. Things remained that way as the visitors took the spoils by the narrow margin of 0–7 (1 penalty and 1 drop goal). The Ferry team was selected from fullback and captain T. Griffiths; backs W. Millet, I. Jones, Lion Rees, W. Adey, J. Down and C. Richards; half-backs Tuan Thomas and Dick Butler; and forwards P.C. Kay, D. Roberts, M. Watkins, A. Edwards, C. Bannister, S. May, E. Gill, B. Davies, S. Diamond, D. Thomas, J. Mort and D. Jones. The month ended with an away fixture with Loughor.

Also in November back row forward Dick Jones played for the Blacks against the Whites in the first of several Welsh trials. These took place after the second-class clubs of South Wales insisted that they get more recognition. So the WRU arranged several matches involving only non-international players, there were Western District and Eastern District trials and the final trial was an East v. West game.

Ferry suffered another narrow defeat at the start of December, 0–9 away to Skewen. This was followed by a first visit to the Ferry of the Welsh Universities, who had only been beaten by Abercarn and Ferndale during the season. The game was preceded by the varsity team giving their "college cry" to the Ferry supporters. The home team were without skipper Tom Griffiths, who was injured, or centre Lion Rees, who had "missed his train". The final score was 9–5 to the Ferry, with tries from Adey, Meg Watkins and Idris Jones.

A return match with Bryncethin was another narrow defeat, this time by 8–9. Charlie Bannister scored a try, Arthur Thomas converted and trialist Aaron Williams kicked a penalty. It was reported as being a most exciting game in the opinion of referee Mr Dewitt of Swansea. There was also praise for the playing arena, quoted as one of the "best in Wales".

Games over the Christmas period were against Aberavon at the Mansel Ground on Christmas Day, in which they were heavily defeated 0–20; then away to Newport side Pill Harriers on Boxing Day morning, again they suffered defeat, this time by 6–19, with Adey scoring two tries.

The New Year started with a game played in terrible conditions at home to Maesteg, which Ferry lost 0–7. Followed by a narrow 0–3 away defeat to Swansea Second XV. Johnny Flynn came into the backs, along with W. Wellington, K. Collins and A. Phillips. Admission charges for this game were advertised at St. Helens for 8d. and in the Grandstand 8d. extra, including tax.

Pill Harriers then paid their first visit to the Ferry and the home team were forced into changes due to the loss of a number of good players. New faces in the side were fullback. L. Prosser, half-back W. Bevan and forward J. Jones. But the Monmouthshire side were victors on the day, 7–9. The Ferry only had a drop goal and a penalty.

February started with a cancelled game against Loughor at home due to the Wales v. Scotland game being played followed by a visit to Cardiff Varsity, Next up was a home game against Aberavon, watched by a large crowd, reportedly numbering several thousand, many of whom were Aberavon supporters who had all walked to the game! They saw their team home with just a drop goal the difference between the visitors and the home side; Ferry also lost the return game by 0–13.

Loughor were the next visitors to the Ferry in a rearranged match and the home side were victorious by 18–0. Tries came from Evan Williams, Jim Mort, Handford and Adey, and a conversion and a drop goal from Tuan Thomas. The month ended with a visit to Blaina on a Monday evening. The home side were defending a four-year ground record. The Ferry snatched it from them with a 5–3 victory.

In a home game with Neath at the beginning of March, the Ferry were once again victorious. A drop goal from Flynn gave the winning score, 4–3. Jim Johns played, although he had also been for Swansea on this Saturday. The game was slightly marred when, after the final whistle had been blown, the experienced referee, MrW.J. Llewelyn, was jostled by Neath supporters as he left the field and he had to be protected by members of the Glamorgan Constabulary!

The next games were a visit to Pontypridd and a home game with Ebbw Vale, before the return match with Neath on Good Friday on the Gnoll, this time the Welsh All Blacks were the winners. A home game against Blaina on Easter Saturday completed the month.

The first match in April was to have been against Cardiff Scottish, but no agreement on the guarantee was given, so the game was cancelled.

In April, the club played a home fixture against Pontyclun. The game kicked off late due to the late arrival of the away team. After a 4.30 kick-off the Ferry won comfortably by 23–8, even without Jack Jones and captain J. A. Thomas, who was playing for Neath that day. Johnny Flynn was the star of the game. Unfortunately, inside-half Shon Thomas injured his leg badly and was out for the rest of the season.

Other April games were all away. Against Maesteg, which Ferry won, and against Tredegar and Ebbw Vale.

Other players to help Neath out that season were fullback Gwyn Thomas, wing Vernon Hill, prop S. Dymond, flanker T. Jones and no.8 W.E. Thomas.

VERNON HILL was a POW in Karlsruhe in 1917. He played for the Royal Flying Corps in 1916 and then for a South Wales XV v. a New Zealand XV and for a North of England XV v. Anzacs. He went on to captain Neath and to represent the Barbarians. He became a successful businessman in the steel and tinplate industry.

Other news

Ferry's soccer team also rose in the ranks in late autumn, and the press reported that a first-class football side would be run the next season and would play on the rugby pitch at a cost of about £10,000. And that they would enter both the Southern and Welsh Leagues.

Tuan Thomas was reported to have been "poached" by Rugby League scouts and offered the sum of £800 if he would return to his position of inside-half, but he declined the invitation.

Mr G. Llewelyn indicated that he intended to become a candidate for a seat on the WRU committee in place of W. Williams, who had resigned. He didn't succeed, a certain Mr J. B. Williams (who co-incidentally was instrumental in forming Neath C.C.) was elected.

1921/22

The Ferry started the season with a game against local rivals Skewen, which was played at Neath. The game was apparently a niggly affair in which the forwards' struggle was the focal point of the game. W. Richards of Skewen was ordered off in the first half for a late charge on Dobson, the Ferry fullback, but the final score favoured Skewen 3–6. Jack Flynn kicked a penalty very late in the game for the Ferry. The Ferry team were assisted that day by Aberavon captain Jim Jones (who lived in the Ferry at that time and who had been awarded his Glamorgan County cap while playing forward for Aberavon), and by Jim John, the Swansea forward. This helped them dominate up front, but half-backs Shon Thomas and Charlie Heard were outplayed by the Skewen halves.

This was followed by away fixtures with Maesteg, then Treherbert, then at St Helens against Swansea Second XV, in which the Ferry triumphed with 1 try, from Millet, and 1 drop goal to 1 try – 7–3.

October continued with a tough home game against Monmouthshire giants Pill Harriers. The Ferry dominated all aspects of the game. They started well when Charlie Heard kicked a penalty and then scored a try, which he also converted. Following a disallowed try from Adey, W. Millet plunged over for another try, which went unconverted. In the second half their defence shone and gave Ferry an 11–0 victory.

Resolven away ended in a 0–0 draw. Then Ystalyfera were visitors to the Ferry and the start was delayed until 4 p.m due to heavy rainfall. The Ferry were resting several of their top players in light of an upcoming fixture with Neath,

Captains
Morgan Watkins
Llewelyn Thomas

and the game ended in a draw. New wing Adolf Roberts from the Briton Ferry Welfare XV played well.

At the next fixture, a midweek home game against Neath, centre Flynn had to drop out of the game for the Ferry, so once again they had the services of Jim Jones. Ferry started well with a drop goal from Charlie Heard, followed by a T. Thomas try that went unconverted. But Neath pulled back with a try of their own, before Millet scored once again, an unconverted try, to a penalty for the Ferry, to notch up a famous 10–6 win.

Earlier that week Ferry forward Mog Watkins had been selected for the reserves squad in the WRU trials. There were rumours that both Welsh international Ambrose Baker and Sam Thomas of Neath were about to transfer to the Ferry.

October ended with a 0–12 away defeat at Mountain Ash. The team was selected from the following squad: backs Tom Griffiths, W. Millet, D. Jenkins, D. Handford, Tuan Thomas, W. Adey, A. Roberts and A. Thomas; halves Shon Thomas and Charlie Heard; and forwards Morgan Watkins (captain), S.L. Thomas, W.J. Thomas, R. Thomas, R. Davies, G. Bansey, T.J. Jones, Carter Williams, J. Mort and A. Edwards. The referee, Mr Ben Davies of Maesteg, accused skipper Morgan Watkins of kicking an opponent during the game.

> Because Watkins was playing while he was suspended from Neath, he was suspended by the Ferry until the WRU hearing. He was found guilty of playing while suspended and was also put on a report from the Mountain Ash game, and was subsequently banned until the end of the year. The WRU also reprimanded club for playing him while under suspension, and were told that any repetition of this offence would be severely dealt with.

November started with an away game with Morriston, which was drawn 3–3. A. Roberts scoried the only try for the Ferry. On Wednesday 9, Mr Hamilton Morgan's Briton Ferry XV played in Brecon against Christ's College Brecon XV, some well-known players were assisting the Ferry that day and the Collegians had put out their strongest team. In the first half Hamilton Morgan scored two unconverted tries for the Ferry, while two tries by wing W.S. Bevan were disallowed. Play turned a bit more even in the second half. The Ferry added to their score with tries by Novel Jones and Dick Thomas, A. Edwards converted one. The college replied with two tries and converted. The final score was 14–8 to the Ferry. Halves W.H. Thomas and Edwin Thomas had given really good displays.

Match results place BFRFC scores first

The rest of November witnessed a narrow 6–11 defeat at Bridgend and a 12–5 home win over Llanelli Second XV, in which new fullback Bob Richards and centre G. McGrath made their debuts. Charlie Heard kicked a penalty in the first half and Richards kicked one in the second half, while wing Adolf Roberts scoried a try double. November closed with a 1-point defeat, 11–12, on an away trip to Pontyclun.

Ferry made a complete turnaround in December, starting with a home win over Bryncethin. They had to play without outside-half Charlie Heard, who was assisting Neath, and both centres W. Millet and D. Jenkins. Despite this they won 8–7. E. Williams scored 1 try and Bob Richards 1 lovely drop goal in the first half. Then, in the dying minutes of the second half, Lang Thomas scored a try that Richards converted to win the game by a point. The game didn't kick-off until 3.30, as the opponents were late arriving, and most of the second half was played in semi-darkness. Their next games were at home: a first encounter with Pontardawe at home, which they lost 0–3; then against Swansea Second XV, with the Ferry Town Silver Band were in attendance! They went on to complete the double over Aberavon's Whites by 6–3, with Adolf Roberts and Millet the try scorers.

On Christmas Eve, at the beginning of a very busy week, Ferry suffered a heavy 3–21 defeat away at nearest rivals Skewen. On Boxing Day, they travelled up to Newport to play the return game against Pill Harriers, before a squad left to go on tour.

The tour party made the return journey home on the Thursday – as arranged by their secretary. Mr Phil Jenkins – for a home game on Saturday against Ogmore Vale, whom they duly beat by 6–3. Once again, kick off was delayed by 45 minutes by the late arrival of the visitors. The try scorers were Dick Thomas and Carter Williams.

Ferry got off to a winning start in the new year with an 8–3 home defeat of Tredegar. This was an eagerly awaited match as Tredegar's reputation had gone before them, and indeed they were in the lead at half-time by 3–0. A try by Charlie Heard had been disallowed but he got himself on the score sheet in the second half with a fine try, which he also converted. Tuan Thomas completed the scoring with a further try. The home side were minus five of their normal pack and had even recruited centre D. Jenkins into the pack. Skipper Mog Watkins returned from suspension for this game.

Further games in January were away fixtures at Cwmavon and Ogmore Vale and a keenly fought home game in atrocious conditions against Resolven, which they won by 9–8. Charlie Heard crossed for two tries and Jim Jones one. There were a few new faces in the side, such as A. Huxtable and Jon Thomas up front and T. Daniels and F. Gibbon behind. Two Resolven players were reported for dangerous play, which resulted in bans until the end of the season, while Ferry's Euan Davies was banned until 4 March for misconduct.

At home during February, Ferry lost to Glynneath (5–9) and won against Mountain Ash (13–3) with tries from W. Millet and Shon Thomas, a conversion by D. Williams and a drop goal from D. Handford. They lost all their February away games: Ystalyfera (4–6), Treherbert (0–3), Glynneath (5–15) and Llanelli Second XV (3–13, D. Jenkins kicked a penalty).

Ferry turned the tables in March during the return fixture with Bridgend and won well (15–3). The home side were without forward Arthur Edwards, but Bridgend were also shorn of their star as Delahay, the Welsh outside-half, was injured and had to watch helplessly from the touchline as Tom Jones scored a first half try, converted by Bob Richards. Further tries came from Lang Thomas and E. Williams and a drop goal from Dai Handford. A 0–15 defeat at Tredegar followed as they paid the price for travelling with a weakened team. They suffered further as one of their forwards was injured and had to leave the field just before half-time. Outside-half L. Thomas disputed a refereeing decision by Charles Sowerby of Newbridge and was subsequently banned until 9 April. Ferry finished the game with thirteen players.

Ferry then took a midweek trip up the Gwent valleys to play a match against Ebbw Vale that had been held over from the previous season. Home dates with Treherbert and Pontyclun followed, before ending the month with a midweek fixture at home to Aberavon that had been arranged to boost the Ferry's finances. The match was well attended and, although Aberavon were without several of their usual players, it proved to be a cracking contest. The Ferry came out on top by 7–0, with Carter Williams scoring the only try and Shon Evans dropping a goal.

The WRU announced that the season was to be extended until 6 May due to the inclement weather.

April started with a home game against Maesteg. They then hosted a first visit from Gowerton, in which the visitors took the spoils by a point 6–7. Dick Thomas scored a try and Shon Thomas kicked a penalty. The Easter weekend was busy, with an away game on Good Friday against giants Neath, an Easter Saturday away fixture with Bryncethin, then an Easter Monday home game against Morriston. Fullback P. James and forward Reggie Davies joined the squad. In the Neath fixture they had been helped out by Aberavon forward Jim Jones and Jim John of Swansea – the latter was knocked out during the game in a collision for the ball with Neath player Llew Edwards. The Ferry was unlucky to lose 3–9, with Huxtable crossing for the Ferry. The Morriston team were victorious by 6–7 – Moses Davies scored a try and W. Adey kicked a penalty. WRU representative Mr J. B. Williams was an interested spectator. Again the Ferry was shorn of a few players and in came wing W. Millard, outside-half J. Nettle, hooker F.L. Thomas, and forwards S. May and M. Davies.

An extra fixture was arranged for later that week to raise funds for Swansea hospital. A Jim Jones XV drew 13–13 with a Briton Ferry XV. Dai Jenkins, Ivor Davies and E. Gill crossed for the Ferry. The season ended with the return fixture against Gowerton.

Tour

4.1 West of England tour, December 1921

Standing: G. Llewelyn, D. Watkins, T. Daniels, E. Williams, T Thomas, E. Davies, A. Edwards, S. Williams, G. Williams, R. Davies, A. Roberts, J. Jenkins, T.J. Jones, D. W. Hanford; Sitting: B.Richards, R. Thomas, M. Watkins, D.B. Davies, T. Thomas, P.G. Jenkins, W. Millett, A. Myerscough, D. Jenkins, A. Huxtable, J. Thomas, R. Morgan, S. Thomas, J McGrath

On Boxing Day, after the match against Pill Harriers, a squad of 21 players left Newport for Bristol, where they caught the Cornish Riviera Express to Falmouth. They arrived at 10 p.m that night and booked into the Royal Hotel. They played a couple of games that week against Falmouth and Redruth, captained by Tuan Thomas in the absence of Mog Watkins. At Falmouth it was the home team's biggest crowd of the season. In true 'Welsh style' Ferry threw the ball about and were much the better team, however, the home side were awarded a try at the end of the game, which they converted. The referee immediately blew the whistle, leaving Ferry defeated by 3 points.

AGM

The AGM was presided over by Mr D. Davies. The balance sheet showed a deficit of £133 2s. There had also been some difficulties about a ground to play on, as the old rugby ground had been taken over by the local welfare association, and no arrangements had been made for its use. It was hoped that this would be sorted out very soon and that the club would be back playing on the old field. The only alternative was to use the old soccer ground at Brynhyfryd, which was neither very flat nor so easily accessed as the welfare ground.

Mr Jenkins was asked to continue as secretary and the following were elected to the committee: W.J. Hill, Hamilton Morgan, Rees Jones, W.S. Bevan, C. Callaghan, F. Llewelyn, D.D. Davies, Rees Phillips, R. Thomas, R. Jones, J. Digman and R. Phillips. The likely captain for the next season, to be decided in the players' meeting, was ex-Aberavon captain, Mr Jim Jones.

The *South Wales Daily Post* on 27 March printed an interesting article about events before and during the France v. Wales match the previous weekend. The writer was from Briton Ferry, then resident in Paris. She described how the streets of Paris were covered in snow on the Thursday, but how the Stade Colombes ground was perfect, with lush green grass. She recounted how the battle for the best seats started at 11.30 p.m.! She conjured up a little white monument in one corner of the ground, dedicated to the football players who had fallen during the Great War, and how the banners beside it and the conscripts in the crowd, the gendarmes, the soldiers on guard and the bands all gave a military air to the place. She also mentioned that Wales won the game and that it was the Welsh team who paraded through the boulevards covered in confetti!

1922/23

The club held a practice match on their new ground off Old Road at the beginning of September, on which the posts had not yet been erected. Club captain Jim Jones refereed the game, which ended in a 9–9 draw. W. Adey was among the best of the backs on the day, and ex-Swansea player Jim John was prominent up front. The ground was officially opened the following Thursday 7 September with a game against a Jack Jones Neath XV, which was kicked off by Mr G. B. Marsh. Ferry were defeated by 2 tries to 0.

The season started on a miserable, windy, wet day when they met Bryncethin at home in a match that ended in a 0–0 draw! Outside-half Shon Thomas was playing for Aberavon that day so Tuan Thomas took his place, up front Jim John had recently joined from Swansea, and Evan Harris had recently returned from India.

Captain
Capt H. Rawlings

Next up was another home fixture. The visitors were Amman United, who arrived late, delaying kick-off by an hour. The ensuing game was hard and keenly fought. A player from each side was dismissed and the visitors got so upset that the whole team went to the touchline and had to be induced to return by their committee. The Ferry won an unconvincing match, with a solitary try from E. Gill. Ivor Thomas was subsequently banned for attempted punching and suspended until 30 November, as he had already served a ban for another offence.

The next opponents were Bridgend (away) and in atrocious conditions the Ferry suffered a narrow defeat by 3–5. Vice captain Willie Millett was the try scorer for the Ferry. Two home wins followed, the first over Pill

Harriers. The second over Ammanford by 12–11, despite being down to seven forwards for most of the second half due to an injury to long-serving player Dick Thomas, and being without half-back W. McGrath or Captain Jim Jones, who was assisting Aberavon. Prominent in this game were fullback Bob Richards, half-back Con Evans, and forwards J. Slater, E. Williams, Evan Harris, E. Davis and A. Jenkins.

October continued with fixtures at Skewen, which they lost 3–10 (Hurford kicked a penalty), and then at home to Ystalyfera.

P. Cantle come into the side at half-back for a November away game at Resolven. Ferry then lost the next two away games, at Ammanford 5–11 and at Pontypridd 0–25, before completing the month with a disappointing home 3–3 draw with Kenfig Hill, for which the homesters failed to raise a full team.

Welsh trials were held in Port Talbot during November. A Probables XV played a West XV, and Harris of the Ferry was on the Probables bench.

Mountain Ash at home was the first challenge in December. It was reported that a good gate should be expected, along with an equally good game, as the Ferry forwards – which included E. Harris, R. Thomas, S.L. Thomas, E. Williams, A. Salter, R. Jones, captain Rawlings, M. Watkins, A. Huxtable, J. Groves, Downey and Skipper Jim Jones – were reputed to be as good as any in the district. But the game proved disappointing for the Ferry because, despite monopolising all of the play and the possession, they could only manage a try from Dai Jenkins which was converted by P.C. Hurford. While the 'Mount' managed a try and a penalty goal to win by 5–6.

Gowerton away were next up, before Ferry lost once again to Skewen (away 3–21). Then followed the return fixture away to Amman United, before playing Treherbert at home just before Christmas.

On Christmas Day they played Aberavon away. On Boxing Day they drew 0–0 with a strong Dulais United XV at home. For the last game of the year, at home to Ogmore Vale, they received a telegram informing them that Ogmore could not raise a side to travel and therefore had to cancel the fixture.

Just before Christmas it was reported that, for the previous few months, the town of Briton Ferry had had the unique experience of having no unemployed people, but that, sadly, the Albion Steelworks had announced in November that due to a temporary depression in trade, they were to make over 500 men redundant.

On New Year's Day, new faces Pep Mellin and A. Soper up front and H. Marsh (a Brecon Collegiate) on the wing appeared against Neath at the Gnoll.

A good win at Maesteg was followed by a visit from Pontypridd to the Ferry in a game that they won 6–4 (after being earlier defeated 0–24 by the same opponents). Another late arrival delayed the kick-off until 3.30 p.m. After a strong surge by Jim Jones, Huxtable followed up to score for the Ferry, this was followed by a second half penalty kick from the touchline by Hurford to give Ferry a deserved win. They then defeated Cwmavon 11–6 at home, with Tuan Thomas, Mog Watkins and G. Davies the try scorers, Thomas added a conversion. G. Ireland came in at fullback for this game. Ferry finished the month off with a 3–11 defeat at Pill Harriers, a Jim Jones penalty was Ferry's only score.

They also played Ystalyfera away.

February fixtures were against Maesteg (lost 5–9) and Resolven (home 3–3, Jim Jones scored a fine try. Ferry had to use seven reserves against Resolven due to player unavailability. They then lost 8–12 to Glynneath away, in which Jim Jones and Huxtable scored tries, with McGrath converting.

In early March, a game with Neath had to be postponed to rest the pitch at the Gnoll. A home defeat (0–11) to Skewen got them off to a bad start. A home game with Ogmore Vale started an hour late, but the visitors were heavily defeated by 32–0. Team changes were made for the Glynneath game, with Adolf Roberts coming into the back division and new half-backs W. Edwards and E. Cross, and forwards A. Soper and P. Button. Cross and Huxtable scored a try in the 8–8 draw.

They played Mountain Ash in March and lost 0–6. Tom Collins of the Old Firm (Maesteg) stood down from the game as he was selected to get his first cap for Wales v. Ireland the following Saturday.

An away trip to rugged opponents Bryncethin was the final away game of the month.

Ferry faced Aberavon on Good Friday, in front of the biggest home crowd of the season, and then Skewen on Easter Saturday at home, which ended in a 3–0 win and a 5–19 defeat, respectively.

Ferry ended the season with all away games against: Kenfig Hill; Bridgend (lost 14–20, Huxtable, Morgan, Crabtree and Evans scored tries, Adey converted); Treherbert (lost 3–8, Dai Harris the try scorer); Cwmavon; and Neath. The final game against Skewen was cancelled.

Making his debut for the club against Aberavon was ARTHUR LEMON from Tonna. He was just short of his eighteenth birthday and was a steelworker at the Briton Ferry works. He gained his first Glamorgan County cap before joining Neath in 1925/26. He was selected for his first Welsh cap against Ireland in 1928/29 and went on to win 13 caps. It was said that he was one of the best exponents of

lineout play in the four nations. He played against the touring Springboks in 1931/32. Benny Osler, the Springbok captain, described him as "like a tank". Arthur was not averse to entering into the physical side of the game and said of a game against France in 1930, "You had to join in and punch otherwise you would have ended up on the floor!" It made later battles in Paris in 1981 and Twickenham 1980 look like vicarage tea parties. He joined St Helens in 1933, when he was 28, and played there for two seasons before joining Streatham/Mitcham Rugby League Club, who were trying to get a foothold in London. But they only lasted for one season and Lemon returned home to work as a steelmaker in Neath.

4.2 Arthur Lemon

AGM

At the AGM on Tuesday 3 July it was reported that the balance sheet, which had started the season with a deficit of over £50, was in credit by 6s – despite spending £38 on fencing off the ground.

- Income – £387 15s 9d
- Expenditure – £387 9s 9d.

Mr J. B. Williams was thanked for making the playing ground available once more. Outgoing secretary Mr Abraham Owen was thanked for his services and Mr Willie Millet unanimously voted in to his place. Mr W. Rhys Jones was re-elected as treasurer and they were joined on the committee by: chairman Mr W.J. Hill, D. B. Davies, James Thomas, Ben Phillips, W. Thomas, Hamilton Morgan, Evan Thomas, R. Morgan, T. Thomas, Dan Phillips, and G.F. Llewelyn as captain (to be announced at a later date by the players). There was also the prospect of a tour to Cornwall at the end of the season.

Other news

During the close season Mr W.J. Hill was voted on to the Neath & District committee.

1923/24

The season started with a novelty, the first annual sports day instead of the annual trial match at the club.

Athletes from all over the area participated. The 100 yards open handicap was won by J. Rapey from Abergwnfi, who netted the prize of £5. Cochrane of Neath came second (£1) and I. Thomas of Penygraig third (10s). In the 220 yards open E. Thomas of Aberavon was first past the line, netting £3, with J. Youatt of Neath second (£1) and Cochrane third (10s). In the 410 yards race, first place and the £3 prize went to R. James from Aberavon, Youatt came second again (£1) and G. Mumford from Pontardawe third (10s). In the Under-16s 100 yards open the first prize of 10s went to Tommy Martin from Pontardawe, with Burrows from Neath second (5s) and Tommy Thomas of the Ferry third (2s 6d). They even had a 100-yards open whippet race, which was won by Somo Scraps (Purcell) who netted £5, with Little Prince (James) second (£1) and Will Eira (Snow) third (10s).

Captain
Capt H. Rawlings

Jim Jones brought a Neath XV to start the rugby season – and they left with a 0–13 win.

Ferry had a good start to the season proper with an 11–6 home win over Pontycymmer. This was followed by difficult away matches at Maesteg (lost 7–27, Crabtree 1 drop goal and McGrath 1 try) and at Bryncethin before meeting old rivals Skewen at home (lost). Prominent in these opening games were backs Bob Smitham, Jas McGrath and Dai Harries and forwards Morgan Watkins, Sam Lang Thomas, Jack Harris and H. Lemon. Also coming into the side at this early stage were A. Williams at fullback and forwards S. May and W. Gleaves.

In October, the side was strengthened for the away game at Bridgend with the inclusion of Levi Phillips at half-back, ex-Welsh international and Aberavon forward

Jim Jones and ex-Neath captain Jack Jones up front. But Ferry lost the game by a single point, 11–12, in a game that was voted the best seen at Bridgend that season. Dai Harries scored a hat trick of tries in the first half, W. Adey converted one. But a drop goal at the end of the game put paid to their efforts.

Then they faced a visit from East Wales rivals Pill Harriers. Bryn Kleiser, the ex-Skewen and Swansea outside-half, played for the Ferry alongside Bob Smitham. The first half ended scoreless, but Kleiser scored a lovely try and then kicked a late drop goal to win the game for the Ferry by 7–5.

There were sweeping changes to the team for the next match away to Ammanford as Kleiser had decided to return to Skewen, Smitham had transferred to Swansea, and Charlie Heard had returned from Neath. So, in came Arthur Williams at fullback and J.W. Jones, P.C. Hopkins and Glyn Williams up front. But Ferry were defeated 3–15.

The month ended with a home game against Tredegar in a rain storm. Rice-Evans scored the only try in a 3–3 draw. New to the team that day was back H. Marsh.

During October J.M. WATKINS, the Ferry forward, was selected to play for the Whites in the second West Wales Welsh trial. He was reported as being to the fore of the action throughout. He was later selected to play for Glamorgan County at Neath against Western Counties, alongside him that day was last minute replacement wing Dai Harries and centre Bob Smitham. That game was won 38–6 in controversial circumstances as the Western XV had six Llanelli players pulled out of the team the day before the game.

BOB SMITHAM went on to impress for Swansea for the rest of that season and also played for the victorious West Wales XV against the Welsh Probables in a trial match at Llanelli in November. He then made the reserves for the Probables against the East Wales XV.

Neath paid a visit to the Ferry on Thursday 1 November, and went away with a relatively easy win, 0–12, although the Ferry had kept them pointless in the first half. Ex-Ferry player Charlie Heard made 1 drop goal at the end of the match for Neath. Wing Dai Harries joined the Neath team later in the season.

The following Saturday Ferry visited Aberaman and lost 0–6. And then lost their next game at home to visiting Maesteg 3–10 (W. Adey was the try scorer). Changes were again made for the next game at home to Ammanford, with Tom Jones at fullback, W. Paisley at centre, B. Denby on the wing and PC J. Hopkins and A. Phillips up front. But they failed to prevent the visitors from doing the double and lost 0–6.

The frost beat them in the next two games, away at Pontycymmer and home to Skewen, as they were both called off.

In a cold December, games against Glynneath and Resolven at home both ended in a 3–3 draw. Wing Jos Hughes made an excellent debut in the Glynneath game and Tom Jones kicked a penalty in the Resolven game for the only score.

The annual Christmas period challenge was next for the team that had last won a game on 13 October. First up were Aberaman and a 0–0 draw ensued. Then they faced the local Workingmen's club on Christmas Day. Unfortunately, their Boxing Day opponents Pontardulais sent a telegram on that morning to say they couldn't raise a side, so the game was cancelled. Ferry visited Aberavon on the 27th, and were defeated 4–13. Jim Jones' drop goal was the only Ferry score. The month ended with a visit to Treorchy.

A home game with Pontypridd was quite a start to the new year. They rose to the occasion by winning 10–7. Forward Jim Lemon got a goal from a mark (3 points), PC Will Perry added 1 try and Tal Harris 1 drop goal. It was said that the combined forwards experience of the two ex-Welsh internationals, Jim Jones and PC Will Perry, helped greatly to gee up the youngsters in the pack. There were three other policemen in the side that day, three-quarter Evan Grey, and forwards S. J. Hopkins and Goodwin.

Pill Harriers at home was followed by a Thursday away clash with fierce rivals Skewen, which they lost 7–22 in front of a large crowd. Jim Jones got 1 try and Paisley 1 drop goal. Ferry then played at Neath the following Monday. A home win over Bryncethin the following Saturday raised hopes, with wing Sam Jones and centre Evan Grey the try scorers.

February continued with a home game against Treorchy, followed by the return match with Pontypridd, before yet another defeat, this time away to Glynneath 0–12. They finished the month with another Thursday fixture, this time against Aberavon. The match was to have been played in the Ferry, but thanks to the kindness of the Neath committee it was played on the Gnoll where a bigger crowd could be expected. The Ferry had the services of Llanelli forward Ivor Jones for this game (as he had relatives in the Ferry), which brought the number of Welsh internationals in the pack up to three. Tal Harris scored the only try in a 3–0 victory.

March started with a rearranged game against Swansea Uplands. Their opponents that day should have been Ogmore Vale, but they had been disbanded. Ferry were without fullback Tom Jones as he had transferred to Swansea, but they still managed to win 11–8. H. Rice–Jones scored a try, converted by W. Paisley, then C. Lewis and Ivor Davies added further tries. March ended with an away fixture at Tredegar sandwiched between home and away fixtures with Pontardulais. Ferry lost the away game 0–8, featuring that day were wing Vernon Preece and forwards I. Hopkins, D.R. Murphy and Tim Bright.

Ex-player **ROBERT SMITHAM** was still pushing for a Welsh cap, as he was selected in the centre for the Rest XV in the final Welsh Trial.

Referee **ALBERT FREETHY** was selected to take charge of two internationals on the same day – England had contacted him to referee their home game with France, then Scotland asked him to referee their game against Ireland. He opted for Twickenham, and another Welshman took his place at Murrayfield.

4.3 Referee Albert Freethy

The club was also represented in an international match between Wales Civil Service and their English equivalents at Bristol (26 March 1924). Forwards **JACK JONES** and **H. RAWLINGS** were both capped in a Welsh victory, despite going down to fourteen men after half-back Albert Owen from Swansea collapsed due to an injury sustained in a tackle.

The final month of the season started in confusion as opponents Bridgend had double-booked fixtures. So Ferry played Maesteg instead. The following Monday they hosted original opponents Bridgend and beat them 8–6. Jim Lemon and Charlie Heard were the try scorers. Into the side that day came three-quarter D. Poley and forward Moses Davies.

For the next game Ferry visited Resolven before a clash that should have been with Kenfig Hill. But they managed to slip in a return fixture with

Briton Ferry Workingmen's club, which they won 18–13. Lemon, A. Bray and Jenkin Hopkins were the try scorers, W. Paisley added two conversions. The penultimate match was against Kenfig Hill away. They wrapped up the season with a midweek away fixture against Neath RFC. It was reported that the players treated this game quite lightly and that there were many amusing incidents, such as PC Marcus Cole sitting in the mud and spinning like a top! A certain Mr J. Bancroft refereed the game. The result went Neath's way, 0–12.

AGM

The AGM in the Royal Dock Hotel had a record attendance. Chairman Mr W.J. Hill stated that the balance sheet was looking healthy and that the election of a strong committee meant the new season was looking good. Mr Millet was re-elected as secretary, and Rhys Jones as Treasurer.

Other news

There was a move afoot to create a rugby league, as in the South Wales and Monmouthshire areas, and one immediate suggestion was to form a league system and/or a knockout cup, but these did not come about until much later.

1924/25

The Ferry team used to change in the Royal Dock Hotel in Villiers Street, from where they travelled by coach to Old Road, Cwrt Sart playing field. There were four cut-off baths in the Dock Hotel for the players after the game. MR JIM JONES ran the hotel (ex-Aberavon captain and Welsh international no.8/flanker; first capped in 1919 against the New Zealand Army XV; he won five further caps, one against England, two against Scotland, one each against France and Ireland, the last in 1921; he also later turned out for the Ferry). Sadly, he died in 1933, aged only 40.

Jim Jones' son, also JIM, strayed over to soccer and played for Cardiff City during the Second World War, alongside the likes of Alf Sherwood. He made his debut at Ashton Gate, Bristol, on 13 February 1943, before the Welsh rugby team made theirs. His manager was Cyril Spears, who offered Jim a contract worth £1.50 per match, at today's rate!

Captain
Adam Bray

Vice captain
W. Paisley

The club played a trial game on the evening of Saturday 30 August. Quite a number of new players from the district turned up and impressed the selection committee. The Probables won by 3 tries to 0, but there was little to choose between the sides. It was reported that the pack was equal to any in the county and that, with a mixture of new and old talent, they should do well in the coming season. The find of the game was fullback Len Shipton from Neath, who was outstanding in defence and a strong kicker; stand outs in the three-quarter line were PC Evan Grey, Tommy Evans, A. Bray, Davies and Jeffs; young Denby played well at half-back, and should be pushing Tal Harris for a place, alongside W. Paisley. A meeting of the players elected their captain and vice captain.

The first challenge of the season was an away fixture at Treorchy with Shipton being given his first start at fullback. Unfortunately, they lost a narrow game by 1 drop goal to 0.

The next game involved a trip to Barnstaple, which meant a journey from Swansea to Ilfracombe by boat on Saturday morning. They were without some first choice players but Joe Hughes and J. Groves were drafted into the team. Groves scored one of the two Ferry tries, Davies grabbed the other, but it was a 9–6 defeat.

A midweek match at home against Hendy was next. Neath players Dai Hiddlestone and Glyn Jones appeared for the visitors. Ferry were without Tal Harris, Jim Jones or J. Hopkins. Arthur Edwards was the only try scorer for the Ferry in a 3–3 draw. Two away defeats followed, one against Maesteg, and then Bridgend in which they started with 14 players and were down to 13 after the first minute of the game.

The following Saturday they met Neath at the Gnoll and gave their illustrious opponents a real fright. The first half was all Ferry, but the second half belonged to Neath, who scored an unconverted try and kicked a penalty to win by 0–6.

A return game with Treorchy ended in a 0–0 draw– a try by wing Preece was disallowed. The following week they were defeated at home by Aberaman, 0–6, who were unbeaten at that time.

The final game in October was a home one against Ammanford in which they were back to full strength. The game was kicked off by the prime minister, Ramsey MacDonald! It brought in the biggest gate of the season. Tal Harris scored the only try with a brilliant run from his own 25-yard line in a 3–0 win (see Figure 4.1)

November started with a visit to local rivals Skewen, followed by a midweek fixture against Glamorgan County Police, which they lost 4–6 – Tom Davies 1 drop goal. They then faced an unbeaten Aberaman side away. They won Pontardawe at home by 4 points, even though they were without four of their regular forwards in captain Rawlings, Jim Jones, A. Edwards and C. Bannister. The Briton Ferry Welfare club recruits played well, such as Len Shipton and Bryn Bazzard.

The following week they were again at home, this time to Kenfig Hill. They emerged as victors by 9–0, despite being without Rawlings, Evan Grey, Jenkin Hopkins and Tom Jones, the latter two were playing for Neath. Two tries from wing T. J. Davies and one from Syd Jenkins secured the win. They ended the month with an away game at Resolven.

4.4 Briton Ferry v. Ammanford 1924 – Ramsay MacDonald is holding the ball

December was a tough month, with games against Pontypridd and Treherbert at home, followed by Ammanford away. On Christmas Eve, Aberavon away, they lost 5–14. On Boxing Day it was Carmarthen away and on the 27th Bryncethin at home (3–9, Pascoe penalty). They defeated Pontypridd 3–0, with centre Paisley scoring a dazzling try, but lost the next two games by 0–5 and 0–11, in the latter match Ferry was again without Rawlings, Tal Harris, Tom Jones and Jenkin Hopkins, as they were all due to be playing for Neath in a match at Bath. P. Griffiths, D. David, R. Llewelyn and W.C. Thomas came into the side.

The new year began with a visit to Pontypridd, then further visits to Resolven (3–3) and Glynneath (3–14, Cross with a try), and home games with Ystalyfera (0–4), Skewen (0–8) and Maesteg. Despite the assistance of twice-capped flanker/lock Dan Pascoe, who had previously played for Llanharan, Bridgend and Neath, and was to go north to play for Leeds Rugby League in 1927. New players drafted in included W. Bowen, PC J. Hopkins, E. Bourdon, PC E. Jones, W. Edwards, E. Cross, A. Jeffs, W. Ball and S. James, some came from the Welfare club. This allowed Tal Harris and others to play for Neath.

These were hard times in the Ferry as the recession started to bite with 2,000 men laid off during February and the threat of more to come. The Villiers, Ferry and Baglan Bay tinworks all closed down and the Albion and Briton

Match results place BFRFC scores first

Ferry steelworks both lay idle. That only left the Briton Ferry ironworks, the Whitford galvanising works and the Gwalia tinworks still active.

A scheduled match against Neath at the Gnoll had to be re-scheduled due to the massive interest in the Neath Ex-schoolboys game against Christ's College Brecon Boys, which was played on the Gnoll instead of the Ferry game! Neath won 6–3, with two tries to one. So Ferry's only two games in February were both away, at Pontardawe and Bryncethin. They won both.

March was a busy month in which Ferry at home defeated Resolven by just 1 try to 0. A. Jeffs was the scorer. Reggie Davies came into the side. In an away 16–8 win at the Dingle against Morriston, Pascoe scored a try and then converted it. A. Morgan was also among the try scorers. This was followed by two away games at Kenfig Hill and Aberaman and home games against Carmarthen Quins (3–0, Bryn Bazzard was the try scorer), for which there was a poor crowd. Then the return with Morriston and finally the much-awaited visit to the Gnoll to play Neath, which they lost 4–11, Adam Bray 1 drop goal.

April was equally as busy, starting with a home win over Cwmavon by 10–4. Policeman Evans 1 drop goal, PC Ivor Thomas and PC Evan Harris 1 try each. A trip to Treherbert followed.

On Good Friday they entertained local rivals Aberavon. This was regarded as the chief fixture of the season and a special train was commissioned from Aberavon to arrive at the Ferry in time for a 4.30 p.m. kick-off as a very large crowd was expected. Unfortunately, Ferry lost 6–14 (E. Harries and E. Selby were the try scorers).

Ferry then made a trip to Ystalyfera, before a home win over Glynneath by 6–0, then a midweek visit to Bridgend, which they lost 0–8. The season ended with two visits that ended in defeat: to Hendy, 0–21; and at Skewen, 0–8.

A sad end to the season was the announcement that Ivor Davies had been suspended until the end of September for striking an opponent in the game against Morriston, the recipient of the punch, Tom Morgan, was also banned – until the end of October!

Youth rugby

Neath Schoolboys played in the Ferry during January and won 8–5 against their close opponents, Aberavon, in the Dewar Shield competition.

Around the district

During March the Welfare side scored a good victory over Neath Banks by 5 tries to 0. A number of the Ferry players were selected to play for Neath

Borough Police against their counterparts from Monmouthshire at Neath, refereed by Mr Freethy. Hollingdale and Grey were included in the side. It was reported that after the game the players were entertained in the Bird in Hand by their captain, and Chief Constable for Neath, Rawlings!

During this season Mr W.J. Hill was elected to the Glamorgan County committee and Evan Grey played for Neath v. Aberavon.

During November, Tal Harris was selected to play for Glamorgan County against Western Counties at Ammanford. As outside-half he scored 1 drop goal in a 19–21 defeat.

In December, Tom Jones transferred back to the Ferry and Len Shipton transferred out to Swansea. Briton Ferry Welfare had an interesting fixture when they hosted a Public Schools XV at the Welfare ground, refereed by none other than Albert Freethy, who had selected the school team with Mr Gwyn Thomas, a former Neath fullback. A number of school internationals were selected. Mr Freethy was to infamously send off New Zealander Cyril Brownlie against England this season.

Other news

In February, the International Board met to consider new reforms, including: reducing drop goal points to 3 from 4; appointing referees for all international matches; and preventing a charge when taking a penalty.

In May, whippet racing was held in the Ferry as a novelty, with the proceeds going to club funds. The handicapper was Mr W.J. Lewis of Merthyr.

Captain W.J. Rawlings was nominated for one of the five positions as WRU vice president, but his 38 votes were not enough, therefore he was not elected. He was also active at the WRU AGM. First, he opposed a motion by the general committee to secure that members should be elected to the match committee – all thirteen for a period of three years instead of the current one year. But again he was defeated, this time by a large majority. Second, he led the opposition to a general committee proposal to increase the selection committee from five to seven. His felt that if the right five people were on the selection panel that any extras would merely add two more unsatisfactory workers. The vote went against him again, but not with a sufficient majority to be carried forward so it was defeated, and the panel was to carry on with a 'big five'. Then, on behalf of Briton Ferry RFC and seconded by Mr W.J. Hill, Rawlings moved that in future those five should be selected by a ballot vote taken at the annual meetings of the union. He expressed the view that if this motion was carried forward it would get rid of the "terrible feeling that we must be represented on the committee". He also argued that such a system would be a means of doing away with the pernicious system of canvassing for positions and that only persons with a sound practical knowledge of rugby football would stand a chance of election. The feeling of discontent with the selectors had largely grown out of the last two teams fielded by the Welsh side – again he was defeated by an overwhelming majority.

4.5 1924/25

1925/26

A fete and sports day on Bank Holiday Saturday in August raised funds for the club.

At a meeting in August chairman Captain H. Rawlings announced the election of the captain and vice captain and that there would be a practice match at the end of the month. Many Neath Harlequins members were expected to attend as their club had become defunct for lack of a ground to play on. T. Ireland and Evan Thomas were appointed as trainers. The meeting was attended by W. Paisley, the Ferry outside-half who had just signed for Swinton Rugby League Club. Although the Ferry were sad to lose him, they wished him all the best in his new venture.

Captain
Jenkin Hopkins

Vice captain
Tal Harris

The practice match was a success as the numbers of players far exceeded two teams. The stripes took the game 12–3 over the whites and outscored them 4 tries to 1, but plenty of fire from the forwards and skills from the backs were in evidence.

The season opened with an away fixture at Pill Harriers, which Ferry narrowly lost 3–6, with Tom Hollingdale the try scorer. Tom Jones, the first-choice fullback, had been selected to play for Swansea Second XV, so a couple of new three-quarters, Sam Jones and Glyn Morgan (formerly of Neath RFC) were selected, as was Glyn John up front, Penry Davies replaced W. Paisley at outside-half partnered by Tal Harris.

In the first home game of the season Treorchy were the visitors and Adam Bray scored a try for the Ferry in a tight game which ended even at 3–3.

Match results place BFRFC scores first

On the next Saturday fixtures were swapped and the Past v. Present game was brought forward a week. Neath were the next opponents and they went down to them 3–11. Returning players were to the fore, such as Glyn Morgan at centre, Syd James in the backs and J. Lemon, A. Lemon, B. Burton and B. Bazzard up front. Wing W.D. Denby had a trial for Swansea. Charlie Heard scored the Ferry try.

That same week W.J. Hill was re-elected to the Glamorgan County RFC committee.

Newbridge were the next opponents away, which Ferry lost. This was followed by a visit to Skewen, again lost, 6–22. S. Jones and T. Hollingdale scored tries, J. Harries got himself sent off and Dan Richards was taken off injured.

There was a bit of controversy that week as Swansea had asked for a permit to play **TAL HARRIS**, but they were refused.

4.6 Tal Harris: Briton Ferry, Aberavon and Wales

A drawn game at Cwmavon followed, with a 3–3 score. E. Thomas kicked a penalty. Cwmavon's try was controversial as the touch judge had held up his flag to indicate touch as the Cwmavon player went over the line, but the referee overruled him and gave the try. Treherbert were the next opponents away. H. Smith came in at fullback.

The Ferry won a home midweek match with Bryncethin, 12–3. A. Jeffs made two tries and Charlie Heard and Crabtree grabbed one each. H. Rice-Evans made his debut for the Ferry. Also that week, A. Lemon was selected to play for Glamorgan County against Gloucestershire at Cardiff, which they won 12–5, he also played for them against Western Counties.

The Ferry's next three games were all away, against Pontypridd, Maesteg and Tredegar. Ponty were beaten by 11–3, with Crabtree scoring two tries and E. Thomas kicking a penalty and a conversion. They went down 3–9 at Tredegar and 6–8 at Maesteg.

> Then there was more controversy surrounding TAL HARRIS. The WRU announced that he had been suspended until 28 November for challenging an opponent to a fight in the game against Skewen, but the Ferry secretary then pointed out in the *Daily Post* that this was a case of mistaken identity as it was Jack Harries who had received the ban and not Tal.

In November, Ferry had their first home game on a Saturday for two months and they defeated opponents Pontardawe 13–0. Jim Lemon (2) and Tom Hollingdale were the try scorers and Jenkin Hopkins converted 2. Ferry also triumphed the following week against visitors Glynneath, this time by 16–6. Tries from Hollingdale, Syd James and W. Jones were added to by a drop goal and two conversions. For their third consecutive home game, they defeated Bridgend by 11–0. A. Bray, W.C. Thomas and Charlie Heard were the try scorers and Eddie Thomas added a conversion. Pontypridd were then seen off on their own patch with Bray getting a try for the only score of the game. Ferry then completed their November fixtures with another home game, this time over Treherbert. Tal Harris and Eddie Thomas were the try scorers, Thomas converted one, for an 8–3 victory.

Still at home for the first game in December and facing the formidable challenge of their closest rivals Skewen, the *Daily Post* picked the match as the fixture of the day. S. Smith came in at fullback. There was a huge crowd as large numbers of Neath and Aberavon supporters came along after their teams' games were abandoned due to heavy frost. It was also touch and go whether this match was going ahead. Charlie Heard 1 neat drop goal for the Ferry, but they lost their ground record by 4–14.

> About a month previously they had been presented with a new set of jerseys with black and amber hoops. These clashed with their rival's colours and they had to change for this match to a set of green jerseys. One wag stated that they probably would have won if they had kept their new colours!

The following week Ferry travelled to Bridgend for a return match, but this game turned into a dour, no score draw. The following Saturday, the week before Christmas, they decided to experiment with playing two games in one day: an away game at Kenfig Hill, which they lost by 5 points; and a return fixture at home to Newbridge, which they won 9–0. Bray, W.C. Thomas and Lemon were the try scorers. Over Christmas they entertained Kenfig Hill to a return match on Christmas Eve, a home fixture against Cwmavon on Christmas Day, and Cardiff Grange (the holders of the Mallet Shield) on Boxing Day – ending up with three wins of 10–3, 13–6 and 32–3, respectively. The last was a record home score and try scorers were Gibbon (3), Jeffs, Tal Harris, Lemon, E. Thomas, Crabtree, Foley and Syd James – only one try was converted.

January started with a 20–0 win over a full Penygraig side in an outstanding display of rugby. Wing Gibbon made two tries by, with further tries from centre W.C. Thomas and A. Bray, two conversions from Eddie Thomas and a drop goal by Tal Harris. The game was delayed and subsequently shortened due to the late arrival of the away side as their charabanc had broken down on route! Outstanding for the Ferry were forward Lemon, who had played for the county earlier in the season, and half-back Charlie Heard, in their first fixture against Penygraig.

Skewen (away) was next up and the Ferry won well, 9–4, with tries from Tal Harris, Heard and Sid James. A visit to Bryncethin was the next fixture before they faced Pill Harriers at home and defeated them 6–0, Eddie Thomas and Bray the try scorers. The game did get a little rough towards the end and the referee had to speak sternly to the players. But in true Ferry fashion there was a dinner after the match at the Dock Hotel and the Pill Harriers players all attended.

> Ferry chairman Captain H. Rawlings presided, supported by the Mayor, Alderman D.G. Davies JP, Alderman B. Bowen, and councillors R. Jenkins (ex-mayor), W.H. Waring and W.J. Hill, with Messrs Walter E. Rees and T.W. Hubert of the WRU, and G.F. Llewelyn and J. Glover. The chairman presented Mr W. Millett, the club secretary, with a silver-mounted, ebony walking stick, suitably engraved as an appreciation of his splendid work in

the club's interest. Millet was lauded by all the speakers. Then former player Llewelyn presented Captain Rawlings with a large framed portrait of himself in club colours and praised his great service to the club. He hoped that the portrait would remind him of the jolly time he had at the club with the boys.

On Thursday 28 January they were awarded a fixture against Swansea at St. Helens, and they faced a strong All Whites side. This was their first ever fixture with the senior club, and they were keen to give a good impression. Within seven minutes of kick-off they scored a fine try through their captain, Rawlings, which W.C. Thomas converted. But the lead didn't last long and at half-time they were 5–8 down. A further try from Swansea made the final score 5–11.

The following Saturday Ferry drew 3–3 up in Penygraig. Sam Jones scored the only try. Pontypridd then visited the Ferry and, after arriving late for kick-off, went away the losers by 9–0. Charlie Heard, Arthur Lemon and Gibbon were the try scorers. The following week Tredegar were the visitors and they also went away defeated by 15–0. The Ferry scored 4 tries and 1 penalty.

There was no fixture on the next Saturday, so they hastily arranged a game against a Gwyn Thomas XV. Maybe the ex-Neath and Glamorgan County player was sorry to have brought a scratch side to the Ferry as his team were put to the sword to the tune of 73–5. This record for the Ferry came from W.C. Thomas scoring 5 tries, his centre partner Eddie Thomas scoring 3 and converting 10, Gibbon scored 3 tries on the wing, the other scorers were Charlie Heard, J. Harris and J.H. John. Neath player Dan Pascoe, who was guesting for the Ferry, converted 1.

Maesteg were the visitors the following Saturday and they were defeated 8–0. Eddie Thomas scored 1 try, converted it and added a penalty. A couple of the WRU committee watched this game with an eye on the Ferry backs.

March started with a narrow home defeat of 0–3 to great rivals Skewen, in a very rough game that ended in darkness. On Saturday 6 March, a try from W.C. Thomas with a conversion by Eddie Thomas gave Ferry a 5–0 away win at Pontardawe. This was followed by a midweek visit to Gowerton, who were also defeated, this time by 4–0 from a Charlie Heard drop goal. Dan Pascoe played on permit again from Neath, and Tal Harris was sent off and subsequently banned until 1 May, which sadly ended his season.

The next game was a first fixture against Aberaman, which should have been played up in Aberaman, but due to a change of fixture they played in the Ferry and then played in Aberaman the following week. The first game was a bit scrappy and ended in a narrow 6–3 win for the Ferry (A. Bray and Crabtree were the try scorers). The away game ended in a 9–17 defeat. PC Barrell scored 2 tries and G. Davies 1. Arthur Harris was deputising at half-back for Tal Harris.

Neath and a home midweek match with Skewen were the next two fixtures, before the club embarked on a tour to Cornwall.

Back home the following week they were pitted against Aberavon Quins, who were a plucky side but no match for a Ferry on form. The final score was 14–0 to the Ferry. Lemon and Joseph Harris scored tries, which Eddie Thomas converted, he also produced a neat drop goal. Thomas was still on form in the next game, as he scored two tries and another drop goal in a 19–0 home win over Gowerton.

The biggest game of the season was billed as the away fixture against Aberavon. Disappointingly, the Ferry went there with a very weak team and actually had to borrow six Aberavon reserve players. Aberavon were also suffering from absentees from their XV, which made the game less important. Aberavon duly scored 31 points without a reply, which ensured that the last kick of the game gave them 500 points for that season.

Ferry's poor result and turnout continued into the next game, another away fixture and a midweek match at Neath. Ferry arrived with four or five players missing, but at least they battled a little harder, despite losing outside-half Penry Davies with a broken finger, and only lost to the tune of 0–13.

> Dinner at the Cambrian Hotel followed this match. Councillor W.J. Hill presided, and the guest of honour was Chief Constable H. Rawlings, who was off to become the new Chief Constable for Derby. PC Jenkin Hopkins the Ferry captain, presented him with a cigar case and spoke of their regret at losing this fine man, A number of speeches followed from Councillor Richard Jenkins (ex-Mayor), PC Tom Hollingdale (later to become Ferry vice president along with Albert Freethy of the Crawshays), Charlie Heard and Harold Crabtree who all spoke in glowing terms of the recipient.

Then Ferry visited Treorchy for the final game of the season.

On tour

In Cornwall, Ferry defeated Redruth in their first match by 5–3. The game turned very rough and the referee, Mr Rogers, actually left the ground for a talk with the home team. The following two games on tour were against Penryn and Camborne.

AGM

The AGM was on 13 July and the chairman, Councillor W.J. Hill, pointed out the fine season on the field that the club had just completed, scoring a record of over 400 points, with Eddie Thomas scoring well over 100 points.

However, off the field the club had a deficit of £45 as reported by the secretary, Mr W. Millett. Elections resulted in a committee of: Mr Bob John (treasurer), W.J. Hill, G.F. Llewelyn, W. Glover, Rhys Phillips, W. Watkins and H. Thomas. The players had also been busy voting and had elected Eddie Thomas as captain for the next season, with Jenkin Hopkins as vice captain. Charlie Heard was elected as player's representative on the committee. The next Easter tour was announced as visits to Derby, Chesterfield and Burton.

Other news

Ex-player Tom Hollingdale played for Neath and Aberavon combined XV versus the New South Wales Waratahs and went on to win six Welsh caps. He became a reverend in Colchester and president of Colchester RFC.

Future player Charlie Banfield won his Welsh Schools cap this season.

In May, G. Llewelyn was selected as a candidate for the role of Mid-Glamorgan Division of the WRU committee, but his bid failed.

A number of players had distinguished themselves by playing for select teams during this season:

- Jim Lemon played for a West Wales XV against a Welsh Probables XV in a trial match in November at Carmarthen, which they lost 15–27. One of the stand out players that day was ex-Ferry player Ivor Jones who, following the game, signed professional forms for Swinton Rugby League for £450

- Arthur Lemon was selected for Glamorgan County along with W.C. Thomas, Captain Rawlings, A. Jeffs and Tal Harris. They defeated Monmouth at Cardiff 20–5, Western Counties 24–18, Monmouth again, but at Newport, 20–14, and Western Counties again 10–6 (when Lemon was a try scorer)

- H.R. Crabtree (of Neath Post Office) was selected to play for the National Civil Service XV against the Police of Great Britain XV at Newport on Thursday 3 December, and again against the Royal Navy at Chiswick on 20 February. The King was expected at this match to open the new ground.

- Captain Rawlings, Tom Hollingdale and Ivor Davies all played for Neath against Pontypool during the season.

- W.C. Thomas gained further honours as he was selected to tour with Captain Crawshays XV to Torquay, Camborne and Devonport Services – they lost this last game 4–11 having beaten Camborne 32–3. He was also invited to practise with the Welsh XV at Cardiff Arms Park as a reserve centre prior to the England match.

1926/27

The season's fixture list included Maesteg, Glamorgan Wanderers, Bryncethin, Kenfig Hill, Treorchy and local rivals Skewen, Resolven, Glynneath and Cwmavon.

There was a good turn out of players in August for a practice match against a team drawn from all the local Welfare clubs. It was a good win for the Ferry. Unfortunately, they lost some fine players at the beginning of the season as both Tom Hollingdale and Arthur Lemon transferred to Neath – and both were on the score sheet in their first game. While W.C. Thomas, E. Thomas, Tal Harris, Willie Chance-Thomas, Eddie Thomas and Sid James went to Aberavon.

It was reported that the club would have become defunct that season, had it not been for the enthusiasm of the then Mayor of Neath, Councillor W.J. Hill, and his great interest in the workings of the club, coupled with the work of a faithful few.

The club also lost a wholehearted supporter in Chief Constable Rawlings (ex-captain of the Ferry in 1922/23 and 1923/24) when he left for Derbyshire to take up a new post in the police force.

The season started with a home game against Amman United. New players added to the squad included backs Ivor Rees and A. Jewett, forwards W. Jones, R. Evans, D. Worth, D. Watkins, T. Vaughan and B. Burton, and the brothers Youatt. On this occasion the players were not quite good enough and lost 0–8.

The next fixture was Resolven at home, at an interesting kick-off time of 3.40 p.m. The Ferry triumphed 9–7. Tom Youatt 1 drop goal and converted an Ivor Rees try.

Captains
Ivor Davies
Adam Bray

Vice captain
Jenkin Hopkins

Match results place BFRFC scores first

During the second week of September the referees invited all the club captains to three meetings in Cardiff, Newport and Neath to discuss law changes.

The next visitors were Neath, who went away with the spoils 11–17. But the Ferry did go down fighting, with Youatt scoring a try and both Tom Thomas and Selby dropping goals. A visit to Maesteg and 0–0 draw at Gowerton followed.

The first game in October was against Pontardawe at home, which they won 3–0. Vaughan was the try scorer. Penygraig provided the next opposition in an away fixture which Ferry lost 0–6. Tom Rees came in at fullback and J. Mainwaring on the wing, alongside Adam Bray (captain), G. Vaughan, Ivor Rees and Joe Hughes. The Youatt brothers were at half-back, and T. Beddoe and D. Worth up front.

Ferry then lost at home to Kenfig Hill, 8–18. Huxtable had a try and conversion, and they added a penalty try. H. Thomas came in at fullback for this match and D. Denby on the wing.

Two draws followed. First at Skewen in a midweek match, 3–3. Lemon was the try scorer. Then at home in the return fixture with Penygraig, 9–9, with a T. Youatt try, J.H. John converting and an E. Youatt drop goal. Neath fullback Tom Bowen played for the Ferry in this game. In the final game of the month, Ferry visited Cwmavon.

November should have started with an away game at Bridgend, but there was a mix up in fixtures so Ferry stepped in to play at Aberavon instead (who should have been playing Cardiff). Ferry lost 3–18. Selby kicked a huge penalty from near the halfway line. Four ex-Ferry players were against them in this game, including Tal Harris, who dropped a goal.

For the next fixture at Bryncethin, Rowland Hill and R. Curtis came into the backs, but Ferry lost again, 0–3. They were then heavily beaten by Gowerton, 4–19 at home, before entertaining Dulais United at home in a 6–6 draw. Jack Williams and Joe Hughes were the try scorers.

December started with an 3–18 defeat at Skewen (E. Youatt was the try scorer), before facing Blaenavon and losing 3–8 at home. Jim Lemon kicked a penalty. They faced Skewen on Christmas Day morning at home and gained revenge by defeating them.

In a New Year double header against Aberaman, the first away from home ended in a 0–16 defeat. They then found themselves without a game for the next three weeks due to adverse weather and a free fixture.

In February Skewen visited the Ferry, but the match had to be abandoned just before kick-off as the field was waterlogged. The following week Treorchy visited the Ferry and left narrowly defeated, 5–0 (despite Ferry being down to 14 men for much of the second half, due to an injury to centre A. Mellin). W.J. Youatt scored the Ferry try, which C. Williams converted. Maesteg were their next opponents. Again Ferry ended up with 14 men on the field (this time the injured player was Aubrey Davies), but again ended the victors, this time by just one point 7–6. Their pack contained a good mix of youthful players from the Welfare club.

February ended with a fixture against Glamorgan Wanderers at home. Three new players were selected for the Ferry: wing Norris Bazzard; his brother, forward Bryn Bazzard; and fellow forward from the Welfare club, T. Salter. The game was played in sodden conditions, but Ferry won 5–3. Wing Bazzard was the try scorer, converted by C. Williams. Other players who impressed were the Youatt brothers, R. Hill, A. Mellin, Ivor Rees, Ivor Thomas, J. James, D. Denby, Jim Lemon, J.H. John, E. Evans, E. Selby, W. Jones, G. Worth, W. Bright, A. Davies and A. Huxtable.

March included away fixtures against Kenfig Hill, Amman United, Glamorgan Wanderers and Glynneath (9–3, Ivor Thomas, Denby and A. Davies the try scorers) and at home against Treherbert.

In a busy April, the Ferry defeated Glynneath in the return match by 9–7. T. J. Youatt 1 drop goal from a mark, D. Youatt and W. Youatt each scored a try. Further wins came against Treherbert away, Bryncethin at home (8–6, Albert Davies the try scorer with Youatt converting and kicking a penalty) and, their eighth win on the trot, Cwmavon at home on Good Friday (11–3, Mellin, Selby and Ivor Thomas the try scorers, Evan Harris converted one).

On Easter Saturday they visited Resolven before travelling up to Derby for an Easter Monday match with the local team, which was refereed by ex-Ferry player, now Chief Constable of Derby, H. Rawlings. Ferry lost the game 3–14. Adam Bray was the try scorer.

The following week they visited Treorchy before losing 0–17 at home to Cwmavon and then bringing the curtain down on the season with a visit to Amman United.

Other news

Once again, players were honoured during the season by various teams. In a Welsh trial at Gowerton in December 1926, ex-players Tal Harris and T.

Match results place BFRFC scores first

Hollingdale and current player Jim Lemon all featured in the reserves for the West XV against the Welsh Probables. Harris scored a try in a 19–8 win.

Hendy Harris and Lemon both played for Glamorgan County v. West Counties in another 19–8 win, with Harris again scoring a try.

1927/28

The season had not started when the club was thrown into turmoil as, up to the Tuesday prior to the first game against Aberavon, the Ferry were not sure that they would be able to field a side. They called a crisis meeting at which it was decided to disband due to the general lack of interest. But George Llewelyn, Jim Jones the old Welsh forward and secretary M. Watkins got to work and between them raised a side, to be called Briton Ferry Wanderers. Reports through the season do not indicate that this name lasted for more than one game. The team was selected from: fullback Rowland Hill; threes A. Gibbon, Morris, Norris Bazzard, A. Mellin, D. Youatt, J. Broad and M. Hughes; halves T.J and E. Youatt; forwards Ivor Davies, Jim Jones, E. Evans, Ivor Jenkins, Bryn Bazzard, S. James, A. Davies, O.L. Davies, M. Watkins, C. Williams and G. Worth. Unfortunately, they were not strong enough to defeat Aberavon in that first game and lost 0–12.

Their next opponents were Gowerton away and C. Williams and Idris Morgan came in on the wings, with A. Hopkins, J. Slater and D. Phillips up front. Ivor Davies was captain. But again they tasted defeat.

Their next game was cancelled as Treherbert had a problem with their ground. To complete their September fixtures they drew 3–3 at home to Ystalyfera. Tom Youatt was the try scorer. Further changes were made to the team with S. John and T. Jeffreys into the backs and H. Bevan and A. Hughes up front.

Ferry were still struggling to get that first win as they were defeated at home by Bryncethin, then away at Pontypridd (8–24, Sam and Tom Jones both scored tries,

Captain
Ivor Davies

Match results place BFRFC scores first

Sam converted one) and at Cwmavon. Then two further home defeats to Maesteg (4–11, T. Youatt drop goal) and Gowerton (4–12, E. Youatt drop goal).

In November, Ferry visited Cinderford before a home game against Kenfig Hill, both of which ended in defeat. Finally they got their first win of the season by defeating Aberaman at home, 3–0. H. Morgan scored the try. E. Wilkins came into the side that day. They then faced Aberaman in the return fixture, before losing 0–3 at Glynneath.

Gordon Thomas and Idris Morgan came into the side in December. The Ferry ended the month with games against Resolven and Ammanford away, and Kenfig Hill and Cwmavon home. They were due to play Carmarthen Quins away on Christmas Eve but couldn't raise a side, so the fixture was cancelled.

January started with some confusion as their fixture list stated that they were due to play Resolven at home, but the WRU handbook stated Ammanford at home. After much telephoning Ammanford provided the opposition, which meant the team arrived late and the game didn't start until 4 p.m. The away team stole the glory with a 5–0 win. Two away games at Kenfig Hill (lost 0–14) and Treorchy followed, with Norris Bazzard back in the team. A game at home to Melyn Barbarians, arranged at the last minute, ended the month. Tom Youatt scored a hat trick of tries and Tom Jones scored 1 to win the game 12–0.

Glynneath defeated Ferry away 6–7 in February (H. Morgan scored a try and B. Williams a penalty). Then Ferry squeezed a narrow 5–3 win at home against Glamorgan Wanderers. Tom Youatt scored all the points with a try and a conversion. They then faced an away trip to Maesteg.

Pontypridd were the first visitors in March, and they went away with a 6–14 victory. Ted Youatt was the try scorer and Edgar Evans kicked a penalty. The Ferry then played a home midweek match against Aberavon, which they narrowly lost 3–6. To help club finances, kick-off had been arranged for 5 p.m. to allow people to get to the match.

There was another change of fixture the following Saturday after the original opponents, Carmarthen Quins, cancelled. Ferry played an away match at Porthcawl instead. They then faced another four away fixtures to see out March, against Treherbert, Glamorgan Wanderers (lost 0–11), Kenfig Hill and Ystalyfera. Cochrane came in for this game and captain Ivor Davies came back from an injury.

April started with a midweek game at home to Skewen. Then another home fixture with Resolven, which Ferry won 6–3. Jack Jones was the try scorer and T. Youatt kicked a penalty. Ferry then played three away fixtures, at Bryncethin, Skewen (lost 0–3) and Bridgend (lost 0–29) before finishing the season with a return home match against Bridgend.

T. Slater was suspended for one month after the Skewen game for fighting an opponent, I. Nicholls.

Other news

Mr W.J. Hill was elected to the Glamorgan County committee in September.

At the end of October, J.H. John, I. Morris and E. Jenkins all represented Glamorgan Police against W. Faull XV in Glais, in aid of funds for Clydach Hospital.

1928/29

The following players featured in the season's team selections: hooker Edgar Evans (captain), Edgar Gill, J. Evans, Rowly Hill, W.V. Williams, A. Mellin, I. David, G. John, B. Thomas, F. Norman, H. Morgan, Jim Jones, W.J. Thomas, I. Evans, G. Watkins, D. Bray, H. Bray, Edwin Selby, E. Harries, J. Callaghan, A. Thomas, T. Norman, T. John, L. Davies, J. Abseil, Ivor Davies, Ivor David and three celebrated Youatt Brothers – David and half-backs Edward and Tom.

> Tom Youatt was selected to play for Glamorgan County v. Gloucester in Cardiff in October, which they lost 26–9. He also finished as the season's top scorer with 74 points. Brother Edward was selected as a reserve to Tal Harris.

Ferry held a series of trial matches, the final one was arranged to replace a cancelled fixture. Their original opponents, Skewen, were offered a match against Aberavon, whose game against the County Police had been cancelled. This meant that Ferry's season was late starting.

The season finally got underway with an away fixture against Kenfig Hill, which they narrowly lost 0–3. They then managed an away draw at Loughor, 5–5. Tom Youatt converted a Frank Norman try. J. Bancroft was referee.

October started with a home game against Bridgend, before which the Ferry Town Silver Band accompanied the teams to the ground. The Ferry lost the game 10–12. Harry Morgan scored the Ferry try, Tom Youatt kicked 1 penalty and Ted Youatt 1 drop goal. They lost the next match at Pontypridd and again at home to Gowerton by 0–6. Ivor David slipped to fullback, D. Bray went into the

Captain
Edgar Evans

Playing record
P 38
W 18
D 6
L 14
Points for 293
Points against 201

centre and Ivor Olsen up front. The Ferry ended the month with a 6–3 home victory over Blaengarw. D. Bray and Ted Youatt were the try scorers. Norris Bazzard moved to centre and ex-Neath Wanderers forward E. Selby featuried up front as the Wanderers had just been disbanded.

November started with a home game against Treherbert, which Ferry won by 2 tries to 0 (G. Watkins and I. David the scorers), even though they played most of the game with thirteen men as Ivor Olsen and G. Watkins were taken off injured before half-time. They then played Porthcawl away, before getting another home win over Kenfig Hill by 9–0. D. Bray got 1 try and I. David 1 fine drop goal. Then the away game at Glynneath was postponed due to the bad weather. Forward J. Callaghan was to have come into the side for this game.

December was a busy month as they faced Cwmavon at home, followed by away games at Blaengarw, Resolven and Ystalyfera. They played Briton Ferry Workingmen's club XV at home on Christmas Day, winning 17–0 with a hat trick of tries from I. David, and further tries from G. Watkins and E. Youatt, T. Yoautt converted one. They then shared a 3–3 draw with visitors Ystradgynlais on Boxing Day.

The New Year started with a dour 0–0 draw at home to Skewen, followed by a home defeat to Resolven by 0–11, in which they lost left wing Vernon Williams to injury. To complete the month they defeated Glynneath at home, 16–0. I. David got a try double, H. Bray added another try, Ted Youatt 1 drop goal and his brother Tom kicked 1 penalty.

Unfortunately, their first February game, against Loughor at home, was called off due to an international fixture. They then lost 5–17 at Gowerton (D. Bray was the try scorer). The next fixture was frozen off, against Ystalyfera at home.

This game was to coincide with the opening of the club's new headquarters in the Grandison Hotel, which included two splendid changing rooms with central heating, showers and baths. Newspapers called it one of the best and most convenient buildings in the county. Mr D.M. Evans-Bevan was due to open the facility, but the ceremony was postponed.

Ferry completed the month with their first ever win against Ystradgynlais away from home, 14–8, with tries from H. Bray, D. Bray, S. Davies and George Watkins, with 1 conversion from Tom Howard.

Changes were made for their first game in March against Bridgend (away). G. Wagstaffe and T. Rees came into the backs, with T. Slater, J. Gleaves and C. Chegwidden up front. E. Gill captained the side. They then played a midweek game against Loughor at home and won 9–5. Watkins, H. Bray and E. Youatt were the try scorers. Ferry then faced a trip to Maesteg, where they lost 0–5, before another trip to Pontardawe. Cwmavon were the visitors on 23 March, and they were defeated 8–3, which completed the double over them. I. David scored two tries and Tom Youatt converted one.

Over the Easter holiday they beat Pontardawe at home on Good Friday by 16–0, with tries from Ted Youatt, F. Norman, Jack Evans and G. Wagstaffe, and Tom Youatt converting two. They visited Aberaman on Easter Saturday before finishing with an Easter Monday morning 30–0 victory over the Neath Borough Police XV, which included try hat tricks for George Wagstaffe and H. Bray, and tries from W. Williams and F. Norman. Tom Youatt converted three.

April continued with a 6–3 home win over Crynant. Ivor Davies was the try scorer and Youatt added the extras. Then a return home midweek fixture with Ystalyfera, before facing Treorchy, champions of the Glamorgan league, away. The Ferry lost narrowly, 0–3. The season was then brought to a close with a visit to Treherbert, and home games with Treorchy and Maesteg (won).

Ferry played Neath at the end of the season in a game which they lost 0–34 to the eventual Welsh Champions.

> It had been hastily arranged to accompany the rearranged opening of the new changing rooms. The opening ceremony was to have been performed by Mr D.M. Evans-Bevan, the High Sheriff of Brecon, but he couldn't make the new date. So Alderman J. B. Williams, alongside Councillor A.J. Morris MBE, Secretary of Neath RFC did the honours. The Ferry Town Silver Band, led by Mr G. Thomas, entertained the large crowd.

AGM

The AGM at the end of the season was held at the Grandison Hotel on a Saturday night. Chairman Mr George Llewelyn (who had been a member of the club for thirty-five years, five as captain and nine as chairman) praised the work of the secretary, Mr Osborn Davies, and offered a vote of thanks to Mr J. B. Williams for his sterling work in fencing in the ground area at Cwrt Sart. He urged all the players to put in strict training and to play the game, as he was certain that they would have a side equal to any in the district since most of the old players were available and this, along with the new members who were wishing to join, would ensure that competition for places would be fierce. He also appealed to all the supporters to rally around and get behind the team. And there was a hint that a supporters' club might be formed.

The accounts were presented and showed a debit balance, which was considered satisfactory with so much unemployment in the district.

The officials elected for the following season were chairman George Llewelyn, honourable secretary Osborn Davies, treasurer Syd Abraham, with a general committee of: T. Cole, Stan Davies, G. Smart, W.S. Davies and Ivor Olsen. Mr W. Hill had been voted on to the Glamorgan County committee during the season.

Other news

The local press were caught up in a saga involving the club's ex-captain, HORATIO RAWLINGS, who had gone to Derby as Chief Constable. He was reported to have been applying himself with considerable assiduity by studying modern traffic control and introducing some successful innovations. There was a rumour that in October 1928 he'd been in line for Chief Constable of Hull, with an annual salary of £900, and that he'd turned down an offer from Leicester because it was £100 less a year. He was reportedly then offered a deal to stay in Derby of £700 on appointment and another £50 every two years! He was also on the shortlist for the same job in the Nottingham force. He subsequently joined the Worcestershire regiment for four years and was awarded the King's Jubilee medal in 1935 and the Coronation medal in 1937. He was appointed as Chief Officer of the Fire Brigade, which he left in 1939. In 1941 he received the King's Police and Fire Services medal and in 1943 he was seconded to H.M. Forces in the Civil Affairs Organisation and was promoted later that year to Colonel. In 1945 he returned to police duty and received another Coronation medal in 1953. He retired from the police force in 1956 and passed away late in 1960. His funeral was held on 7 October at Derby Cathedral. The police lined the streets prior to the service and the police choir led the procession.

Neath Borough Police played a few games in February at the Ferry. First, they won 7–5 against a D.J. Rees XV that contained a number of Ferry players. Second, against a Local Transport XV, which they also won, 3–0. As a result, they played a game on the Gnoll against a Ferry Workingmen's XV, which they lost 3–5. Ferryites Evan Harris, A. Harris, Joe Hughes and Mog Watkins featured strongly for the Workingmen's, while international Tom Hollingdale played for the Police. The game was to raise money for the Swansea Hospital Radium Fund, and managed a sum of £40. After the game, the teams were entertained to dinner at the Bird in Hand Hotel in Neath.

In June 1929 Mr W.J. Hill was presented with a photograph at Briton Ferry Workingmen's Club, in recognition of his being an ex-mayor of the borough.

There was a storm brewing between the Welsh Union and the RFU as there had been a growing feeling that the English clubs were poaching players, and that it was a step towards professionalism! In particular, Cheltenham RFC

Match results place BFRFC scores first

had acquired the services of seven Aberavon players over a couple of weeks. Among them ex-Ferry player Tal Harris, who had played against Gloucester the previous weekend and had his jaw broken, but was playing instead of a player who had broken his leg! Cheltenham's defence was that these players were out of work and had come to their town to obtain employment in the local motor works.

Another former Ferry player was called up for his first cap against Ireland, quoted as being one of the best exponents of lineout play in the four nations. This was none other than Arthur Lemon, who was in his fourth season with Neath RFC and was working as a steelworker at the Briton Ferry works.

Ex-player Tom Hollingdale was selected to tour with the Crawshays Welsh Squad.

1929/30

In the season the twenties came to a close the strength of the team was in the forwards, led by the virile Edgar Evans. Other players to shine were: fullback Rowly Hill, in his fourth season with the club, who was also pushing hard to get selected for his county cap; and the Youatt brothers, Edward and Tom (Tom proved a popular choice as captain among players and supporters alike and was a well-known Powderhall runner). Evan Harris and Edwin Selby both had trials for Neath prior to the season starting.

Briton Ferry's season started with a visit to Cwmavon, and their first defeat. This was followed by a midweek game at Skewen, which they won 6–3. A.F. Norman and W.V. Williams came into the side. Williams scored the only try and E.J. Youatt kicked a penalty. They won again the following Saturday in a home game with Pontardulais, 11–8. Williams was the try scorer again and Tom Youatt added 2 penalties and 1 conversion.

October was a good month for the club with the likes of L. Goodreid coming into the side up front and G. Vaughan behind. They started with a narrow 3–0 win at home to Kenfig Hill, but were then defeated by the same score at Llanelli New Dock Stars. A really tight game followed at Crynant, where they shared the honours in a 0–0 draw, before returning to winning ways away at Gowerton (won 6–3, with Youatt kicking a penalty) and Cardiff Varsity (won 23–0), in which both T.P. Jones and C.H. Harris featured prominently.

In November they drew a return game with Skewen at home, 7–7. Jack Evans was the try scorer and Ted Youatt 1 drop goal. They then had a new fixture at Newport

Match results place BFRFC scores first

United, before playing unbeaten Cwmavon. That was a tight game that ended in a 3–3 draw, with the Ferry's Wagstaffe scoring the only try of the game. This was followed by a narrow 6–9 defeat at the Old Parish against Maesteg, with tries by George Vaughan and R. Jones. The Ferry pack were in great form and, according to the match report, didn't deserve to lose. Another player in great form that day was fullback Rowly Hill. A 0–0 draw then ensued at Kenfig Hill before ending the month with a fine win over Cardiff XV at home, 9–6. D.F. Lewis and V. Williams were the try scorers and Tom Youatt kicked a penalty.

December was a busy month. The Ferry suffered the first home defeat of the season against a strong Pontypridd side by the narrowest of margins, 5–6. A Williams try and a Youatt conversion were the only scores. Then came another draw, 3–3 at Pontardulais. Vernon Williams received the ball from the kick-off in the second half and ran the length of the field to touch down.

After this game it became evident that there was a split at the club. It was reported that the brothers Youatt had failed to appear for the game at Pontardulais and it was alleged that they had severed their connection with Ferry and applied for transfers because their brother Dai had not been selected for the match. The club responded by selecting a new pair of half-backs, Abraham and Ivor Thomas. However, in a later interview Tom Youatt stated that they had left because of the re-instatement of a previously barred player, which went against the direct orders contained in the committee minutes. The disappointment worsened when they both joined deadly rivals, Skewen.

Just before Christmas, Ferry had a 6–17 defeat at Bridgend, with Vernon Williams and Ivor Thomas scoring a try apiece.

The Christmas period proved to be a very strange time as the town was suffering from the indefinite closure of Albion Steel, with the loss of 400 jobs, followed by Whitford Galvanising, 500 jobs, Briton Ferry Steel and four other tinplate works. This meant that nearly 3, 000 men were out of work.

A match was arranged to take place in the Ferry on Christmas morning against a Chief Constable P.D. Keep XV prior to the club leaving on Christmas Day night for a three-day tour to Somerset and Devon.

The New Year started with a bang as they took Cwmavon's ground record with a 6–4 win (H. Bray and Wagstaffe were the try getters).

On the same day Neath and Aberavon were involved in a controversial game when, after the final whistle was blown, a fight broke out between the two teams on the field. This allegedly continued into the changing rooms, followed by some of their supporters. The Neath committee met a few days after the match and decided that the club would not honour the final match with their opponents and would be cancelling futures fixtures with them. Aberavon's reaction was swift and they made a formal complaint to the Welsh Rugby Union. Neath were fined £10 and ordered to play the match within 10 days, which they did, and they were defeated.

Resolven were the Ferry's next opponents and S. Bates came into the backline with R. Harding up front. Unfortunately, foul weather stopped both this match and their next scheduled game against Pontypridd away.

West Wales League leaders Ammanford were their next opponents at home before a 3–3 home draw with Maesteg (Wagstaffe was the try scorer).

They continued their great form into February, with a fine 6–3 win at home to Gowerton. Dil Jones and Sam Bates were the try scorers. Ferry then pushed Aberavon all the way at the Talbot Athletic ground before succumbing to a 5–11 defeat. This match featured some good moves among the Ferry backs, mostly initiated by half-back I. Thomas and A. Thomas, and fullback Hill, with wing Vernon Williams always a source of danger. There were other moments worth mentioning and T.O. Jones featured in two of them. First, he collided with a goalpost in an attempt to prevent a try. Then, just before the end of the game, a Ferry forward accidentally jammed his knees into Jones' stomach with such violence that he had to be carried off the field in agony. There was also a hint of controversy over a conversion by the Ferry which was allowed, but apparently the referee sought to change his mind over the decision after the game – the score stood!

Their next opponents were Cardiff XV and they completed a famous double by winning away 5–3. W.E. Evans, the captain was the try scorer, with R. Hill converting.

At long last some local steelworks started their furnaces back up for production in February and men were returning to work after a lengthy lay off.

In March, the Ferry secured the rubber against Cwmavon with yet another draw, 3–3 at home. Wagstaffe was the try scorer again. They then lost a penalty ridden game at Newport United 0–3. In a midweek away match with a weakened side at Bridgend, the home team secured a double over the Ferry, winning 4–11. G. Vaughan 1 drop goal.

Another defeat followed at Resolven before completing their own double over Cardiff University by 11–6. It was an excellent game, with tries from forward D. Jones and George Vaughan, one of which was converted by Rowly Hill. Ivor Jones kicked a penalty to seal the win.

To complete the March fixtures they played an away game at Maesteg.

Match results place BFRFC scores first

April home fixtures were against Llanelli New Dock Stars and a Norris Buzzard International XV. Unfortunately, the Union ordered the international players not to play at all before their game against France. Howie Jones ran the line for this one and Albert Freethy was referee. The try scorers were G. Vaughan (2), Vernon Williams, A. Thomas, Ivor Thomas and G. Wagstaffe, two of which were converted. Buzzard added a try for the International XV.

Ferry ended the season with a 3–13 defeat to Skewen.

AGM

At the AGM, chairman Mr G.F. Llewelyn congratulated the players on a good season, but expressed disappointment at the loss of good gates due to inclement weather. The secretary, Mr Ossie Davies submitted a balance sheet that showed the club in debit, but not too much! He also remarked how unbelievable it was that only one away game was played in wet weather, yet a large percentage of the home games where ruined by the weather. He was subsequently re-elected as secretary, and Mr Sid Abraham as treasurer. The following were elected as committeemen: G. Smart, I. Olsen, J. Lewis, T. Hughes, J. Hill, D. Lloyd and J. Wozencroft. The players then met and selected Rowly Hill as their captain, and Edgar Evans as vice captain.

Around the district

Among the junior clubs in the area to make use of the Ferry facilities were Briton Ferry Workingmen's club, who played the Neath Borough Police XV twice and defeated them twice – their only defeats that season. They won the first game 25–0, which was a fundraiser for the Boys Welfare. Evan Harries led the side to a 19–8 win in the second game. Sadly, this season also saw the demise of the Briton Ferry Welfare XV. Other junior sides playing at the time included Neath Rovers, NOR, NSA, Melyn Barbarians, Neath Wanderers, Gnoll Athletic GWR and Abergarwed. Neath Rovers and Melyn Barbarians contested the Neath Cup final, which the Rovers won 11–3.

Youth rugby

Cwrt Sart Central School was also prevalent this season. They won the Neath Schools Championship for the Roger's Shield with a 26–0 victory over Cadoxton Central. Gwyn Thomas scored a hat trick of tries in the first half, followed by another two tries in the second half. A. Biggs and Clifford Jenkins also scored tries and Richard Howells converted one. Their winning team was: fullback Stanley Parry; wings Clifford Jenkins and Gwyn Thomas; centres Ken Jones and A. Biggs; half-backs Harold Jenkins and K. Colwill; the forwards consisted of V. Pulman, J. Keep, Leslie Price, Richard Howells, Harold Davies, W. Bessell, Melvin Rees and J. Keneally.

The 1920s had produced the best organised, most regularly coached, most attractive and consistently successful side of the era in this team of ex-schoolboys, gathered together and trained under the watchful and authoritarian eye of Albert Freethy of Cwrt Sart School, Neath.

ALBERT FREETHY's own playing career as a fullback had been cut short by injury, but he went on to make more than a name for himself as one of Wales' finest referees. He was the first WRU referee invited to control a club match in England (Blackheath v. Cardiff, 6 November 1920). He officiated at six Varsity matches, the Paris Olympic Rugby final of 1924 and sixteen internationals between 1924 and 1931. He immortalized himself by sending off Cyril Brownlie, of the 1924/25 All Blacks, in the eighth minute of their international at Twickenham, in front of the Prince of Wales. Freethy instructed his boys in technique on the field and tactics on the blackboard. They played exciting, attacking, running rugby. In their first full season, 1922/23, they played on the Gnoll and made £100 for Neath and £700 for charities. They went undefeated for four years. In February 1925 they met a star-studded Christ's College, Brecon, at the Gnoll and beat them 6–3 in front of a crowd of 5,000. In one week in February 1926, they beat Llandovery 18–4 and Christ's College 18–5. Such was the success, and the attractiveness, of Freethy's brilliant youngsters that friction developed with the Neath club. Understandably, Neath wanted to include some of them on its own side, but Freethy felt that 'the spirit of Welsh rugby was not what it should be', and asked to be allowed to keep his side together for a couple more seasons. Smarting at Freethy's refusal, Neath denied him the use of the Gnoll, so they played at Cwrt Herbert, where the 'Invincibles' still drew larger crowds than the town team. They lost their invincibility at Cardiff Arms Park on 30 April 1927, to a Cardiff ex-schoolboys team, including Norman Fender and Tommy Stone. It marked the end of an era of ex-schoolboy rugby, and the concept of youth rugby would not be revived until the 1940s. But several of Freethy's stars orbited into senior football. Neath certainly owed its great season of 1928/29 (when only four matches in forty-nine were lost and 930 points were scored), to an influx of ex-schoolboys such as Howie Jones, Arthur Hickman and Tom Day – all of whom went on to win full international caps in the early thirties.

On tour

The tourers played Wellington on Boxing Day (lost 7–11, Tom John scored 1 try and Ivor Thomas 1 drop goal), then Newton Abbott on the following day (won 12–9, A. Thomas, T. John, D. Jones and Edgar Evans were all try scorers), ending at Wiveliscombe (3–3, an Abraham Thomas try).

Other news

Some of the Ferry players to feature for Neath RFC in the twenties included locks Harold Thomas (who won six caps for Wales in 1936/37, and then went on to play for Salford Rugby League in 1937; he was also a Regimental Sergeant Major in the Royal Marines and was mentioned in dispatches in the Second World War) and his brother, Dai Leyshon Thomas, who also played for Bridgend and had one cap v. England in 1937, alongside his brother.

No.8/flanker PC Tom Hollingdale won six caps for Wales between 1927 and 1930. His brother Albert, also a flanker, won two caps in 1912 against South Africa and England while playing for Swansea. Albert was originally from Ammanford and reputedly one of Neath's finest forwards, alongside the likes of Arthur Lemon.

PART 5: 1930–1940

Throughout the 1930s Briton Ferry RFC ran an annual jazz band competition.

5.1 1930/31

1930/31

The club's playing standard remained high, as can be seen by the strength of the fixture list, which included first-class sides in Neath, Aberavon, Maesteg and Bridgend. Ex-chairman Morgan Jones was an ever-present club member during this period, when the Ferry proved more than a match for such opposition.

Fullback Rowly Hill captained the side for the first season of the decade. Mr Ossie Davies filled the secretary's role, as he had done for ten years. He also filled any vacancy in the pack as required and was the only life member of the club.

The club held two trial games before the start of the season and they revealed that there was a good deal of talent in the town, such as Ivor Watkins (brother of ex-Ferry player Mog Watkins), Idris Evans, (the younger brother of Jack Evans the Ferry wing), D. McArthur (a useful forward from Newport High School, who was now employed at a local bank) and Emrys Hill. The local papers said that the club was in good hands with players such as Rowly Hill, centre G. Wagstaffe and inside-half A. Thomas, but that they needed to fill the gaps at centre and outside-half, due to the likes of Ivor Thomas leaving the club. The club's strength lay in their forwards, such as lock Dai Leyshon Thomas (who went on to represent Neath and Bridgend, and one cap for Wales v. England in 1937) and his brother, lock Harold Watkin Thomas.

> HAROLD W. THOMAS also represented Neath, Cimla and Wales (six caps between 1936 and 1937), then Salford Rugby League club in 1937. He served in the Second World War in the Maritime Royal Artillery as a regimental sergeant major and was mentioned in dispatches for bravery.

Captain
Rowly Hill

Vice captain
Edgar Evans

Playing record
P 41
W 9
D 7
L 25

Other players who were prominent during the season were: George Vaughan, a fine wing and a product of Gnoll Road rugby team, who later represented the famous Neath Wanderers (who went undefeated for three seasons in the 1920s) and then Neath RFC; and the other wing, Vernon Williams, was also a bit of a flyer and used to put in a lot of track training to assist his lightning speed.

5.2 1930/31

The fixtures in September included a 3–19 defeat by Aberavon in which Rhys Harding and W. Evans were the pick of the forwards and Wagstaffe, Bray, and Abraham Thomas in the backs. Six successive home games in September resulted in three wins (including 12–8 over Newport United and 19–8 over Neath Borough Police), two defeats and one draw against Bridgend. The defeats were blamed on poor scrummaging by the forwards.

> The papers noted that attendances had improved markedly for this early part of the season, but that many supporters were watching from the main road. So the committee deliberated closing the ground in with fencing on the main road side.

In October there was a win over Gowerton by 10–6. N. Bazzard scored a nice interception try, which was converted by Harding who also converted the try by centre A. Griffiths.

November included an 0–11 defeat by New Dock Stars.

Match results place BFRFC scores first

At an exciting game with Pontypridd in December the scores were level at half-time, 6–6. Then Ponty pulled away to a 6–14 victory. Dai Leyshon Thomas scored the try and Harding kicked a penalty goal for the Ferry. Forwards McCarthur and Edgar Evans were prominent. During this month a new forward emerged in the shape of Bob Gibb, a product of Bursall School, Fleetwood, Lancashire. He was described as

a fine type of forward, well over six foot tall, useful in line outs, speedy, possesses a good kick, and works hard in the scrummages.

The Christmas Day game with Treorchy took place in a sea of mud and ended in a 3–3 draw. Sion Evans, the Ferry juniors centre, played for Treorchy and scored their only try. A. Morgan kicked a goal for the Ferry.

The New Year started with a 6–3 win over Tredegar. Prominent players were Edgar Evans up front, Bazzard behind and young Rees at scrum-half. One paper reported that ex-Ferry player and captain, H. Rollings (then Chief Constable of Derby), came to this match from Swansea, where he had been staying, and ended up kicking off to great cheers.

Pontypridd away again ended in defeat, 3–9. R. Gibbs scored the only try for the Ferry and Bray and Buzzard showed up well again with their clever tackling. This was followed by another defeat on the road, this time to unbeaten Newport United, 8–16.

February opened with another narrow 3–4 defeat to Cwmavon (1 drop goal to 1 try by the Ferry). Pick of the Ferry XV were half-backs D.J. Rees and George Vaughan, and Edgar Evans. This was the second home defeat in a row as they had lost 3–6 to Skewen in January. Bray scored the only try after a break by Vernon Williams down the wing. February concluded with a drawn match at Kenfig Hill in a fast, exciting game, in which Dai Leyshon Thomas scored a try and Rees Harding kicked a penalty and a conversion.

March brought defeat in a freezing cold, snowbound Tredegar, 3–9. Followed by another defeat at Cardiff University, by a single point 14–15, with tries from Gibbs (2) and Morgan Jones, who also kicked a conversion.

In the absence of captain Edgar Evans, the team for the next game at home to Loughor was selected from: Morgan Jones, W.V. Williams, W.N. Buzzard, P. Waters, T.J. Hughes, H. Bray, P. Davies, D.J. Rees, G. Jefford, Dai Leyshon Thomas, D.J. Jones, R.M. Gibb, C. Harris, W. McArthur, T.T. Jones, W.H. John,

T. John, Emrys Hill, W.E. Harding and Rees Harding. The team rallied around and a Rees Harding try was enough to earn them a 3–3 draw.

Another 3–3 draw against Skewen at home started the final month of the season, Vernon Williams was the try scorer. The Ferry were handicapped by the absence of scrum-half D. Rees. The match became a bit over-vigorous and Edgar Evans was sent off for striking an opponent, the first time in five seasons a Ferry player was given their marching orders. The team then suffered three consecutive defeats at both Treorchy and Maesteg and at home to Llanelli New Dock Stars. They conceded 64 points across the three games, with only three points to show for themselves. Yet another home defeat followed at the hands of Swansea Second XV (3–9), with Rees Harding again the try scorer.

Ferry finally ended the season on a high note by defeating Barry in a stirring game by 27–5. Harding, Morgan Jones and L. Thomas added conversions to tries from W. Griffiths (2), T.J. Hughes (2), Vernon Williams, Morgan Jones and G. Wagstaffe.

This was the worst season in the club's history, which then resulted in poor attendances at all matches.

AGM

At the June AGM in the Grandison Hotel, the chairman Mr Jones stated that the general consensus was that a lack of training had resulted in the absence of organised play, and suggestions for remedying this were adopted unanimously. The committee elected for the coming season were: president Major J.M. Bevan MC, chairman Mr Jones, honourable secretary Ossie Davies, treasurer Sid Abraham. With a general committee of: M. Griffiths, Dick Thomas, Jack Wozencroft, Morgan Powell, David Lloyd, Percy George, Sid Oakes, George Smart, Will Davies, P. Steer, Dick Jones, Alderman W.J. Hill, George Lodwick, Llew John and George Llewelyn.

Around the district

Junior clubs in Neath & District were: Neath Allied Traders, Seven Sisters II, Cimla, Resolven Cubs, Cwmavon Juniors, Berni Stars, Crynant II, Park Juniors and Neath Rovers. Two clubs were re-formed, Neath Baa Baas (after three seasons) and the Melin Boys RFC.

Two new junior clubs were formed for the coming season: Castle Stars and Neath Harlequins. The Quins contained two ex-Ferry players, including captain J. Rees at scrum-half. Both clubs were seeking a suitable playing ground near Tonna.

1931/32

Junior league

During this season for the juniors, all games for the Briton Ferry Supporters Cup were to be played at the Ferry's Old Road ground, with all the proceeds going to the club. The Castle Stars beat the GWR XV. The cup had been won twice on the trot by Neath Abbey, then controversy struck. On 4 December 1931 the *Neath Guardian* reported that the Neath & District league had told all junior clubs in the area that they were not allowed to enter the Supporters Cup on the grounds that there were already two league cups to play for and that Briton Ferry were not allowed to put up a cup to benefit their own funds. The article suggested that this was another instance of interference by the junior leagues in what would have been a fillip to all rugby clubs between Neath and Aberavon and would actively encourage defunct clubs to reform. It was also not hailed as very commendable attitude by the leagues and that it would kill rugby enthusiasm ! A later appeal by BFRFC to the Welsh Football Union was upheld and the competition was back up and running. Unfortunately, this happened too late for some clubs to raise a team or to organise their kit. So teams such as Melin United and Neath Baa Baas, who'd been in full swing up until the ban, had to forgo the competition.

In the new draw for the Supporters Cup, teams involved in the preliminary rounds included Aberavon CYMS, Tonmawr, Neath Excels (who included ex-Ferry player Mervyn Youatt), Castle Stars, Taibach and Neath Quins. A couple of early matches were Neath GWR v. Margam Works and Allied Traders v. Aberavon Central. The final

Captain
Rees Harding

Playing record
P 41
16 9 (13 home/23 away)
D 7
L 18 (9 home/9 away)
Points for 292
Points against 3

Scores
Tries 72
Conversions 20
Drop goals 3
Penalties 8

was contested between Aberavon CYMS and Taibach before a record crowd. The Taibach XV were led on to the field by a goat mascot wearing the club colours and Councillor J.D. Williams performed the kick-off. Alderman W.J. Hill kicked-off the second half. The match ended in a narrow 0-3 win for Taibach.

Senior league

Meanwhile, on the senior scene, the early season trials indicated that there was plenty of young talent in the area to ensure that things were looking a bit brighter. So that, along with old stalwarts such as Willie Griffiths and with the talented V.G. Davies and Vernon Williams in the three-quarters, this would add attacking thrust to the team. There was also talk of Phil Griffiths (ex-Newport) joining the Ferry, as he had recently accepted a post at Cwrt Sart School. The second trial was played against Neath GWR XV, which Ferry won 23-3. Tries were made by W. McArthur (2), S. Anthony, W. Jefford, V. Williams, Emrys Hill and T. Hughes, with Rees Harding converting one.

Season 1931-1932

O.L. DAVIES(SEC) E.HILL. D. THOMAS. R. GIBB. C. CHEGWIDDEN T. JONES.
I. WATKINS. W. MACARTHUR.
G. BLIGHT. W.V. WILLIAMS. N. BAZZARD. E. EVANS(CAPT). W. GRIFFITHS.S. BAKER.
D.J. REES. M. JONES. G. VAUGHAN. R. HARDING. T. JOHN.

5.3 1931/32

The season then started with a 3-23 defeat in the first game against Aberavon. But an 18-3 win over Cardiff Athletic followed. A superb all-round team performance set them back on the road to recovery. T.J. Hughes, D.J.

Match results place BFRFC scores first

Jones and E. Selby (ex-Maesteg) were the try scorers and Rees Harding added 2 conversions and a penalty.

Two more wins followed: over Pontardawe away, 11–9; and in midweek over Gowerton by 10–3, Selby was among the try scorers again, Rees Harding kicked a penalty and T.J. Hughes slotted a drop goal (4 points). Then came two defeats in a row, against Treorchy away, 10–13, and Maesteg at home, 0–5. This surrendered their short-term home record. W.J. Griffiths 1 drop goal and W.V. Williams scored 1 try and kicked 1 penalty.

Next up were local rivals Skewen, which ended in a 0–0 draw.

The *Neath Guardian* reported that the tussle had been an extremely bad advertisement for Welsh rugby with both teams indulging in such uncalled-for actions on the field. Many unpleasant incidents took place that resulted in some nasty injuries. They called it "rugby of the worst kind".

A mixed bag of results followed: defeat at home to Tredegar, 3–4; an away win over Cwmavon 6–0 (the MP for Aberavon, Mr W.G. Cove, kicked off the second half); and finally a 3–3 draw at home with the Rhondda champions, Pontypridd. Among the scores in these games were tries from Gwyn Vaughan, H. Morgan and E. Thomas, and a penalty kick from Rees Harding.

The mixed results continued in November with a fine 5–0 win over Swansea, followed by an 8–9 defeat at Cae Syr Dafydd to Cardiff University, a 3–3 draw at Gowerton and a 9–3 home win over Kenfig Hill. Among the scores were tries from Jack Lowry, W. McArthur, Bryn Jones, D.J. Rees, W.J. Griffiths and George Vaughan, and two conversions by Rees Harding.

Ferry ended the year with a Christmas Day win over Taibach at home by 19–8 and a 0–0 draw up in Maesteg against 13 players and in monsoon conditions. Scorers for the Ferry were W.J. Griffiths with 2 tries and a try apiece from Charlie Banfield, Edwin Selby and George Vaughan, Rees Harding converted two of them. The Christmas period ended with a 0–6 defeat at home to Gowerton, which squared up their matches at one win each away from home and a draw.

In the new year, a strong Newport United side defeated the Ferry 5–13 in Newport. Rees Harding scored the only try which Hill converted. They then achieved an 11–3 home win over Swansea University, in which Harding scored two tries and converted one. Ferry then completed January with a 6–3 home win over Cwmavon, tries by Charlie Banfield and George Vaughan clinched the win. This completed the double after they'd taken their unbeaten home record by 6–0.

There was little real success for the Ferry in February as a 6–15 defeat at Ynysangharad Park against Pontypridd was followed by a home defeat to Newport United, with only a Rees Harding penalty to show. Then another defeat, this time at Resolven 14–20, while a friendly with Neath County School OB XV ended in a draw.

When the Ferry's original opponents, Carmarthen Quins, didn't turn up later in February, a match was set up between a Neath Baa Baas XV (made up of players from the Ferry, Cimla, Castle Stars and others) and Neath Allied Traders. They played on the Gnoll in front of a big crowd and it ended in an 8–0 win for the Baa Baas. Both try scorers were Ferry players, centre Charlie Banfield and fullback Mog Jones.

March started in style with an 11–8 home win over NOR Skewen (with tries for E. Hill, W. McArthur and Rees Harding, who also added a conversion). Then came a 3–6 midweek defeat at home to Cardiff University (try by W. McArthur), and an 11–11 draw at home with Treorchy. The kick-off was delayed because Treorchy arrived late and the match didn't end until nearly 6 p.m. The best try of the match was scored by Ferry's new outside-half T. McNulty, who had signed up from Aberavon CYMS. Tries by E. Selby and the Neath County schoolboy Vernon Friend (who gained a Welsh Schools cap this year v. Yorkshire), and Mog Jones' conversion completed the scoring. In a 22–5 home win over Swansea Uplands the away side contained ex-Ferry player, V.G. Davies, who had left to play for Swansea and had decided to end his playing career with the Uplands.

Ferry suffered two defeats over Easter. Away against Kenfig Hill on the Saturday, 8–27, and at home on Easter Monday to tourists Catford Bridge from London, 6–9, with Banfield and Vaughan the try scorers. Further defeats followed, this time at the Ynys against Aberdare by 0–3, at home to Cwmavon 0–10, and in a midweek game with Aberavon 8–9, with tries by E. Hill and E. Selby and a conversion by Rees Harding.

The Ferry then got back to winning ways up in Tredegar with a 3–0 score, a Selby try separated the sides. The season finished without defeat: a 3–3 draw with Skewen (S. Anthony try); a midweek win over Bridgend by 19–6, with tries by D.J. Rees (2), Bryn Jones, E. Selby and Charlie Banfield and Rees Harding adding 2 conversions; finally, an 8–0 home win over Pontardawe (with tries by E. Hill and S. Anthony and a conversion by Rees Harding) brought the curtain down on the season.

Season's end

Top scorer was Rees Harding with 62 points (1 try, 17 conversions, 9 penalties) and top try scorer was W.J. Griffiths with 10 tries.

It is also worth mentioning the 19-point victory over Oxford University and that Morgan Jones and Charlie Banfield played in every game.

George Llewelyn was made a life member of Briton Ferry after forty years' service to the club.

Mr Llewelyn Griffiths spearheaded an off the field effort to raise funds to erect a grandstand.

Other news

Throughout the season the local news kept readers informed about former Ferry players who were doing well for themselves, such as:

- Tal Harris, the Aberavon and Wales scrum-half (originally a Ferry player) and E. Youatt the Neath scrum-half

- PC Ivor Thomas, the scorer of many a try became an accomplished cricketer and captain of the Neath Borough Police XI

- They lauded 23-year-old Morgan Jones as a safer player than the Neath fullback Myo Abraham (who was to play for the Ferry) – Mog also helped out Neath Police and Neath Workingmen's XV

- Harold, the brother of D.L. Thomas, made his debut for Neath in March and went on to play for Wales as well as for the Ferry!

5.4 The Thomas brothers, Harold (left) and D.L. (right), were both capped for Wales

1932/33

The season started with a bang by beating Treorchy 13–8 and robbing them of their proud unbeaten home record (Steve Anthony made 2 tries, E. Selby 1, T. John converted 2). The *Neath Guardian* acknowledged the victory with a stirring call for local support to get behind the Ferry for the rest of the season! But Ferry were defeated in their next two matches against Ystalyfera (one at 6–9, when Rees Harding scored all the points) and Skewen 14–15. In a forwards-dominated game they defeated Tredegar by 6–3 – Emrys Hill scored both tries. Then defeat once again up in Newport United, 6–10, McNulty was the try scorer, and Harding kicked a penalty.

Captain

Emrys Hill

Playing record

P 37

W 18

D 0

L 19

The *Guardian* noted that speedy young wingers, such as Harold Powell, should be considered for Neath RFC and gave credit to the Ferry's rugby committee for always giving local juniors a "try out". The paper pointed out how playing the Ferry Supporters Cup on their own ground gave them the opportunity of watching such up and coming youngsters as Aberavon CYMS' outside-half McNulty, the Allied Traders' wing H. Powell and Taibach Juniors' W.S. Anderson. All of which turned out to be good boys, who then formed a Second XV to play cross fixtures. They won their first game 3–0 on October 21 against Neath Excels, with J. Dempsey being hailed as the outstanding player with a fine physique! However, two 0–3 defeats followed, against Neath Harlequins in the Cimla and Castle Stars.

Meanwhile Ferry's First XV were suffering consecutive defeats against Carmarthen Harlequins and Maesteg, both by 5–6 (tries by T.J. Rees and R. Harding, both converted by T. John).

The shortest match on record happened at the end of October at home against Treorchy. A terrific downpour

Match results place BFRFC scores first

prompted both sides to agree to play fifteen minutes each way, just to get a decision. A decision that went the Ferry's way 3–0, with a McNulty try.

November proved to be an excellent month in which the First XV went unbeaten with wins over Newport United, Cwmavon 14–3, Kenfig Hill 9–0 and Bridgend 6–3 at the Brewery field by. S. Anthony (2), D. Rees (4), C. Harris, T. John, D.J. Jones and R. Harding were among the try scorers.

December started with a win and Ferry taking another ground record. Gowerton were the victims by 8–3, D.J. Rees and Griffiths were the try scorers and Griffiths added a conversion. But a 3–5 defeat by Cardiff Athletic followed, after a sole try from D. Jones.

One prominent player was REES HARDING, who'd started his career with the Gnoll school, went on to play for the Neath Schoolboys XV and then joined Neath Rovers. He was only sixteen when he was chosen to tour Devon with Briton Ferry. He captained the Ferry in the 1931/32 season and also finished as top scorer – on top form at 20 years of age, 5'8" tall and weighing no more than 12 stone.

A new player joined the club in December, Bryant a good lineout forward signed from Neath Quins.

The new year started badly with defeat at Carmarthen Quins by 0–3, although only 40 minutes were played due to the bad weather. Ferry bounced back the following week at home, defeating Aberdare 6–3. Absent from that match was D.J. Rees as he was assisting Aberavon. Another away defeat followed at Cwmavon, again by 0–3. The match was played before a large crowd and put Cwmavon 2–1 up in the series for the year. Fullback Mog Jones was outstanding in defence for the Ferry.

There was a sad start to February as the club mourned the passing of their committeeman and secretary of the Supporters' club, MR PHILLIP A. STEER (he'd been wounded in battle during the First World War, while serving in the Dardanelles). There was further sad news in March as MR GEORGE P. LLEWELYN also passed away. As a long-standing loyal servant to the club and an ex-captain he'd been made the club's first life member only two years previously. The further loss of two former players, CHARLIE BANNISTER and DAI POLEY, made this a miserable early year.

Also in February, the Supporters Cup hit the headlines because of a drop in the number of entries, which cost five shillings per club. Only eight had signed up and two of the strongest teams, Taibach and Neath Quins, were notable absentees. The papers speculated that this was probably due to the fact that all the money raised during the competition went to the Supporters' club and that no trophies were awarded. This story was rebuffed when the new secretary of the Supporters' club, Mr A.G. Richards, reported that in fact 12 teams had entered, including Taibach, that the entry fee was 2s 6d and that medals were awarded to the winners. He also stated that the reason the cup was run was to keep the noble cause of rugby in the Briton Ferry district and to help the club continue to foster rugby in the Ferry. Taibach retained the cup, as Port Talbot Centrals failed to turn up!

The First XV suffered a home defeat to Gowerton by 0–11 (a revenge for their only home defeat of the season, so far) and then another defeat, 3–5 to Bridgend Athletic, with only 1 try from Emrys Hill.

Next up was a home match against Cwmavon. In this tough encounter the famous referee Mr Ivor David needed to use all his experience and ended up sending off four players, two from each side. It was a 6–5 victory to the Ferry, with tries by Steve Anthony and Gwyn Thomas.

> The same Gwyn Thomas was in prominent form for Cwrt Sart Central School against the County School in an 18–3 defeat, also in February.

In March, Ferry took a revenge win over Penclawydd by 3 tries to 0, two by Charlie Banfield and one by Gwyn Thomas to seal the win, but they were missing the influence of Vernon Williams at outside-half. Next up were Neath at the Gnoll in a midweek friendly, which Ferry narrowly lost 6–13, with a try by Vernon Case and a penalty by Rees Harding. Reports said that outstanding players were G. Harris in the Ferry pack, Rees Harding and in the back division, Rees and Gwyn Thomas at half-back and G. Anthony in the centre. "Ginger" Thomas went on to play for Neath in the Easter Monday fixture against Ebbw Vale alongside County School centre Vernon Friend, who went on to represent Wales Schoolboys and Briton Ferry. One of Neath's tries that day was a spectacular effort by fullback Arthur Basset, brother of Welsh international Jack Basset.

Then a welcome first visit to the Ferry by Merthyr, in which an 18–3 win was ground out to revenge an earlier away defeat (tries scored by W.J. Griffiths (2), D.J. Rees, Bryn Jones, Rees Harding and Gwyn Thomas). Ferry also lost at home 3–18 to Aberavon.

Two Easter wins followed over Ystalyfera, 11–3, and Tredegar away, 5–3, with McNulty scoring a try, converted by Rees Harding. There was also a 0–13 defeat to local rivals Skewen.

They finished the season with impressive wins over Cardiff Athletic (8–5, Anthony and McNulty tries, Harding conversion) and Maesteg 24–0, with tries from D.J. Rees, Ivor George, B. Brian, C. Banfield, Bryn Jones and Mog Jones.

Ferry played a game to raise funds for Port Talbot hospital, at Cwmavon against a combined Afan Valley XV, which they lost 6–10 (C. Banfield and R. Harding were the try scorers).

On the junior scene

There was a good 13–3 win over Cymmer by an improving Second XV, who were also doing well in the Rogers Cup. They only lost one match after Christmas and reached the semi-final of this competition, which they lost to Neath Allied Traders by 4–7, their only score a drop goal by P. Walsh.

AGM

Chairman Mr J.B. Williams presided over a large attendance at the AGM. There was disappointment with the balance of funds, which was in the red. This was put down to poor gates due to a trade depression in the town. One suggestion was to turn the pitch around, widening and lengthening it, to enable a bigger crowd to watch. Officers elected for the following season included: president Major J.M. Bevan MC, honourable secretary O.L. Davies, assistant secretary Ivor Dargavel, treasurer Syd Abraham, with a general committee consisting of Alderman W.J. Hill, W.S. Davies, R. Phillips, J. Anthony, Dick Jones, Llew Griffiths, T. Ireland, D. Lloyd, B. Grey, J. Thomas, J. Evans and B. Rosser.

Top scorers for the season were Rees Harding, 37 points, and D.J. Rees with 30 points.

Around the district

This season there was a one and only mention of a team called the Ferry Paupers, who lost to Neath Traders in the Supporters Cup 6–3 and then drew with Banwen away.

The season also witnessed the demise of Neath Rovers, Neath Stars and Cimla (due to four of their star players being suspended for not paying subs to a former club).

Among the ex-Ferry players featured in the *Neath Guardian*'s sports gallery were Harold Powell, stand-off Tommy Hughes of Allied Traders who'd spent two seasons with the Ferry, and one of the finest forwards in the district at that time, W. Bowden of Neath Old Boys RFC, who had been hooker for Neath, Skewen and Briton Ferry.

1933/34

Rugby league reared its ugly head again this year with wingers Harold Powell and Vernon Case being made offers of £200 from Salford and £300 and £350 from Broughton Rovers and York, respectively.

5.5 Harold Powell (photo: Harry Jones, Neath)

Captain
Edwin Selby

Vice captain
Mog Jones

Junior's playing record
P 39
W 28
D 4
L 7
Points for 293
Points against 98

The season started with a visit by Merthyr, which Ferry won 17–9. Morris and Charlie Banfield scored a try apiece and wing Vernon Case scored a brace, Rees Harding added a penalty and a conversion. Then came the result of the season, a visit to Talbot Athletic ground to face an Aberavon side who had not tasted defeat for over a year at their own patch – until now! What a win, 16–12, with tries by D. Rees, H. Powell, V. Case and B. Jones, and again Rees Harding adding 2 conversions. Outstanding were both wings, Powell and Case, and up front, Jones and Ned Selby. The Ferry had included eight youngsters from local junior sides: Harold Powell (Neath Traders), Dai

Rees and Vernon Case (Neath Quins), Mog Jones (Neath Barbarians), Ned Selby (Wanderers) and Gwyn Thomas, Charlie Banfield and Rees Harding (County School). A week later Harold Powell was selected to play for Neath against Aberavon, but this time he was on the losing side. Both Powell and Gwyn Thomas continued with Neath after featuring in a midweek win over Pontypridd.

Season 1933-1934

J. Callaghan, L. Drew, W.S. Davies, E. Thomas, B. Grey, E. Gill, V. Griffiths, T.Lewis,
T. Morris, E. Hill, G. Thomas, A. James, V. Friend, R. Phillips, M. Jones, W. Bryant,
E. Selby, S. Anthony, V. Phillips, J.S. Anthony, D. Lloyd, G. Blight, A.McArthur
I. George, T. John. D. Rees.

5.6 1933/34

Two more wins followed, 6–5 over Maesteg with 2 tries by Case, and 6–0 over Resolven, another try by Case and one from Bryn Jones. Ferry then travelled up to Treorchy, who were protecting a ground record. The game ended in an 8–8 draw, with yet more tries for Case and D. Rees, Harding converted one. In the midweek previous to this game two players were loaned to Aberavon, who took Pontypridd's home record – Rees Harding at hooker and wing Vernon Case, who scored two tries. Case played for Neath against Exeter in another midweek match and was on the scoreboard yet again.

Next up for the First XV was a home game with Morriston, which they won by 14–5 with tries by Ivor George, Emrys Hill, D.J. Rees and Steve Anthony, and a Bryn Jones conversion. Another home win followed, 22–3 over Cardiff University. Ivor George and D.J. Rees were again among the scorers, with tries added by C. Banfield, Bryn Jones and Rees Harding, who also scored 1 penalty and 2 conversions. They continued this winning streak over Kenfig Hill (17–0), Gowerton (6–0 before one of the largest attendances of the season), Cardiff University (3–0 to complete the double), Cwmavon (8–5).

After an away win at Blaengarw, 6–0, at the end of November their unbeaten run was halted by fierce rivals Skewen on 1 December, 0–3, who kicked a penalty with five minutes to go to full time.

The Ferry XV saw December out with another defeat away, again by 0–3, this time to Cwmavon. They defeated the juniors on Christmas Day by 12–0 and then gained revenge over Cwmavon on Boxing Day with a 6–5 win. Among the scorers during this run were Ivor George 5 tries, C. Banfield 2 tries, Dil Jones 1 try, Rees Harding 1 penalty and 1 conversion, Tom John 2 tries, Ned Selby 1 try and D. Rees 2 tries.

Ivor George started the first game of the new year as he had finished the last, with a hat trick of tries in an 11–3 away win over Glynneath, Mog Jones added the conversion. Then the First XV lost their next game, at home to Bridgend 3–16, in heavy rain on a field like a mud heap. Prominent players were forwards S. Selby, T. Morris and A. McCarley, backs Mog Jones, I. George and C. Banfield and half-backs Dai Rees and Gwyn Thomas.

The next home match, against Treorchy, was marred by the late arrival of the away side, which meant a 4 p.m kick-off and a 35-minute game, but a 3–0 win for the Ferry. George scored the only try.

February started with a 17–3 win over Abercrave – C. Banfield scored a try, D. Rees and Bryn Jones added 1 try, 1 drop goal and 2 conversions. The Ferry XV continued in this vein with further wins at home over Cardiff Athletic 10–7 and Aberdare 24–0 (which completed another double for the season) and finally beating Maesteg 3–0. Scorers in these games were I. George 2 tries, D.J. Rees 2 tries, C. Banfield and W.J. Griffiths 1 try apiece, and 3 conversions and 1 penalty from the boot of Bryn Jones.

March brought the sad news of the death of JIM JONES at a young 41, who had played for Aberavon, Briton Ferry and Wales.

Another defeat to Skewen by 3–10 in March. The following match was played at the Gnoll in aid of the Neath Rugby Supporters pavilion fund and Neath won 11–13. E. Selby and I. George scored tries and Bryn Jones kicked 1 conversion and 1 penalty. Both teams then went to a dinner at the Cambrian Hotel to celebrate and honour three members of the Neath XV who had gained their Welsh caps, D.R. Prosser, Glyn Prosser and A. Hickman.

A home win (6–0) over Glynneath completed another season double, despite fielding six reserves. This was the first match Charlie Banfield missed in three seasons and Edwin Selby was in for Edgar Evans, who was playing for Swansea. They then lost to Resolven 0–14.

At Easter ex-Neath player Mervyn Stevens assisted the Ferry for a few games on his return from Moseley. On Good Friday, Ferry defeated London County Council XV 11–5 (tries by Jefford, D. Jones and I. George, conversion by Mog Jones). On Easter Saturday, Ferry drew away to Carmarthen Quins. Easter ended with a heavy defeat of Bath Non-Descripts, 48–0, with a hat trick of tries for W. Green, and a pair each for D. Rees and I George, and further tries from E. Hill, Griffiths, Jefford and Mog Jones (who also added a conversion), McNulty with 3 conversions and a drop goal by Selby.

In April, Ferry were defeated at Worcester Field by Morriston, 3–6, with I. George scoring the only try. The First XV's season ended with a defeat to Carmarthen Athletic, and yet another I. George score, and a 3–3 draw with Carmarthen Quins.

In May, members of the club were summoned to Neath Borough Police Court accused of misappropriating funds. Gate money had been collected during a local derby in November 1933, which had produced a large crowd. All tickets sold should have received an excise revenue stamp. Most of the sixpenny tickets were stamped, but many of the threepenny ones weren't – it seems the club officers had underestimated the likely sales. This was picked up by a customs and excise officer during a visit to the club. They were found guilty of a technical offence and ordered to pay costs and to refund the unpaid excise tax.

Junior league

On the junior front, the teams competing in the Neath league were Allied Traders, Neath Quins, Crynant Juniors, Banwen, Bryncoch, Resolven Cubs, Glynneath Juniors, Taillwyd Crusaders, Neath OB, Cwmgrach and, of course, the Ferry Juniors.

The Ferry juniors were playing well in the local cups and during the season, after losing four of their first six games, they went unbeaten for 24 games.

In late September they defeated Maesteg Celtic by 13–0 (Phillip Walsh scored all the points with a try hat trick and a drop goal), but lost their next match 0–10 against Heol Las. Prominent in these games were Hill, Williams and

Sandham. After a 0–3 defeat to Cwmgrach away they then began achieving some success with wins over Cymmer, Aberavon Quins (8–0, which featured an outstanding solo try by Sandham in which he reportedly picked up the ball on the halfway and then went on a swerving and sidestepping run past at least six defenders on his way to the line), Neath Unemployed (3–0), Margam Works (8–0, the fifth game on the trot without a point being scored against them), Ystalyfera Whites (17–0, with a length of the field interception try by Walsh; after the match the Whites invited the juniors to their annual dinner dance as guests of honour) and a final 12–6 win over previously unbeaten Cwmavon (there'd been a 0–0 draw between these teams in November) – before their eventual defeat by the First XV on Christmas Day.

Outstanding for the juniors during this period were: Vernon Phillips, Dai Matthews, Reg Jones, Shon Evans, V. Collins, R. Brian up front and Sandham, W. Hill, P. Walsh, W.C. Thomas, J. Evans, D. Morris, W. Ram, fullback Tom Watkins and Tom Donovan.

5.7 Briton Ferry Juniors 1933/34

In the Neath Supporters Cup the Juniors beat Neath United (22–0), then Crynant (13–0), Townhill (8–3) in a friendly, followed a 9–9 draw at Ogmore Vale, with reports of a 3,000-strong crowd! They reached the final, where they faced Town Juniors.

In the Rogers Cup they defeated holders Cwmgrach 6–0 (A. Stevens 1 try, D. Morris 1 penalty) in a rough match, which augured well for the Ferry. The Cwmgrach outside-half was sent off after several warnings to all players about foul play. In the semi-final they defeated Neath Unemployed 11–0 which took them to the final, also against Town Juniors.

Internationally famous Ivor David refereed both cup finals, and Ferry completed the double, the first time any side achieved this. They won the Neath Supporters Cup 16–3, with tries by G. Jefford, Ram and a double from J. Evans. D. Morris converted 2. They won the Rogers Cup 11–5, with Ivor Morris, Roger Parker and A. Stevens scoring tries, and Stevens converted one. There were complaints about poor attendance and rough play throughout the Rogers Cup tournament and some clubs disbanded – Cimla, The Quins, Berni Stars, Neath Stars and Taillwyd. Resolven had withdrawn earlier in the season.

5.8 Referee Ivor David

The Juniors also had a friendly win over Nantyfyllon, 3–0, with a solitary penalty by Walsh. Gwyn Walters played in this match on his return from army duties in India, where he'd represented the service in both boxing and athletics!

Other news

In January, the 19½-year-old, 6'1" policeman Vernon Case (then playing for Neath) joined Wigan RLFC for the princely sum of £300 (£4 a week, £3 for a draw and £2.10s for a defeat).

1934/35

This was the season that the club were elected to join the West Wales League.

Juniors

The Juniors changed their name to Briton Ferry Wanderers RFC. Quite a few new clubs were added to the fixture list: Trebanos, Bethel (Port Talbot), St. Mary's, Heol Las, Oystermouth, Glyncorrwg, Ynys United, Elba and Cymmer.

Under captain Tom Donovan, the Wanderers started off the season with a 25–0 win over Bethel, but a narrow defeat to Kenfig Hill 0–3 followed. They then beat Birchgrove 12–3, but lost 0–3 in a foul-tempered game against Oystermouth. They bounced back at home and defeated Townhill 6–0. They finished the year in style with wins over St. Mary's (Aberavon) 8–0 and Abergarwed 25–0. Donovan, Walsh, Beer, A. Stephens, Watkins, M. Stephens, J. Hill, J. Evans, W. Hill and R. Jones were all prominent players.

The Wanderers started 1935 as they'd finished 1934, with a 10–0 win over Maesteg Celtic, thus winning the double, the first team to inflict that on Celtic for six years. Jefford and Donovan were the try scorers. A smoker night for both teams followed in the Grandison Hotel, entertained by fine renditions from J. Brimm, Ben Morgan, Reg Jones, Tom Donovan, and Len Stephens, with Dai Llewelyn at the piano.

In early February they won against Crynant 19–0. A 0–0 draw with Trebanos completed the March fixtures. Their season ended in April with a rare 0–3 defeat by Ynys (Port Talbot).

Captain
Edgar Evans

BF Wanderers playing record
W 12
D 2
L 4
Poins for 138
Points against 30

Match results place BFRFC scores first

During the season two Cwrt Sart schoolboys were selected to play for the Welsh Under-15s Schoolboys, fullback Tom Morgan and 12-year-old Rees Stephens.

Seniors

Hooker Edgar Evans was in for a difficult season as captain because, over the months, more than a dozen players transferred to first-class clubs. Emrys Hill went to Aberavon, while Steve Anthony and H. Morris joined ex-player McNulty at Cheltenham.

Ex-players E. Youatt and Gwyn Thomas, who were with Neath, both had Welsh trials and played for the Rest of Wales XV against Wales XV on 4 May for a Jubilee celebration.

Season 1934-1935

Top Row:- Ray Rees, M. Jones. I. George. M. Abraham.
2nd Row:- J. Arthur. T. Morris. V. Phillips. L. Drew. D. J. Randall. C. Harris.
3rd Row.- S. Anthony. E. Selby(V/Capt) W.E. Evans(Capt) O.L. Davies(Sec) T. John. B.S.Jones.
Seated:- T. Lewis.   D. Morris.

5.9 1934/35

The Ferry XV got off to a bad start by losing 0–7 to Morriston and 0–6 to Aberavon 6–0. But they bounced back with a good win over Merthyr, 24–3, with an Ivor George hat trick and tries from S. Anthony, Tom John and E. Selby, with 3 conversions by Bryn Jenkins. The following week only a Bryn Jenkins penalty gave them a score in a 3–12 defeat at Maesteg. The next Saturday they were an hour late arriving at Lydney and lost narrowly by 0–3, in a game in which a certain Myo Abraham at fullback was to the fore. Yet another 0–3 defeat followed to Pontardawe before a visit from Tenby a week later ended the drought. In an excellent 15–0 win, tries came from G. Rees, Mog Jones, J. Richards and Steve Anthony, who also kicked a penalty.

While several Ferry players were assisting some local first-class clubs, they narrowly lost to Cardiff University 3–8, D. Rees was the solitary try scorer. Next up were Newport United and, despite being a man down for the whole of the second half, a Bryn Jones try and conversion were enough to make it a 5–3 victory. Ferry then played local rivals Skewen at their venue and an even game resulted in a 3–3 draw, with D. Anthony the try scorer. This was followed by a trip to Pontypridd, where an E. Selby try and a B. Jones conversion were not enough to prevent a narrow 5–7 defeat. Back home against Aberdare a B. Jones try and 2 conversions and a Steve Anthony try were enough to overcome the opposition by 10–8. A player from each side was sent off (D. Jones for the Ferry).

News filtered through from Neath in November that ex-Ferry player Charlie Banfield, after an excellent trial match in which he enabled ex-Welsh wing J.C. Morley to score 5 tries, had signed for Wigan RLFC for £250.

Pontypridd were the next visitors to the Ferry and they were defeated 5–0. I. George scored a try after a kick through by Roy Rees, which B. Jones converted. Yet another defeat followed in the return match at Newport United, 5–13. Selby was the try scorer, again converted by Jones.

5.10 Bryn Jones (photo: Imperial Studios, Aberavon)

The Ferry XV finished the year off with two wins: 8–0 over Kenfig Hill (E. Evans and Ted Morris tries, B. Jones conversion); and 11–0 over Glynneath, with the only try scored by I. George, B. Jones kicked 1 conversion and 2 penalties – another match in which a player from each side was dismissed from the field.

The new year started with a 9–6 win over Gowerton, with tries by E. Richards, I. George and J. Harris. Seventeen-year-old ex-Neath Grammar schoolboy D. Jones featured at inside-half (he'd been capped at schoolboy level in 1930). They then took a revenge win over Lydney at the Ferry by 9–3.

The Ferry made a new signing from Neath Quins, scrum-half D. Morris.

Defeats in February – 9–16 at Resolven (Selby try, M. Jones conversion, John drop goal) and 3–5 at home to Aberavon – were followed by a midweek defeat by Neath, 3–20.

They completed the March fixtures with an 8–5 win over Skewen (tries by S. Anthony and Ned Selby, 1 conversion by B. Jones) and a 0–0 draw with Trebanos.

April started badly with two defeats: 3–20 away at Treorchy (M. Thomas try); 3–6 away at Glynneath (M. Jones try). Ferry then made it two Easter weekend wins, 14–3 over Treorchy (tries by S. Anthony, D. Morris and R. Rees and 1 conversion and 1 penalty for B. Jones) and 11–6 over Upper Clacton (London) (tries from W. Gregory and I. Morris, conversions from T. Drew and B. Jones)

The season ended in style with wins away at Resolven (11–6, with 2 tries and 1 conversion for Bryn Jones, 1 try for I. George) and 6–3 at home to Aberavon.

1935/36

Captain Morgan (Mog) Jones' season started with controversy as the Ferry Wanderers were in dispute with the senior side about the use of the pitch. They agreed on a fee of £2 10s to use the field.

The First XV lost their first game at home to Amman United 8–11, Edgar Evans and G. Nicholas scored tries and B. Jones converted 1.

More defeats followed for the Ferry XV: to Neath 0–17; 3–6 up at Resolven, T.J. Davies, Reg Rees, W. Cousen, V. Williams, T. John, M. Thomas and E. Evans were prominent; and Crynant away, 6–8, with Dai Morris and L. Morris the scorers.

Captain
Morgan Jones

Playing record
P 43
W 18
D 4
L 21

The First XV managed their first long-awaited win in October, 6–0 against Pontardulais, with tries by Williams and Anthony. A 3–3 draw with Kenfig Hill followed, in which Vernon Friend kicked two penalties, but then another defeat, 3–17 up in Merthyr. They did go on to defeat local rivals Skewen, at home 11–6. Two away defeats followed, 3–13 to Newport United and 3–18 to Skewen.

Roy Rees scored two tries in a 6–11 home defeat for the First XV to Cardiff University, which featured brothers Ted and Tom Youatt at half-back. Next up were Cwmavon, who boasted an unbeaten home record for the season. A try from S. Anthony and 1 conversion and 1 penalty from B. Jones weren't enough for Ferry to break that record and they lost narrowly, 8–9. Another defeat completed a miserable November, this time 6–9 at home to Treorchy, with an E. Selby try and a B. Jones penalty.

December didn't start too well either as they suffered another home defeat. Ferry's only score was a T. Youatt try for 3–13 against Maesteg. The year finished with a 3–3 draw with unbeaten Cwmavon, in which B. Jones kicked a penalty.

> The club held a dance for players and supporters on New Year's Eve at the Public Hall, which had been decorated in club colours.

The new year started with a 13–3 home victory over Newport United, with tries by Teddy Morris, Tom Youatt and B. Jones, who also kicked two conversions. It was noted that no fewer than five players from the senior Newport side were playing, including Welsh international A. Fear!

In a midweek match hung over from the previous season, they lost 6–10 at home to Gowerton, with S. Jones and Tom Youatt the try scorers. Fullback Mog Jones was carried off injured. The month ended badly with a 3–8 defeat in Crynant (I. John scored the only try).

February started quite brightly with a 7–3 win at Cardiff University, from a D. Jones try and a Youatt drop goal. In the second half of a home match against Pontardawe, the Ferry made a remarkable recovery to achieve a 6–6 draw. Mervyn Youatt scored the best try of the match and another by D.J. Randall made them level. At the previous fixture between these teams the referee for the day hadn't turned up and, in an amazing coincidence, this happened again. So the match was refereed by an official from each club, who did one half each.

> Schoolboy Rees Stephens of Cwrt Sart School played for (and captained) Neath Schoolboys. He also captained Welsh Schools to a victory over England Schools.

The Ferry XV were defeated again, 0–3 by Gowerton, before managing a 14–6 home victory over Merthyr in March – the try scorers included E. Evans, R. Rees, G. Jefford and B. Jones, with E. Evans converting one. Outstanding players that day were A. Clarke, B. Jones and T. Donovan. In a 3–3 midweek draw with Resolven, D. Jones was the try scorer, and then Aberdare were defeated 12–3, with 2 tries and 1 penalty from B. Jones and 1 try from E. Selby. The conditions dictated that this was a kick and rush game and fullback Myo Abraham was outstanding for the Ferry.

In another midweek game at home Neath won 0–20, then Maesteg also inflicted a 0–15 defeat on the Ferry. Ferry bounced back to take the honours over Penygraig by 7–3, with Syd Harris the try scorer and Tom John dropping a goal. G. Rosser was brought in at fullback and L. Drew in the forwards for this game.

The end of April spelt defeat away from home yet again, 5–9 at Amman United (John scored 1 try, converted by B. Jones). Although the forwards were well on top, Amman proved to be smarter in the backs.

Ferry bounced back yet again to win the penultimate game of the season by 6–0 over Gowerton, in a rain-sodden match. E. Jenkins crossed for a clever solo try and Bryn Jones kicked a penalty from a difficult angle. This made it 60 points for Jones since his return to the team at Christmas after scoring 100 points in the previous season. The two Selbys, Ned and D., were in fine form in the backs, as were half-backs Arthur Stephens and M. Youatt.

The final game of the season was a rearranged match from Christmas Day against Aberavon, which Ferry won 6–3. E. Jenkins scored both tries for the Ferry. Aberavon finished sixth in that year's merit table.

The Ferry finished twenty-third in their first season in the West Wales League.

The Wanderers

The Wanderers played a drawn game, 3–3, up in Penygraig in which the outstanding players were Willie Hill, Joe Hill, Deg Jones and Goddard. They maintained their unbeaten start with an 18–3 win over Abergarwed, but it didn't last as they lost their very next game up in Ogmore Vale 0–3.

The Wanderers also lost at home in October, 0–3 to Pencoed, before defeating Three Crosses by a narrow, one-point margin, 4–3.

AGM

The AGM reported that the top scorer was 42-year-old Bryn Jones, with 62 points (all scored since Christmas).

Of the £175 13s 3d received, £41 15s 7d was gate money.

The officers elected were W.S. Davies as secretary and H. Bevan as treasurer. The committee elected were Jack Evans, Jack Anthony, Sid Abraham, George Ireland, Vernon Williams, Harry Thomas, W.J. Hill, Eddie Hughes and Emrys Hill. Mog Jones was elected captain for the following season, with Bryn Jones as vice captain.

1936/37

During this season ex-Ferry player Harold Thomas, still only 22, was elected captain of Neath RFC and became a Welsh international.

Ferry's season opened with a home game against Ystradgynlais, the first match between them in ten years. Ferry's captain, Mog Jones, was indisposed and their vice captain, Bryn Jones, was playing on permit for Swansea. An early try from wing E. Jenkins was not enough as two tries from Ystradgynlais gave them a 3–6 victory. Ferry won the next game 14–6, again at home, against Ystalyfera, with tries from I. George and R. Harding, who also kicked 1 conversion and 2 penalties.

Amman United should have been the next visitors, but their bus broke down in Garnant and the match had to be postponed. This was a shame because the game was to have been kicked off by ex-Ferry player and captain, H. Rawlings, Chief Constable of Derby and former Chief Constable of Neath.

The next game was also postponed as Aberdare could not raise a side, so a home game against Swansea United was quickly arranged. The Ferry won 3–0 with a very late try by S. Anthony. Two away defeats followed (0–12 at Glynneath in front of a large crowd, then in midweek to Aberavon by 0–5), before a 3–3 away draw with Skewen settled things down a bit (Tom Donovan was the try scorer and outstanding for the Ferry were E. Gorman and Max Arnold).

Cilfynydd were the next visitors to the Ferry. They left with the spoils after inflicting a 0–14 defeat on the Ferry. Another draw followed, 6–6 with Maesteg, J. Evans and

Captain
Ivor Jenkins

Vice captain
Brian Jones

Playing record
P 41
W 11
D 3
L 27
Points for 170
Points against 249

M. Arnold were the try scorers. Penygraig visited the Ferry in late October and were defeated 10–3. E. Jenkins and Selby were the try scorers and a fine drop goal from Ivor George completed the win. October ended with a tight away win at Cwmavon, 7–5. Hooker R. Jones 1 drop goal and D. Selby scored 1 unconverted try.

> Several Cwrt Sart boys were selected for a Neath Schoolboys XV match against local rivals Aberavon on the Gnoll, which ended in a 3–3 draw. They were fullback F. Poley, wings Roy Evans and V. Hendre and forward A. James.

In November, a weakened Ferry team (with five reserves) visited Cwmamman Park to play Amman United. They were defeated 3–8. Centre D. Selby was the try scorer. Another away defeat followed at Aberaman, 0–7. To end November they got back to winning ways at home to Cwmavon, 12–0. Max Arnold 1 drop goal and 1 try, which Tom Donovan converted. Ivor George also crossed for 1 unconverted try.

December got underway with an at home 0–0 draw with Gowerton, before another narrow away defeat against Cardiff University 0–3, and a 3–11 defeat at home to Resolven, Steve Anthony the try scorer. Cwmavon were Boxing Day visitors and Ferry had already defeated them twice this season. The game was kicked off by the Chief Constable of Derby, ex-Ferry player H. Rawlings. It was a tight affair and a late score from Cwmavon gave them a 3–0 victory over the Ferry.

The new year started with a 5–0 win over Skewen, the try scorer was second row M. Thomas, T. Donovan made the conversion. It was followed by another close defeat, 0–3 away at Penygraig.

Their next opponents were Cardiff University and unfortunately the Ferry were unable to field their strongest side so the team was: fullback Id Evans; threequarters E. Jenkins, V. Friend, George Beer, I. George; half-backs S. Harris, M. Arnold; forwards V. Phillips, T. Donovan, R. Collins, W. Amphlett, K. Nesbitt, J. Evans, M. Thomas and M. Jones (captain).

In the next game, away to Resolven, Ferry were defeated 0–8. Half-back S. Harris was not playing as he'd been selected to play for Neath against Aberavon. Yet more away defeats followed, 0–3 by Gowerton and 0–8 by Maesteg. Then Skewen managed to win 0–3 at the Ferry, to even up the series for the season. A notable absence from the Ferry team was Vernon Friend, who'd been selected to play for Swansea against Leicester.

5.11 Vernon Friend: Welsh Secondary Schools, Briton Ferry and Neath

February ended with an overwhelming 32–0 victory over visitors Treorchy. Scorers were: single tries from Haydn Williams, E. Jenkins, D. Davies, S. Anthony and T. Donovan; V. Friend with 3 conversions and 1 try; George Thomas with 2 tries; and Mog Jones with 1 conversion.

Merthyr were the next home opponents and they were also defeated, 14–5. G. Thomas scored 1 try, while T. Donovan scored 2, converted 1 and kicked 1 penalty. Skewen then managed to get ahead in the series of games with a 0–6 win over Ferry.

To start the Easter holidays at the end of March the Ferry defeated Glynneath at home, 5–3, with Vernon Phillips scoring 1 try and Tom Donovan 1 conversion. A 6–11 defeat at Cwmavon on Easter Monday followed, with Tom Donovan scoring 1 try, converted by Rees Harding.

The next visitors were Aberaman who went away with a 5–6 win, although a Tom John try and a Rees Harding conversion had given the Ferry a lead. The losses continued. First, 0–3 to Crynant in a rearranged midweek match for which the Ferry only managed to field 14 players. Second, on the Saturday in Merthyr 0–5. Third, the following week up in Cilfynydd by 0–14. They ended a poor season by losing 0–6 at Crynant when, to rub salt into the wound, they also lost centre D. Selby with a fractured cheekbone and back rower D. Collins with fractured ribs. They also lost a return game at Ystalyfera.

The Ferry finished twenty-sixth in the West Wales League.

In April, the editor of the *Neath Guardian* had written an open letter decrying the disgusting incidents that had started to creep into the game in West Wales, and imploring both club committees and all the players to clean up their acts and to stamp out the violence, as people were starting to drift away from the game and were turning to other sources of entertainment.

AGM

The Mayor of Neath, Councillor J.B. Williams JP, presided over the AGM held at the Grandison Hotel on 5 July. After the playing record for the season was announced (top scorer was Tom Donovan with 28 points), the secretary added that the results would have been different if all the selected players had given their support by turning out regularly.

Ex-sergeant A. Bevan, the treasurer, reported a debit of £9 9s 5d, the lowest funds for a few years.

All committee officers were re-elected for the coming season. The general committee members were: Councillor John Shea, Sid Abraham, Percy George, Jack Evans, E. Cledwyn Davies BA, George Ireland, Harry Thomas, Eddie Hughes, Ivor Olsen, Ned Selby and William Griffiths.

1937/38 – 50TH

The club were quite optimistic about their chances for the coming season as all last year's players were available and a number of new players joined. They held a trial match on Saturday 28 August and a further trial on Wednesday 1 September.

The first match was against Aberavon at the Talbot Athletic ground. Reports said that Aberavon had a depleted side but also, arguably, the fastest pack in Wales. Ferry fought hard to achieve a result with a promising pair of half-backs in Max Arnold and H. Parker (brother of Dai the Neath scrum-half), but it was W. Bansi and Tom Donovan up front who got Ferry's only points with a penalty in a 3–25 defeat.

Two more defeats followed. First, 8–14 at Maesteg (away), with Cockett scoring a try, converted by Tom Donovan, who also kicked a penalty. Then in midweek at Bridgend, 6–33, with Steve Anthony and Ernest Jenkins the try scorers. Then, at last, a win in the first home game against Pontardawe, 3–0, with Rees Harding kicking a penalty. A a mixed bag followed in the next two home games with a 3–3 draw with Resolven in the West Wales League and a 3–14 defeat to Glynneath. Hooker Rees Harding kicked a penalty in each game. Prominent players were backs Vernon Williams, E. Jenkins and S. Anthony and, up front, Harding, Donovan and Phil Lewis.

Cardiff Athletic were the next opponents and the Ferry went down to a heavy defeat, 0–22. Reports described how the Cardiff three-quarter (Rev. John Roberts, a Welsh international and Cambridge Blue, who had recently returned from China after five years of missionary work)

Captain
Tom Donovan

Playing record
P 37
W 12
D 5
L 20
Points for 173
Points against 336

was having trouble with his boots and so played the closing stages of the game in stockinged feet!

Ferry were away in the next league match, in Cwmamman Park to Amman United, and they managed another 3–3 draw. V. Williams kicked the equalising penalty.

Gowerton were the next home opponents and, in front of a record crowd, Ferry won 10–0. There was a bit of controversy when Gowerton pressed hard near the Ferry line and H. Parker, endeavouring to clear, was struck a violent blow to the chest when he was tackled and fell to the ground. All the players stopped, with the exception of Lee who, in the process of gathering the loose ball, knocked it on. Unfortunately, the referee didn't spot it and allowed the resulting score to stand.

Ystradgynlais were the next league opponents at the Ferry and Rees Harding kicked the only penalty in a 3–12 loss. This was followed by another defeat, 0–13, this time away to old rivals Skewen. Ferry were unfortunate as they lost forward M. Thomas midway through the first half and finished the game with fourteen men.

Ferry then drew with visitors Kenfig Hill. Rees Harding kicked a penalty and converted an Ernie Jenkins try for an 8–8 score. Again prominent for the Ferry were John Evans and Les Drew up front and fullback E.C. Roberts.

The next game was the league return match with Resolven which ended in another defeat for the Ferry, 3–8. Phil Lewis scored their only points with a late try. Once again, injuries didn't help as two Ferry forwards were off the field by the end of the match.

A rare double for the season was recorded in the next game over Pontardawe, as Ernie Jenkins scored the only try and Bryn Jones converted and kicked a penalty for an 8–3 Ferry victory.

The front page of the *Neath Guardian* on Friday 10 December 1937 ran an advert stating that Neath RFC were to play the Ferry on the Gnoll on 11 December with a 2.45 p.m. kick-off, tickets in the stand were 2 shillings (ladies and boys 1 shilling), in the field 1 shilling and inside the ropes 1 shilling and sixpence – all inclusive of tax. Lessons learnt from 1933 then!

Over Christmas there was a 0–0 draw at home on Christmas Day with Crynant, then a 0–8 defeat away to Cwmavon on Boxing Day.

At New Year, the Ferry managed a good victory over visiting Penygraig, 6–0. Outstanding for the Ferry were fullback E.C. Roberts, wing Ernie Jenkins, and Phil Lewis (who suffered an ankle injury that eventually forced him off the field) and Max Arnold at half-back, with Rees Harding, G. Griffiths and J. Evans up front. Ernie Jenkins and G. Griffiths made a try apiece.

A visit to Gowerton was next, and a 3–6 defeat. Tom Donovan scored the only Ferry try. Harold Parker came in at half-back for the injured Lewis.

Ystalyfera were the visitors for an exciting drawn game (5–5) in deplorable conditions. H. James scored the only try, converted by B. Jones. There were quite a few changes from the previous game: Mog Jones came in at fullback and was made Man of the Match; G. Gifford, G. Thomas, H. Jones, G. Fisher, I. Morris and D. Morris came in to the back division; and G. Daymond, D. Collins, A. Clarke, D. Selby, V. Phillips, A. James and H. Thomas all came in up front.

Aberaman were the next opponents at the Ferry and they went away with a six-point victory (5–11). Dai Selby was Ferry's try scorer, converted by Brian Jones converting. Once again luck went against them when they lost half-back Harold Parker to a knee injury.

Home team Glynneath triumphed at Abernant Park, 3–8. Ferry made many changes: J. Arnold came in at half-back and Hughes, M. Randall, D. Llewelyn, S. Barry, J. Evans, C. Harries and W. Shewry all came in up front. The only scorer for the Ferry was hooker Degwel Hughes, with a try.

5.12 Charlie Clarke

The first game in February (Ferry v. Maesteg) clashed with a trip to Scotland for the internationals, which depleted both sides. Two local lads, W. Rothero and Charlie Clark, had to play for Wales. To add to the problems the appointed referee, Mr J. Bancroft of Swansea, didn't turn up so the teams agreed to local referee, Mr O. Davies, taking charge of the game. The result was a 6–6 draw. Brian Jones kicked a penalty and Ernie Jenkins grabbed a try to draw the game. New players to feature were T. Ireland on the wing and A. Poley up front.

Despite more bad weather at the end of February, Ferry defeated old rivals Skewen in the last game of the month at home, 8–0. An early interception try by Max Arnold was converted by Brian Jones. In a brilliant solo effort, centre Dai Selby dummied his way past four defenders to score a sensational try.

Selby featured heavily the following week against Skewen at Tennant Park, but as is the fickle way in rugby, as he was attempting to score in the final stages of the match he was knocked unconscious and carried from the field. It was reported that it took him nearly an hour to regain consciousness! The game went the way of the home team (0–5), whose win put them 2–1 up in the series. G. Barry and P. Roderick showed well up front for the Ferry.

Amman United visited the Ferry at the end of March for a thrilling game in which the home team were victors by 14–9. Tries from half-backs and brothers, Geoffrey and Max Arnold. Max also 1 drop goal. Brian Jones kicked 2 conversions.

This was followed by another home victory over Ogmore Vale, who were defeated 14–6 with tries by A. Clarke, Steve Anthony, Mog Jones and Brian Jones, who also kicked a conversion. But the Ferry were then defeated at home by a strong Ebbw Vale side, who were the victors 3–21. The only points for the Ferry came from a Rees Harding penalty. Harding and fellow forwards Aubrey Clarke, Edwin Selby and Dan Griffiths were outstanding throughout.

Easter weekend at home saw a defeat by a single point on Good Friday, to local rivals Skewen, 5–6. D. Griffiths was the try scorer, with Brian Jones converting. Then on Easter Saturday a strong Cardiff Athletic side visited the Ferry. Up until this point in the season Cardiff had only lost once, but they went home well beaten by 11–3. The Ferry's try scorers were Harold Jones, with a double, and I. Drew, with Rees Harding converting one.

Ferry then closed the season with a rearranged game at Maesmawr Field against Crynant and were narrowly defeated 6–9. Ferry played the full game with only fourteen men, albeit against a Crynant side who were also struggling. Max Arnold scored a try and Dan Griffiths a penalty for the Ferry.

Top scorers for the season were Brian Jones (46), Ernie Jenkins (25), Max Arnold and Rees Harding (20)

The 50th AGM

Monday 18 July 1938 was a significant date in the history of the club, the fiftieth Annual General Meeting. Mr W.J. Hill chaired it at the Grandison Hotel, in the absence of vice president Councillor J.B. Williams.

Treasurer Mr Abraham Bevan stated that, after expenditure, the club was left with a credit balance of £42 0s 7d. Also, they were awaiting the result of the jazz band competition, which would probably yield about £20 and that gate receipts amounted to £40 1s 6d.

The chairman's address included tributes to some of the early names connected with the club, in particular to the dedication shown by ex-secretary Mr Ossie Davies, who had become the club's first life member. The club had also decided to honour his brother, the current secretary Mr W.S. Davies, by presenting him with a token of their appreciation. He had chosen a writing desk, which had been suitably inscribed, but as it was impossible to bring this to the meeting, he was presented with a cheque for £10 15s, which was the value of the desk. A vote of thanks was also made in his absence to Councillor J.B. Williams who had done a great deal for the club, particularly in his capacity of agent to the Jersey Estate where the ground was concerned.

Officers elected for the coming season were: president Major J.M. Bevan, vice president Councillor J.B. Williams, chairman Mr W.J. Hill, vice chairman Mr Ossie Davies, secretary Mr W.S. Davies, assistant secretary Mr W.R. Lewis, treasurer Mr Abraham Bevan. The general committeemen were Sid Abraham, Percy George, Jack Evans, Ned Selby, Harry Thomas, Cledwyn Davies BA, Eddie Hughes, Jack Anthony, Vernon Davies, D.J. Jones and Morgan Jones. Captain for the fiftieth anniversary was to be Brian Jones, with Max Arnold as vice captain.

Other news

W.J. Hill, who'd served the club since the 1920s, was secretary of Glamorgan County RFC.

In September, ex-Ferry and Neath international Harold Thomas went north to Salford for the reported sum of £375!

1938/39

The fiftieth season started on Saturday 3 September with a home game against Crynant, which Ferry won 8–0. D. Llewelyn and E. Jenkins were the try scorers and Rees Harding converted one. Ferry were then heavily defeated by Aberavon, 0–34, at the central athletic ground, and at home by Ystradgynlais, 0–3.

The season didn't improve with a 3–19 loss against Gowerton, but Ferry managed a narrow win at home to Kenfig Hill, 5–3. Max Arnold was the try scorer and newcomer John Griffiths converted. The new forward, young Phil Lewis, was very prominent up front for the Ferry. More defeats followed: at Skewen by 0–3; by unbeaten Gowerton for the second time in the season, 6–12 (Brian Jones kicked two penalties); at Bridgend in midweek, 0–14.

On Saturday 22 October, Llandybie made their first visit to the Ferry and were defeated 8–3. Brian Jones kicked a penalty and converted a Jefford try.

Ferry ended October with an away defeat, 0–3 in a rearranged game at Mountain Ash.

November saw another narrow defeat to Skewen, 0–3. The only score of the game came in the very first minute with an interception try by G. Howells, the Skewen right wing. Ferry had a new no.8 in F. Latty.

A solitary penalty goal by Rees Harding was all Ferry had to show in the next outing, away to Resolven, which they lost 3–9.

Then came another first visit to Briton Ferry, of Abercrave who were defeated 8–3. Ernie Jenkins scored a try, which was converted by Rees Harding. A. Clarke

Captain
Brian Jones

Vice captain
Max Arnold

Playing record
P 41
W 9
D 8
L 24

added a second try. Reports said that the liveliest player on the field was Spaniard A. Duenas, the Abercrave scrum-half, who was all of five feet tall!

Llandybie were the next opponents and, despite losing two players to injury, the game ended in a 0–0 draw – it also ended in darkness.

Ferry then had a narrow defeat at West Wales table toppers Ystalyfera, 3–6, with Brian Jones the try scorer.

The year ended with a home defeat to Ammanford, who were visiting the Ferry for the first time in ten years. The Ferry were without five of their regulars, and fielded new players in I. Jones on the wing, R. Collins at prop, G. Woodhouse and A. Jones at second row and V. Phillips at no.8. Their try was scored by G. Jefford, converted by Rees Harding who, along with opposite number Euric Thomas, was sent off later for over-vigorous play!

5.13 1938/39

At the end of January, a fourth round Welsh Rugby League match was delayed by almost three-quarters of an hour due to the late arrival of Kenfig Hill. Ernie Jenkins was the try scorer in a 3–3 draw.

A narrow 0–3 defeat at Ammanford in February was followed by a narrow defeat at Abernant Park, where Glynneath were the victors 3–6 – the only score came from centre H. Jones. New faces in the side were S. Harris at outside-half, A. James in the second row and W. Nicholas at flanker. This was the eleventh time in the season that Ferry had lost 3–6.

An R. Jones try converted by Rees Harding was not enough to defeat home side Amman United, who won 3–9. They'd played at the Ferry a few weeks previously and drawn 3–3, when Gwyn Thomas scored Ferry's try. They'd fielded a very young and inexperienced side, including J. Morgan at fullback, the Morris brothers at half-back and T. Thomas at prop.

GWYN THOMAS celebrated his 100th birthday in June 2016 and died in Cardigan in November.

March started with a midweek 9–12 defeat at Aberavon. Arthur James and Morgan Jones scored a penalty each, and John Griffiths a try. Two days later they lost 0–1 away, to Loughor's solitary penalty goal.

Two heavy defeats followed at the end of March and beginning of April: to Cwmavon in a midweek home match by 6–14 (Brian Jones scored two penalties); and on the Saturday 5–19 away to Skewen (a Godfrey Thomas try and a Brian Jones conversion). The Ferry fielded a depleted side in both games, containing such youngsters as wing Godfrey Thomas, D. James and A. James in the second row, and D. Moron and W. Hill as flankers.

The Easter programme started with a 5–4 home win on Good Friday over Glynneath. A Rees Harding try was converted by Brian Jones. On Saturday Ferry entertained Loughor and lost 3–5, with just a Brian Jones penalty to show for their efforts. On Easter Monday they visited Maesteg and went down to a narrow 10–12 defeat (Griffiths converted tries from Harold Jones and Ernie Jenkins). To end the Easter period Ferry went down 3–9 away to Cwmavon (E. Griffiths' penalty kick was the Ferry's only score).

Ferry achieved a rare double win over Pontardawe. A try from newcomer D. Shea, a penalty by Brian Jones and a late drop goal from Max Arnold gave them a 10–0 score. Shea had featured for Aberavon Quins earlier in the season in the Burton cup final, along with the Arnold brothers. They lost to GKB (Margam) 4–9, Max Arnold's drop goal was their only score.

Neath RFC asked the Ferry to play them at the Gnoll on the last but one Saturday of the season after Cardiff made a late postponement. Ferry sportingly changed their original away fixture with Aberaman and gave a very good account of themselves before going down 8–9. D. Selby and Brian Jones scored tries and Jones added a conversion. Some new players featured strongly in this game, such as Albert Williams in the centre, D. Prosser in the back row and A. Thomas as hooker. Albert Williams went to Aberavon and became a Wales international – he was awarded a Glamorgan County cap in 1947.

Ferry ended the season as they'd begun, with a 3–6 defeat at Abercrave.

The season's top scorer was skipper Brian Jones with 47 points. He'd also represented Neath as flanker against Cardiff during the season.

AGM

No changes were made to the committee during the AGM, and the new captain elected for the coming season was wing Ernie Jenkins.

There had been a large decline in gate receipts compared to the previous season, as they reportedly only took just over £11. The club were left with a £7 balance at the end of the season.

1939/40

The season got underway a month late and in their first appearance Ferry drew 8–8 at home to old rivals Skewen, with two tries and a conversion apiece – Ferry scorers were W. Davies and J. Drew with a try each and Drew added a conversion. There were old and new faces in the Ferry side: Duckfield and Arthur Lemon did not turn out as expected; two ex-Neath forwards were in the pack, T.O. Jones and H. Bowen, and in the back row with Bowen were C. Denner and D. Moran; J. Drew and W. Davies formed the centre partnership.

A narrow 3–0 victory over Crynant at home followed, with J. Jones getting the only try of the game. Back in the line up were D. Webber at no.8 and flanker H. Thomas, while Godfrey Thomas went into the centre for W. Davies, who replaced M. Arnold at half-back.

Ferry then drew again with Skewen. The game had to switch to the Ferry as the Skewen ground was unplayable. This time the game ended 3–3, with D. Selby scoring the only try. J. Drew was played at inside-half for this game and there was also an appearance in the centre by ex-player Charlie Banfield (who had been playing for Wigan). There was an underlying edge to the game and several regrettable incidents were reported.

Kenfig Hill were the next visitors and they were sent packing with a resounding 19–6 score line – and against only fourteen men as the Ferry played the whole game a man short! The try scorers were Charlie Banfield, Dai Selby and John Jones with a hat trick. J. Selby kicked two conversions. Up front G. Morgan, P. Griffiths and J. Slater

Captains

Geoff Arnold

Morgan Jones

were outstanding. The return game also went the way of the Ferry, although Griffiths was the only try scorer in a 3–0 win.

A visit to Skewen was the usual tough encounter between these old rivals and the Ferry just edged it by 8–6. Both wings, J. Jones and G. Thomas, scored tries and W. Davies a conversion. A feature of this game was the appearance at scrum-half for Skewen of Dai Parker, the ex-Neath and Warrington player, who had a fine battle with his opposite number, his brother Harold Parker the Resolven scrum-half, who was making an appearance for the Ferry. New players taking part were W. Jones at fullback and prop W. Evans.

Ferry triumphed in yet another encounter with Skewen in December at home. The only score in a tight 3–0 game came from a brilliant run from his own 25-yard line by fullback Mog Jones. He fielded a high kick and then took off downfield, beat everyone and scored the winning try. Dai Selby filled in at scrum-half for Geoff Arnold, who had transferred to Aberavon.

Mr **ALBERT OSBORNE HUTCHINSON**, of 11 Lowther St, brother of Fred the ex-Welsh international and once a member of the terrible eight (as the Ferry pack became kown), made and laid the first step of the Briton Ferry War Memorial.

In the New Year, the Ferry kept their unbeaten record intact with a 6–0 win at the Brewery Field against Bridgend Sports. Godfrey Thomas and Dennis Moran were the try scorers.

They lost their unbeaten tag on 10 February at home to Swansea University, 0–16. They were suffering from a lack of match practice as they had not played any games for a few weeks. But they bounced back and inflicted the double over Bridgend Sports, 9–3. Godfrey Thomas was on the score sheet again with a try and Phil Griffiths added another. Scrum-half Idris Evans kicked a penalty.

On the day that Wales lost to England at Gloucester, the Ferry entertained the RAF XV in a game refereed by Ivor David of Neath. Ferry beat them convincingly, 19–5. They were better all round and worked smoothly in attack. The scorers were wing J. Jones, centre T. Lewis and wing C. Anthony. No.8 V. Phillips ran three-quarters of the length of the field to touchdown for the final try. Rees Harding converted 1 and added 1 penalty. Morgan Jones also kicked 1 conversion. Centres T. Lewis and D. Madden combined well, as did the half-backs Idris Evans and M. Arnold. Up front, captain Rees Harding, H. Thomas, P. Griffiths, T. Slater, A. Williams, B. Ireland and B. Evans all played well.

A hard fought 10–8 win over Felinfoel was the highlight of April. A. Williams intercepted the ball on his own line and raced half the length of the field before passing to T. Lewis, who scored the try under the posts and then converted it. Wing G. Thomas added a second try, also converted by Lewis. Outstanding that day were back row forwards, Dennis Moran, W. Evans and Dai Selby, also H. Edwards in the second row and half-back B. Davies.

Annual dinner

At the annual dinner, held at the end of November at the Grandison Hotel, Mr William John Hill, club chairman, was presented with a grandmother clock by the committee and members, as he had been actively connected with the club for over thirty years. Councillor J.B. Williams JP made the presentation, in the absence of Major J.M. Bevan. Former club secretary Mr O.L. Davies remembered how Mr Hill had once had the doubtful honour of winding up the club as gates were extremely poor, and on one occasion the take was only two pence! However, after some good teamwork from the supporters' club over two seasons the £200 debt gave place to several pounds in the bank, and it was noted at the time that for rugby to survive they must have a league or turn professional.

Musical entertainment for the evening was provided by the Stuart Brothers, Morgan Jones, Dennis Madden, Bob Rees and Fred Meyrick, accompanied by Mr W.H. Williams.

PART 6: 1940–1950

1940/41

There was very little rugby played during the war years, but the Ferry did decide to carry on during the 1940/41 season in October and actively sought fixtures via the *Neath Guardian*. They did play a strong RAF side, and the team was selected from: Morgan Jones, G. Thomas, I. Anthony, Albert Williams, B. Madden, J. Jones, G. Arnold, J. Drew, H. Thomas, T. Slater, V. Phillips, D. Selby, D. Williams, D. Griffiths, A. Clarke, B. Ireland, A. Pullman and H. Edwards.

They also played fixtures during November and December, on several occasions against a Military XV and a Home Guard XV. Other players to feature included D. Madden, S. Williams, G. Thomas, D. James, A. Kennefic, B. Evans, D. O'Neill and S. Anthony. A regular referee was Mr Ivor David of Neath.

The only reports of games during the season came in January, saying that the Ferry was one of the few clubs still playing, and that they had an enviable record thus far as they were undefeated. It was noted that the club had a full list of fixtures until the end of April. They had just beaten Swansea University, 7–0. Prior to that they had beaten Felinfoel away, 9–0, and were due to play them again in January at home.

The very prominent referee Mr Ivor David was in charge of the game against Felinfoel. The team was selected from: captain M. Jones, W.E. Jones, S. Williams, B. Madden, S. Williams, J. Jones, G. Arnold, D. Madden, A. Thomas, T. Slater, J. Rowlands, C. Phillips, D. Griffiths, V. Phillips, L. Kennific, D. Selby, and S. Anthony.

Captain
Morgan Jones

During 1940 the press reported on the misgivings expressed by many Welsh clubs that, by winding up until the war was over, they now felt could jeopardise the future of the game. But some leading game administrators reminded everyone that after the same sort of pessimism during the First World War public interest in rugby football and soccer grew so fast that some clubs had to increase their ground capacity to cope with the demand and that more teams were formed and fixtures became more attractive. Some clubs still actively sought fixtures and it was reported that many servicemen were eager to see clubs continuing to play throughout the war years. One regimental side, led by former England scrum-half Captain Alan Key and Sergeant Davies, arranged games against Swansea, Birchgrove and The Ferry. The Borough police also arranged fixtures.

In August 1941, the death of 'Jaypee' was reported. This was the 'nom de plume' of journalist MR JOHN PERROTT, who had written about the Ferry for over 30 years.

M.E. Rees a clothier of Maesteg once provided the Ferry with their kit when they were struggling financially.

1941 TO 1944

The debate continued about whether to play matches during wartime. Some argued that by keeping things steady it would help with morale and complement the nation's military and industrial performances, so club games were resumed in September 1945.

During the 1941/42 season, the Ferry played a match at the Gnoll against a Welsh Guards XV, and won narrowly, 6–5. The team selected that day was Morgan Jones, Dai Morris, Willie Lee, Bernard Madden, George Williams, Geoff Arnold (captain), Bridgeman, Vernon Phillips, Ernie Slater, Albert Morgan, George Brown, D.M. James, Harry Edwards, John Rowlands and Dennis Madden. Bernard Madden scored a try in each half for the Ferry. Sergeant Harris on the left wing opened the scoring for the Welsh Guards and Lance Corporal Roberts added a conversion. Once again, the game was refereed by none other than the famous Ivor David of Neath.

The press noted that most Ferry players were employed locally and did not have the time to pursue intensive training and so it was to their credit that they managed to defeat such a fine body of men as the Guards – especially as they finished the game with two men down due to injury.

It was reported that the Ferry were unbeaten throughout the war years, when they played mostly against service teams. The club were able to call upon the likes of Aussie start Dennis Madden, and many guest players from Rugby league. The wholly unbeaten season was 1942.

Other news

In January 1943, a collection for POWs was taken around the area and a donation of £15 was made by the BFRFC athletes – the second highest figure in the collection.

Captains 1941/42
Morgan Jones
Geoff Arnold

Captain 1942–45
Morgan Jones

In April 1943, in the Briton Ferry Constitutional Club, Lieutenant W.J. Hill of No. 2 platoon 'G' company of the home guard at Briton Ferry was presented with a case of pipes as a token of esteem from his NCOs and men.

In 1944, BFRFC donated one guinea towards expenses for an East v. West secondary schools match to be played on the Gnoll on 30 December in aid of the Red Cross and the St John POW fund.

In the August prior to the 1945/46 season, a jazz band character competition was held at the ground for prizes totalling £49. The parade left Victoria Park and then proceeded along the main street before entering the Old Road ground.

6.1 1941/42

1945/46

The team started with some intensive training for the first game of the season, against Neath, but they lost by 3–26. G. Arnold scored the solitary try. Ferry also lost the return match in October, 0–11.

Other news

Later in the season centre Alfred Duemas went to play for Neath, while wing John Evans went on to have a long and successful career with Aberavon.

Windsor Major, "The Flying Carpenter", later played for Wales, Aberavon, Bridgend, Neath, Glamorgan County, the Army and Combined Services, to name but a few. He'd made his debut for Maesteg at 16, alongside his father Gwilym in 1946 against the Ferry.

John Stockham and Vernon Friend both played for Neath in 1946, and front rower Doug "The Champ" James played for them in 1948.

In 1946 Briton Ferry Athletic FC secured a 30' x 18' hut from the Air Ministry and the Ministry of Works. It had been at King's Dock Swansea during the war and was eventually erected at the edge of the current cricket field, near the site of the clubhouse.

Captain
Howie Thomas

1946/47

The Ferry again started the season with a game against Neath at home, and were defeated again, 3–23 (Mog Jones was the try scorer). This was followed by an away defeat at Aberavon, 3–21, during which forward Glyn Rees fractured his hand. Prominent players were Jack Thomas, in his first game for the club, Llew Llewelyn, Mog Jones, Evan Harries (who kicked 1 penalty), Howie Thomas and A. Morgan. The team were: M. Jones, E. Jenkins, M. Jones, D. Samuels, J. Evans; C. Wathan, J. Thomas, H. Thomas, P. Griffiths, L. Pearce, G. Rees, L. Llewelyn, A. Morgan, J. Griffiths and E. Harries. Ivor David refereed the game.

6.2 Wing John Evans in action against Neath, 1947

In October, St. Athan RAF XV visited the Ferry for a tight-fought game and came out on top, 13–16. Brian

Match results place BFRFC scores first

Jones, Merlin Jones and Doug Phillips were prominent. Both Brian Jones and John Griffiths scored and converted 1 try.

In November at home, the Ferry defeated Felinfoel by 8–7. Wing Albert Williams and Llew Llewelyn made tries and B. Jones converted 1.

December started with a bang at home by defeating Gowerton 11–6. Pritchard, Harold Jones and Johnny Evans made tries and Jones converted 1.

Aberavon were the visitors in January and they won convincingly, 0–15. Aberavon wing Danny Shea was the star of the game. Unfortunately, Ferry's own star, back Ernie Pritchard, had to go to hospital with an injury, which left them with fourteen men for a large chunk of the game.

After a succession of defeats the Ferry played Vardre at home in late January in the West Wales Cup and defeated them 16–6. A new record for an individual's scores was set by flanker Brian Jones, who scored all the Ferry's points with 3 tries, 2 conversions and 1 penalty. Ferry's new outside-half, Ellis Thomas, also had an outstanding game. The club reached the quarter-finals of the West Wales Cup.

Ferry played Ystalyfera away and lost.

The following year Ferry played Ystalyfera in the West Wales League and beat them 12–6 at home and 3–0 away. In 1948/49 they lost to the same opposition at home 0–11 and ended up twenty-ninth in the league. The following season they finished twenty-sixth. In 1950 the West Wales League was renamed the West Wales Championship.

Around the district

The Neath & District competition, which had originated in 1910, was re-established.

The Neath Supporters Cup was won for the first two years by Seven Sisters, who defeated Tonna 3–0 in the second match of the series, and were then defeated by Cwmgrach in the 1948/49 season. Cwmgrach went on to win the league and the Dewar Challenge Shield.

Other news

At the ground in May, BFRFC again hosted a carnival with a jazz band competition, which some six bands entered.

1947/48

Captains

Albert Williams

W.J. Howells

The season started at home with a 14–3 victory over Pontardawe, albeit with a weakened team as four of the previous season's players were assisting Aberavon. Tries came from Jack Thomas, wing Dick Rees (2) and Ernie Pritchard and A. Jones converted 1. Albert Williams (captain) was outstanding.

The Ferry followed this up with another victory at home, this time 17–10 over Carmarthen Quins. Try scorers were Albert Williams (2) and H. Powell, W.E. Rees 1 drop goal and 1 conversion, A. Jones also converted 1. Outstanding in this game were newcomer Bryn Jenkins and D. James.

They then completed a double over Pontardawe by defeating them 14–3 in the return match. Alcwyn Jones kicked 1 penalty from his own half, Glyn Rees made 2 tries and Albert Williams 1, with 1 conversion from W.E.

Match results place BFRFC scores first

Rees. However, Ferry finished the game with fourteen men, as outstanding centre Harold Powell fractured his collar bone. Powell came to the club from Swansea as a record try scorer during the 1930s. Forward Lewis Thomas was outstanding. This good start to the season was put down to up to twenty players turning out for training every Tuesday and Thursday, despite losing four players to Aberavon and one to Neath.

Then Ferry then defeated Kenfig Hill at home 9–6, before a narrow 9–6 away win at rivals Skewen. Albert Williams and Will Paisley scored tries and Mog Jones kicked a penalty. They then defeated Gowerton at home, 12–10.

Two tough away matches followed, at Amman United (lost 7–8) and at Brynamman, before they returned home to hammer RAF St. Athan, 36–10. Try scorers were Albert Williams (3), D. Selby, E. Jenkins (3) and J. Stockham. Newcomer W.J. Howells converted 5 and Les Pearce 1. Outstanding were Stockham and C. Phillips in the pack.

The following week had the biggest gate of the season so far for the visit of Mountain Ash, who came with an unbeaten record, but left narrowly defeated 8–6. Dicky Rees and Ernie Pritchard scored tries and Les Pearce converted 1. It was a tough game and I. Rees at stand-off had a fine game.

Ystalyfera visited the Ferry in November and the home team won 12–6. Dicky Rees scored 2 tries and Les Pearce added 1 and converted 1.

Earlier that week ALBERT WILLIAMS made his second appearance for Glamorgan County during the season.

Another home win followed over Resolven 11–3, even with fourteen men from the second minute onward after Jack Thomas had to leave the field with a large gash under his eye. Outstanding up front were Doug James and George Brown. Albert Williams, John Stockham and Dicky Rees each scored 1 try, W.J. Howells added the extras.

Former player JOHN WATKINS died in November. He had also played for Neath in the 1880s and was thought to be the only surviving member of the team from that era.

The final three games in November all ended in defeat. First, a narrow away loss to Carmarthen Quins, 0–6. Ferry were down to thirteen men at one point due to injuries. Second, they visited Aberavon and lost 0–3. Finally, they lost their home ground record to Swansea University, 8–19. Dicky Rees and Doug James were the try getters and Howell converted. Ferry were without their captain for this game as he'd transferred to Aberavon, while centre Harold Powell was assisting both Neath and Swansea.

During this season, ex-player and committeeman **ED SELBY** became a WRU referee, the first from BFRFC for a number of years.

December started with a 3–3 home draw with Amman United. Five team changes were made, including Jim Tandy coming in on the wing, Les Jenkins up front and C. Wathan at centre. W.J. Howells kicked a penalty for the home side.

For their next game, the Ferry returned to winning ways at home by beating Treorchy 19–6. Try scorers were Dicky Rees, Jack Thomas, Les Pearce, Glyn Rees and the new centre, Lieutenant R.S. Roberts. Howells converted 2 and kicked 1 penalty. George Brown was again to the fore among the forwards.

Season 1947-1948

H. Thomas, C. Phillips, G. Thomas, J. Stockham, B. Phillips, D. James, G. Rees, G. Brown.
L. Pearce, D. Selby, C. Wathan, A. Davies(Ref).
R. Jenkins, M. Davies, H. Poewll, WS. Davies (Sec), W.J. Howells(Capt) E. Jenkins.
A. Thomas, R. Rees. J. Griffiths(Trainer), Ivor Rees, Jack Thomas.

6.4 1947/48

They ended the year with fixtures against Skewen at home (which Ferry won 27–6 on Christmas Day), Cwmavon away on Boxing Day (which Ferry lost 0–6) and then a 0–0 home draw with Bridgend. Prominent in these games were half-backs Jack Thomas and H. Greenslade, fullback Lieutenant R.S. Roberts, and Harold Powell and J. Stockham in the centre.

New year fixtures were at home against Gowerton (0–0 draw) and away at Mountain Ash (lost 6–8) and Ystalyfera (Ferry won 6–3). Then a West Wales Cup match away at Crynant, who were unbeaten at home. This was a hard-fought game and the Ferry triumphed 3–0 (Jack Thomas was the try scorer).

February home games were against Cwmavon in the second round of the WWRU Cup (won 5–0) and Brynamman. Away fixtures were at Kenfig Hill (lost 7–11) and Tredegar (won 4–0).

6.5 Match in 1947/48

The first game in March was a West Wales Cup quarter-final at home to Amman United. This was the first time that the Ferry had reached this stage of the competition, and the crowd turnout at the Old Road ground, apparently over 2,000, was said to be the largest of the season thus far. A successful penalty kick by Amman put Ferry 0–3 down. Then, with ten minutes to go, a kick ahead by Jack Thomas was gathered by Ivor Rees, who passed it to Harold Powell in the centre, who passed to his fellow centre Arthur Thomas, who raced over in the corner to equalise the score at 3–3. Captain W.J. Howells failed to make the conversion to win the match.

The tie went to a replay. Unbelievably, the rematch at Amman ended in a no-score draw, so a further replay was booked. This game was played at Vardre and after a brave display against the former winners Ferry were defeated 6–9.

Wing Ernie Jenkins scored a try and W.J. Howells kicked a penalty. Howells almost won it for the Ferry at the death with a beautifully struck drop goal from the halfway line, but he missed by inches.

The Ferry were due to play at home to Tredegar, but the opposition couldn't raise a side, so the game was cancelled at the last minute. Ferry also played at home against Treorchy and Pontardawe.

> A film on rugby was shown at the Briton Ferry Workingmen's Club in March.
> Ferry secretary Mr W.J. Hill presented it and Wilf Wooler and referee Ivor
> David were commentators. A good crowd came to this fascinating event.

In April, during the first game back home after a tour, Aberavon narrowly defeated the Ferry 0–3. It was a controversial win as the Ferry linesman judged that a penalty kick from "Junior" Howells for the Ferry had crossed the posts, but the Aberavon linesman judged that it hadn't. The referee then ruled against the Ferry. George Brown and Les Pearce were outstanding for the Ferry up front and scrum-half Harold Parker worked manfully behind.

Further fixtures during April were games against Cwmlynfell, Cardiff Athletic and Maesteg at home and away games at Bridgend, Treorchy, Resolven (lost 3–9, H. Phillips scored a try) and Cwmavon.

The final game of the season was at home in May, against Felinfoel.

On tour

6.6 Tour team before their first game v. Garryowen at Limerick, 27 March 1948

Match results place BFRFC scores first

At the end of the March the club embarked on their first trip to Ireland over the Easter period. A party of 32 left Neath on Thursday 25 March and arrived at Cork on Good Friday, the next day they played Garryowen RFC at Limerick, in front of 5,000 spectators. This was a massive game for the Ferry as the Irish team was rated one of the best in the country and had already produced no fewer than 22 internationals. In fact, they fielded five internationals against Ferry, who were defeated 6–13 in a tense game.

The Garryowen club then entertained them with a dinner and Irish dance, which went on until the small hours.

6.7 Tour posters v. Garryowen

The next day they watched their opponents defeat London Irish 17–5, and after lunch they carried out the ceremony of trooping the Ferry's colours at their hotel, and spent a good hour singing Welsh hymns, to the delight of the crowd of hundreds.

On Easter Monday, the Ferry travelled to Tipperary for a game against Clanwilliam, the Munster Junior Cup Holders and Garryowen Cup holders. This opposition was not as stiff as the previous Saturday, even though they had strengthened their team with players from other clubs in the area, and the Ferry triumphed 6–3.

6.8 Clanwilliam RFC Programme, 1947/48

6.9 Players in Tipperary, 1948

The tour party arrived back home on Thursday 1 April after enjoying a wonderful welcome on this first venture.

AGM

In June, the president, Mr O.L. Davies, stated that this was the fortieth AGM in the recorded history of the club – as records had not been kept prior to 1908. A statement supported by chairman Mr W.J. Hill, as both a life member of the club and a member of the Glamorgan County Rugby committee.

The finances were very satisfactory, with a debit balance on the season of £20, due to expenses incurred during the Irish trip, and a balance in hand of £377 19s 10d. The club had also received grants from the WRU of £50 and the West Wales RU of £12 guineas.

Mr W.S. Davies and Mr G. P. Hemming were re-elected as secretary and treasurer, respectively. Elected to the committee were Messrs Morgan Jones, J. Griffiths, George Ireland, T. George, M. Powell, W.L. Williams, C. Callaghan, E. Adams, E. Jones, E. Selby, E. Davies and M. Abraham. Mr Harold Powell was elected as captain for the forthcoming season.

School rugby

During April, Neath Schools made their first tour to the East Midlands to play against Leicester and Coventry over two days. They lost both games, 8–0 and 14–11 respectively. John James of Cwrt Sart represented the Ferry in the Neath Schools squad.

1948/49

The 1948/49 season started with a 6–9 defeat at Aberavon. W.J. Howells kicked a penalty and Llew Llewelyn scored a try. The team that day was W.J. Howells, D. Amphlett, H.M. Powell, D. Davies, E. Jenkins, Ivor Rees, J. Thomas, H. Thomas, C. Phillips, A. Thomas, M. Davies, R. Jenkins, L. Llewelyn, G. Brown, H. Watkins.

A trip up to Mountain Ash was followed by a narrow home defeat to Tredegar (5–6). An Amphlett try was converted by Howells.

Neath were their next opponents at the Gnoll, and Ferry were well beaten, 9–19, despite the home team losing fullback Granville Jones just before half-time, with a broken and dislocated jaw, and scrum-half W.J. Darch with a dislocated shoulder. Howells and Alan Davies each kicked a penalty goal and E. Jenkins scored a try.

Ferry then lost away to Skewen, 0–5, and played Morriston at home two days before entertaining Crynant, who went away with the spoils 6–14. Ferry had a depleted side as several top players were unavailable. D. Amphlett and E. Jenkins were the try scorers.

October started with a West Wales League game at home to Gowerton, which Ferry lost 6–8. Howie Thomas scored a fine try and D. Amphlett added another near the corner flag. Defeats to Maesteg and Amman United gave them a miserable start to the season.

A desperately unlucky 14–16 defeat at home to Cardiff University continued the sad run. Skipper Harold Powell scored a try, Ivor Rees a drop goal, D. Amphlett another try, Llew Llewelyn did the converting and Doug James kicked a penalty.

Captain
Harold Powell

Points for a drop goal were reduced to 3

Match results place BFRFC scores first

Ferry then faced Gowerton away in a return fixture, before the month ended in a home defeat to Cwmavon by 0–12.

November didn't start any better. In fact, they were heavily defeated at Aberavon, 3–36, the only score came from an H. Watkins penalty. The Wizard's centre Gerwyn Rees set a new individual points scoring record with 21 points (Johnny Ring had been the record holder).

Ferry then faced a return match at Cwmavon, during which John Stockham had his nose broken, Ernie Jenkins broke his shoulder, and scrum-half Jack Thomas was sent off (coincidentally John's brother, Fred Stockham, was also on the injury list with a fractured collar bone). Ferry then fell to a narrow 0–3 defeat at Resolven. They ended the month with a home game against Cardiff Athletic.

Season 1948-1949

N. Phillips(Ref). M. Davies. H. Watkins. D. James. L. Jones. L. Llewellyn. J. Stockham.
E. Pritchard. G. Brown. C. Phillips.
H. Roberts. Jack Thomas. H. Powell(Capt). D.Staines. I. Rees. R. Jenkins.

6.10 1948/49

In December, the Ferry met Penygraig at home and away, and lost the home game 9–11 (D. Staines, R. Jenkins and T. Shufflebotham all scored tries). Then Kenfig Hill away and Skewen home.

They were due to play Cwmavon at home on Christmas Day, but the visitors cancelled the match. Given the pre-existing tension between the teams after the away game in November it was felt that the opponents had cancelled the game for fear of repercussions. As a result it was reported that the Ferry would not include Cwmavon in future fixture lists.

In the new year Pontardawe were the first visitors, followed by away games at Cwmlynfell and Penclawydd, before ending the month at home to Bridgend.

February started with tough away fixtures at Morriston and Felinfoel before meeting local rivals Skewen in the West Wales Cup at home. Ferry narrowly defeated Skewen 8–6, in front of a large crowd (over 3,000). L. Llewelyn scored a try, converted by H. Roberts, then Jack Thomas scored an interception try to win the game.

> REG JENKINS, the Ferry second row, was selected to go to France the following week for two games with Glamorgan County, the third time he had played for them. He had previously played for Taibach but had been with the Ferry for the last three seasons. During his Army service he had played for Kilmarnock.

Ferry then faced Resolven at home, before meeting Ystalyfera at home in the next round of the West Wales Cup, which Ferry lost 0–11. The month ended with a home fixture against Penclawydd.

March was a busy month, with home games against Kenfig Hill and Mountain Ash, and away games at Bridgend, Pontardawe, Ogmore Vale and Amman United.

April started with a 0–0 draw at home to Carmarthen Quins. Returning to the side from Cwmavon was former player Albert Williams. A new recruit to the side was wing forward Esmore Lewis, who had played a game or two the previous season.

> ESMORE LEWIS joined from Neath Grammar School, where he had also been a successful cricketer, and the previous year he had represented Glamorgan Secondary Schools in the high jump at the Welsh Sports, Wrexham.

Felinfoel were the next opponents at home and the Ferry were the victors, 11–3. Harold Thomas scored 1 try, added 1 conversion and 1 penalty. John Stockham added 1 try.

> Before the game both teams had made a gentleman's agreement to keep the wing forwards in the scrums until the ball had been heeled, which produced a much more fluid and enjoyable game for the spectators. They were following a similar policy to several other clubs, including their neighbours, Neath.

Ferry ended the season with an away fixture against Vardre United and home games against Maesteg (won). The final game ended on a high note as they beat Tredegar 15–6. L. Llewelyn, D. Morgan and D. Steer scored tries, and H. Thomas and D. Staines both kicked penalties.

Ferry ended twenty-ninth in the league, which was a disappointment.

AGM

During the AGM at the Grandison Hotel on 30 May the club president, Mr O.L. Davies, stated that he was not happy with the attitude of Neath and Maesteg RFCs with regard to the confirmation of fixtures for the upcoming season. He let it be felt that Neath RFC in particular should give the Ferry a fixture every year. There was a happy note when the hatchet was buried after the bad feeling of the previous season and Cwmavon were welcomed back on to the fixture list. He then went on to thank both players and committee for sticking with the club through a difficult season on the field results wise and hoped that fortunes would change for the better the following season. He also noted that, with the advent of rugby league in the Neath area, it would be a little more difficult to draw in both players and crowds. He hoped that the club would continue with their gentleman's agreement with regard to wing forwards at scrum time to provide a more open game.

It was also noted that the club had been spending money every season on entertainment for the players and he felt that this should cease and the money be spent on pitch improvements.

6.11 Commiteemen Geoff Hemmings, W.J. Hill, W.S. Davies

Congratulations were given to the outgoing and incoming captains, Harold Powell and Reg Jenkins. Two players who had recently got married, Howie Thomas and John Stockham, were each presented with an electric clock.

The treasurer, Mr G.P. Hemming, showed that the club had made a profit of £48 3s 8d during the season and now had a healthy balance of £426 3s 6d. Gate revenue had yielded £259 2s, the highest figures came from the Neath game at £77 8s 7d, and the Skewen West Wales Cup match at £40 8s 3d – while the lowest was the Carmarthen Quins game on a very wet day, which only yielded 4s 6d.

Player subs were fixed at 2/6d, and non-players 10/6d, This was their last season in black and amber hoop jerseys as it was decided to go back to the club's original colours of royal blue, gold and white.

Congratulations were extended to secretary W.S. Davies for his twenty-first year of service. The president was then re-elected, along with Ewart Adams as assistant secretary. Both secretary and treasurer were re-elected for another five years. Elected to the committee for two years were Bert Anthony, C. Callaghan, V. Davies, Ewart Jones, Harold Powell and Jack Watkins, and for one year were E. Richards, Roy Thompson and Les Morgan.

Notes on some players of the era

- Harold Powell was a pre-war county player who went on to become a Neath RFC committeeman
- Harold Roberts was the brother of the Neath and Wales wing Cyril Roberts, who also played in a few games for the Ferry
- Hugh Watkins was known as "Steel Girder", after Bodger, and his only party piece was a near-perfect rendition of a Tchaikovsky piano concerto.

Other Clubs at a Glance

BRITON FERRY.—Because of the death or departure from the town of so many of the old timers, the origin of Briton Ferry Club is very vague.

It seems that in the 80's and 90's the Ferry had several Rugby teams—Mr. W. H. P. Jenkins's XV., Briton Ferry Athletic, Briton Ferry Excels and Briton Ferry All Whites— but there are conflicting reports as to their headquarters and where they played. While some say that the present Briton Ferry R.F.C. was originally Briton Ferry Athletic, others believe it originated from the All Whites. But there seems to be one good reason for saying that, if not actually the " father " of the present club, Mr. W. H. P. Jenkins's team had a strong " blood relationship."

The exact date of the founding of Briton Ferry R.F.C. is also unknown, but what is known is that it was in 1906 that it became a member of the Welsh Rugby Union. One of its present day claims is that it was one of the first of the second-class clubs to join the W.R.U.

The present secretary of the club is Mr. W. S. Davies, and the club's colours blue and gold. Their headquarters are at the Grandison Hotel, Briton Ferry.

BRITON FERRY R.F.C., 1948-49

Standing—T. H. Phillips (referee), Morlaid Davies, H. Watkins, Dick James, Les Jones, Llew Llewellyn, John Stockham, E. Pritchard, George Brown, C. Phillips
In front—H. Roberts, Jack Thomas, Harold Powell (captain), D. Staines, I. Rees, Reg Jenkins (next year's captain)

6.12 Extract from "South Wales Rugger Souvenir" by Emrys Evans, 1949

Tour

The Ferry embarked on a second tour to Ireland. A party of 20 players and trainer Jack Budge left Neath on Wednesday 13 April and boarded the SS Great Western at Fishguard, having reserved berths and supper on board. They arrived at Waterford on Thursday morning to a free day and then travelled to Kilkenny on Friday. They played a game on Saturday and were hosted for dinner that night. On Sunday they moved on to Enniscorthy, and played against them on Monday – again followed by a dinner and dance in their honour. On Tuesday evening they left Enniscorthy for Rosslare, from where they sailed overnight and arrived back in Neath on Wednesday evening.

6.13 Ireland Tour 1949, complimentary ticket to Grand Carnival Dance at Enniscorthy

Match results place BFRFC scores first

1949/50

A trial was held at the Old Road ground early in September. It was thought that the season would be a good one given the potentially sound players in the side, such as forwards Morlais Davies, Doug James, Llew Llewelyn and Reg Jenkins, and backs Jack Thomas, Harold Roberts and newcomer D. Steer.

The West Wales League was renamed the WEST WALES CHAMPIONSHIP – and the Ferry were to finish twenty-sixth.

During September JACK THOMAS represented Glamorgan County against Warwickshire at the Gnoll in a game that ended 0–0.

HUGHIE "CRACKERS" WATKINS made his debut for Neath this season.

The season started with a 3–17 away defeat at Aberavon – Harold Roberts was the try scorer. The first home fixture ended in a 6–6 draw with Glais before an away defeat at Glynneath. There then followed a string of home games:

- against Tredegar
- Carmarthen (won)
- Pontardulais – the first game between the two for twenty years, which Ferry won 21–6 with J. Evans, H. Roberts, Rosser and E. Pritchard (2) scoring tries, Roberts converting two
- Ogmore Vale (won)
- Merthyr (won 10–5)
- Mountain Ash (won 8–3) – Watkins and Stockham the try getters and Roberts converting 1

Captain
Reg Jenkins

Vice captain
Jack Thomas

Playing record
P 38
W 15
D 5
L18
Points for 239
Points against 271

- and finally a 6–13 defeat by Kenfig Hill – Pritchard and Staines the try scorers for the Ferry.

October finished with an away fixture at Merthyr and a home game against Cilfynydd.

Ferry's November started with two away fixtures, at Tredegar and Pontardawe, before a depleted team met and lost to Gowerton at home (6–16) – Reg Jenkins got a try and H. Roberts kicked a penalty. To end the month they drew 11–11 at home with Blaengarw – Dick Rees, Arthur Owen and H. Roberts scored tries, Roberts converted 1.

During a busy December, the club first defeated Pontycymmer at home, 8–0. Phil Griffiths and J. Madden scored tries and Roberts converted 1. Then away fixtures at Crynant, Resolven (lost 12–3, Roberts penalty, ex-Neath forward J. Brennan and Ira Hopkins of Tonna were playing for the Ferry), and Cwmavon on Christmas Eve, followed by the return with Cwmavon on Boxing Day. The year ended with an away match at Gowerton.

Season 1949-1950

J. Budge(Trainer) L. Llewellyn. L. Lewis. F. Hoare. G. Rees. G. Davies. H. Davies.
W. Brennen. H. Davies. E. Thomas. A. Donovan(Ref).
A. Owen. Dick James. Jack Thomas(Capt) D. Steer. D.W. Roberts. J. Madden.

6.14 1949/50

The new year started with a home game against Resolven, followed by a visit to Skewen, where Ferry lost narrowly, 3–6 (Roberts was the try scorer). Then Bridgend at home and finally another visit to Skewen, this time in the West

Wales Cup, which was postponed due to the weather. The rematch replaced an away game at Felinfoel on 11 February and the Ferry gained revenge by winning well, 11–3. Howe and Steer each scored 1 try, Roberts converted 1 and added 1 penalty. The previous week had seen an away game at Vardre United. Ferry completed the month with away fixtures at Pontardulais and Ogmore Vale and a home game with Crynant.

March was again a busy month for the club, with three home games in the first week – against Felinfoel, Pontardawe and unbeaten Maesteg. In front of the best gate of the season (2,000), a plucky Ferry side nearly defeated Maesteg (8–9), with Arthur Owen kicking a penalty and converting a fine try scored by Llew Llewelyn. Outstanding for the Ferry were fly-half D.M. Roberts and forwards Doug James, Llew Llewelyn and Gwyn Lewis.

6.15 Try scored 1949/50

Their next fixture was an away match at Cilfynydd, before entertaining Aberavon at home, narrowly losing by 3–6. Arthur Owen was the try scorer. Outstanding in this game were forwards Hugh Watkins, Morlais Davies and P. Hoare. Both sides had a guest player in their side, fullback Viv Evans of Neath played for the Ferry and Alun Thomas the Swansea fly-half for Aberavon – indeed Thomas supplied all their points by kicking two penalties! Two away games then followed against Mountain Ash and Glais, before ending this busy month with an away fixture against Neath, which Ferry lost heavily, 3–28 (forward Cyril Phillips scored a try for the Ferry).

6.16 Viv Evans

The final month of the season started with two home games against Skewen and Tredegar, before the tour. On their return they ended the season with two home games against Vardre United and Glynneath and away games at Blaengarw and Pontycymmer.

Ferry also competed in the Cup final, drawing with Crynant, the previous season's winners, which was to be replayed during the next season. Crynant won and were then runners up to Tonna in the league.

6.17 Match in 1949/50

Tour

On another Easter tour to Ireland, Ferry played County Carlow (winning 9–3 with three tries from G. Madden), and Enniscorthy (won 9–3, with Madden again on the score sheet and D.W. Roberts also bagging a pair).

AGM

The club was still housed at the Grandison Hotel and played at its Cwrt Sart playing field (they changed in the room above the stables) through the 1950s. The club also featured on the front page of the *Welsh Rugby* magazine around about 1950 wearing their new broad band jersey, which were sometimes used by Glamorgan County in their games.

6.18 Committeemen W.L. Williams, W.S. Davies (honorary secretary) and Morgan Jones (vice chairman)

Criticism had been levelled at the club by those who thought they should provide better accommodation on their ground rather than spend money on tours to Ireland. At the AGM on 15 May the reply by secretary Mr W.S. Davies was that the club had been informed by the owners of the ground that they would not be allowed to erect a press box let alone a stand. He added that if they were given permission, then a stand would have been erected within a few months!

The season's record was better than the previous one and top scorer was Harold Roberts with 59 points, who had joined the club from Bryncoch two seasons previously and also represented Neath. Jack Thomas had played in 37 out of 38 matches for the club this season. Wing Jack Madden ended with seven tries and just missed out on becoming top try scorer. The following season's fixtures would total 42 games against 22 different sides.

The financial report stated that they had a balance of £376, despite having a deficit over the season due to purchases of equipment. Vice chairman Morgan Jones presented another clock, this time to Phil Griffiths on the occasion of his marriage.

Club patrons at this time were The Right Hon. Earl of Jersey, Briton Ferry Constitutional Club, Briton Ferry Workingmen's Club and Baglan Bay Tinplate Co. Ltd.

Assistant secretary J. Adams was re-elected, while elected to the committee were M. Jones, W.S. Jones, Les Morgan, N. Selby, E. Richards and M. Abraham. Idwal Morris was elected as players representative.

Llew Llewelyn was elected as captain for the new season, with Harold Roberts as his deputy.

LLEW LLEWELYN had joined the club from Cimla Barbarians three
seasons previously and had played several games for Neath and
represented Glamorgan County against Gloucestershire.

Around the district

- Tonna won the District Shield
- Hughie "Crackers" Watkins made his debut for Neath
- A Neath Rugby League side were formed for the 1949/50 season, who played on a pitch at Caewern. One of the group who formed this team was Mr Bill Farmer, chairman of the Neath Rugby League Supporters' Club, They played their first game against Cardiff at Cefn-y-Ysgyrn in Crumlin Road, Skewen, and held a celebration dance at the Gwyn Hall in Neath on 11 November
- The Boys Club of Wales played their first game against England on 19 November and a Ferry representative was at the initial meeting. They won 9–3 and their captain was centre Graham Michael, who was a centre with Neath Youth, had been a Welsh Schoolboy cap in 1948, and had also skippered his school XV and the Neath Schools XV
- Cwrt Sart School Youth Club defeated Coedffranc Youth Club 5–3 in their first game of the season – centre Trimnell and outside-half Rees were the pick of the backs, along with scrum-half Millett, up front Broad, White and R. Rees were prominent and hooker Wybron monopolised the scrummaging

- A team called Cwrt Sart Apprentices played in October, and were defeated 0–6 by Coedffranc

- Another side formed this season were Eaglesbush RFC, who later in the season were to have the loan of the Old Road field to play a game against fellow newcomers Neath Anglers RFC in a game to raise funds for Neath's £25,000 War Memorial Fund, which was followed by a grand variety concert in the Gwyn Hall at Neath

- There were thoughts about Neath RFC forming a Second XV, but this did not reach fruition

- During September Jack Thomas represented Glamorgan County against Warwickshire at the Gnoll in a game that ended 0–0.

6.19 Jack Thomas in action (top and bottom right); in a Glamorgan County jersey against Warwickshire (back row, bottom left)

Season 1950-1951

J. Budge,(Trainer), P. Hoare, Dick James, R. Griffiths, R. Griffiths, A. Jones, B.Phillips,
Doug James, D.W. Roberts.
A. Jones, (Ref) H. Watkins, A. Owen, Llewellyn Llewellyn(Capt) J. Madden, R. Thomas,
H. Roberts.   In Front. Ellis Thomas, Jack Thomas.

7.1 1950/51

PART 7: 1950–1960

1950/51

Captain
Jack Thomas

Playing record
P 38
W 15
D 5
L 18
Points for 239
Points against 271

Scores
Tries 24
Conversions 12
Drop goals 1
Penalties 15

**Playing record
in WWRU**
P 17
W 8
D 3
L 6
Points for 84
Points against 74

Pre-season training in August was followed by a trial match in the first week of September, during which the year's captain Jack Thomas, Llew Llewelyn, A. Jenkins, E. Thomas, L.J. Jones and W. Sparks all made an impression.

Club secretary Mr W.S. "Spam" Davies announced some new fixtures for the season ahead, such as Blackwood and Ammanford.

> THE DAVIES BROTHERS were quite a club fixture: O.L. Davies had been secretary for nine years before Bill succeeded him; Trevor was to take over from Bill; and Vernon was involved in the club in later years.

September saw home fixtures with Neath and Cwmlynfell (which they won). Then away at Aberavon, Ferry lost 0–16. Reports say that the pack, known as the terrible eight, were really strong. Stars of the game were Michael, the centre, and the forwards A. Jones and E. Lewis. Ferry lost both away games at Ogmore Vale and Blackwood, but drew at home against Felinfoel.

In October they started with a revenge win at home to Ogmore Vale, then lost away at Tredegar, before beating both Vardre United and Pontardulais at home.

The Ferry excelled against the Welch Regiment in a November fixture at Brecon by scoring 39 points without reply. Man of the match was deputy outside-half Ellis Thomas, who replaced D.W. Roberts. Harold Thomas scored a hat trick of tries and converted 1, wing David Parker and Jack Thomas 2 tries each, while J. Madden, Dick James, Peter Hoare and Doug James each added 1, both Arthur Jones and Llew Llewelyn made 1 conversion.

They followed this up with another victory at home to Tredegar, 8–3. Arthur Jones scored a try, converted by H. Roberts who also added a penalty. They were then defeated away at Glynneath and ended the month with a win up at Treorchy.

In December, the Ferry lost at home to Felinfoel, 3–9. Fullback Ron Thomas, H. Watkins and Bryn Phillips all played well, and H. Roberts kicked a penalty. They beat Vardre away, lost away at Merthyr and at home on Christmas Day to Cwmavon. They then beat Skewen at home on Boxing Day and ended the year with an away game at Aberaman.

> G. HEMMING passed away in December after six loyal years as club treasurer following the end of the war. Ewart Jones (ex-London Welsh) was elected in his place in January.

The new year started with a 3–3 home draw with Amman United. Again, Roberts kicked a penalty. They then defeated Pontardawe, 14–3, away. Ron Griffiths, Jack Thomas and Roberts were the try scorers. Roberts added a conversion and Griffiths a drop goal. January ended with a scoreless home draw with Skewen in the West Wales Cup. The team included future Welsh international and Neath player Cyril Roberts, alongside his brother D.W. Roberts. Ferry lost the replay a week later.

The first visit of Blackwood to the Ferry in February was a dour game that ended in a 3–3 draw, with another penalty goal from Roberts. But they did pick up three wins, one at home to Brecon and two away, at Cwmavon and Pontardulais.

In March, Ferry produced a good home win over Crynant, with tries from Ron Griffiths and J. Madden, both converted by Roberts who, for good measure, added yet another penalty to end with a 13–5 score line. They then lost away at Ammanford, followed by a 3–3 draw at home with Treorchy, Madden produced the try.

The club ended the season with a glut of fixtures. Home games with Ammanford, Merthyr, Aberaman, Pontardawe and Carmarthen. Away at Cwmlynfell, Carmarthen and Amman United.

They finished the 1950/51 season in fourteenth position in the Welsh Wales Rugby Union (WWRU) championship table.

Tour

7.2 Tour group 1951

The Ferry embarked once again on an Easter tour to Ireland, their fourth trip to the Emerald Isle. They left Neath on Wednesday 21 March and returned on Wednesday 28. They played against Clontarf on Good Friday and against Carlow on Easter Monday.

7.3 Match in 1950/51

AGM

Fred Stockham, Ron Griffiths, Dickie Rees and Harold Roberts were presented with the traditional clocks at the AGM at the end of May. D.W. Roberts received gifts from the club and the supporters for reaching a club record points total of 144 points, which consisted of 24 tries, 15 penalties, 12 conversions and 1 dropped goal. Jack Thomas was well behind in second place with 39 points. Mr Davies stated that this was the best record he had seen in his eighteen years as secretary.

Club president Mr O.L. Davies felt that dropping out of the West Wales competition would enable them to strengthen their fixture list and become a first-class club.

The treasurer gave the bank balance as £162 2s 11d and stated that it would have been healthier if the weather had been a little more clement, as the gate receipts had been hit badly with only £128 18s 3d taken, compared with £250 the previous season. The Irish tour had cost £338 12s 4d and the club president stated that as the tours were a drain on the club's resources, he thought they should be suspended. Instead, blazers should be awarded to players who had rendered loyal service and accomplished notable achievements on the field. This proposition was to be brought to the committee.

Newly elected to the committee were Glyn Thomas, Harry Davies and Cyril Phillips. All others were re-elected, along with new captain Llew Llewelyn and vice captain Harold Roberts.

Around the district

- Mr W.J. Hill was re-elected vice president of Glamorgan County, his seventh year in office after forty years of service with the Ferry.

- During the season Neath Rugby League moved to a new ground at Cefnyrysgyn, on the Old Road at Skewen, near Neath Abbey.

- There were moves to form teams at Skewen and Glynneath, Ystradgynlais and Aberavon having already formed teams.

- Within the Neath District, Tonna beat Bryncoch in the league shield final by 6–0. Tonna had been re-formed in 1946 by ex-Ferry player D.J. Daymond. He was fulfilling the results of a discussion he'd had in the Middle East during the war and he became club chairman.

1951/52

Captain
Llew Llewelyn

Vice captain
Harold Roberts

Playing record
P 44
W 27
D 4
L 13
Points for 369
Points against 245

Scores
Tries 79
Conversions 27
Drop goals 3
Penalties 23

Hopes were high for a good season, which started with a tough challenge, a home fixture against Neath. But there were a few setbacks as both Joe Owen and Arthur Jones up front were missing with injury and fellow forward Peter Hoare was forced to retire from the game through injury. Ferry were defeated 0–29. Neath's forwards got the better of the Ferry pack with the likes of Roy John and Rees Stephens.

Ferry then had three home games – with RAF St. Athan, with Pontardawe (which the Ferry won 16–9 with a Jack Thomas try double and skipper Llew Llewelyn adding another, Roberts converting two and Ron Thomas kicking a penalty), and losing to Aberavon – before facing a tough away challenge at Mountain Ash. They finished a long month with two further home fixtures, against Pontardulais and Carmarthen. Ferry won the Camarthen game 11–6, with Cyril Roberts bagging a try (which his brother Harold converted) and a penalty and wing David Parker scoring the final try after a brilliant bout of passing among the backs.

October started with a midweek away fixture against Crynant with a depleted team, which Ferry lost 3–12. Roberts kicked a penalty. They then won a home game with Hendy (16–6, J. Madden, C. Roberts, S. Thomas and A. Owen the try scorers, with a conversion each from H. Roberts and R. Thomas), before beating Carmarthen in the return match. The month ended with a home victory over Blackwood (17–3, J. Madden (2), L.Llewelyn and H. Roberts tries and Roberts converting 1 and adding 1 penalty) and a 0–6 away defeat in a robust game at

Match results place BFRFC scores first

Skewen (Howard John was outstanding up front for the Ferry – brother of Roy John, he was the latest addition to the ranks and a doctor in Neath General Hospital).

A return fixture with Crynant was first up in November and the Ferry conceded the double, 8–11, and lost their unbeaten home record. Ellis Thomas and Harold Roberts made tries, Roberts converted one. They then won away fixtures at Porthcawl and Amman United, before facing Aberaman at home to end the month with a 6–0 victory – W. George and L. Llewelyn were the scorers.

The team kept busy in December with home fixtures against Mountain Ash (won 10–5, Roberts 1 try and 2 conversions and Jack Thomas 1 try), Kenfig Hill (won) and Porthcawl on Boxing Day (a draw). With away games at Pontardulais (won), Crynant, Cwmavon (on Christmas Day) and Pontardawe (won).

In the new year Cwmlynfell visited the Ferry and were well beaten by 25–3. Cyril Roberts grabbed a brace, Phil Griffiths, Doug James, and Ellis Thomas all added tries, H. Roberts converted two and Ron Thomas added a drop goal. There were then fixtures away at Aberaman and home to Gowerton before the first round of the West Wales RU cup, all of which they won. Ferry were up to sixth in the table having, only lost three league games so far this season.

February saw home games with Merthyr (won) and Felinfoel (drew), and away fixtures at RAF St. Athan, Kenfig Hill (won) and Hendy (lost).

Then three away games on the trot in March, against Gowerton (won), Blaenavon and Blackwood (lost). Followed by a home fixture against Amman United and ending with a losing trip to Felinfoel.

Six games in April brought the season to an end. Game one was a home fixture against Cwmavon before a double header with Skewen. The Ferry won the first 8–0 away, which kicked off late (4.40 p.m) due to the broadcasting of the Grand National! Ferry lent Skewen two forwards to make up their pack. D. James and J. Madden were the try scorers and Roberts converted 1 – they also took their home ground record with this win. On Good Friday Ferry pulled off the double by winning 19–0 in front of one of the best gates of the season. David Parker, Cyril Roberts and Sam Thomas (2) were the try getters, Roberts added 2 conversions and 1 penalty. Skewen went on to win the Championship, the Shield and the Cup.

7.4 1951/52

Back: J. Budge (trainer), P. Hoare, Dick James, R. Griffiths, R. Griffiths, A. Jones, B. Phillips, Doug James. D.W. Roberts. Centre: A. Jones (referee), H. Watkins, A. Owen, Llewellyn Llewellyn (captain), J. Madden, R. Thomas, H. Roberts. Front: Ellis Thomas, Jack Thomas

This was followed by away games at Merthyr and Cwmlynfell and the curtain came down with a home tie against Blaenavon.

Annual dinner

During a dinner in April at the Grandison Hotel players and officials were presented with club blazers for the first time since 1928 – at a cost of £170 2s! Club president Mr O.L. Davies said, "We have experienced our lean times and we have had our differences of opinion between players and officials, but I am confident that very few clubs in South Wales can boast of the happy association which exists now in the Briton Ferry Rugby Club." He also praised the work of the Welsh Union in giving encouragement to the game.

In response, Mr W.R. Thomas MBE, JP, vice president of the Welsh Union and chairman of Aberavon RFC, stated that he had been associated with the Ferry for many years and had always found them "a wonderful tactful body" who were closely allied with themselves and Neath and that they always played with a "great sporting spirit".

The Mayor, Councillor Ben Morris JP, then proposed a toast to the club. Other speakers were: Albert Freethy of the WRU; Mr Morgan Jones, club vice chairman; Ewart Jones, treasurer; Mr W.L. Williams, committeeman; and Mr Cyril Michael, chairman of Neath RFC. The toastmaster was Mr T.R. Vernon Davies.

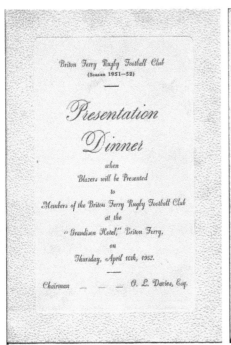

7.5 Presentation night menu 1951-52

7.6 Blazer badges, designed by Graham Davies, 18-year-old son of club secretary Bill

The players who received blazers were Messrs. Llew Llewelyn, Harold Roberts, Howie Thomas, Ellis Thomas, Hugh Watkins, Jack Thomas, Arthur Owen, Doug James, Dick James, Jack Madden, Arthur Jones, Phil Griffiths, Cliff Thomas, Ron Thomas, Alan Davies, Cyril Roberts, Sam Thomas and Ron Griffiths. The president, the assistant secretary Mr Ewart Adams and the trainer Mr Jack Budge were also presented with blazers.

AGM

The AGM took place in the Grandison Hotel on 19 May. Bill Davies, the secretary for the last nineteen years, stated that the last season had been one of the most successful he had known, despite sometimes fielding a weakened side due to the unavailability of players. For the third year in succession Harold Roberts was top scorer with 141 points, having scored 8 tries, 20 penalties and 27 conversions along with a single drop goal. His brother Cyril was in second place on 45 points and Jack Madden was third.

Club president Mr O.L. Davies announced that after some wangling and squeezing the club had gained a seven-year extension on the lease of the Old Road ground. He added that, despite a certain amount of antagonism between the club and Neath, he hoped they could look forward to a renewed friendship.

The treasurer's report from Mr Ewart Jones showed that the club had come through the best season financially for years, and had a bank balance of £186 17s. It was also pleasing that gate receipts had increased by £76.

Officers re-elected were the president, chairman, secretary, assistant secretary, treasurer and committeemen Morgan Jones, W.L. Williams, W.S. Jones, E. Richards, C. Callaghan, H. Davies, V. Davies, C. Phillips, and G. Thomas. Elected to the committee were H. Thomas, W. Thomas and D. Davies. E. Selby was elected as honorary vice president. Captain for the upcoming season was Jack Thomas, with Doug James as vice captain. As usual, the four players who had married during the season were presented with electric clocks: Llew Llewelyn, Ron Thomas, Alan Davies and Cyril Roberts.

J. Budge.(Trainer). D. Rees. L. Lewis. P. Hoare. J. Madden. B. Phillips. A. Jones.
Morgan Jones(Chairman).
R. Griffiths. J. Owen. Doug James. Llew Llewellyn(Capt) H. Watkins. A. Owens.
Ron Thomas. H. Roberts. Jack Thomas.

7.7 1951/52

Other news

In September, Staines and Steer, left the Ferry to join junior club Cimla.

In October:

- Mr W.J. Hill was elected as a life member of Glamorgan County RFC after 28 years of service
- Both Viv and John Evans played for a Combined Neath/Aberavon against the Springboks.

JOHN OAKES, aged 62 of Penrhiwtyn, was the first man in Neath to win the Carnegie Hero Fund Trust's bronze medal "the highest award for bravery" and the George medal for pulling out a fellow worker trapped in the middle of a fire at the Albion works.

1952/53

The 1952/53 season got off to a good start with twenty-two forwards to choose from. Dick Jones, Ellis Thomas and Arthur Jones had all retired, but new wing John Hill seemed promising and Terry Collins of Baglan looked the part as the new hooker.

> This year saw the tragically early death of former player and Welsh International **DAI LEYSHON THOMAS**. He'd suffered serious burns after gas bottles exploded at Calor Gas at the NOR. He'd been one of the first players to transfer to Neath as a prop, where he was captain during the 1937/38 season.

The first game of the season was a change to the original fixture (Pontardawe away) and they drew 3–3 at Cwmavon. Ferry followed that with a narrow 0–3 defeat at Aberavon. Ex-Aberavon player Llew John played against his old club at scrum-half. Ferry then inflicted the same score line at home on Cwmlynfell (John Hill scored a try and centre Sam Thomas was outstanding). Ferry's next test was an away fixture at Mountain Ash, a narrow 0–3 loss, before a 14–0 home win over Blaengarw, in which Ron Thomas 1 drop goal, Harold Roberts converted 1 Sam Thomas try and kicked 1 penalty, and wing Cyril Roberts added another try with a run from all of 75 yards. They ended the month with a 12–8 win at Pontardulais – Llew Llewelyn, Sam Thomas and Jack Madden were try scorers and Ron Thomas kicked a penalty.

In October, the Ferry were pitted against Gorseinon in the first round of the Welsh Wales Rugby Union cup. They defeated them at home 6–0. Cliff Thomas dabbed down 1 try and Dai Hill 1 drop goal. Ferry then defeated Gowerton 8–0 with tries from Cyril Roberts and Jack Thomas and 1

Captain
Jack Thomas

Vice captain
Doug James

Playing record
P 42
W 28
D 7
L 7
Points for 399
Points against 208

conversion from Thomas. Merthyr were the next visitors and the Ferry were triumphant again, with a bigger score of 22–0. Young Brian Tobin of Aberavon made his debut in the centre and scored 2 tries. Hughie Watkins, David Hill, Cyril Roberts and Jack Madden added tries, Doug James converted 2. Aberaman were the last visitors of the month and they were defeated 11–0.

November started with a 3–3 home draw against Kenfig Hill. Harold Roberts kicked a penalty, but Ferry lost their unbeaten league record the following week at Amman United, 3–5. A Jack Madden try was the only score. Despite the defeat Ferry were still sitting joint top in the league with Carmarthen. They then paid visits to Aberaman (won 22–5) and Crynant (3–3), before ending the month with a 16–3 home win over Ystrad Rhondda. Arthur Owen, Cyril Roberts and Jack Madden made tries with 2 conversions and 1 penalty from Harold Roberts. D.S. Thomas played well in this match – up to this point he had played in every position behind the scrum this season, including one game at wing forward.

After the game **REG JENKINS**, Ferry skipper in 1948/49, was presented with his Glamorgan County cap by club chairman Mr W.J. Hill. Reg had played ten games for the county between 1946 and 1950 and had also picked up a schoolboy cap.

Fixtures for the final month of the year were at home to Carmarthen (3–3), Mountain Ash (11–5), Pontardawe and Cwmavon (17–9 on a midweek Boxing Day; with tries from D.S. Thomas, J. Madden, Arthur Owen and Doug James, 1 conversion by L. Mogford, Llew Llewelyn kicked 1 penalty). Then away games at Cwmlynfell (3–0) and Skewen (on Christmas Day).

The new year brought a spate of away challenges as the Ferry faced

Rory O'connor
Briton Ferry-Aberavon - WALES
7.8 Rory O'Connor

Merthyr, Tredegar (drew 6–6, D. Hill and J. Madden tries), Ystrad Rhondda and Ystalyfera in the second round of the WWRU Cup (won 12–11). They won their only home game, 20–6 against Ystalyfera.

This took the club into February and their next opponents were Gowerton, away, which Ferry won 11–6 with 2 tries from Arthur Owen and 1 from Harold Roberts, who also converted 1. They then met Crynant at home, whom they defeated 11–6. Rory O'Connor, Llew Llewelyn and Jack Thomas were the try scorers and Roberts converted one.

Match results place BFRFC scores first

The next visitors to try and take the club's ground record were Treorchy but, despite seven players being unavailable, the Ferry triumphed 6–0. Cyril Roberts and David Hill scored tries. Dai Poley, Phil Griffiths and Alan Davies were outstanding up front alongside Hughie "Crackers" Watkins. Their final game of the month was another home challenge against Pontardulais. Ferry defeated the visitors 9–3 in a dour game, with tries scored by Jack Madden, Cyril Roberts and Doug "the Champ" James.

March and April were busy months on the field for the Ferry, starting with three away games. They won 6–5 at Kenfig Hill (Dai Poley with a try and Roberts kicking a penalty), then a trip to Cwmavon. Finally a 13–8 win at Ammanford, with Mel Pugh coming in at scrum-half and Wyndham Morgan at centre. Cyril Roberts played out of position in the centre and bagged a hat trick of tries and dropped 1 over the line, Arthur Owen converted 2. In a 3–3 home draw with Carmarthen, Alan Davies kicked 1 penalty. Then followed an away fixture at Blaengarw before March ended with a 9–8 home win over Amman United to retain their home ground record. Dai Poley, Harold Roberts and David Hill were the try scorers, and Ira Llewelyn was outstanding up front.

April started with another home win, this time over Ystalyfera on Good Friday, before going on tour.

In the final run-in to the end of the season Ferry lost the semi-final of the West Wales Championship to Loughor at Vardre in a rearranged fixture (the first was cancelled due to the death of Queen Mary) and they ended in third place in the league. Then an away fixture at Blaenavon, followed by a crushing blow when Ammanford took their home ground record by 3–16 – Wyndam Morgan was the only try scorer for the Ferry. A 6–0 home win over Tredegar with a Cyril Roberts try and D. Hill penalty, led to the final home game with Skewen and an away date at Treorchy.

The club was just shy of 400 points for the season. They'd been in the league play-offs, finishing third, and had only lost one league game.

Tour

The remainder of Easter was spent on tour to the Isle of Man. The Ferry won the Invitation Sevens tournament with a team of John Madden, Cyril Roberts, David Hill, Arthur Owen, Cliff Thomas, Terry Collins and Morwyn Morgan. They also played fixtures against the Old Instonians and an Isle of Man XV.

Isle of Man tour 1953-kindly loaned by Brian Tobin

7.9 Isle of Man tour, 1953, (bottom right) Sevens winners

AGM

The AGM at the end of May showed a healthy balance. Treasurer W.L. Williams stated that a wonderful effort had been made by officials and members that season to raise £338 16s 6d. Gate takings of £141 2s 6d were down on the

Match results place BFRFC scores first

previous season by £60, which was disappointing considering the season that the club had just completed. Club president Mr O.L. Davies felt that the only explanation for the lack of support was that the rugger fans weren't fully aware of the standard of play that the Ferry were involved in! Treasurer Ewart Jones stated that a wonderful effort had been made by officials and members to raise £338 16s 6d by outside efforts and new kit had cost £109 1s 9d.

For the third season in succession Harold Roberts finished as top scorer with 85 points (4 tries, 11 penalties and 20 conversions), and his brother Cyril was next on 81 points from 21 tries.

Young John Nash of Baglan, son of Ferry member W.Nash, was presented with a new kit bag to celebrate him representing Welsh Schools against England.

Season 1952-1953

W.S. Davies (Hon. Sec.) M.Jones (Chairman), A. Owen, D. Jones, D.S. Thomas, C. Thomas,J.Hill,
A. Davies, H. Davies, R. Thomas, J.Budge(Trainer) E. Adams.
P. Griffiths, H.Watkins, J.Thomas(Capt.),J.Madden, C.Roberts.
Front: T. Collins. L. John.

7.10 1952/53

Officers re-elected included the club president, chairman and secretary. Due to the retirement of Mr Ewart Jones, Mr Ewart Adams was elected treasurer. Elected to the committee were B. Williams, V. Davies, R. Jenkins, I.

Llewelyn, J. Thomas and D. Roberts. Mr Cliff Jones was elected captain for next season, with Cyril Roberts as vice captain.

In the district

Cwrt Sart school visited Resolven secondary school and took their ground record 9–5. J. Harrison scored 2 tries and D. Harding 1.

Tonna defeated Cimla Barbarians 15–6 in the cup final.

Other news

The rugby club organised a children's party and dance at the Public Hall in Briton Ferry for the Queen's Coronation in June. A Coronation Fairy Queen was chosen by the judges, Police Inspector Hedley Onions and Mr and Mrs O.L. Davies. An adult dance followed at 9 p.m.

Cyril Roberts
Briton Ferry-Neath RFC & Wales

7.11 Cyril Roberts

In June, speedy Ferry wing Cyril Roberts, while walking along the Neath Canal with his wife, heard children screaming eighty or so yards away and saw the head of a child bobbing in the water. He raced to the spot, grabbed the little girl's dress and pulled her out of the water. He applied artificial respiration and saved her life. That little girl was two-year-old Sonia Godbear of Cecil Street in Neath. Roberts had also played a few games for Bryncoch and was no.6 for the Training Battalion RASC during the 1950/51 season, when he scored a total of 55 tries. He'd clocked 10.3 seconds for the 100 yards!

1953/54

The new season started with two home wins and a home draw. Ferry defeated Cwmlynfell 6–3 (new boy Brian Start 1 drop goal and wing Howard Jones scored 1 try, which Ron Trimnell failed to convert) and then Llandybie 8–0 (D. Hill drop goal and conversion, C. Roberts try) in between these wins they played Aberavon at home. Ferry then drew 3–3 at home with Ystalyfera, with forwards Bob White, A. Davies, P. Vaughan, Gwyn Davies and Cliff Thomas all prominent. This put them third in the league.

Ferry then paid a friendly visit to Penygraig, before returning to a first round Welsh Wales Rugby Union cup game against Ammanford (because vice captain Cyril Roberts had played for Neath in an earlier round, he was cup-tied for this match). Forwards B. Tobin, A. Clarke and G. Francis, backs D.O. Taylor and C. Evans, along with new boy in the centre Graham Michael, were playing well and the match ended in a 0–0 draw.

Neath were then entertained and proved too strong on the night. The best try of the match was scored by, now ex-Ferry, wing Cyril Roberts. Scrum-half Brian Tobin played well, as did forwards L. Llewelyn, B. Hire and Graham Francis. Ferry also lost away at Carmarthen, 0–3, but ended the month with an excellent 5–3 home win over Merthyr, with a Francis try converted by Arthur Owen. D.S. Thomas and Jack Thomas played well.

December saw an 8–12 away defeat at Skewen. H. John and D. Poole scored tries and Arthur Owen converted 1.

The new year didn't prove to be a happy one. In March, a double header against Crynant ended with two defeats, 3–14 at home and 3–9 away. D. Taylor scored 1 try at

Captain
Cliff Thomas

Vice captain
Cyrill Roberts

Playing record
P 35
W 13
D 5
L 17
Points for 233
Points against 206

home game and H. Roberts 1 away. The following week they defeated Swansea Uplands at home, 17–13. Fullback Don Taylor added 1 try and 1 conversion, Harold Roberts and Alan Davies 1 try, Sam Thomas 2. Ex-Ferry player John Stockham did well for the Swansea side. But the Ferry then slipped up at home to Carmarthen by 3–14 – Bob White scored the only try.

season 1953-54

M.Jones. G.Francis.D.S.Thomas. A. Davies. B. Hire. J. Thomas. C. Thomas.
C.Evans. T.Parfit.(Ref) J.Thomas. G. Michael. J. Jones. (Captain)
A. Thomas. B. White. M. Thomas. M. Pugh.
Inserts. R. Trimnell. L. Llewellyn. R. Mears. B. Tobin. R. Owen.J. Hill.
D. James. H.D. Watkins. D.J. Poley. R. Evans. A. Owen(Who later became Canf

7.12 1953/54

In the final month of the season the club played in a seven-a-side tournament at the Gnoll, run by Neath RFC. They entered both an A side and a B side and did quite well. The A side played Cwmgrach, Trinity College and Swansea University and won them all, but lost to the eventual winners Seven Sisters. Surprisingly, Seven Sisters' opponents in the final were the Ferry B team. The Bs had played Crynant A and Trebanos (twice), winning them all and receiving a bye in the semi-final.

AGM

At the Grandison Hotel in June club president Mr Ossie Davies stated that Briton Ferry was not the place for league football and we would be better off just playing friendlies. The club had gained £17 13s 7d as a result of membership of the Welsh Wales Rugby Union, and he complained that the club was not well placed in between the likes of Aberavon and Neath. He worried that stopping internationals in St. Helens would be detrimental to the game in the West. The club had suffered on the field this season, as shown by the playing record – they'd lost nine games by only three points and had failed to score on seven occasions. Players had left the club for other local teams and gate receipts were down, not helped by poor weather.

In time-honoured fashion, clocks were presented to the two players who had got married that year, Hugh Watkins and Mervyn Thomas. Thanks were given to outgoing captain Sam Thomas, trainer Cyril Beasley, groundsman A. Kennedy, touch judge Morgan Jones, and Mr and Mrs I.J. Morris of the Grandison Hotel – and the press!

The president was re-elected as were the chairman (Mr W.J. Hill in his forty-sixth year), the secretary (Mr W.S. Davies), the assistant secretary (Mr Ewart Adams), the treasurer (Mr W.L. Williams), and committeemen Morgan Jones, W.S. Jones, Emlyn Richards, Howie Thomas, William Thomas and Ron Reed. The honorary auditors, Messrs Morgan and Ewart Jones, were also re-elected.

Top scorer was Sam Thomas with 41 points, Arthur Owen was second with 27. Arthur Owen was elected captain for the next season, with Thomas as his deputy.

In the district

Crynant won the Neath Rugby Supporters Cup and the Challenge Shield.

1954/55

Captain
Arthur Owen

Vice captain
Cliff Thomas

Playing record
P 36
W 17
D 7
L 12
Points for 220
Points against 180

Scores
Tries 47
Conversions 14
Drop goals 0
Penalties 17

The season started with the club setting out on a new venture, running a Youth XV. The young squad struggled a bit against bigger opponents and lost home and away to Pontrhydyfen by 33–11 and 20–0 respectively, in October and November.

The First XV defeated Ystalyfera at home in October by 11–3. Gwyn Morris, Arthur Owen and Graham Michael scored tries and Algie Baker slotted a conversion. Playing well through this period were fly-half Louis. S. Daniel and forwards Bryan Hire and G. Reed.

The Ferry lost their next home game with Carmarthen, 0–3, in which scrum-half Roy Evans was prominent. October ended with a big win over Ystradgynlais at the Ferry, 26–0. Young Cyril O'Connor, a former youth cap, scored a hat trick of tries on his debut at wing forward. Bryan Hire Sam Thomas and Graham Michael added 1 try apiece and Baker kicked 4 conversions.

November brought a double header against Crynant, but Ferry lost both games – 3–13 at home (L. Daniel try) and 0–9 away. They'd played them earlier in the season, also at home.

In December, 47-year-old chairman Morgan Jones took over the fullback position when a player didn't turn up for an away game at Vardre. The match ended in a muddy 0–0 draw, although the Ferry had won the home game earlier in the season.

Ferry ended the month against Porthcawl and lost at home on Boxing Day (in the process losing their unbeaten home record). Ferry got their revenge in the first game of the new year, the return fixture at Porthcaw,l by winning 5–3. Winger C. Evans was the try scorer and Fraser converted.

Ferry went to Aberavon Quins during March and lost 0–13. Fraser and M. Thomas played well up front.

In April they defeated Llandaff at home, 6–3. Gwyn Morris kicked two penalties.

The Neath RFC Supporters' Club ran a sevens competition again and again Ferry entered two teams. In the draw, the A team got a bye to the semi-final, where they met the B team who had earlier defeated Tonna 10–0. It was the B team who succeeded in getting to the final with 6–0. They played Seven Sisters and lost 0–6.

A disappointing eight games were called off during the season and the club finished eighteenth in the league.

AGM

The AGM in June was again held at the Grandison Hotel, and, with only nineteen players all season, the club's playing record for the season was disappointing. The top points scorer was Gwyn Morris with 36 (made up of 8 tries, 2 penalties and 3 conversions). Douglas Fraser was second on 33 (scoring 1 try, 8 penalties and 3 conversions). For the second year running Graham Michael was third on 26 (with 5 tries, 3 penalties and 1 conversion). Algie Baker also had a good record for the season.

President Mr Ossie Davies said that the club would not be playing for points in the West Wales competition next season but would enter the cup competition. Morgan Jones agreed, stating that this year's champions, Seven Sisters, had received no less than £251 from cup and championship games, compared with the Ferry's £11. In fact, two-thirds of the gate money had come from just two matches against Neath and Aberavon.

Treasurer Mr Bill Williams presented the accounts, which showed a satisfactory balance, mainly due to the supporters' dance committee donation of £53 10s 6d, and supporters' other efforts that raised £ 257 12s 7d. Gate receipts were £109 16s 6d. The youth section had cost the club £24 16s 6d, but was regarded as a good investment. As usual, players' weddings were celebrated with clock presentations, this year recipients were Bryan Hire, Gwyn Morris, Arthur Williams and Algie Baker. Hughie Watkins was presented with a WWRU tie.

All officers were re-elected and the usual thanks given to trainer Cyril Beasley, groundsman Tom Kennedy, kit man Morgan Powell and Mr and Mrs Idwal Morris of the Grandison Hotel.

Tour

The Ferry also went on a tour to Ireland during 1955, hosted by Bandon Rugby Club in County Cork. The Ferry had defeated Charlesville on Saturday by 14–0. On Easter Monday they played the Bandon XV, which included D. Barry of Munster and lock Michael Madden (who had three caps for Ireland that year). The Ferry team was: backs A. Baker, G. Michael, R. Mears, D.S. Thomas, G. Morris, D. Parker and R. Evans; forwards M. Thomas, D. "the Champ" James, H. "Crackers" Watkins, D. Fraser, A. Williams, B. Hire, D. Poley and Bob White.

In the first half the Ferry scored 2 tries through D. Parker and Bob White and 1 penalty by Barry. In the second half Ferry really took control and their speedy backs were no match for the opposition. Parker added 2 tries for a hat trick, 1 of which was converted. After spectacular handling by the whole team M. Thomas scored 1 other. The final score was 30–3 to the Ferry, with Parker scoring 22 points.

7.13 Touring party arriving in Cork, 1955

Morgan Jones. E. Richards. E. Adams. A. Williams. Ernie Jones. Roy Evans.
D.J. Poley. D. Parker. Doug James. B. Hire. R. Mears. C. Beasley(Trainer)
P. George. Algy Baker. W.S. Davies(Sec)
Hugh Watkins. Mervyn Thomas. D. Fraser. W.L.Williams. D.S. Thomas(Capt)
G. Michael. Bob White. Batchwbin (G) (G-Guests)

7.14 Team photo before the game on Easter Monday 1955

Sadly, not long after this tour **DOUG FRASER** died at too young an age.

In the district

In the cup and shield finals Tonna played Crynant. The latter won the shield, but the cup was delayed until the following season.

1955/56

In a tough start to the season the club took on the might of Neath with a team that included newcomers N. Phillips, W. Brennan, Dennis Hare, Bob White and A. Williams.

They then entertained Aberavon and, despite an E. Mosley try, went down 3–14. Swansea Uplands were the next visitors and Ferry defeated them 24–3. Doug Fraser, Arthur Williams, Mervyn Thomas (2), Hughie Watkins and Ernie Jones all scored tries and Fraser converted 3. Ferry then defeated Merthyr, again at home, 11–0. Fraser was again among the try scorers, along with Doug James and Brennan, Graham Michael converted 1.

In October they played Kidwelly at home in the Welsh Wales Rugby Union cup, and drew 6–6. Michael kicked two penalties. Ferry then lost 0–11 at home to Carmarthen, and 8–14 to Llanharan (Brennan and wing Bob Burns scored tries and Michael converted 1).

Captain
D.G. Thomas

Ferry defeated Pontardawe 8–3 at home in November. New fullback John Selby, son of Edwin Selby, and new centre Doug Allin, from Neath RFC, played their first game for the Ferry. Hughie Watkins was the try scorer and Michael added the extras.

> Ferry boy J. SELBY was selected later to play in the centre for Neath Youth against Aberavon and then in a match against Pembrokeshire – when he was joined by another Ferry boy, fullback JOHN HARRIS.

December saw a return match with Carmarthen and another defeat, this time by 3–32, with Watkins making the only try. They went away for this match and seven regulars were missing, so trainer Cyril Beasley, among others, had to play, but they only had fourteen on the field.

Their fortunes swung the following week as a new-look away side defeated Gowerton 13–11. Prop Alan Davies, Bill Brennan and Michael all touched down, with Michael again adding the extras. The weather got the better of the Christmas fixture at home to Cwmavon. On Boxing Day they played Skewen at home, but unfortunately lost 6–8 – Cyril Michael and Sam Thomas were the try scorers.

Ferry ended the year with a change of fixture as Merthyr could not play. Instead, they entertained Blaengarw and beat them 16–13, with tries from Ron Trimnell, Doug James and Mervyn Thomas. Michael converted two and added a match-winning drop goal.

The new year started with a 3–0 home victory over Gowerton, Michael was the try scorer. Ferry were also victorious against Resolven at home, 6–3. Sam Thomas and Arthur Williams got tries.

> The conditions were so atrocious that the only way the teams could cross the Pantyrheol stream in full flood and reach the ground from their changing rooms at the "Grando", was to use a rope swing attached to a large branch, which some local boys provided!

Ferry then ended a good month at home by defeating Loughor 8–0 in the second round of the WWRU Cup. Sam Thomas got a try, which was converted by Michael, who added a penalty. Ferry had lost 3–12 at home to Ystalyfera earlier in the season, but defeated them away this month.

During March, in a first home game for weeks, they defeated Kenfig Hill 3–0. Michael again kicked 1 penalty, but Algie Baker had a try disallowed. Ferry then played Crynant in the semi-final of the WWRU Cup on the Gnoll and drew 3–3. Ron Trimnell got the try, set up by Brennan. H. Watkins and M. Thomas were outstanding in the front row.

In April they were defeated 3–6 at home by Ystradgynlais, with Baker kicking a penalty.

They were due to play a fixture at home to Ogmore Vale in May, but this was cancelled as the Vale couldn't raise a side.

In the district

The District Shield was won 3–0 by BP A against Tonna.

Youth team

The new Youth XV reached a milestone by getting to the Neath & District Cup final, where they lost narrowly to Resolven, 0–3.

7.15 Youth 1955/56

(back) Billy Lipton, E.C. Jones, Barry Nicholas, Sam John (secretary); (middle) Matt Roberts, Geoff Thomas, Rob Hughes, ?, Peter Roach, John Hill, Clive Thomas, John Harris, John Dugmore; (front) Viv Jenkins, Harold Gorman, Dudley Mills (captain), Gwyn Jenkins, Terry Sampson

Match results place BFRFC scores first

1956/57

The season started with three trial matches, for which players were invited to send their particulars to the club secretary prior to being allowed to play. The club was in a good position with regard to numbers of players.

> The Ferry were re-elected to the Welsh
> Wales Rugby Union for the season.

The first match was an away fixture at Tenby, followed by a trip to Felinfoel. Then home fixtures against Aberavon and Gowerton, the latter were defeated 14–9, with Arthur Williams, Graham Michael and Trevor Thomas scoring tries and Michael adding a conversion and a penalty. Then a home fixture against Neath and two trips to Ystrad Rhondda and Ystradgynlais, before ending the month with another home win over Penygraig. Hooker Trevor Thomas was again on the try sheet, along with Youth XV player Alan White and D.S. Thomas. Roy Evans converted 1.

October started with a home fixture against Amman United in the first round of the West Wales Cup and the Ferry won 3–0 (try scored by Dai Newton). Next up was a visit to RAF St. Athan, before meeting Amman United again the following week. After a visit to Kenfig Hill they ended the month with a 15–12 home win over Resolven. Tricky wing Dai Newton score a hat trick of tries and Howard Burt bagged a brace, but every kick at goal failed.

November saw three away fixtures against Amman United, Carmarthen and Penygraig and an 11–6 home win over Ystradgynlais with three Youth XV players in the side, Dudley Mills, Alan White and John Harris. Harris kicked a

Captain
Hugh D. Watkins

Playing record
P 43
W 26
D 5
L 11
Points for 332
Points against 299

conversion of Dai Newton's first try, he added another later, as did Dennis Hare after a scoring pass from outside-half Howard Burt.

Season 1956-1957

G. Beasley (Trainer) D. Newton, E. Jones, D. Poley, D. Mills, D. Hare, T. Woodlands,
B. Hire, D. James, C. O'Connor, A. Williams, W. Jenkins(Ref) M. Thomas, M. Jones (Chairman)
H. Watkins (Capt) W.S. Davies (Sec) G. Michael, D.S. Thomas,
Front: Roy Evans, F. Rees, H.Bunt, G. Norman

7.16 1956/57

December was to be a busy month with seven fixtures, four at home against Felinfoel (won 13–0, with Newton scoring a brace, Roy Evans adding another and Doug James kicking 1 goal), Ystrad Rhondda (won 18–3, Michael kicking 2 goals and Roy Evans, Newton, Sam Thomas and centre Elwyn Branford adding tries), Llanharan and Pontardawe, and three away fixtures at Aberaman, Pontardawe and Skewen. They completed a winning December double over Pontardawe (the away game by 6–3, with a try from Bryan Hire and a penalty from Graham Michael).

The Ferry played Loughor in the new year and drew 3–3 at home, with Bob White notching a try and fullback John Harris fitting in well to replace Michael. Followed by an away fixture at Llandaff and then the home game with Cwmavon had to be cancelled to play a cup round against Ammanford at home.

Match results place BFRFC scores first

What an occasion that was. There are reports of about 1,500 people attending the game, the best crowd since 1947 when 2,000 watched another cup match with Amman. But the best crowd ever was reported as being for the visit of unbeaten Maesteg just before the Second World War, in which the visitors took the spoils and stayed unbeaten, but only just.

A 3–0 win saw Ferry through, and they drew with Neath at the Gnoll a week later! The Ammanford game ended in a splendid 12–6 win for the Ferry. Roy Evans returned from an injury and combined well with fellow backs Dennis Hare, Dai Newton and Ron Trimnell. Evans dropped 1 chance goal, Arthur Williams added 1 try, along with Newton and Dai Poley.

DAI NEWTON was a convert from soccer and he was proving to be a class act. He scored 19 tries this season alone, and he trialled for Neath at the start of the next season.

In February the club took on Gowerton and Resolven away and Carmarthen and Kenfig Hill at home. The original date for the Kenfig game had been cancelled due to West Wales Cup duties (at home to a strong Seven Sisters side, losing 0–1) and Ferry were the victors by 9–5. Roy Evans scored 1 try and kicked 1 penalty, and then sold a dummy to the Kenfig defence and dropped 1 goal to seal the game.

In another rearranged match, Ferry entertained Blaengarw in early March and defeated them 8–5. D. Sam Thomas touched down, H. Watkins converted and Evans kicked a penalty. Newton was not available for these games as he was on loan to Maesteg.

Later in March, following two away games at Cwmavon and Crynant, Ferry entertained Llandaff and Aberaman, winning the latter at a canter, 32–3. Newton scored a brace, and D. James, E. Jones, H. Burt, T. Thomas and G. Michael all added tries. Michael also kicked 1 penalty. A. Williams converted 1 and H. Watkins converted 3.

April saw away games at Llanharan and Ogmore Vale and home fixtures with RAF St. Athan, Crynant, Ogmore Vale (won 9–8, Ron Trimnell with a drop goal and a try and Michael kicking a penalty) and Skewen.

Ferry completed the season with an away fixture at Blaengarw.

In their last six matches 66 points had been scored against the club. The Ferry ended tenth in the league.

There was a joke among the supporters that they should keep an eye on the posts during games in case they went missing. This was because ball after ball had disappeared from the field during matches, and a bench that had been used when taking a team photo had gone missing, and the remains of the gangway spanning the brook along the main road side of the field had been removed – very inconvenient for the older supporters!

Youth team

The Youth XV were playing well and defeated BP Llandarcy by 3–0 at home, with Harris kicking a penalty. This was their fifth win on the trot and they were to play Cornelly in their next game. D. Mills and D. Jones were selected as reserves for the Neath & District side to play Aberavon, and they also played a game at Briton Ferry against Swansea.

There was a little confusion about the Youth XV fixtures and Maesteg came to the Ferry during early February only to find that the club were already playing away at Pontrhydyfen!

Tour

This year's tour was back to the Isle of Man to take part in their annual sevens festival. The team stopped for lunch at the Old Nag's Head in Chester on the way up to Liverpool to catch the Ferry.

The tournament was held on the King William's College playing fields on three pitches and the winners were to receive the F.M. Cubbon Shield.

Their first fixture was against Port Sunlight on the Good Friday in Douglas. They then split into A and B squads. The As played Old Wirralians A in the second round, and the Bs played Liverpool Collegiate Old Boys A in the first round. There is no record of the final result.

7.17 Programme of Isle of Man 7th Annual Seven-a-Side Tournament

A mixed Ferry team then played an Isle of Man XV at Quarterbridge in an additional fixture on the Easter Monday.

After a free day on Tuesday they departed Douglas on Wednesday morning and stopped off in the Angel Hotel in Ludlow for high tea on the journey home.

The touring party consisted of committeemen (Morgan Jones, Edward Selby, W.L. Williams, Ewart Adams and W.S. Davies), the trainer Cyril Beasley and the following players: Hugh Watkins (captain), Graham Michael (vice captain), Dai Newton, Ron Trimnell, D.S. Thomas, Elwyn Bamford, Mal Phillips, Roy Evans, Howard Burt, Fred Rees, Trevor Thomas, Mervyn Thomas, Doug James, Ernie Jones, Bryan Hire, Arthur Williams, Dai Poley, Dennis Hare, Dudley Mills and Barrie Nicholas.

7.18 1956/57, behind the Grandison changing rooms

AGM

The fifty-sixth AGM was again held in the Grandison Hotel presided over by Morgan Jones in the absence of club president Mr O.L. Davies. He thanked everyone for their continuing support and hard work during the season. Attendance was good, despite the hot July weather.

The club had suffered a small financial loss, which was put down to the bad weather when they played against Neath that probably cost them £50–£60 in gate money. Although, in general, gate receipts were up on the previous year. Some people blamed the cost of the annual tour, although there'd not been a tour the previous season. Others pleaded a case for spending money on the ground, but what needed to be done wasn't quite clear.

The season's top scorers were Dai Newton with 76 points and Graham Michael with 57. There was mention during the AGM that a reason for some of the match defeats was the lack of a reliable kicker. Mr Ned Selby was congratulated on his selection as a linesman at the Empire Games in Cardiff.

Officers re-elected were president O.L. Davies, chairman Morgan Jones, vice chairman Edwin Selby, secretary W.S. Davies, assistant secretary Ewart Adams and treasurer W. Williams. Messrs Ewart Jones and Ron Edwards were appointed as auditors. The committee consisted of T.R. Vernon, L. Llewelyn, Percy George, Jack Thomas, Con Callaghan, Albert O'Shea, Ron Edwards, Edwin Selby, Emlyn Richards, Sam Jones, Avon Roberts and W. Thomas.

1957/58

Wing **DAI NEWTON** had a trial for Neath before the season started and played a few games during the season for Maesteg, but he continued his rich vein of form for the Ferry through the season.

The first match was a 24–0 home win over Aberaman, with tries from Mel Phillips, Hugh Watkins, Elwyn Bamford and Graham Michael, who also added 1 penalty. G. Morgan kicked 1 other penalty and added 3 conversions.

In a 9–9 draw at Tenby tries came from D.S. Thomas and B. Hire and another penalty from Michael. Neath were the next opponents, followed by a 15–0 home win against Resolven – tries from Michael, Mel Richards and G. Morgan, who converted all three.

October started with a home Welsh Wales Rugby Union Cup game with Hendy that ended in a draw. In the replay the following week, also in the Ferry ground, the away side took the spoils 0–11. In a rearranged midweek home game with Crynant both sides had to make changes, but the away side won 0–8. Next up was a visit to Carmarthen, where they drew 3–3. Mervyn Thomas bagged a try on a day when kicks at goal kept hitting the posts, twice for Carmarthen and three times for the Ferry.

Also this month, Neath & District faced Bridgend District for the first time in fifteen years, and two Ferry players were selected, hooker **DENNIS PRICE** and fullback **JOHN HARRIS**.

GWYN MORGAN completed his transfer from BP Llandarcy, where he'd plied his trade as a fullback, but the Ferry converted him to outside-half to play alongside Mervyn Thomas.

Captain
Graham Michael

Playing record
P 38
W 19
D 2
L 17
Points for 289
Points against 208

In a good start to November the club defeated Blaengarw at home, 11–3, with a double from Dai Newton, and 1 conversion and 1 penalty from Michael.

Meanwhile, the new Quins (the re-formed Second XV) lost at Bryn, 0–9. But they defeated them in the return match and notched up a win over Vardre.

During December, future Welsh International BRIAN THOMAS led his Neath Grammar School team on an historic unbeaten tour to France, thought to be the first of its kind.

Brian Thomas
Briton Ferry Youth - Cambridge Univ Blue
Neath RFC & Wales

7.19 Brian Thomas

December started badly with a fire in the changing rooms. Among the items it destroyed were treasured photographs of past teams, four sets of jerseys, five balls, track suits, boots and souvenirs of post-war tours, valued at about £200. A fire survivor came to light on Boxing Day, a statue of a fisher boy named "The Colonial Boy", a gift from an admirer during a tour to Cork – he was put in the care of the landlady of the Grandison Hotel, Mrs Alberta Morris.

Because of the fire Ferry had to borrow a set of jerseys from Aberavon to play against Ystalyfera, which put them back in their old strip of black and amber. The Ferry won 6–5, Newton was a try scorer again, along with Clive Thomas. The opposition scrum-half that day was Clive Rowlands!

There were home Christmas games against Cwmavon and Taibach. To end the month they lost 0–6 at Resolven.

The new year started a little sourly during a home game against Gowerton, which Ferry lost 0–3.

The referee, Mr Trevor Jones of Skewen, came in for some heavy criticism and Billy Williams, the club treasurer, said that his refereeing was the most atrocious exhibition he had seen over the last twenty years! Bryan Hire had only just returned to the field after treatment to a cut eye, allegedly sustained from a kick to the face, and got involved with the opposition scrum-half, Reg Jones, and was immediately sent off with two minutes of play left. The club were waiting for the match report to be sent to the WRU before making any sort of official protest. Coincidentally, Dr Nathan Jones of the WRU was at the match.

In a busy March, Ystrad Rhondda were defeated at home 24–8. Emrys Collins, Mel Phillips (2), Roy Evans and Doug James all scored tries, and Gwyn Morgan converted 3, Michael added 1 penalty. Ray Woodward, a newcomer from the Quins, made an excellent debut at scrum-half. The Ferry then drew 6–6 at home with RAF St. Athan – Michael got a try and Trimnell a drop goal. This was followed by a home game against Llandaff.

For all these games they were given the use of the Briton Ferry Steel Cricket Club pavilion to change in.

Season 1957-1958

C.Beasley(Trainer) G. Morgan, L.Llewellyn, B.Hire, M.Jones(Chairman), E.Jones, W.S.Davies (Sec) A.Williams, A.O'Shea,M.Phillips, D.Hare, D.S.Thomas, D.Newton, M.Thomas, G.Michael (Capt) T. Woodlands, J. Harris, J. Williams, Front: D.Jones, R.Evans,(V.Capt) R.Woodward. A.Watkins. E. Collins.

7.20 1957/58

The Ferry then played Loughor at home and had to lend them Bryan Hire to make them up to fifteen. Ferry nearly came a cropper, but managed an 8–3 win. Terry Woodland and Ernie Jones got a try apiece and G. Morgan converted 1. They then lost to Porthcawl, 9–11 – Michael kicked 2 goals, Dai Poley added 1 try.

In April, Ferry lost 5–9 to Skewen at home – Doug James scored 1 try, which Roy Evans converted.

Top scorers were Graham Michael (with 70 points for 3 tries, 19 penalties and 5 conversions), Gwyn Morgan (64 points with 3 tries, 6 penalties and 17 conversions). Top try scorer was the prolific Dai Newton with 9 tries.

The club finished twenty-fifth in the league.

Presentation supper

A presentation supper at the Grandison in May celebrated Cyril Roberts, ex-Ferry player, now at Neath and recently capped against Ireland. He was presented with a canteen of cutlery. Mr Morgan Jones presided. He stated that the club's future was looking good as they did not have to look around for players and the supporters' club was really stepping up to the mark with their spirit and untiring efforts.

Edwin Selby then congratulated Cyril and described his joining the club after leaving the army (RASC) and how he had impressed everyone with his play, following in the footsteps of Tal Harris, Tom Hollingdale and Arthur Lemon.

Ron Trimnell then thanked the press for their recognition of the club, nestled as it was between Neath and Aberavon.

Responses came from Neath and Aberavon representatives, Mr A. Davies and L. Morgan, respectively. WRU members, Messrs Raynor Jones, D.J. Phillips and Arthur Griffiths, were welcomed by club treasurer Mr Billy Williams, and they reciprocated with good wishes to the club. The club thanked the WRU for their invaluable financial aid to second-class clubs.

A toast to the club was proposed by Mr T.L. Roberts, who stated that the spirit of good fellowship within the club was bigger than the game and that it was perfect training for the battle of life in its demands for loyalty, team work, courage and fair play.

Mr D.J. Phillips then praised the work of Arthur Griffiths in getting Cyril Roberts into Neath, and how close both clubs were – despite all the poaching and pinching!

Club secretary Mr Bill Davies then thanked the chairman and closed the evening's speeches. A trio of Morgan Jones, Trevor Haywood and Briton Ferry Steel CC secretary Fred Hill provided the entertainment.

At this time, a certain **DOUG JONES** was getting his Boys Club of Wales cap against England, and a certain **ALBERT GLEAVES** was representing the Neath Schools team, who only lost two games out of the seventeen played that season.

Doug Jones
Youth, Briton Ferry, Neath & Swansea

7.21 Doug Jones

AGM

In June, the AGM was held at the Grandison Hotel. It was allegedly slightly disturbing, more like a game that had got out of hand than a quiet review of the season. One of the most notable issues was chairman Morgan Jones not being re-elected to the committee – even though he had stood in that night for club president Mr Ossie L. Davies, had been chairman for the last four years after taking over from Mr W.J. Hill, and had been connected with the club for the last thirty years in one capacity or another. There was also the fact that the team were not ready to announce their captain for the next season and secretary Mr W.S. Davies announced his disappointment, first with the turnout of players that night and second with the lack of training within the players' group, which he felt was one of the main reasons for the season's poor playing record.

Morgan Jones praised the efforts of the loyal bunch of players who had turned up week in week out, no matter the weather, and he thanked captain Graham Michael for his leadership, and also club members such as Doc Cyril Beasley, groundsman Tom Kennedy, baggage man Morgan Powell, Geoff Thomas, Sam John for his work with the Junior XV and club landlord Idwal Morris. He then thanked Briton Ferry Steel CC for their unstinted help with the use of their cricket pavilion following the fire they'd suffered earlier in the season. He also reiterated that this was the first time in the club's history that the team captain had not been chosen on the night.

The ballot for the committee then resulted in the election of committeemen Sam John, Afan Roberts, Mervyn Thomas, Sam Jones, Emlyn Richards and Percy George. The failure to re-elect Morgan Jones after all the work he'd put in was greeted with slight disdain by Billy Williams. Edwin Selby then proposed that Jones be elected as a life member – joining himself and Mr W.J. Hill – which was passed unanimously. The club officers were duly re-elected, and a notice of motion was given by Davies that anyone who nominated someone for the committee had to have been a member of the club for at least a year.

On a happier note, scrum-half Roy Evans was presented with an electric toaster to mark his recent marriage.

Following a committee meeting after the AGM, Evans was announced as club captain for the next season with Bryan Hire as his deputy, and Morgan Jones was elected as a life member and back into the club chair!

7.22 (main picture) Against Seven Sisters 1957; (inset) Dai Newton against Seven Sisters

1958/59

The club started the season with a tough away game at Neath in which ex-Ferry player Cyril Roberts notched up a hat trick of tries against his former club. Ferry worked hard up front (Bryan Hire, Ernie Jones and Huw Watkins) and behind (danger man Newton scored 1 try, as did Ray Woodward). John Harris at fullback 1 drop goal, but Ferry lost 9–29.

Next up was a home game against Resolven, which Ferry won 6–0. Newton was the try scorer and newcomer Doug Frazer kicked a penalty. Two forwards made there debut that day, J. Nash and G. Burns. A home draw with Burry Port followed – Ernie Jones and Gordon Matthews bagged tries and Gwyn Morgan converted 1. Meanwhile, the Quins lost at Tonmawr, 0–3.

October saw home wins over Penygraig 3–0 (Frazer penalty) and Gowerton 6–0 (tries for Trimnell and Arthur Williams), and a defeat to Amman United 8–9 (again Trimnell and Williams the try scorers, Morgan converted 1) and at home to Ystalyfera.

The Ferry XV played the Cimla in November, while the Quins lost 0–18 in Bryncoch. Two Quins, D. Dugmore and John Selby, then made their debut for the First XV in a 0–0 home draw with Llandaff.

December started well for the club with a 21–6 home win over Swansea Uplands. Newton got a hat trick and D.S. Thomas, D. Poley, G. Matthews and Bryan Hire all added tries –none were converted! The half-backs that day were Bird and Pugh of the Quins. There was also an away win at Ystalyfera, and a 6–6 home draw with Skewen on Boxing Day, in which both Charlie Hanford and Gordon

Captain
Roy Evans

Vice captain
Bryan Hire

Playing record
P 46
W 24
D 6
L 16
Points for 377
Points against 324

Scores
Tries 89
Conversions 30
Drop goals 3
Penalties 17

Matthews scored 1 try. The following day Ferry played a home friendly with Llangennech and beat them 5–3 – Matthews was the try scorer again and Morgan converted. This match turned a little nasty towards the end and three players were sent off the field, two from the Ferry.

January was a wet month and 18 tonnes of sand had to be spread on the pitch before a match against Resolven, which Ferry lost 6–11 – Arthur Williams and hooker Charlie Teale were the try scorers.

E. Selby, A.N. Other, G. Pugh, W.S. Davies(Sec) B. aHira(V.Capt) B. Donovan, E. Jones, A. O'Shea, D.J. Foley, V. Davies, Doug James, E. Adams, A. Williams, C. Thomas J. Sparkes. SEATED, H. Watkins, G. Matthews, Roy Evans(Capt) M. Kerr, R Trimnell, FRONT. B. Nicholls, T. Dowrick, D. Newton, G. Morgan, C. Hanford.

7.23 1958/59

In February, the First XV defeated Cwmavon 5–3 – Dai Newton with a try, converted by Hanford. The half-backs for this game were promoted from the Quins XV and both Terry Dowrick and Granville Pugh did really well, along with fellow Quins players Albert Williams and Max Kerr. The Ferry XV also drew 11–11 at home to Ammanford. Roy Evans was the try scorer and Morgan kicked 2 penalties and 1 conversion.

The season was ended in April with an excellent win at home over Kidwelly, 21–11. Both Dowrick and Kerr from the Quins were on the score sheet with a try apiece, Newton added another. Hanford scored the last try after making three conversions and a penalty. The Quins beat Dunvant at home, 17–14.

Quins

The Quins played Trebanos in early December and then lost away to Crynant, 6–8. They'd also reached the semi-final of the Neath & District cup and were to play either Bryncoch or Seven Sisters.

In January they played Maesteg CYMS, Gowerton, Abercrave, Nantyfyllon and Cwmlynfell, and, in February, Banwen and Gurnos Aces (won 6–0)

Into March and the Quins' playing record in the league (played 11, won 7, drew 2, lost 2) got them to the semi-final play-offs for both the Neath & District Supporters' Club Cup and the Neath & District Cup. Both were played in Skewen, but Quins lost 0–3 to Bryncoch in the Cup and then lost to Tonna in the Supporters' Cup. Banwen were to meet Bryncoch in the Cup final and Tonna in the Supporters' Cup final. Controversially, Neath RFC cancelled the Supporters Cup final, which was held over until the following season.

Tour

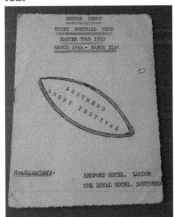

TEAM

Full-back — Ron Trimnel

Threequarters — Dai Newton, Charlie Bamford, Roy Evans (Captain), Gwyn Morgan, Gordon Matthews

Half-backs — Ray Woodward, Terry Dowrick, Granville Pugh

Forwards — Hugh Watkins, Doug James, John Scannel, Clive Thomas, Clive Cooper, Brian Hire (Vice Captain), Ernie Jones, Brian Donovan, Arthur Williams, D.J. Poley, Max Kear

Trainer — C. Beasley

7.24 Easter Tour 1959

The Easter tour was to the Southend Rugby Festival at the end of March. On the way they stopped in Cheltenham for lunch at the Belle View Hotel and then stayed in London. They played Gidea Park on Good Friday and won 19–8. They then moved to Southend, where they dined at the Royal Hotel and on Saturday played Old West Cliffians, and lost 0–9. After a free day on Sunday they played Leicestershire Lions on Easter Monday, beating them 27–3. They left Southend on Tuesday, lunching in Cheltenham again on the journey home.

The tour party consisted of committeemen Morgan Jones, Edward Selby, W.L. Williams, Ewart Adams and W.S Davies, and trainer Cyril Beasley. The playing squad were Ron Trimnell, Dai Newton, Charlie Hanford, Roy Evans (captain), Gwyn Morgan, Gordon Matthews, Ray Woodward, Terry Dowrick,

Granville Pugh, Hugh Watkins, Doug James, Barrie Nicholas, Clive Thomas, Clive Cooper, Bryan Hire (vice captain) Ernie Jones, Brian Donovan, Arthur Williams, Dai Poley and Max Kier.

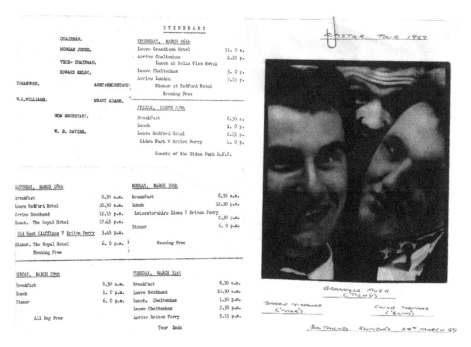

7.25 Itinerary Easter Tour 1959 with Granville Pugh (Tichy), Barrie Nicholas (Nick) and Clive Thomas (Slim)

AGM

The fifty-eighth AGM was again held in the Grandison Hotel during July – again chaired by Morgan Jones in the absence of Mr Ossie Davies. The club reported a small loss of £23 19s 6d, although a lot of good work was going on within the club. Apart from making a substantial donation to the general fund the Supporters' Club had raised £856 12s 3d – the cost of building a new boundary wall and playing field fence. Gate receipts were £117 13s 3d. Quins' expenses had accounted for £115 3s 11d, but they had supplied valuable aid to the senior side and, as Sam John pointed out, the club were lucky to have them..

Percy George (with 30 years of service) and Jack Thomas were elected life members. All the officers were re-elected, with a committee of Vernon Davies, Llew Llewelyn, Ron Edwards, Jack Thomas, Albert O'Shea and Phil Griffiths. Mr Edwin Selby presented wedding gifts to Terry Woodland and Max Kerr, and the chairman handed over a gift to Mr Selby's son John. Thanks were accorded to Cyril Beasley, Morgan Powell and Mr and Mrs Morris of the Grandison for services rendered.

Top try scorer was Dai Newton again (with 22) and with 66 points he was also top scorer, followed by Charlie Hanford and Gwyn Morgan, both with 52 points.

In the district

In November, the Ferry was represented in the Neath & District XV for game against Pembrokeshire by M. Bird at centre, T. Dowrich at 10, G. Pugh at 9 and second row J. Price.

7.26 Clive Stuart, Graham Jones and David Joseph

1959/60

Captain
Roy Evans

Vice captain
Bryan Hire

Playing record
P 41
W 24
D 5
L 12
Points for 336
Points against 235

Scores
Tries 76
Conversions 24
Drop goals 3
Penalties 17

With Evans and Hire still at the helm the club ventured into the new season with great hope, but they had a tough start with an away game at Neath, which they lost 5–24. Flanker Dennis Hare was the opening try scorer and fullback Les Doughty's conversion had given them a 5–0 lead seconds after kick-off. Half-backs Dowrick (at 9) and Bernard Hill (at 10) had an excellent game, along with flankers Hare and Brian Donovan.

Two days later they began a run of three home games. First against Cwmavon, then two days after that with Risca and, to end the month, they defeated Kidwelly 6–3, with tries from Max Kerr and Bryan Hire.

October began with a tough tie in the West Wales Cup, away to the holders Ammanford. The Ferry XV were defeated 0–11. But they beat Llandeilo 15–3 away in the next game. Hire was on the score sheet again, along with D. Poley and Ron Matthews, Algie Baker converted all three. A 3–3 draw at home with Glais followed – Matthews a try scorer again. Then defeats at Resolven, 0–6, and at home to Pontyberem, 3–18 (only 1 Algie Baker penalty).

The First XV had away fixtures against Amman United and Ystradgynlais and home games with Penclawydd (won 6–0, John Simonson and Matthews tries, hooker Dai Williams played well), and New Dock Stars (won 11–6, Simonson and Brian Donovan tries, Baker penalty and conversion).

December brought away fixtures at Kidwelly and Glais and home games with Llandeilo, Kenfig Hill and Cwmavon (unfortunately, bad weather on Christmas Day caused the cancellation of this game).

Match results place BFRFC scores first

The First XV started the new year with a home revenge 9–3 win over Resolven. Charlie Hanford scored 2 tries, one of them from 75 yards out, Baker added a penalty. Forward Barry Nicholls played well, alongside Matthews and Hire. After three away games, at Pontyberem, Felinfoel and Gowerton, the month ended with yet another away game, at Blaengarw (won, with tries from Ken Smith, Haydn Walters and Donovan). This game replaced an original match with Swansea Athletic that had been cancelled due to a mix up in the fixture list.

In February, the club played home games with Amman United and Ystradgynlais and away fixtures at Penclawydd and RAF St. Athan.

> The Council were making plans for the Briton Ferry Welfare Ground. They wanted to incorporate a new football pitch and pavilion for the Ferry Athletic and a new full-size rugby pitch alongside the cricket ground and a new clubhouse (which the cricket club had already requested). Boundary fences would be provided so the pitches could be leased separately by each club. The cost of the scheme would be approximately £2,800.

The March fixtures were home games with Felinfoel (won 8–3, C. Hanford try and conversion, John Simonson try) and RAF St Athan, and away fixtures at Carmarthen, Kenfig Hill and Penygraig.

The final month of the season started with a 24–6 home win over Llandaff. Matthews notched a double, Ernie Jones, Arthur Williams and Roy Evans added further tries and Hanford kicked 3 conversions and 1 penalty. Then two away fixtures at Pontardawe and Tenby before the return home fixture with Penygraig.They completed their fixtures with a home game against Carmarthen and an away game at Llandaff.

The club finished thirteenth in the Welsh Wales Rugby Union table.

Quins

The Quins played SCOW, Gowerton and Cimla (won 39–0) in September.

In October the Quins defeated Scow at home, 24–0, and then played Trebanos. In November they defeated Brynamman 9–3 and played Abercrave. In December they lost at home to Bonymaen, 3–8, and played Glynneath away. They also lost to Bryncoch in Skewen in the semi-final of the Neath RFC Supporters' Club Cup. Bryncoch eventually retained the cup.

They were also lying third in the league having played 11, won 6, drawn 2 and only losing 3. They also defeated Nantyfyllon 6–3.

AGM

During this year's AGM in July at the Grandison Hotel, Mr W.L. Williams (treasurer) stated that televised sport was the Goliath in every home as it was ruining local support for the various clubs. This comment followed from the accounts showing a drop in gate receipts, coinciding with a drop in the vice president's list and in the membership in general, while expenditure for the year was £975 4s 1d, but the club still showed a profit of £30 11s 6d. Income other than gate money had to be found to help with the running of the club.

Morgan Jones presided again in the absence of the club president, and club secretary Mr W.S. Davies gave the club record for the season. Top scorer was Algie Baker, with John Simonson and Gordon Matthews in second place. Mr Davies said the club's table position could have been improved on if some of the players had not "fallen off" during the season. Morgan Jones replied that it had been one of the best seasons for a while and that if more goals had been kicked they could well have been in line for honours. He stated that another successful tour had been enjoyed by all. He also expressed his disappointment with those players who had not turned up during the season – indeed, only two playing members had paid their annual membership fees of half a crown, and that "as they are here to play the game if they cannot pay their subs then they should all call it a day." He also mentioned that training turnouts were very poor and one week just a solitary player had turned up. He went on to thank the official supporters and the press.

Vice chairman Edwin Selby then presented clocks to the players married that year – John Nash, Dai Williams, Dudley Mills and Clive Cooper.

The president, chairman, vice chairman, secretary, assistant secretary, treasurer and auditors were re-elected. Committee members elected were Avon Roberts, Emlyn Richards, Mervyn Thomas, Sam John, Eddie Clements and George Brown. Mr W.S. Jones was then thanked for his service over the past couple of years and Vernon Davies was elected to replace Ron Edwards, who had asked to stand down and was thanked for his service. The new captain was announced as Bryan Hire, with Algie Baker as his deputy. Mr Les Morgan then gave notice that he would move a motion at the next AGM that nomination papers for the committee should be sent through the post to each member.

Easter tour to Ireland

BRITON. FERRY.
RUGBY. FOOTBALL. CLUB.

IRELAND.

EASTER.TOUR.   1960.

HOTEL C?

THE GR?

PRESIDENT.
O.L.DAVIES.

CHAIRMAN.
MORGAN JONES.

TREASURER.
W.L.WILLIAMS.

VICE-CHAIRMAN.
ED. SELEY.

SECRETARY.
W.S.DAVIES.

ASST. SECRETARY.
EWART ADAMS.

Committee.
Avon Roberts.
Evlyn Richards.
Llew Llewellyn.
T R V Davies.
Sam John.
Jack Thomas.
Ron Edwards.
Mervyn Thomas
W.S.Jones.
Albert O'Shea.

P L A Y E R S.

Full Back.
Algi Baker.

Three Quarters.
Lawrence Morgan.
Haydn Walters.
Roy Evans. (Capt)
John Simonson.
Charlie Hanford.
Ken Smith.

Half Backs.
Terry Dowrick.
Granville Pugh.

Forwards.
Hugh Watkins.
Douglas James.
Terry Woodland.
Gareth Burns.
Brian Hire. (Vice-Capt)
Brian Donovan.
Gorden Mathews.
Ernie Jones.
Max Keer.
D.J.Foley.

Trainer.
Cyril Beasley.

Monday. April 18th.

Breakfast.	8.30.a.m.
Lunch.	12.0. m.d.
Match. Kick off.	3.0. p.m.

THURLES. V. BRITON FERRY.

Guests of the Thurles Rugby Club.

DINNER.

Tuesday.April 19th.

Breakfast.	8.30.a.m.
Lunch.	12.30.a.m.
Depart Nenagh.	4.55.p.m.
Arrive Dublin.	6.5. p.m.
Dinner.	6.30.p.m.

Wednesday. April 20th.

Breakfast.	8.30.a.m
Lunch.	12.0. m.d.
High Tea.	4.15.p.m.
Special Coach from Grovenor Hotel to Airport.	
Leave Dublin Airport.	5.55.p.m.
Arrive Rhoose.	7.45.p.m.
Arrive Home.	approx. 9.15.p.m.

Please be on time at all points

7.27 Easter Tour to Ireland 1960: players and committee, programme cover, list of players and itinerary

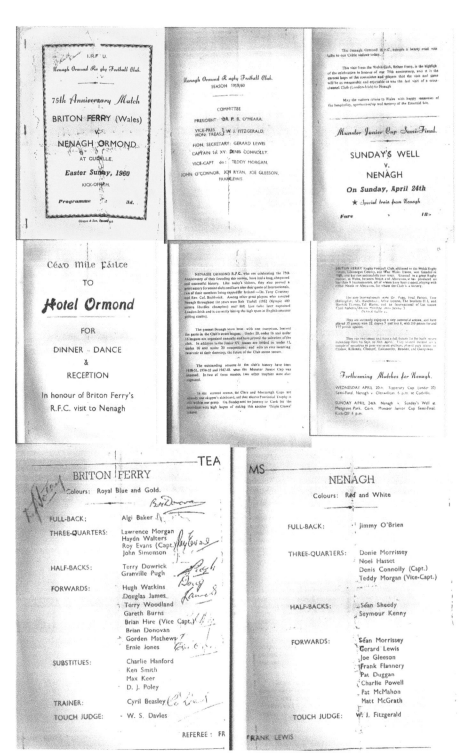

I.R.F.U.

Nenagh Ormond Rugby Football Club.

75th Anniversary Match

BRITON FERRY (Wales)
v.
NENAGH ORMOND

AT CUDVILLE

Easter Sunday, 1960

KICK-OFF P.M.

Programme   3d.

Gleeson & Son, Nenagh

Nenagh Ormond Rugby Football Club.
SEASON 1959/60

COMMITTEE

PRESIDENT: DR. P. B. O'MEARA.

VICE-PRES.
HON. TREAS. J. W. J. FITZGERALD.

HON. SECRETARY: GERARD LEWIS

CAPTAIN 1st XV.: DENIS CONNOLLY.

VICE-CAPT. do.: TEDDY MORGAN.

JOHN O'CONNOR, JOE RYAN, JOE GLEESON,
FRANK LEWIS

The Nenagh Ormond R.F.C. extends a hearty céad míle fáilte to our Celtic visitors today.

This visit from the Welsh Club, Briton Ferry, is the highlight of the celebrations in honour of our 75th anniversary, and it is the earnest hope of the committee and players that the visit and game will be as memorable and enjoyable as was the last visit of a cross-channel Club (London-Irish) to Nenagh.

May the visitors return to Wales with happy memories of the hospitality, sportsmanship and scenery of the Emerald Isle.

Munster Junior Cup Semi-Final.

SUNDAY'S WELL
v.
NENAGH

On Sunday, April 24th

★ Special train from Nenagh

Fare   1/8-

Céad Míle Fáilte

TO

Hotel Ormond

FOR

DINNER · DANCE
&
RECEPTION

In honour of Briton Ferry's
R.F.C. visit to Nenagh

NENAGH ORMOND R.F.C., who are celebrating the 75th Anniversary of their founding this season, have had a long, chequered and successful history. Like today's visitors, they also proved a great nursery for senior clubs and have also their quota of Internationals, two of their members being capped for Ireland —Dr. Tony Courtney and Rev. Col. Bushwick. Among other great players who assisted Nenagh throughout the years were Bob Tisdall (1932 Olympic 400 metres Hurdles champion) and Biff Lyne (who later captained London-Irish and is currently hitting the high spots in English amateur golfing circles).

The present Nenagh team have, with one exception, learned the game in the Club's street leagues. Under 20, under 16 and under 14 leagues are organised annually and have proved the salvation of the club. In addition to the Junior XV, teams are fielded in under 15, under 16 and under 20 competitions, and with an ever recurring reservoir at their doorstep, the future of the Club seems secure.

The outstanding seasons in this club's history have been 1930-31, 1934-35 and 1947-48, when the Munster Junior Cup was annexed. In two of these seasons, two other trophies were also organised.

In the current season, the Clare and Murroe Cups are already our skipper's sideboard, and that shows Provincial Trophy is well within our grasp. On Sunday next we journey to Cork for the semi-final with high hopes of making this another 'Triple Crown' season.

BRITON FERRY Rugby Football Club, affiliated to the Welsh Rugby Union, Glamorgan County, and West Wales Union, was founded in 1880, and has run successfully ever since. Situated in a great Rugby district, in Wales, between Neath and Aberavon, it has produced no less than 9 Internationals, all of whom have been capped, playing with either Neath or Aberavon, for whom the Club is a nursery.

The nine Internationals were Dr. Perry, Fred Perrett, Tom Hollingdale, Wm. Hutchings, Arthur Lemon, the brothers D. L. and Harold Thomas, Ted Harris, and an International of East season Cyril Baptists (brown Hooray (now Swansea).

They are currently enjoying a very successful season, and have played 35 games, won 22, drawn 5 and lost 8, with 519 points for and 177 points against.

They ran two senior and have a full fixture list for both teams extending from 1st Sept. to 30th April. They expect (visited) as a couple of occasions at present two years and have played such teams as Chelow, Kilkenny, Clontarf, Enniscorthy, Bandon, and Garrymen.

Forthcoming Matches for Nenagh.

WEDNESDAY APRIL 20th. Tipperary Cup (under 20)
Semi-Final. Nenagh v. Clanwilliam. 5 p.m. at Cudville.

SUNDAY APRIL 24th. Nenagh v. Sunday's Well at Musgrave Park, Cork. Munster Junior Cup Semi-Final.
Kick-Off 4 p.m.

TEA—————————MS

BRITON FERRY

Colours: Royal Blue and Gold.

FULL-BACK: Algi Baker

THREE-QUARTERS: Lawrence Morgan
                  Haydn Walters
                  Roy Evans (Capt.)
                  John Simonson

HALF-BACKS: Terry Dowrick
                  Granville Pugh

FORWARDS: Hugh Watkins
                  Douglas James
                  Terry Woodland
                  Gareth Burns
                  Brian Hire (Vice Capt.)
                  Brian Donovan
                  Gorden Mathews
                  Ernie Jones

SUBSTITUES: Charlie Hanford
                  Ken Smith
                  Max Keer
                  D. J. Poley

TRAINER: Cyril Beasley

TOUCH JUDGE: W. S. Davies

REFEREE : FRANK LEWIS

NENAGH

Colours: Red and White

FULL-BACK: Jimmy O'Brien

THREE-QUARTERS: Donie Morrissey
                  Noel Hassct
                  Denis Connolly (Capt.)
                  Teddy Morgan (Vice-Capt.)

HALF-BACKS: Seán Sheedy
                  Seymour Kenny

FORWARDS: Seán Morrissey
                  Gerard Lewis
                  Joe Gleeson
                  Frank Flannery
                  Pat Duggan
                  Charlie Powell
                  Pat McMahon
                  Matt McGrath

TOUCH JUDGE: W. J. Fitzgerald

7.28 Programme 75th Anniversary Match v. Nenagh Ormond – Easter 1960

PART 8: 1960–1970

Highlights of the decade

- BFRFC were semi-finalists five times in the Welsh Wales Rugby Union Cup
- The Ferry reached the top four play-off's on three occasions
- The club opted out of the WWRU twice, 1955 and 1967

Season 1960-1961

Lllewellyn. E. Clements. A. O'Shea H. Walters. C. Hanford. G. Pugh. A. Baker. J. Simonson.
R. Carr. T. Dowrick. C. Beasley(Trainer) M. Jones(Chairman). W.S. Davies(Sec).
B. Donovan. D. J. Poley. D. Jones. B. Hire(Capt) E. Jones. H. Watkins. E. C. Jones.

8.1 1960/61

1960/61

The season started with a 14–9 home win over Cwmavon (C. Hanford and H. Watkins tries, Ernie Jones 2 penalties and 1 conversion). Hooker Doug James and Granville Pugh were to the fore.

This was followed by fixtures against Carmarthen at home (won 23–3, Ken Smith, C. Hanford, Dennis Hare and Doug Jones were the try scorers, Ernie Jones added a penalty and 3 conversions and Algie Baker 1 conversion) and Ystalyfera away (won 45–0, try scorers were Bryan Hire with a hat trick, C. Hanford and John Simonson with a brace each, and 1 each from Doug Jones, Terry Dowrick, Ray Carr and Dudley Mills; conversions added by Ernie Jones (5) and Hanford).

October also started with a bang as Ferry defeated Llandeilo at home in the first round of the West Wales Cup by 8–3. Ernie Jones kicked a penalty, John Simonson added a try and Graham Michael a conversion. It was looking like the Wednesday evening circuit training with Norman Biggs was paying off! Gowerton at home ended in a 3–3 draw (1 Charlie Hanford try), followed by away games at Burry Port, RAF St. Athan and Vardre and a home fixture with Skewen (another 3–3 draw, a Gordon Matthews).

So, into November and still unbeaten. Their first test was against Crynant at home, which Ferry won 14–8. Hanford, Brian Donovan (2) and Haydn Walters were the try scorers and Baker added a conversion, In round two of the West Wales Cup they were at home to Llangennech and triumphed again, 5–3. It was a tight game and Ken Smith got the try, which Baker converted. Trebanos

Captain
Bryan Hire

Vice captain
Algie Baker

Playing record
P 41
W 24
D 5
L 12
Points for 336
Points against 235

Scores
Tries 76
Conversions 24
Drop goals 3
Penalties 17

were the next visitors and they went home empty-handed as the Ferry once again produced the goods to win 9–0. Doug James and Emrys Jones made tries and Baker added the extra points. Ferry ended the month with a trip to Carmarthen.

> A local paper noted that the success of the team thus far this season was down to their brand of attractive open rugby and to the formation of a youth team five years previously, which was now paying dividends.

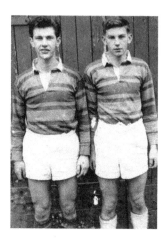

8.2 A young Emrys Jones and Allan Hopkins

December away games were at Felinfoel, Gowerton and Cwmavon, with home fixtures against Ystalyfera (won 24–0, tries from Simonson (3), Walters, Pugh and Carr, 2 conversions from Baker and 1 from Hanford), Burry Port (won 8–3, Simonson and Roy Evans with tries and Baker converted 1) and Felinfoel.

> This year also saw the passing of **NED SELBY**, former Ferry player, club vice chairman and life member. He'd been capped by Glamorgan and been a WRU referee. He had also played for the famous Albert Freethy's XV and a few games for Maesteg. His son John went on to become a committeeman with the club and his son Clive became a well known and respected local GP.

In the new year Cyril Roberts returned from Neath, unfortunately to a first defeat at Skewen. Then a trip to Amman United before playing Vardre at home, and winning 14–0. Tries from Hanford, James and Roberts (his first back at the club), with Baker adding the extras.

February started with away games at Kenfig Hill, Crynant and Trebanos and a home game with Loughor (won 13–0, Simonson (2) and Hire with tries and Baker converting 2). Then the quarter-final of the West Wales Cup against

Match results place BFRFC scores first

Ystradgynlais, which Ferry won 6–0 with tries from Hughie Watkins and Charlie Hanford.

Into March and home games with RAF St. Athan and Llandaff (won 8–5, Hanford 1 try, Baker 1 penalty and 1 conversion) before meeting a powerful Cefneithin side, inspired by a certain Carwyn James at outside-half, at St. Helens in the semi-final of the West Wales Cup. Ferry lost 3–17. A home game with Amman United followed before more quarter-final action, in the Glamorgan Silver Ball competition. But Ferry came up short and lost to Bargoed (who eventually lost to Glynneath in the final). They ended the month with a home game against Loughor and an away fixture at Pontardawe.

> Neath Council's tender for the works on the Briton Ferry Welfare Sports Ground at a cost of £8,129 17s 3d were approved in April (in the previous year the cost was quoted as £2,800). Work to lay out a rugby pitch and a football pitch would proceed as soon as possible.

The season closed with fixtures at home to Kenfig Hill, Risca and Pontardawe and away at Llandaff and Felinfoel. Ferry were also involved in a West Wales Championship semi-final play-off game at the Gnoll against Seven Sisters, which they lost and ended third in the league. So the club had played in five semi-finals and lost them all – First XV three, Quins two.

8.3 1960/61 Cup Final

Quins

The Quins drew 8–8 at BP Llandarcy in a Neath & District Cup match, then lost at the Cimla by 3–8 (young Emrys Jones bagged a try). They got their revenge by beating them 6–0 in the return match with a Howard Burt try and a Baker penalty.

Tour

The Easter tour this year was a visit to old friends at Nenagh in Ireland, and the accompanying Figures (8.3–8.6) show the close relationship between the two clubs..

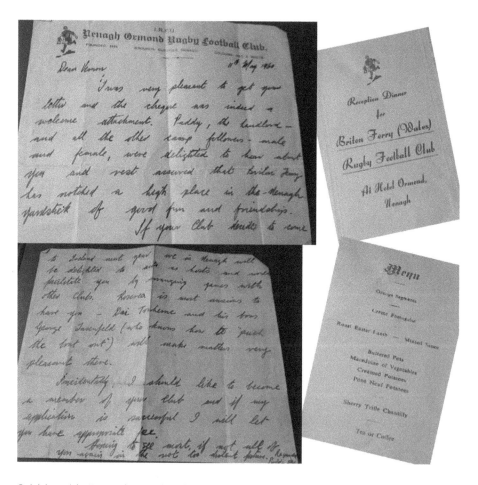

8.4 (above) Letter and reception dinner menu; (opposite) Programme for Easter Tour 1961

Match results place BFRFC scores first

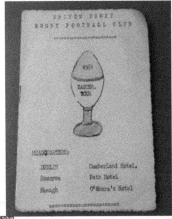

PRESIDENT

O. L. DAVIES.

CHAIRMAN	VICE CHAIRMAN
Morgan Jones	Avon Roberts
HON. SECRETARY	ASSIT.SECRETARY
W.S. Davies	Ewart Adams

HON. TREASURER

W.L. Williams

COMMITTEE:
Vernon Davies
Llew Llewellyn
Enlyn Richards
Jack Thomas
Mervyn Thomas
Sam John
Albert O'Shea
Ron Edwards
Phil. Griffiths
George Brown
Ed. Clements

***

I T I N E R A R Y

SATURDAY 1ST APRIL

Leave Grandison Hotel	9. 0.a.m.
(Private Coach)	
Arrive Rhoose Airport	10.15.a.m.
Depart Rhoose Airport	11. 0.a.m.
Arrive Dublin	12.30.p.m.
Private Coach to	
Kingsbridge Railway Station	
Deposit all Baggage	
Lunch Cumberland Hotel	1.45.p.m.
Depart Kingsbridge Station	5.30.p.m.
Arrive Roscrea	7.30.p.m.
Dinner	7.45.p.m.

SUNDAY 2ND APRIL

Breakfast	8.30.a.m.
Lunch	12.30.p.m.
RUGBY MATCH	3.30.p.m.
ROSCREA v BRITON FERRY	
Dinner – Guests of The Roscrea Rugby Football Club	

***

MONDAY 3RD APRIL

Breakfast	8.30.a.m.
Leave Roscrea	12. 0.m.d.
Arrive Nenagh	12.23.p.m.
Lunch	1. 0.p.m.
RUGBY MATCH	3.30.p.m.
NENAGH v BRITON FERRY	
Dinner Dance – Guests of the Nenagh R.F.C.	

TUESDAY 4TH APRIL

Breakfast	8.30.a.m.
Lunch	12.30.p.m.
Dinner	6. 0.p.m.
ALL DAY FREE	

WEDNESDAY 5TH APRIL

Breakfast	8. 0.a.m.
Leave Nenagh	8.50.a.m.
Arrive Dublin	11.30.a.m.
Lunch	1.15.p.m.
Leave Kingsbridge Station	4.15.p.m.
Members make their own arrangements to Station	
Leave Dublin Airport	5.55.p.m.
Arrive Rhoose Airport	7.45.p.m.
Arrive Grandison Hotel	9.15.p.m.

PLAYERS

FULL BACK	Algi Baker (Vice Captain)
THREEQUARTERS	Colin Gregory
	John Simonson
	Charlie Hanford
	Clive Stewart
	Ray Carr
HALF BACKS	Roy Evans
	Les Doughty
FORWARDS	Hugh Watkins
	Douglas Jones
	Terry Woodlands
	Bryan Hire (Captain)
	D.J. Poley
	Brian Donovan
	Ernie Jones
	E.C. Jones
TRAINER	Cyril Beasley

8.5 On tour 1961

These stories from Irish tours also show the close relationship:

- Bill Brennan in a shop in Waterford, looking at the assortment of cigarettes, which were unobtainable at home, and asking the girl behind the counter, "Have you any Pasha?"

- the stunned silence as Peter Hoare sung, "The Yeomen of England" at an Irish Easter party

- the whole tour party on stage at Courtown Harbour singing "Music Man"

- and Howie Thomas lecturing a big audience on the art of hooking

1961/62

In September, three games in five days ended with a 6–18 home defeat to Pontardulais (Gordon Jenkins 1 try, John Harris 1 penalty). Llew Llewelyn had to play in this game. Then another home defeat, 3–11 to Felinfoel (skipper Hire on the score sheet with 1 try).

The Welsh Wales Rugby Union Cup started in October and in the first round Ferry were drawn at home against Vardre (ended 0–0). Then an away fixture at Aberavon Green Stars, before a defeat at home to Llandybie (3–13, Graham Jones with a try).

In November they suffered yet again with a lack of player commitment and lost 0–11at home to Cwmlynfell. This culminated in a December defeat at home by the same margin to Llangennech, who had to lend Ferry two players as they only had thirteen of their own! Allegedly, this led to some of the committee going elsewhere to watch a game.

The game against Taibach on Boxing Day was cancelled so an inert club game was played between the First XV and the Quins.

In the new year, the First XV struggled once again and a 0–0 draw at home with Abercrave and a 12–20 home defeat to Tumble in February, was a poor return.

The local press stated that the indifference of the players in failing to turn up after they were selected was very strange, as the club was financially more secure than in the past. Club spirit and loyalty were both lacking and running a second string as a feeder for the senior side appeared to be working against them.

Captain
Bryan Hire

First XV playing record
P 32
W 5
D 8
L 19

Quins playing record
P 25
W 14
D 4
L 7

Then, in March, sickness created eight absentees from the team. The Quins game against Banwen had to be cancelled so that the players could move up into the First XV to play against Ystradgynlais at home (but they lost 6–16, Dudley Mills with 1 try and Charlie Hanford kicked a penalty).

More upset occurred in April. A game at home to Risca had to be cancelled due to an outbreak of smallpox so a hastily arranged game between the First XV and the Quins was organised.

> During the game someone broke into the dressing rooms at the Grandison and stole wallets, rings, money, watches (including one worth £30) and even premium bonds! As club secretary Mr Bill Davies said, they'd used the same dressing rooms for the last thirty-five years and this was the first time anything had been taken. It seemed that the thief was already hiding inside the building and after the teams left for the game he filled up a duffle bag and broke out.

Season 1961–1962

H. Watkins. B. Hill. A. Hopkins. G. Thomas. A.Gleaves. B. Hire. E. Jones. H.Walters. G. Jones. D.Mills. L. Llewellyn. T.Woodlands. Roy Evans. G. Jenkins.(captain). G.Pugh. A. Thomas. A.Jefford.

8.6 1961/62

The Ferry finished thirtieth in the league.

Quins

In the first half of the season, the Quins lost to the Cimla twice, 0–11 away and 0–6 at home in the cup. They also lost 8–16 at Pontrhydyfen (L. Doughty 1 conversion and 1 penalty, D. Thomas 1 try). The Quins also had only thirteen

Match results place BFRFC scores first

men, and had to borrow two from the opposition. D. Poley, G. Burns, R. Barton, G. Stuart and M. Price played well. In the new year they drew 8–8 at home with Pontrhydyfen (Algie Baker converted 1 of the 2 tries scored).

AGM

The AGM in June was very volatile as the loyalty of both players and committeemen were called into question. Receipts showed a slight loss and gate takings totalled £32 0s 6d. Records show that a postal ballot for the committee would cease. Added to the committee that year were Mervyn Thomas, Avon Roberts, Sam John, John Selby, Hughie Watkins and Ted Clements.

Gordon Jenkins was to be club captain, with Granville Pugh as his vice.

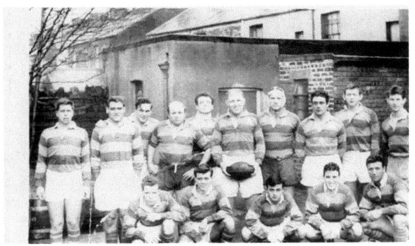

Briton Ferry RFC 1961-62– Behind the Grandison Hotel changing rooms

Standing– Ray Carr, Doug Jones, Charlie Hanford, Hughie Watkins, Doug James, Brian Hire (Capt) , Dai Poley, Algie Baker , Brian Donovan, Emrys Jones

Kneeling– Haydn Walters, Ken Smith, Granville Pugh, Roy Evans, Ernie Jones

8.7 1961/62

The move

In 1962 the local authority suggested to the club that they move from the Old Road ground to a piece of land behind the Briton Ferry Town cricket pavilion – the council needed the Old Road field for an extension to the local hospital. After several meetings, the rugby club agreed to move and built the present clubhouse in partnership with the cricket club.

8.8 Borough Engineer's letter

In the district

In April two future Ferry players were representing a Neath YMCA team in the Welsh Association of Youth Club's sevens tournament at Stradey Park (they reached the semi-finals). Both David Parker and Brian Evans were to give long service to the club.

Seven Sisters won the Neath & District Cup.

The *South Wales Echo* did a focus article on the Ferry in 1961 (see Figure 8.9), which also featured a caricature compilation of the Ferry committee.

Match results place BFRFC scores first

8.9 *South Wales Echo* caricature compilation

1962/63 – 75TH

Captain
Gordon Jenkins

Vice captain
Granville Pugh

Playing record
P 36
W 23
D 2
L 11
Points for 263

Scores
Tries 54
Conversions 31
Drop goals 0
Penalties 13

The seventy-fifth anniversary season started with a fixture against Kenfig Hill at home (lost 6–14, Haydn Walters and Mike Price touching down). Frankie Thomas and Barry Nicholas played well. Then an 11–0 home win against Cefneithin (Hanford bagged 1 try and 1 penalty, Bernard Hill added 1 try converted by Terry Woodland. Then a 6–6 draw at home with Cwmavon (Doug Jones 1 try and Terry Woodland 1 penalty) and a trip to Hendy.

In October, Ferry visited Kidwelly in the West Wales Cup, and made trips to Ammanford and Morriston, with a home game in between against Brynamman, which Ferry lost 6–12 (Haydn Walters bagged both tries).

November was the time for return trips to Cwmavon (won 3–0, Granville Pugh 1 try) and Cefneithin and home fixtures with New Dock Stars (won 10–8, Hanford 1 try and 2 conversions, Mike Price 1 try) and Seven Sisters (won 9–8, Allan Hopkins and Mike Price bagging tries and Hanford kicking 1 penalty).

December was a very busy month with home fixtures against Hendy (drew 0–0), Ammanford (won 3–0, Granville Pugh, Barrie Nicholas and Alan Jefford played well) and Porthcawl; and away matches at Pontardulais, Brynamman (won 5–0, Terry Woodland bagged all 5 points), Taibach and Kenfig Hill.

The new year kicked off with atrocious weather and the first five Saturday games were all postponed. The first match happened on 16 February at home to Aberaman. Tries from Granville Pugh and Roy Evans and a penalty goal from D.L. Thomas gave Ferry a 9–5 win. Four further games at home followed, against Swansea Uplands,

Cwmavon (won 14–3, tries from Allan Hopkins, G. Pugh and H. Walters and a conversion from Terry Woodland; the visitors turned up two players short so Gwynfryn Thomas and Bryan Hire played for them). Then a rearranged game with Morriston (won 6–3, G. Jenkins and Pugh tries) and one against Llandaff (won 3–0), before visiting Porthcawl and Llandaff. Another run of four homes games followed: Taibach (lost 0–8, Billy Fleming of the Quins stood in at scrum-half for Roy Evans); Aberavon (lost 0–26), Amman United and Pontardawe.

The Ferry completed the season with home games against Porthcawl and Crumlin and away games at Cwmavon and Amman United.

Ferry had climbed back up to fourth in the league and again reached the play-offs. Once again the club had reached the semi-final of the Welsh Wales Rugby Union Cup.

Tour

The Easter tour returned to the Isle of Man Sevens and a full fixture against Douglas RFC.

Quins

The Quins had had a full fixture list up to this point with home games against Nantyfyllon, Bridgend Sports, Hirwaun Welfare, Mumbles, Taffs Well, Brynamman, Metal Box and Dunvant; and away trips at Gowerton, Ystalyfera, Crynant, Taffs Well, Brynamman, Dunvant, Hirwaun Welfare, Maesteg CYMS and Heol-Y-Cyw. Fixtures booked for the new year were at home to Bonymaen, Ystalyfera, Cimla, Nantyfyllon, and Crynant and trips to Maesteg CYMS, Ystradgynlais, Heol-Y-Cyw, 3M's Gorseinon, Bridgend Sports, Abercrave, Metal Box, Bonymaen, Mumbles and Cimla.

The Quins ended the year with a disappointing two home defeats, both 3–8, against Metal Box and Baglan Youth. Flanker A. Davies got a try against the Box and J. Bond a drop goal against Baglan. Ronnie Breach, Terry Ellis and L. Ayres were prominent during these games.

AGM

The AGM was held in the Grandison Hotel for the last time and Mr and Mrs Idwal Morris were thanked for their support over the years. Thanks were also given to helpers L. Beasley, Dai Evans and Tom Kennedy, and to the local press for their past coverage – and hopes were expressed for future coverage!

In the absence of the president, Mr Ossie Davies, chairman Mr Morgan Jones stated that new club members were needed to keep the momentum going and that ordinary members could join for 11s per annum, or indeed could become vice presidents. The supporters' club, with the great help of Albert O'Shea, had raised £450. Gate receipts were low, at £35, while vice president's subscriptions totalled £76 12s 6d, compared to membership fees of £62 10s.

The season's weather had affected income and expenditure, due to cancelled fixtures, and secretary W.S. Davies pointed out that only 36 games had been played out of the 43 organised. Expenditure had gone on: £81 18s travelling expenses, plus; £68 11s 3d on equipment, such as boots and jerseys; laundry costs were £16; gas and coal £18; labour and dressing rooms £53; printing etc. £24; insurance £61; telephone £26. The Quins' expenses were separated out: £54 for travel; £23 for insurance; £5 10s 1d for kit; and £3 8s 6d for postage and telephone.

Costs for the new ground and preparation for next season were: £10 for the lease; £18 15s rent; £22 8s 6d for fertilisation.

This left a credit balance of £12 1s 6d.

After running through the season's playing record Mr Davies said it was unfortunate that Allan Hopkins had not joined the club sooner as, undoubtedly, he would have altered the final results, given that he was top scorer, with 48 points. Bernard Hill came next with 30 points and 10 tries, and Charlie Hanford third. The new captain for the following season was to be Terry Woodland, with Roy Evans as vice captain.

Morgan Jones praised the committee for their fine work during the season. He made special mention of treasurer Mr W.L. Williams who, for some time, had being carrying the heavy burden of a seriously ill wife in hospital and yet the accounts were still in really good order – as accredited by auditors Mr T.R. Vernon Davies and Mr Ewart Jones.

Six committeemen had been returned unopposed by postal ballot: T.R. Vernon Davies, Llew Llewelyn, Phil Griffiths, Jack Thomas, Albert O'Shea and George Brown.

Talk then turned to the new field, which Morgan Jones called "Twickenham", compared to some West Wales grounds. Mervyn Thomas' and Gordon Jenkins' hard work was appreciated. The new ground was probably going to cost the club around £18 a week to maintain, so Morgan Jones urged everyone to bring in one new member during the coming season.

Mr Les Doughty put in a notice of motion to discontinue with the postal vote, which was carried unanimously. He then presented Mr Dai Poley with a handsome pewter mug for being a great sportsman and a loyal supporter of Briton Ferry. Doughty himself was presented with a club clock in light of his marriage during the season. Charlie Hanford had only recently got married, so he would receive his at a later date.

Mr John Selby then gave a report on the Quins team. Finally, Poley, Howie Thomas and Joe Evans all promised their support for the club the following season.

1963/64

The new season was greeted with great hope and anticipation as the club looked forward to life on their new ground.

> The papers were saying that competition was high for places in the First XV, with experienced men such as Bryan Hire being kept out of the team by youngsters like Phil Chapman and Dai Leyshon Thomas. Fullback Ken Harris and centres Allan Hopkins and Bernard Hill were playing well.

The move

The club were granted a licence in February for their new premises and headquarters at Ynysymaerdy Road, which would be able to take a maximum of 160 people. This move made it an important year in the history of the club.

Captain
Terry Woodland

Vice captain
Roy Evans

Briton Ferry Rugby and Cricket Social Club

The Management Committee of the above Club, requests the pleasure of the Company of

Mr and Mrs T.R.V.Davies.

AT THE

OFFICIAL OPENING

OF THEIR

NEW CLUB-HOUSE

YNYSYMAERDY ROAD, BRITON FERRY

Wednesday, 26th February, 1964 at 4 p.m.

By

His Worship the Mayor of Neath

(Alderman Aneurin J. Rees, J.P.)

R.S.V.P. to Hon. Sec. Mr. W. L. WILLIAMS, 285, Neath Road, Briton Ferry

8.10 Invitation to official opening of the new Club House

The opening ceremony happened on 26 February 1964 and many rugby and cricket notables attended (Figure 8.13: Standing Avon Roberts, Glyn Elias, Ron Edwards,

Billy Williams, Dai Poley, Les Morgan, Hugh Watkins, W.S. Davies and Norman Jones, seated were E. H. James, Morgan Jones, Bob White and T.R.V. Davies, and behind the bar were the new stewards Dick Standing and his wife Stella). The clubhouse was officially opened by the Mayor of Neath, Alderman J. Anuerin Rees, accompanied by club trustee Mr E.H. "Tu" James and social club chairman Mr Les Morgan.

The opening speeches mentioned the hard spade work done by both Morgan Jones (interim chairman) and Glyn Elias (treasurer), and expressed gratitude to the clerk of works, Mr Vernon Davies, who had "watched every brick being laid". Mr Ron Edwards had handled the legalities and Messrs W.H. Snow and Sons of Neath had completed the building.

8.11 Attendees at official opening

Standing Avon Roberts, Glyn Elias, Ron Edwards, Billy Williams, Dai Poley, Les Morgan, Hugh Watkins, W.S. Davies and Norman Jones, seated were E. H. James, Morgan Jones, Bob White and T.R.V. Davies, and behind the bar were the new stewards Dick Standing and his wife Stella

First XV

The First XV defeated both Felinfoel (14–0, tries from Roy Evans, G. Pugh and Alan Jones, with a drop goal from Evans and a conversion from Jones, the team contained four Quins, including Jeff Squires) and Ystalyfera (20–6, tries from Doug Jones, Allan Hopkins (2), Gordon Jenkins (2) and Mike Price, Hopkins kicked a conversion and a penalty). They ended the first month with a 14–11 home win over Llangennech in a tightly fought Welsh Wales Rugby Union match. Dennis Hare, Lyn Jenkins and Mike Price made tries, Woodlands converted 1 and kicked 1 penalty.

Abercrave away were the First XV's next opponents, in a West Wales Cup match. It ended in a 0–0 draw. The replay went the Ferry's way four days later at home, 8–0, with tries from Frankie Thomas and Bryan Hire, Hopkins converted 1. In the next fixture, away at Seven Sisters, another 0–0 draw ensued. They ended October with a 12–6 home win over Aberaman. Terry Woodlands, Doug Jones, Allan Hopkins and a young Brian Evans were the try scorers. Evans caught the eyes of the older players and had a fine game, alongside Frankie Thomas.

TAL HARRIS, one of the Ferry's earlier Welsh-capped players, died in October.

November included two narrow defeats at home, 0–6 to Llandybie and 6–8 to Kidwelly. Flanker Frankie Thomas came to the fore and Brian Evans was a try scorer again. Reg Chapman kicked a penalty on his debut at second row.

The first game in December meant an exit from the West Wales Cup after the First XV were well beaten at home by Pontardulais, 6–20 (D.L. Thomas kicked 2 penalties).They ended the month, and indeed the year, with a 3–0 home win over Seven Sisters – Dudley Mills scored the decisive try.

The First XV lost their first three games in January.

A note in the *Sporting Post* stated that clubs and supporters were bemoaning the fact that nearly every home game was kicking off about fifteen minutes late. They blamed players for not showing loyalty and selectors for picking 18–22 players, so that when players did turn up they weren't selected!

Fortunes changed in February with a 3–0 away win at Llandeilo (1 try by Lyn Jenkins), then home wins over Dunvant (8–3) and Cwmlynfell (9–6, tries from Roy Evans, Lyn Jenkins and Doug Jones; Dennis Hare came in for Graham Jones) and an away win at Llandybie (18–8, Terry Woodland 2 tries, Phil Chapman 1 penalty and 3 conversions), which took away their undefeated home record! Ferry also played a friendly at home to Crumlin.

March 7 was the date of the first game played on the Ynysymaerdy ground, against Morriston. Unfortunately, the first three games ended in defeat, this one by 0–8, then 0–5 to Cwmavon and then to Aberavon (in which Allan Hopkins broke his jaw).

The Ferry's first wins at the ground soon followed and they defeated Pontardawe and then Ystrad Rhondda (3–0, P. Chapman penalty). They finished March with a 6–0 win over Skewen – when referee Harry Trew had to retire injured, his place was taken by committeeman Llew Llewelyn!

> The press was mentioning that it was a pity that Briton Ferry Athletic FC had not joined with the BFRFC and Briton Ferry Town Cricket Club in their new social club venture. It was proving a success and doubts about the £17,000 clubhouse were disappearing. The cricket club's old wooden pavilion had been built around 52 years previously, at a cost of £200, and had been demolished the previous August. The new clubhouse was a shared building and the undoubted interior showpiece are the two huge murals depicting the two sports. It was lovingly painted by that large rugby forward, Mr David Poley, and the club will be eternally grateful to him for this lasting legacy.

By mid-April the First XV had won five out of their last six games and drawn one. They beat Llandaff (13–5, J. Kellaher, G. Pugh tries, K. Parris 2 conversions), and completed a notable double over rivals Skewen. Ferry won the away midweek match, 17–6, with outstanding play from the back row of Dudley Mills, Bryan Hire and Frankie Thomas. Tries came from Thomas, Bernard Hill, wing John Roberts and centre Malcolm Beese, Phil Chapman added a conversion and Dai Leyshon Thomas kicked a penalty.

> Ex-player **ERNIE JONES** started up a new career as a travel agent and reportedly had gone to live in Spain. He'd played soccer for Neath Athletic until he was about 22 years old and was offered a trial with Wolves but he was injured at the time so was not able to take part. He then turned to rugby and signed for the Ferry, but he left in 1960 for Neath Athletic and played one season for Neath.

The club signed the season off with a winning game against Brynmawr, 16–11. Doug Jones scored 2 tries,18-year-old Peter Mends added another, Ken Harris kicked a conversion and Terry Woodland nailed the last try, which outside-half Bernard Lock converted. Malcolm Edwards played at lock for the visitors as they were short.

The club was thirteenth in the West Wales League at the end of the season.

To complete the season a past XV took on the current XV in a highly competitive match. Oldies Ron Trimnell, John Stockham and Gwyn Morgan never gave up, but tries from John Roberts, Roy Evans and Frankie Thomas, all converted by Woodland gave the current XV a 17–5 win, with Morgan getting a try back for the oldies.

Quins

The Quins were defeated 0–5 at home by a Baglan team playing its first-ever fixture – a J. Bond try was disallowed. Unfortunately, the Quins conceded a second defeat, 0–12 to Baglan at end of October.

With a few wins now under their belt it appeared that the training some of the old hands were giving the Quins was paying off. For example, in the Skewen game, youngsters outside-half John Bevan and centre Mike Doyle impressed and Bevan made 1 drop goal. These players ended up playing first-class rugby, Doyle with Neath and Bevan with Aberavon and Wales. Young hooker Malcolm Edwards was also impressive and played for the Ferry until 1974.

> Another youngster to gain a Boys Clubs of Wales cap from Briton Ferry was **CHRIS ABRAHAM**, son of Neath favourite Myo Abraham and brother of soccer star Tony Abraham (who played against England), sadly he never appeared for the Ferry but joined Neath Athletic.

The Quins were defeated at home by BP Llandarcy (5–6, Mike Price try, John Davies conversion), by Cimla away (0–3) and by Baglan at home (0–31, with John Evans and John Carpenter playing well up front).

In the districts

Cimla and Seven Sisters competed in the cup final, which the latter won.

Season 1963-1964

D.L. Thomas. K. Harries. D. Jones. L. Jenkins. D. Williams. A. Hopkins. G. Thomas. F. Thomas. M. Price. D. Hare. B. Hill. Roy Evans(V/Capt) Terry Woodland(Captain) G. Pugh. G. Jenkins. (Insert Bryan Hire)

Malcolm Edwards

8.12 1963/64

Match results place BFRFC scores first

1964/65

The Ferry's first full season at their new headquarters.

Two trial games at the end of August were well attended. The players suggested to the committee that the First XV (which was normally selected on a Monday evening) could play against the reserves and the Second XV on a Tuesday and Thursday as practice runs.

The Ferry then lost the first two games of the season (among them Mumbles). They then defeated Resolven 9–6 at home in the third game, during which wing Brian Evans ran a full 75 yards to the try line, only to be tackled and prevented from grounding the ball. Bernard Locke made a drop goal. The club then made two further home wins; against Morriston at home, Terry Woodland bagged 1 try; and against Mountain Ash.

Prop **DOUG JONES** transferred to Neath this September.

October started with a 0–17 defeat at home to a strong Loughor side, and a heavy 0–22 defeat away at Cefneithin in the first round of the West Wales Cup (Ferry had to field a weakened team, with mostly Second XV playing). They then defeated Abercrave 6–0 (with 1 try from Brian Evans and a Man of the Match performance from scrum-half David Parker), and Bynea 42–0 at home (tries from Allan Hopkins, Brian Evans, Bernard Hill and Bernard Locke, and D.L. Thomas kicked 3 conversions). Ferry then faced away fixtures at Crynant and at Cardiff Athletic (a game which they lost heavily). Meanwhile, the Second XV drew at home to Crynant and then lost away to Nantyfyllon, having defeated them three weeks previously.

Captain
Granville Pugh

Vice captain
Dudley Mills

CARDIFF RUGBY
FOOTBALL CLUB

SEASON   1964 - 1965

CARDIFF ARMS PARK
CARDIFF ATHLETIC
v.
BRITON FERRY

SATURDAY   -   OCTOBER 31st   -   1964
Kick-off 3.30 p.m.

OFFICIAL PROGRAMME   2d.

8.13 Programme for match against Cardiff Athletic

Some necessary changes to the team line up were made for the first game in November: Allan Hopkins into outside-half; Mike Price at centre; and Terry Woodland hooking. Courtney John and newcomer D. Phillips up front played well. They began by defeating Trebanos away, 14–8, and then Felinfoel at home, 8–3 (Allan Hopkins scored 1 try and Chapman kicked 1 penalty and 1 conversion). Ferry then lost away to Pontardulais, 0–16, and drew 0–0 at home to Morriston – Ronnie Breach played well in this game.

> The night before the Pontardulais game the club showed some sports films presented by Mr Ronald Morris. Mr Raynor Jones from the WRU addressed the audience with regard to new rugby laws being introduced. Chairman Morgan Jones made a presentation to treasurer William Williams for his contribution to the club.

> During November, BERNARD LOCKE transferred to Aberavon Quins and ROY EVANS had to retire due to a serious knee injury. Evans then became the club's fixture secretary. RON MORRIS became the club's first coach.

> Sadly, prop TERRY WOODLAND had to retire in December and he followed Evans on to the committee.

The club set up portable training lamps for training sessions on darker nights, which resulted in good turn outs for training – filling both dressing rooms.

On the field of play they started badly again, with defeats away at Cwmavon 3–9, away to Loughor 15–0 (on a ground in a bad state after rain, with new fullback Colin Rees playing well), and at home to Brynamman 3–9.

The new year didn't start any better as they slipped to a surprise defeat away to Bynea 0–8 (new scrum-half J. Lewis played well) A home game with Llandaff was called off due to a frozen pitch but Ferry did defeat Crynant at home, 6–0. Wing Brian Evans scored a great try and made a desperate tackle to save a try in the corner. Roy Evans came out of retirement to play in this game as half-backs H. Richards and P. Lewis were injured. The following week Terry Woodland was also called back in, but the game against Pontyberem was called off.

The Social Club celebrated DAVID EVANS' golden wedding anniversary in January by presenting him with a gift and his wife with a bouquet of flowers. Evans was baggage man for the Ferry and for the Town cricket club, and he always made sure that the players had a hot cup of cocoa waiting for them after training – and gym work and cross-country runs were making sure that training was going well.

The Ferry started to make plans in February for a return to Ireland during the April Easter weekend.

1964-65
Back row –Keith Lewis, Colin Rees, Graham Jones; Lyn Jenkins, Dudley Mills, D.L.Thomas
Middle row-Hughie Watkins; Malcolm Edwards, Bernard Hill; Terry Woodland; Emrys Jones, Dai Phillips, Ron Morris(coach)
Front row-Brian Evans, Granville Pugh (Capt.) , Dai Parker, Hugh Richards.

8.14 1964/65

On the field they defeated Ystrad Rhondda away, then defeated Trebanos at home, 11–0, with C. Rees kicking 1 penalty, B. Pill scoring 1 try and David Parker making his debut at scrum-half. They then lost at Felinfoel by 3–18 (with only a D.L. Thomas penalty to show) and at home to Pontardulais by 5–11 (with Mike Jones playing well). They did end the month with a 12–0 home win over Aberaman. Mike Jones and Lyn Jenkins scored tries and David Parker 1 drop goal.

In February, Quins captain **ERNIE PERRY** was tragically killed in a road accident.

In the final month of the season Ferry defeated Taibach at home before falling to an 8–12 home defeat to Cwmavon. Ferry had to lend Frankie Thomas to the opposition (Allan Hopkins and Brian Thomas scored tries and Chapman converted 1). Aberavon were the next visitors, before they defeated Ystrad Rhondda at home, 14–0 (D. Lewis got a try).

Ruislip came down on tour from Middlesex during April and went away defeated 19–6. B. Evans and L. Jenkins bagged a try apiece, B. Thomas got 2 and P. Chapman kicked 2 conversions and 1 penalty. Roy Evans deputised again for David Parker.

The First XV ended the season with an away fixture at Skewen and as twenty-fourth in the league.

AGM

The club announced at the end of the season that, after only two seasons back in the West Wales set up, they would be withdrawing from competitive rugby as they were carrying out a host of ground improvements, such as new drainage and grass strengthening.

The committee and officials for 1964/65 were president O.L. Davies, chairman Morgan Jones, vice chairman Avon Roberts, treasurer W.L. Williams, secretary W.S. Davies, assistant secretary Ewart Adams, fixture secretary Roy Evans. Committee: Vernon Davies, Llew Llewelyn, Jack Thomas, Albert O'Shea, D.J. Poley, H. Watkins, Phil Griffiths, Howie Thomas and John Selby.

Tour

The day after playing Ruislip in April, the club embarked on the tour to Ireland. They flew from Rhoose airport to Dublin and played old friends Nenagh (losing 11–13) then Birr (winning 8–6). The tour party consisted of fullback Colin Rees, three-quarters Brian Evans, Bernard Hill, Allan Hopkins, Michael Jones and David Lewis, half-backs David Parker and Granville Pugh (captain) and forwards Terry Woodland, Malcolm Edwards, Graham Jones, D.J. Phillips,

D.L. Thomas, Phil Chapman, Dudley Mills (vice captain), Brian Thomas, Lyn Jenkins and Keith Lewis, with trainer Cyril Beasley.

8.15 On tour in Ireland 1965

In the district

A new team was formed in January, Briton Ferry Steel RFC, with chairman ex-Ferry player Arthur Owen and secretary Brian Woolfe (ex-Llanelli, Bridgend and Skewen). They signed up forty-four players and had arranged midweek fixtures in March against Skewen Second XV, Neath Athletic Second XV, Briton Ferry Second XV (which they won), Mumbles Second XV and Baglan. After two practice matches, they played their first competitive game on 10 March against BP Llandarcy Second XV.

Briton Ferry Steel held their first official dinner in July at Bridgend, and secretary Brian Woolfe stated that forty fixtures had been arranged for the following season and no fewer than forty-two players had signed up. They had also arranged a tour to Manchester for March 1966. Their new captain for the upcoming season was wing forward Mike Price.

1965/66

Trials were held during August.

The season started with back to back fixtures against Treherbert, which Ferry lost away but won 3–0 at home – Brian Evans again the try scorer. Half-backs that day were Glanville Pugh and Dai Parker. They then defeated RAF St. Athan away before falling to a narrow 0–3 defeat at home to Carmarthen, with Alan Roper featuring at fullback. The following week Roper was in the pack for a niggling win at Vardre, in which Allan Hopkins took over the goal kicking, Colin Rees played at fullback, Dai Parker scored 1 try and three players were sent off, two from the Ferry.

A home game against Abercrave was the first fixture in October and B. Evans blistered over for another try. In an 8–0 away win at Resolven, Lyn Jenkins scored 1 try and Hopkins kicking 1 conversion and 1 penalty to take Resolven's unbeaten ground record. But the Ferry came back to earth with two 3–9 defeats, to Skewen at home and Cefneithin away. They ended the month with a 6–6 home draw with Gorseinon – outstanding up front were Ronnie Breach, A. Bevan and Courtney John.

Captain
Allan Hopkins

Vice captain
Graham Jones

November also started badly with an away defeat at Cwmavon and they were bemoaning the fact that there was no Quins XV to back up the First XV injuries. Roy Evans helped out again by coming out of retirement. The following week they beat Ystradgynlais, 8–3 at home, with Hopkins bagging 1 conversion and 1 penalty and B. Evans another try.

The First XV's next fixture was against Carmarthen at home. Because 21-year-old Dai Parker had been selected to play for Neath against Maesteg, Roy Evans stepped in again to fill his place. A Bernard Hill drop goal was all they had to show in a 6–3 defeat. Parker was invited to go to Blackheath with Neath again the following week but declined. The Ferry won 11–0 against Vardre. Jon Knight and Keith Lewis were the try scorers and D.L. Thomas kicked 1 conversion. They tried out a new centre in this game, by the name of A. Davey.

The club ended 1965 badly with a 0–3 defeat at home by Resolven. The game featured Youth XV hooker Barry Clements, who played as a trial and put up a good show.

Pitch problems and postponed games meant the new year didn't start any better.

The First XV lost away at Gorseinon, 3–17, then 5–8 at home to Cwmavon (Bernard Hill scored 1 try and Allan Hopkins converted. The team played in their new blue jerseys against Cwmavon, and there were no fewer than four policemen on the field: Hopkins, Chapman, John Knight and Keith Lewis. Ferry ended the month with another home defeat, 0–16 against Mountain Ash. In an effort to give all their players a game the club just about managed two sides and also played an away game at Ystradgynlais with Ray Barton playing at scrum-half and Hubert Davies at fullback – unfortunately they lost this one as well.

Briton Ferry-born JOHN DAVIES, now residing in New Zealand (who had won a bronze medal in the 1500 metres at the 1964 Tokyo Olympics) won the mile race at Madison Square Gardens in New York, clocking in at 4 minutes 4.2 secs.

February didn't see any improvement in the First XV's results as they went down at Kenfig Hill. David Parker played for Neath at Waterloo that day and scored a try. Then they lost 6–19 at home to Blaina (A. Hopkins 1 penalty, B. Pill 1 drop goal), with Roy Evans again filling in for Parker, his outside-half partner was young Haydn Davies. Parker subsequently transferred to Neath. Ferry then played Neath before ending the month with a creditable 3–3 draw at Mountain Ash.

Pitch problems in March caused the club to transfer a home game with Skewen to Skewen, which Ferry then lost heavily. The following week they did host Llandaff, and lost 6–12 (Graham Jones scored 1 try). A midweek defeat at home to Cwmgrach followed before ending the month with a 6–6 home draw with Brynmawr. The side was jigged around a bit for this game with John Simonson playing in the centre, Bernard Hill at 9 and Russell Tustin from Bryncoch up front. Dudley Mills played well.

Some of the stand out forwards during the season were Mal Edwards, Phil Chapman, Dave Phillips, Jim Kelleher and young Keith Thomas, in the backs Bernard Hill again led the way, along with Paul Kyte.

At the end of the month the Ferry played in the National Sevens Competition at Aberavon. They beat Tonna 3–0 and reached the semi-final, where they lost to BP Llandarcy.

The club ended up twenty-fourth in the league.

Youth team

A new Youth XV was formed after trials in August and early September but they struggled to find fixtures and hardly played in the first half of the season. By the new year they were reportedly going along nicely.

On the Easter weekend the Youth XV hosted Neath Colts and lost 0–14. Referee Ivor David come out of retirement to officiate this game. A fourteen-and-a-half year-old David Jenkins played for the Youth XV and went on to play for Neath and Swansea in the centre. The following week David Parker helped out Aberavon against London Welsh.

8.16 Youth team 1965/66

Tour

In April the club toured to Leeds, where they played the undefeated Roundhay on Easter Monday, and lost 3–0 (young outside-half Dean Hoare played well. They lost the Saturday game to Selby Old Boys, 0–12.

The touring party was led by captain Allan Hopkins, whose squad was: fullback Colin Rees; three-quarters G. Pugh, B. Pill, A. Hopkins, Hubert Davies, Richard Barton and John Knight; half-backs Peter Davies, Colin Oates and Peter Lewis; and forwards Russ Tustin, M. Edwards, K. Lewis, D.L. Thomas, Courtney John, P. Chapman, D. Mills, E.C. Jones, Mike Williams and L. Jenkins.

AGM

New members to the committee that year were Bryan Hire, Gwyn Morris, Jack Bevan and Terry Woodland.

Around the district

By the end of January, Briton Ferry Steel were third in the Neath & District League and so entered the playoffs against Glynneath. The other semi was between Seven Sisters and Bryncoch.

After Easter, Peter Dennis of Briton Ferry Steel was selected to play for the Welsh Districts against a Midland County XV.

Cimla won the District Cup, defeating Seven Sisters in the final, and Seven Sisters won the championship.

MR W.S. "SPAM" DAVIES, who'd worked in the pit road at the local Albion steelworks, had proven to be a wonderful secretary and organiser from 1934 to 1966. His name was well known in rugby circles. He organised many Irish tours, to Dublin, Nenagh, Limerick, Cork, Enniscorthy, Carlow, Kilkenny and Tipperary.

8.17 W.S. Davies, Hon. Secretary Briton Ferry RFC 1934–1966

Match results place BFRFC scores first

1966/67

Scrum-half Peter Davies joined the club from Skewen and his first game was against Neath at the Gnoll, which ended in defeat for the Ferry and ex-player D. Parker scoring 2 tries against them!

Two players got lost driving up to the following match at Ogmore Vale, so the Ferry had to play with just thirteen, and lost. They then defeated Porthcawl at home in a midweek match and the following week hosted a strong Cardiff Athletic side and were defeated 5 –30. A little known scrum-half scored a try against the Ferry that day, Gareth Edwards. Young Paul Kyte played well at outside-half for the Ferry and Dudley Mills scored the 1 try, which Allan Hopkins converted. Ferry then defeated Glais 15–0 at home, with Peter Davies featuring at fullback, but they lost at home to Tumble, 3–14, this time with John Noble at fullback and Norman Way at centre. The month ended with a home win over Amman United.

Captain
David L. Thomas

> DOUG JONES featured in this game, after transferring back from Neath. He then transferred to Swansea the following week and later in the season played in a winning Swansea side against the touring Aussies.

Seven Sisters proved too strong for the Ferry in the first game of October, at home, and won 8–32, the first of six defeats this month: away to Ystradgynlais 3–17; away to Bynea 6–9, when they had to borrow a player to make the side fifteen; then at home in the return with Seven Sisters 0–60; 0–19 at home to Kidwelly; and 0–10 to Ammanford.

> Ferry were two props short against Ammanford as Graham Jones and Terry Woodland had gone to Aberfan to help in the disaster. The club held

a two-minute silence before the match against Morriston to reflect the sadness that everyone felt at the sudden loss of so many young lives.

The Ferry made it a 6–0 home win over Morriston – Lyn Jenkins scored a try and A. Hopkins added a penalty. Changes were made for the next game, a narrow 0–3 defeat at Amman United. D. Phillips had a good game in the front row, and new boys P. Lacey and G. Lloyd and new scrum-half C. Oates did well. Ferry then ended the month with another two defeats, at home to Glais 0–3, and away to Tumble 0–19. At this point Russell Tustin transferred back to Bryncoch.

The Ferry ended the year as they had started it, with defeats at Kidwelly (0–3) and Ammanford (0–8), and at home to Ystradgynlais (3–5). The only highlight was a draw at home with Taibach.

Individual performances did indicate some light at the end of the dark tunnel: a new scrum-half emerged in Jack Shore; young Dean Hoare (home from his job in London) had good performances in the centre; and hooker Mal Edwards and Youth XV flanker Phil Green were playing really well up front.

Ferry started 1967 with a bang and a home win over Bynea, 5–0. Scrum-half Gwyn Davies (Glamorgan Police) scored a try that Hopkins converted. In their last-ever game in the Welsh Wales Rugby Union League Ferry won 9–6 at Morriston.

The weather then took January over and games were cancelled or transferred. The Skewen game was played in February and Ferry managed a 5–5 draw. The following week they hosted Bridgend Sports and lost 3–13, then drew 3–3 at Llandaff. The pitch took over again and was reported to be like a paddy field.

The return fixture with Skewen was played in March and Ferry won 9–0 with a Phil Chapman try and an A. Hopkins penalty.

In the final month of a tough season Ferry made it a 6–6 home draw with Ogmore Vale (new hooker John Rue played well and skipper D. Thomas and Norman Way each scored 1 try) a 14–3 home win over Ystrad Rhondda (Hopkins kicked a penalty, tries from Emrys Jones and young Youth XV skipper Roger Amphlett on his debut, he also converted it). The next match, at home to Aberavon Quins, was abandoned due to injury, a nasty head clash between opposing back row men, E.C. Jones of the Ferry and G. David of the Quins. They ended the season with an excellent away win at Kenfig Hill, with wing Vic Hinder playing well.

A past versus present game was organised for Friday 13 May to celebrate the unveiling of a new captain's board that had been prepared and painted by D.J. Poley (who had also painted the two club murals). Hooker Phil Griffiths, who had played for the club 30 years previously, was in top form.

8.18 Past v. Present 1966/67
(back) H. Watkins, D. Hare, D.J. Poley, T. Woodland, G. Morgan; (centre) K. Harris, Howard Burt, Roy Evans, Doug Jones, A Bowen, Phil Griffiths; (front) A. Roper, G. Morgan

Captain and second row D.L. Thomas led a squad of: fullback Vic Hinder; three-quarters B. Pill, Norman Way, Pat Morgan and L. Jenkins; half-backs Paul Kyte and J. Shore; and forwards Alistair Bowen, D. Phillips, M. Edwards, A. Hopkins, P. Chapman, Gwynfryn Thomas, Jack Kelleher, Keith Thomas, D. Mills and E.C. Jones.

Ferry dropped to twenty-ninth in the league, their final season in the West Wales Championship. They had reached the semi-finals of the WWRU Cup on five occasions and been in the top four play-offs in the league three times.

Tour

At the end of March the First XV and the Youth toured to Cleethorpes. The former played Market Rasen on Easter Saturday (lost 15–22) and Lysaghts Steel XV on Monday (won 14–6) – half-backs Jack Shore and Pat Morgan were outstanding.

Youth XV

The Youth XV had a good season under excellent skipper Roger Amphlett, with wins over Tycroes, Hirwaun (twice), Bonymaen, Seven Sisters, Llangynwydd and Morriston. They were defeated by a strong Felinfoel side (containing a certain Phil Bennett), by Aberavon and by Resolven. During their tour, they defeated Lichfield and took Wolverhampton's three-year unbeaten ground record off them, 11–3. The highlight of their season was reaching the Neath & District Cup Final at Glynneath against Neath Colts, which they lost 3–9 – skipper Amphlett kicked a penalty. Other players to shine that year were centre Steve Evans, prop John Lewis, wing Roger Williams and flanker Gerwyn Gullum.

Season 1966-1967

K. Lewis. G. Jones. D. Mills. A. Gleaves. G. Thomas. J. Kelliher. E. Jones. L. Jenkins.
A. Hopkins. M. Jones. P. Chapman. B. Hill(V/Capt) M. Edwards. K. Thomas.
N. Way. P. Morgan. D.L. Thomas(Captain).

8.19 1966/67

Match results place BFRFC scores first

AGM

There was a special social function to unveil the
Captain's Board with former captains present.

New to the committee were Ewart Adams, Ted Richards and Phil Griffiths
(Youth Secretary). Terry Woodland moved to assistant secretary and Jack
Thomas became vice chairman.

In the district

To start 1967, fullback J. Thomas of Briton Ferry Steel was selected to play for
Neath & District against Neath at the Gnoll, another honour for the young club.

Mr H.G. Lewis presented a new cup to the District for use in the cup final.
This year's winners were Metal Box, who defeated Cwmgrach 6–5 (they were
also in the League final against Cimla).

1967/68

Trials were held at the end of August again. Doug Jones rejoined the club from Neath as player coach. Newcomers to the side were centre Peter Chamberlain and no.8 John Stockham.

> Captain and hooker **MALCOLM EDWARDS** had joined the club in 1961 from Trefelin Youth. He'd played for the Quins XV for two years before breaking into the senior side and had only missed six matches in the previous four years.

For the first season out of the Welsh Wales Rugby Union structure, new clubs were added to the fixture list, such as Pontypool United and Swansea Athletic.

Porthcawl visited in September. Then Ferry defeated Glamorgan Wanderers A 6–5 in October. This gave them an unbeaten run of six games (including one draw). They then came up against a very strong Cardiff Athletic side, containing six internationals and a Cambridge Blue, and lost heavily.

Captain
Malcolm Edwards

Coach
Doug Jones

The state of the pitch in November meant another swapped fixture and they losing 6–9 to Aberavon Quins. Scrum-half Jack Shore 1 drop goal and Lyn Davies 1 try. Ferry then lost at home to Pontypool United, 0–6. The back row of Keith Thomas, Johnson and newcomer Clive Lewis and second row Albert Gleaves were in good form. They ended the month with a fine 14–9 win at Resolven, with tries from Hopkins and Stuart Forester.

In December, Doug Jones left the club to go back to Swansea, so Roy Evans took over the coaching duties. With hooker and captain Mal Edwards leading the way on the field, the club was in good hands. Those playing really well were: Albert Gleaves, the strong man in the front row;

locks Howard Mills and Dai Thomas (son of D.L. Thomas and one of the best locks in West Wales at the time); Pat Morgan at half-back; partnering young Jack Shore at scrum-half.

JACK SHORE was in Rugby Training College and made a 260-mile round trip to play for the club every Saturday – he thumbed a lift and was well known to regular motorway users.

December started with a 0–3 defeat at home to Tonyrefail by, which signalled a poor month as they drew 0–0 at home to Aberaman and were defeated in two away games at Cilfynydd and Llandaff. In the latter game young Alan Cowell played his first senior game for the club.

An appeal went out for the players to rally around and commit to training, as only four or five regulars were turning up to sessions, which was having an effect on the way they played on a Saturday.

The club received invites from the Isle of Man, Southend and Fleetwood to play at their Easter rugby festivals.

January didn't get much better for the Ferry as the weather put paid to the club's on-field activities. Home games against Mountain Ash and Resolven were cancelled and the game against Pontardawe ended ten minutes early in a 0–0 draw.

The club had barely played on their own pitch since September, despite all the money spent, the pitch improvements seemed to be ineffective.

Their last home game of the month ended in a 0–3 defeat to Cilfynydd. The knock-on effect of the cancellations and the weather was the postponement of the away game at Neath to later in the year.

Individually however, the front row was playing well – Youth XV hooker Barry Clements, prop Phil Chapman and Alan Ladd in the back row. Young Roger Amphlett was selected to play in the Welsh Youth Trials. Wing Bernard Hill was also playing well.

A strange thing happened at Neath when a certain Brian Thomas was selected to assist neighbours and fierce rivals Aberavon against Rosslyn Park! As anyone from Neath knows, Thomas' constant battles with second row Billy Mainwaring, led to Billy's mother screaming at Brian from the stands to "leave her Billy alone", a standing joke in the area.

It looked as though fortunes might change February when both the First XV and the Youth XV won their first games of the month. But a defeat at Aberaman and a 3–3 draw at home to Skewen ended the month on a more sombre note.

Unfortunately, in this last game Dudley Mills was taken to hospital with a nasty injury that occurred in the first couple of minutes, so they ended up playing almost a full game with fourteen men.

In March, the First XV lost at home to Swansea Uplands, 6–8, and in the rearranged match at Neath they went down to a heavy defeat (fullback Peter Davies played well). In a goodwill gesture, Neath gave the gate takings to the Ferry. They also lost at Porthcawl and at home 6–8 to Aberavon Quins (the team contained five 18-year-olds, including Alan Cowell, Gerald Lewis and Roger Amphlett – who kicked both goals). The month ended with another two defeats at home, to Llandaff (0–11) and to Skewen.

The First XV were defeated 6–10 in the first round of the Welsh Sevens at Aberavon by BP Llandarcy. But they won 10–0 at Cowbridge to notch up a fourth double of the season – scrum-half Mike Nicholas and Keith Thomas played well, while Alan Ladd was outstanding. Nicholas and outside-half Eric Jones bagged 1 try each, both converted by Amphlett. Then they were defeated 13–19 at Mountain Ash in their final game.

Youth XV

In November the Youth XV lost 3–0 at home to Aberavon BC.

In March, the Youth XV won 11–8 at home to Bryncethin. Powerful 18-year-old prop Jeff Stockham scorched in from 30 yards for a winning try.

The Youth XV lost their last couple of games, in the Neath & District Cup final and in the Shield final, both to Seven Sisters – but they'd done really well to make it into both finals.

Tour

In the final month of the season the only good note on the field was the Ferry's unbeaten tour to Cleethorpes, with wins over Grimsby (32–8) and Scunthorpe (44–6). Roger Amphlett scored 20 points from 2 tries and 7 conversions to equal Harold Roberts' individual scoring record in the 1950s. Eighteen-year-old outside-half Dean Hoare (son of Peter) made a promising debut.

This year's squad comprised: fullback P. Davies; three-quarters B. Pill, A. Hopkins, Stuart Forrester, Roger Amphlett and Hubert Davies; half-backs Dean Hoare and Eric Jones; forwards P. Chapman, G. Lewis, M. Edwards (captain), D.L. Thomas, G. Thomas, K. Thomas, P. Green, E.C. Jones, Alan Ladd and Howard Mills.

AGM

At the AGM the club showed expenditure of £905 and a surplus of £151, which was heralded as the best for many years. Chairman Morgan Jones announced that, due to ill health, President O.L. Davies was retiring after being associated with the club since 1925 – as player, committeeman, secretary and president. His brother, Trevor Davies, would take over the reins in his absence. A Life Membership was awarded to assistant secretary Ewart Adams. The chairman praised young Roger Amphlett for his prolific points scoring during the season, as he'd notched up 61 points for the Youth XV and 50 points for the First XV.

Morgan Jones presented a trophy to the club for a new annual award, Player of the Year. Vice chairman Jack Thomas presented clocks to Phil Griffiths and Graham Jones.

The committee and the officials were all re-elected. New members were Harry Melding, Doug James and Dudley Mills..

8.20 1967/68
(back) T. Woodland (trainer), P. Chapman, A. Ladd, L. Jenkins, g. Thomas, D. Jones,
D.L. Thomas, A. Hopkins, P. Green, E. Jones, Roy Evans (secretary0; (front) P. Morgan,
B. Hill (vice captain), Malcolm Edwards (captain), P. Davies, A. Ashton and …

In the district

Briton Ferry Steel were going great guns, which was reflected by the District XV containing four from their team: prop and captain Mike Sambrook; Peter Dennis in the centre; D. Burdon in the second row; and Graham Ellis on the bench.

In March, Briton Ferry Steel defeated Cimla 11–0 in the District Shield semi-final and went on to defeat Neath Athletic 6–3 in the final. They also defeated BP Llandarcy 3–0 in the cup final, with a scoring pass from John O'Sullivan giving Peter Dennis the winning try. This was the first time in 50 years that a team had completed the double. Prior to a presentation evening at the Gnoll they played a District XV and defeated them 14–3. They finished the season having played 31, won 21, drawn 5, lost 5, with 315 points for and 161 against. Alan Jefford was their top scorer with 89 points, with centre Jeff Thomas on 45 points. Peter Dennis headed the try scorer's list with 11. Briton Ferry Steel coach Ron Morris was very pleased, to say the least!

Briton Ferry Steel RFC Neath and District League Champions, HG. Lewis cup winners and Metal Box All Winners Cup winners –"The treble" 1967-68
Back row– Roy Morgan, Keith Bragger, John Budge, John Scott, (Tyfryn Smith, Don Mathias, Jimmy Thomas, Bryn Jones, Emlyn Richards-all committee), Gordon Hill (Fixt. Sec.), Brian Evans, Tony Watkins, Richard Evans
Middle row–Harry Osborne, Elwyn Evans, John O'Sullivan, Dennis Hare, Don Broad, David Burden, Graham Harding, Rowley Adams, Ron O'Rourke, Peter Bevan, Arthur Davies, Graham Ellis.
Front Row– Dai Harding, Peter Dennis, John Turner, Mike Price (v.capt.), Lyton Griffiths (V. Chairman) Mike Sambrook (Capt.), John Wilcock (Chairman), Alan Jefford (treas.), Raymon Davies (Sec) Jeff Thomas, Clive Bevan

8.21 1967/68 The treble for Briton Ferry Steel: Neath & District League Champions, H.G. Lewis Cup winners and Metal Box All Winners Cup winners

Match results place BFRFC scores first

1968/69

Another bad start to a new season with defeat in the opening three games, including at Resolven and 12–13 at home to Treherbert (Graham Jones 1 try, Dean Hoare 2).

New players in the side were centre Alan Ashton and wing Lyn Jenkins. Unfortunately, hooker Mal Edwards had to leave the club to take up work in London, but Ferry did recruit a replacement from Glamorgan Police, Gwyn Morris.

They then drew 11–11 away at Ogmore Vale before defeating Cwmavon 6–5 at home. Eric Jones was outstanding at scrum-half and went on to score a try in his next match – a 6–16 home defeat by Aberavon Quins.

Captain
Peter Davies

Playing record
P 31
W 10
D 1
L 20

Promising youngster Dean Hoare was selected for ABERAVON at Bath, and he went on to play quite a few games for them, including one with fellow ex-Ferry player Mike Nicholas as his half-back partner in a winning match at Neath (who also had an ex-Ferry half-back in David Parker). Aberavon also played Ferry scrum-half Jack Shore and Ferry centres Stuart Forester and John Simonson together later in the season – on one occasion in opposition to Ferry player Allan Hopkins who was playing for Glamorgan Police. In the first game of the season Ferry outside-half Paul Kyte was injured playing for Aberavon and didn't return to the Ferry until the following February.

Cardiff Athletic were Ferry's first opponents in October and they lost prop Jeff Johns to injury during the game. Ferry then lost the next game before winning the following one, thanks to D.L. Thomas and Closs Jones returning from injury and John Simonson rejoining at no.8 after twelve years at Swansea (he'd also represented Wales at table tennis).

During November they lost several matches: 11–14 at BP Llandarcy (D.L. Thomas kicked two penalties); 3–11 at home to Brynmawr (Roger Amphlett kicked a 50-yard penalty); 3–22 at home in the return with Cardiff Athletic; and finally 0–19 away at Swansea Uplands. The Ferry experimented with playing Jeff Stockham at hooker but had to revert to giving a young John Burns the role.

The First XV lost 3–6 at home to Ebbw Vale but on Boxing Day defeated Taibach 9–6 with an outstanding the front row of Youth XV skipper Lewis, Burns and Johns.

Ferry had a good start to the new year with a 14–6 home win over Ogmore Vale. Tries came from centre Forester (once on Cardiff City's books and who'd played in goal for Lovell's Athletic), from flanker Lyn Tregonning on his debut after joining from Cwmgrach (he'd also played for Neath) and back rower Alan Ladd. Gwyn Thomas was outstanding at no.8. Dean Hoare and Stuart Forester had returned from Aberavon. New scrum-half Tudor Phillips also made his debut, he'd played for Fylde RFC and Loughborough University.

The following two weeks were put paid to by the weather, and they ended the month with a home defeat against Maesteg Celtic.

Several debuts were made in February, by wing Steve Roper and by four Youth XV players in their first game against Mountain Ash, including 17-year-old outside-half Rosser. But the game was lost, as was the return game at home later that month (0–18) – despite the returns of Paul Kyte from injury and of Keith Thomas and Malcolm Edwards from London. Edwards had been keeping his hand in by playing for Gidea Park RFC. Once again questions were being asked about player fitness due to lack of training.

In March ex-Ferry player **RON TRIMNELL** resigned as Swansea coach, and ex-Ferry player **DOUG JONES** made a comeback for Swansea after joining them from Mumbles.

An excellent away win at Treherbert was a good start to March. Centre Allan Hopkins kicked two penalties. Then they lost at home, 6–11 to Pontypool United.

The First XV were defeated at home by Llandaff, 9–13. Amphlett kicked 1 penalty and Kyte 1 drop goal. New flanker, Mike Truman, slotted in well to the team. The second row of Amphlett and D.L. Thomas were outstanding. Truman scored an 80-yard try in the next game, although they were defeated yet again, this time by Porthcawl.

Match results place BFRFC scores first

Try-scoring flanker Truman added a brace in the first game of April against Barry, which ended in a 16–9 win for the Ferry.

The club struggled after the tour as some players decided not to turn out and the team lost heavily to both Swansea Athletic and Cwmavon. But they did beat Pontycymmer 27–0 in the first round of the Welsh Sevens at Aberavon.

> A familiar sight every morning was a barefoot BRIAN THOMAS running around the field with his dog, and daughters Sally and Janet following close behind on their tricycles. He was putting in extra training prior to a tour to New Zealand with Wales.

Youth XV

The Youth XV were playing well at the start of the season. Skipper and prop Gerald Lewis led the side and 17-year-old outside-half Peter Rosser was looking good. They defeated Resolven in December.

The Youth XV defeated Hirwaun in February, with wing Steve Roper getting a hat trick of tries.

Tour

The Easter tour was to Manchester, where they played Old Bedians and Ashton-under-Lyne, winning both games with three tries apiece for Lyn Jenkins, Paul Kyte and Dean Hoare. Mal Edwards won the tightheads throughout.

AGM

At the AGM, the absence of Chairman Morgan Jones for the first time in 31 years lent a strange feel to the gathering. He was recovering after being kicked by a horse on the farm. Vice chairman Jack Thomas oversaw proceedings. Yet again, the club had a surplus, of £150, and the supporters' committee had raised £615. The playing record didn't read so well, but top scorer Roger Amphlett had 60 points, closely followed by Dean Hoare with 59, then Lyn Jenkins on 24. The Youth XV was praised, as they had done well yet, and Terry Woodland was commended for his work with them. All the officers and the committee were re-elected, Terry Woodland became Youth XV secretary, and on to the committee came T.A. Roberts and Gwyn Richards.

The Morgan Jones Player of the Year Award was given to captain Peter Davies.

In the district

Briton Ferry Steel defeated Banwen in the Shield semi-finals and then beat BP Llandarcy in the final. They also reached the final of the Cup, beating Banwen again in the semis and then Metal Box in the final.

Bryncoch won the H.G. Lewis trophy for scoring the most tries (44) and the Roger's cup for winning the Sevens competition.

The district committee was president Mr R.W. Winstone, chairman S. John, treasurer T.E.C. Molland, secretary F.J. Squires. The general committeemen were: M. Powells, J. Wilcocks, K. Price, G. Pill, W. Roberts, J. Brown, S. Phillips, P. Jones, H. Britton, K. Morgan, I. David and F. Davies. H.G. Lewis was elected life vice president.

8.22 1968/69

(back) Doc Beesley, Roger Amphlett, Jeff John, Lyn Jenkins, Allan Hopkins, Dai Leyshon Thomas, Gwynfryn Thomas, Stuart Forrester, E.C. Clos Jones, Referee; (middle) Hughie Watkins, John Burns, Bernard Hill, Peter Davies, Phil Green, Alan Ladd; (front) Eric Jones, Dean Hoare

1969/70

The Ferry played in the Bryncoch Sevens tournament during late August and lost to the hosts, 0–21.

New to this year's squad were half-back John "The Rat" Thomas, Leighton "Tiny" Rees, Tom Pollack and skipper and ex-Neath player flanker Lyn Tregonning.

> During this season ex-Ferry player DOUG JONES trialled for Neath (he later signed for Maesteg), as did outside-half Dean Hoare. Other ex-Ferry men JOHN SIMONSON and JACK SHORE played for Aberavon.

Although Ferry lost their first game against Resolven they bounced back to beat Cwmavon in a game where both Malcolm Edwards and Roger Amphlett were in fine form.

> Injuries were starting to take their toll among both the First and Quins XVs; B. Pill, Eric Jones, P. Kyte, A. Ashton, P. Davies, G. Jones and E.C. Jones were all out for four weeks. Even the Youth XV's captain, Leighton "Tiny" Rees, was among the injured.

Captain
Lyn Tregonning

At the end of September the First XV defeated Tredegar Ironsides 11–8 at home. The pack was led by none other than Brian Thomas, who worked well with fellow lock Mal Williams. The try was scored by Lyn Jenkins and converted by Amphlett, Dean Hoare 1 drop goal.

October started with a home win over Ogmore Vale. Returning flanker Closs Jones was outstanding alongside centre Stuart Forrester, who had rejoined the club. Another home win followed, against Ynysybwl 26–3. Among the try scorers were John Barrett and Tregonning with Amphlett converting. College student Keith Evans and lock Keith Thomas played well. Ferry ended the month defeated

9–14 at home by Brynmawr. Closs Jones grabbed his sixth and seventh tries of the season.

To kick November off, two penalties from Peter Davies helped Ferry defeat visitors Mountain Ash, 11–6. But they were defeated heavily in their next game at Aberavon Quins.

The First XV's new scrum-half, John Thomas (Welsh Youth trialist, son of Jack), was impressing everyone with his play. But the Ferry lost at Maesteg Celtic and ended the game with fourteen men after hooker Malcolm Edwards went off injured. They also had a youth forward in their ranks that day, Steve Beckley, who was reported to have played well.

December start with a 3–3 home draw with Cilfynydd, in which guest player Alan Roper played well. Followed by a home defeat to Kenfig Hill. Jack Shore kicked 1 penalty and Dean Hoare 1 drop goal. John Derrick from Bryncoch played on permit in this game.

Ferry came back on Boxing Day and defeated Taibach. New centre Peter Mainwaring was looking good alongside the young teenagers, fullback Dai Davies and flanker Nigel Flowers.

Prop Terry Keefe was in good form in the new year and the club registered an 8–0 home win over Ogmore Vale. Teenage wing Roy Evans and flanker E.C. Jones were the try scorers and Allan Hopkins converted 1. But things turned a little sour as the month wore on with defeats at home by Maesteg Celtic and Porthcawl (16–25, Roger Amphlett kicked 2 penalties).

A number of youth players had to be selected in February as some of the First XV were deemed to be "over the hill" – such as Lyn Morgan and Jeff Williams in the centre, Steve Roper (wing) and forwards Peter Brennan and Leighton Rees (youth skipper). Among the youngsters "blooded" that month were 19-year-old outside-half Peter Rosser and hooker 18-year-old David Mainwaring, who played fixtures against BP Llandarcy and Llandaff.

March started with an 8–8 away draw at Barry. Lock D.L. Thomas was back, and newcomers Tom Pollack, Howard Mills (who had 1 try disallowed) and centre Phil Manning did well. Dean Hoare got 1 try, Amphlett converted and added 1 penalty, while another hit the post. The Ferry then lost 0–5 at Cwmavon before playing the return fixture with Porthcawl, in which Amphlett kicked a penalty.

During the final month of the season Ferry lost at Resolven but won 6–3 against Bridgend Sports in the WRU Sevens at Aberavon (Bernard Hill scored 2 tries).

Tour

The annual Easter Tour went to the West Country, their first tour south since 1921. They played Keynsham (Bristol) and won 14–12. Young wing Roy Evans notched 3 tries and Dean Hoare dropped 1 goal in the closing minutes to win the game and take Keynsham's nineteen-match ground record. Ferry then played Winscombe (won 19–8) and Barnstaple Hornets (won 30–3, with 8 tries). Hoare finished the tour with a personal bag of 29 points.

Youth XV

8.23 Youth team 1969–70
(back) T. Richards, T. Woodlands, N. Williams, H. Thomas, G. Lewis, J. Beekley, N. James, M. Lloyd, N. Watkins; (middle) T. Davies, P. Brennan, L. Rees (captain), G. Llewellyn, P. Nichols, A. Duncan; (front) D. Mainwaring, L. John, B. Morgan

The Youth XV lost at Crynant, 6–26, in October.

In November they drew 8–8 with Llangynwydd and lost 3–6 away to BP Llandarcy – having lost their previous encounter, four weeks earlier at home, by 47 points.

The Youth XV lost to Cwmavon over Christmas.

Unfortunately, due to lack of interest the club had to disband the Youth XV, but they were already planning to run a Second XV for over-19s. The club were also keeping an eye on two Neath Schools players, prop Stephen Smart and lock Cuan O'Shea.

AGM

The AGM was held as usual in June. The club had made a surplus of £142 for the season, due mainly to expenditure being the lowest for ten years, at £779. Chairman Morgan Jones sat in for club president Trevor Davies. He praised the work of Roy Evans and Albert O'Shea.

Top scorer was Roger Amphlett with 97 points, while Dean Hoare was a close second on 93. Lyn Jenkins, the flying wing, was top try scorer with 15. Closs Jones was awarded the double honour of Player of the Year and the captainship for next season. Two new members were added to the committee, Alan Vaughan and Anthony Chick. The Morgan Jones Player of the Year trophy was won by E.C. Jones.

8.24 BFRFC Committee 1969/70
(back) Hugh Watkins, Dudley Mills, John Selby, Gwyn Richards, Ted Richards, Dai Poley, Roy Evans, Albert O'Shea; (front) Llew Llewelyn, Jack Thomas, Morgan Jones, W.S. Davies, E. Adams

In the district

The Briton Ferry Steel XV made a good start to the season by beating Tonna but then lost to Neath Athletic. Newcomers Bob Hopkins and Ray Davies played well.

For Neath & District the representative XV played Aberavon & District in October. Selected that day were P. Dennis, B. Evans, D. Harding, M. Sambrook, B. Hopkins and J. Sullivan and reserves R. Davies and Rowley Addams, all from Briton Ferry Steel. They lost 3–9.

Briton Ferry Steel ended 1969 with success, winning 19–8 at home to Llanelli Wanderers to complete the double over them. Tries came from P. Dennis (2), P. Mahe, P. Harris and young prop Derek Bevan, Dai Harding converted two.

Briton Ferry Steel reached the semi-final play-off in the Neath & District league, but even with new lock Carl Schubert playing well they lost to Neath Athletic.

Briton Ferry Steel started the new year with a fine 13–0 away win at Brecon (Dai Hardin, Mike Sambrook and Ray Davies tries, Jeff Thomas converted 2) and then completed the double by winning 24–6 at home – these were the first ever points scored against them by the Brecon club. Centre Brian Evans set them on their way with a drop goal, followed by tries from Ray Davies (2), Mike Sambrook, P. Dennis and D. Harding. Kicks were added by A. Jefford (1) and J. Thomas (2). They then defeated Neath Athletic in the H.G. Lewis Cup quarter-finals, 24–0, with tries from R. Davies, D. Harding, P. Parris (2) and P. Dennis. Harding added 1 drop goal and J. Thomas 3 conversions. The front row of Roly Adams, Bevan and Ellis were outstanding.

Further wins followed, including against Builth Wells (24–6, Jeff Thomas 3 tries, 3 conversions and 1, Ray Davies and Peter Dennis added further tries), and Cwmtwrch (20–3, tries from P. Parris (2), J. Thomas and P. Dennis, Thomas 1 penalty and 1 conversion). They ended the season defeating Banwen 6–0 in the H.G. Lewis Cup final to retain this trophy for the third year in a row. Their hero was wing Phil Mahe, who bagged 2 tries after splendid work from John O'Sullivan.

Briton Ferry Steel then defeated Neath Athletic 15–6 in the final of the Metal Box Winners Cup, also for the third year in a row (a magnificent achievement). The match was played on their ground as there was no neutral ground available. Briton Ferry Steel fell behind at the start, but they rallied round and tries from prop Clive Bevan and Dai Harding (who also added 1 drop goal) and 2 penalties from Jeff Thomas, eventually gave them the honours.

Briton Ferry Steel ended the season having played 30, won 22, lost 6, drawn 2; scoring 549 points and only conceding 177. Ray Davies broke the club record with 25 tries, Dai Harding and Jeff Thomas both ended on 72 points each for the season. Peter Dennis was top scorer with 91 points, he was also elected skipper for the next season.

8.25 Briton Ferry Steel RFC dinner 1970

Ex-Ferry player Dai Parker had a successful season with Neath and won the Bill Everson cup for player of the tournament in the Snelling Sevens at Cardiff Arms Park. He led the Neath VII to an 18–8 victory in the final against Ebbw Vale.

Three of the Ferry team represented the South Wales Constabulary 'G' Division during the season: prop Terry Keefe, Albert Gleaves and skipper Alan Hopkins.

Back Row.
T.O'Keefe. P.Davies. H.Mills. N.Flowers. E.C.Jones. T.Pollock. L.Rees. G.Thomas.
Middle Row.
D.L.Thomas. C.Schubert. A.Hopkins. L.Jenkins. P.Manning. D.Hoare. J.Thomas.
Front Row.
R.Evans. M.Edwards (Capt.) B.Hill. D.Davies.

8.26 1969/70

PART 9: 1970-1980

- 1971/72 to 1976/77 try increased to 4 points
- 1977/78 to 1991/92 goal from a mark removed from the scoring values with the introduction of the new free kick clause.

9.1 Briton Ferry RFC 1970/71

(back) B. Deeley (referee), R. Tustin, J. Evans, P. Brennan, F. O'Keefe, L. Rees, G. Thomas, L. Jenkins, J. Morris, W. James, T. Ellis, D. Thomas; (middle) T. Woodland (secretary), K. Harris, M. Thomas, G. Williams, G. Jones (captain), L. Tregonning, J. Schmidt, P. Davies; (front) A. Edwards (mascot), M. Edwards, D. Herbert, N. Flowers

1970/71

Trials were held in August and went quite well, and thirty to forty players trained pre-season, so the Ferry were fairly confident of having a reasonable season. The coach was ex-Ferry player and Swansea coach Ron Trimnell.

During August Ferry lost to the hosts in the district sevens at Bryncoch.

The season started with a defeat to Tonna in which new no.8 Justin Schmidt showed up well. Then, in a 6–6 home draw with Crumlin, Roger Amphlett bagged two penalties and had a winning try disallowed. There were reports that the match got quite heated on the pitch (as it also did off the pitch when the corned beef was burnt in the kitchen). Ferry then lost at SCOW Port Talbot 0–3. Two home draws followed: against Barry (8–8, D. Hoare try, Schmidt conversion) and Cwmavon (8–8). Followed by a loss to Abercynon (0–11), in which hooker Hugh Davies made his debut for the Ferry. But the curtain came down on the first month with a 26–0 win at home over Ogmore Vale – Schmidt scored a hat trick and Second XV wing Peter Kops played well.

News filtered through that ex-player fullback Ken Harris was looking to transfer back to the club.

RAY DAVIES was selected to play for a Neath
& District XV against Gwernyfed to encourage
more rugby union in mid-Wales.

October started with a home defeat to Porthcawl in a bruising encounter – and two rival supporters nearly came to blows at the end of the game. Prop Albert Gleaves was taken off after twenty minutes with broken ribs, Howard Mills was sent off for alleged head-butting and Malcolm

Captain
E.C. Jones Junior

Coach
Ron Trimnell

Playing record
P 40
W 19
D 12
L 9

Scores
Tries 73
Conversions 20

Williams for kicking. So Ferry ended the game with twelve players and lost by a point (14–15). The referee was heavily criticised by the home crowd, who threatened to report him to the WRU. The try scorers were guest player Mike Truman, wing Roy Evans and Justin Schmidt.

Ferry then headed west and defeated Llanelli Wanderers 10–9, despite having eight Quins players on the field. Wing Peter Kops and Peter Davies each got 1 try, Steve Smart converted both. They then defeated Aberavon Quins at home, 11–8 (flanker Mike Truman 2 tries, J. Schimdt 1 try, Smart converted 1), before ending the month with games against Gwent opposition, Brynmawr and Tredegar Ironsides (a 3–3 draw, a Steve Smart penalty).

November started with a close win over Taibach, 6–3, which took their ground record. Peter Davies was again on the try sheet, along with Dean Hoare. Next was a visit to Resolven, which they won 6–3 with a Smart penalty, taking their home ground record as well! Ending the month with two home games: against Mumbles (lost 3–13, Smart penalty), and Treherbert.

The First XV ended the year with away games at BP Llandarcy (won 9–6) and Taibach (won 9–6) and home fixtures against Resolven (lost 0–5) and Barry.(drew 6–6, Schmidt try). Playing well in these games were props Leighton Rees and Smart, Peter Brennan, Mal Williams and Quins centre Mike McCarthy.

In the new year the Ferry's First XV had return games with Tonna (lost), Porthcawl (lost), Mumbles (lost), Ogmore Vale (won 20–3 with Dean Hoare's 2 tries, 1 conversion and 1 drop goal, Lyn Jenkins' 2 tries and Bernard Hill's 1 try) and BP Llandarcy (won 11–8 and the double, Dean Hoare scored all the points with 2 tries). They had to play the BP game at Skewen as the Ferry pitch was unplayable.

February fixtures were against Treherbert (won), Dinas Powis (won 17–0, wing Roy Evans 3 tries, Peter Davies and Bernard Hill 1 try, Amphlett 1 conversion), Amman United (6–6, Hoare and John Thomas with 1 try apiece and new prop Clive Anthony doing well), and two matches against Skewen (a 9–9 draw, Evans and Jenkins tries, Hoare penalty, and a 6–0 win, Lyn Jenkins 2 tries; a new Hooker came in for these games, Barton Mills).

March started with home fixtures against Gwent opposition, Crumlin and Brynmawr (lost 9–8), which brought their unbeaten run of eight matches to an end. A 25–9 win of the return fixture against Dinas Powis notched up their fourth double of the season. Outstanding clever play by half-backs Dean Hoare

Match results place BFRFC scores first

and John Thomas often outwitted the opposition. Hooker Barton Mills also had a good game, taking the tighthead count to 3–0. Hoare opened the Ferry scoring with a try and added another cracker towards the end. In between, tries from Roy Evans, John Simonson, Bernard Hill and Roger Amphlett kept the score creeping up. Prop Clive Anthony played well.

The final month of the season was busy, starting with an away win at SCOW to take their two-and-a half-year ground record. On their return from the annual tour they played a combined Neath and Aberavon Police XV and beat them well, 29–3.

The Ferry then had away fixtures at Abercynon and Cwmavon (drew 8–8, Roy Evans achieved his seventeenth try of the season), and a home game with Llanelli Wanderers. They completed another double by winning 17–6. Wings Lyn Jenkins and Roy Evans both got 2 tries, John Thomas 1 and Justin Schmidt added 1 conversion. In the final game they defeated Tonyrefail 9–3 – Clive Anthony kicked a penalty, John Thomas added 1 try and Dean Hoare coolly dropped his twelfth goal of the season to end a good performance. Stand-in fullback Peter Kops, tearaway wing Roy Evans and second row Tom Pollack all had a magnificent game.

Ferry lost 0–13 to Cwmavon in the WRU Sevens at Aberavon, in the first round.

The Quins

The Quins also had a full fixture list which included games against Neath Athletic and Cimla. After defeating Banwen 5–3 in the Neath & District Cup first round they lost to Crynant in the second round. Bryncoch defeated Crynant in the semi-final and went on to win the final to add to their Sevens' and President's trophies.

In September the Quins defeated Glynneath and lock Terry Keefe, Bernard Hill and Tom Pollock showed up well. The following month they drew at Cilfynydd and defeated Banwen in the Neath & District Cup.

In November the Quins drew 6–6 with Neath Athletic.

Tour

Over Easter the club toured the west coast of Lancashire and played Halewood RFC and Port Sunlight RFC.

The touring party consisted of: fullback P. Davies; three-quarters R. Evans, B. Pill, Peter Kapps, Justin Schmidt, Wynn James and Mal Thomas; half-backs D. Hoare and J. Thomas; and forwards A. Gleaves, L. Rees, Clive Anthony,

M. Edwards, B. Wills, T. Pollack, R. Amphlett, Mal Williams, E.C. Jones, A. Hopkins and H. Mills. They won the game against Halewood 6–3. Closs Jones and man of the tour Howard Mills bagged 1 try each.

Unfortunately the tour was marred during the Port Sunlight game when Mills suffered a serious injury and was rushed to hospital. The Ferry were pitted against the champions of the Wirral, but ended the game with an 11–11 tie, with tries from scrum-half Jack Jones and prop Clive Anthony and a superb try by Mills, minutes before being carried off!

> During the tour the club were entertained in a typical Welsh fashion by well-known former Port Talbot businessman George James. At his famous Kingsway Cabaret Room they received a champagne welcome and were invited backstage to meet the star act, Ray Martine.

AGM

Terry Ellis joined the committee and L. Llewelyn was installed as vice chairman. The past versus present match featured hooker Phil Griffiths, who had played in the same match for the opposing team in 1940! W.L. Williams and W.S. Davies were awarded Life Memberships.

The Morgan Jones Player of the Year Award was won by Allan Hopkins.

9.2 BFRFC committee and officials 1970/71

Match results place BFRFC scores first

Presentation dinner

Towards the end of the season a presentation dinner was held in honour of Mr Morgan Jones, the club chairman, who had now served 40 years as player and officer. It was attended by Mr Jack Young and Mr Gwilym Treharne of the WRU, the guest speaker was Welsh international Mr Brian Thomas, and Morgan was presented with the Castello award (an inscribed ashtray and a carton of cigars, although he was not a smoker). Mr Llew Llewelyn presided and also present were club president Mr Trevor Davies, secretary Mr Roy Evans and treasurer Mr W.L. Williams.

Many stories about MORGAN JONES and his on and off field accomplishments were retold with vigour. Morgan told of when he started playing, in the depression era of the mid-1920s, and of squad training with Albert Freethy. Of how, after a campaign of door to door calls to collect a "few pence" he and his mates started a rugby team at the Melyn called the Ba Baas. Their nearest available ground was the Cadoxton Marsh, and they walked to and from there after changing in their own homes! But a number of first-class players emerged out of that team, including Welsh internationals such as Harold and D.L. Thomas. Morgan himself played for Bridgend at fullback –his first game for them was against none other than the Ferry – and he went on to play for Neath. But he served longest as a player with the Ferry with a non-stop run of sixteen years on the field. He even played some games after his retirement in 1947. He was a managing director at the haulage firm of Messrs Jones Brothers in Neath. He was also a quality baritone and had taken leading parts in many Melyn Amateur Operatic Society shows and was a member of the Welsh National Opera Company. As a teetotaller and a non-smoker, he always took care of his fitness and his health.

Briton Ferry Steel

Briton Ferry Steel had another reasonably successful season with wins over Swansea Uplands (29–6, Ray Davies 3 tries, Dai Harding 3 tries, 4 conversions, John Griffiths 1 try), Glamorgan Wanderers (home 24–0, P. Dennis 2 tries, Mike Sambrook 2 tries, John Griffiths 1 try, Dai Harding 4 conversions and a penalty; and away 32–3, Ray Griffiths 2 tries, Mike Barnett 2 tries, and a try apiece for Colin Adams, John O'Sullivan, Brian Evans and Graham Ellis, Harding added 1 conversion and 2 drop goals) and Bonymaen (21–6, tries from J. Turner and R. Davies, Harding 2 conversions and Mike Sambrook 2 penalties, 1 conversion and 1 try).

They had a bye in the first round of the cup and then defeated Skewen heavily, 47–5, in the next round. Their opponents in the semi-final were Gwernyfed and they defeated them 16–5 to reach their fourth final in successive years – only to lose to Bryncoch. In a match against Gwernyfed, tries by Mike

Sambrook, Dai Harding (who also added a penalty and two conversions) and a magical solo effort by fullback Brian Evans saw them home. In the league they found themselves in the semi-final play-offs and defeated Seven Sisters 11–6 (a Johnstone try and a Harding conversion won it for them), to meet Banwen in the final.

> Briton Ferry Steel's centre **PETER DENNIS** had a few games for Neath. He'd been capped at youth level while at Neath Colts, and capped at Welsh Districts level and had gone on tour to South Africa in 1964 as part of a combined Glynneath/Rhymney side.

In the district

The Neath & District League was quite strong and had 16 teams competing in it, with Gwernyfed, Llanwrtyd Wells and Builth Wells in the mix, along with all the local clubs (Briton Ferry, Briton Ferry Steel, Cimla, Neath Athletic, Bryncoch., BP Llandarcy, Tonna, Glynneath, Crynant, Seven Sisters, Banwen, Skewen and Metal Box). There were plans to make four divisions of four teams each for the 1975/76 season.

Briton Steel also had a large representation in the District XV competing in the Districts Cup, with Phillip Mahe, John Griffiths, Peter Dennis, Jeff Thomas, Dai Harding, Mike Sambrook, Bob Hopkins, John Sullivan and Dai Broad, along with Ferry player Graham Jones and future Ferry committeeman Dave Parker (Neath Athletic) as props.

> Griffiths, Sambrook, Hopkins, Jones and Parker were all to work together at BP Baglan Bay along with future and past players and officers, such as secretary Roy Evans, Allan Hopkins, Ron Lilley, Gerald Lewis, Peter Davies, Martyn Bate, Rhys Davies, Dai Jones, George Evans, Brian Makinson and Billy Williams.

1971/72

Coach Ron Trimnell was assisted in training by Brian Thomas.

In their first game Ferry defeated SCOW. John Thomas scored 1 try and went on to make 2 tries in the next game against Amman United, although Ferry lost by 3 points and in which Brian Thomas played on permit from Neath and Dean Hoare broke his jaw. They also lost at Barry, 10–12. John Thomas was on the score sheet again, along with Closs Jones. Albert O'Shea and Mal Edwards were outstanding in this game. Ferry were then defeated in the last two games of the month, against Tredegar Ironsides and Cwmavon.

In October they defeated a new opposition, Clwb Rygbi Caerdydd, 38–9. Ferry fielded a new back line of P. Brennan and John Morris in the centre and half-backs P. Parris and Malcolm Fletcher. Once again Jones was on the score sheet, as were Morris and Smart with 1 conversion. Albert Gleaves was injured during the match.

Disappointingly, training at a local gym was not proving popular as only eight players turned up, which showed up in their games as they were heavily defeated in the next two matches against Tonna and Llandaff. But they picked themselves up and defeated Treherbert 10–0. Peter Bell tackled really well and bagged 1 try. John Morris and Colin Watkins were also prominent. Then, in the new WRU Cup, they defeated Maesteg Celtic, but lost 13–14 at home to Aberavon Quins – Mal Edwards got 1 try and Smart kicked 3 goals. They ended the month with a home fixture against a Welsh Guards XV.

Captain
E.C. Jones Junior

Coach
Ron Trimnell

Scores
Try score increased to 4 points

November saw more defeats. The first in a blizzard, away at Aberystwyth (0–9) – players swore it had been the coldest conditions they had ever played in! The second away at Barry. Ferry then defeated Llanelli Wanderers 16–6 at home. Roger Amphlett was captain for the day and kicked a penalty. Roy Evans bagged 1 try. Newcomer Rees Wynne played well at 10, as did newcomers Colin Stephens (ex-Aberavon and Maesteg), Eifion Jones and Jeff Davies "Olly" in the pack. Ferry ended the month with a 9–18 home defeat by Resolven – Amphlett kicked 3 goals.

9.3 "The day little Dai toppled the greats"
Headline the day Neath won the first WRU Cup against Llanelli. David Parker was the hero and scored the first-ever try at Cardiff Arms Park

Former player and future chairman, **DAVID PARKER**, captained Neath against the Barbarians on the Gnoll during October. Then during December he announced his retirement from the first-class scene with Neath RFC.

He kept fit playing football and the odd game for Vardre RFC, so Neath coaxed him back to help them out during the season. Inevitably, he played at outside-half in the first WRU Cup final at Cardiff Arms Park against Llanelli and Phil Bennett*, ending up on the winning side and scoring the first ever try in a cup final. The following season he was made captain of Neath and played in the early season game against Welsh Wales Rugby Union XV at the Gnoll (alongside a certain Brian Thomas). It was in this match that Thomas famously moved up to hooker when Norman Rees had to leave the field and played with no boots or socks on.

*Welsh international Bennett later played a major part in the greatest try ever in a Barbarian's jersey.

The Ferry then took revenge on Tredegar Ironsides by beating them 7–4 at home. New flanker Colin Stephens played well, and new hooker Paddy Schmidt had a good first game in senior rugby. Amphlett saved the day with 1 try and 1 penalty. Ferry then followed this up by defeating BP Llandarcy 12–10. Roger Amphlett bagged 8 points with his boot, and both wing Peter Bell and scrum-half John Thomas were outstanding. They followed up by defeating Porthcawl 13–4, Bell and Thomas with tries and Amphlett weighing in with 5 points. The back line that day included five Peters: Bell, Kops, Jaynes, Brennan and Davies. Then, sadly, on Boxing Day they lost to Taibach for the first time in seven years.

Young lock CUAN O'SHEA played well over Christmas before returning to Leicester University from where he was selected to represent Midlands Universities against Southern Universities – and became the first Welshman to captain Leicester University. He was selected to play for Neath against St. Luke's College in April.

The new year started with a 10–14 defeat at Aberavon Quins. Then Ferry won against Nantyfyllon, 16–4, but lost the next game against Maesteg Celtic and were defeated 0–16 by Mountain Ash.

Scrum-half PETER HARRIS was selected for the Welsh Junior Rugby Union trials at BP Llandarcy during January and subsequently went on tour with them to Belgium.

A good win over Ogmore Vale got February underway, with John Thomas making 2 tries. Ferry ended the month with wins over Ystalyfera and Ogmore Vale (51–9) – with tries from Kops (2), Lewis (2), Gleaves, Colin Watkins, Closs Jones, Amphlett and Hill (3), Amphlett added 1 conversion and Smart 2 conversions and 1 penalty. This was Ferry's biggest post-war win and beat the 1936 record win of 54–0 over Bath Non-Descripts.

March started with a home defeat by Felinfoel. Welsh international Roy Mathias was playing but he was well shackled by new centre David Lewis, who had transferred from Seven Sisters. Ferry then beat Resolven away, 12–10, Lewis gained another try and Amphlett 1 conversion. Newcomers Jeff "Bonehead" Williams and Dennis Richards and second row Mal Williams played well. The First XV then defeated Porthcawl by 15 points to complete a double. Stand-in fullback Kops and centre Lewis were outstanding again. Brian Thomas also played in this match, on permit from Neath. They then completed another double, 18–12 over BP Llandarcy.

Ferry's injury problems were mounting as John Thomas, Albert Gleaves, Dean Hoare and Colin Stephens were all unavailable.

The Ferry lost to Mumbles (despite Lewis' 2 tries) and also to Tonna (10–16) in the first round of the National Sevens at Aberavon.

Ferry ended the season in style, with wins over Amman United (41–3, Thomas, Hill (2) and Lewis with tries, Amphlett converted 2), then Llanelli Wanderers by 28 points, and Skewen (20–11, Peter Brennan bagged 1 try in this game, new prop Mike Howe played really well).

9.4 1971/72

(back) M. Thomas, P. Cree, G. Lewis, L. Rees, P. Brennan, H. Thomas; (4th row) D. Thomas, T. Pollock, M. Williams, A. Hopkins, W. James, D. Herbert (3rd row) M. McCarthy, M. Edwards, N. Flowers, R. Amphlett, H. Mills, S. Smart, G. Thomas, K. Harris, G. Armstrong; (2nd row) G. Jones, L. Tregonning, B. Hill, E.C. Jones, D. Hoare, R. Evans, N. Davies, P. Probert (captain); (front) P. Davies, P. Kopps, J. Schmidt, J. Thomas, G. Mainwaring, J. Evans, G. Williams

Tour

The Easter tour visited Lancashire again and the club played St Helens and Ruskin Park RFCs. New names on tour were: centre Jeff "Bonehead" Williams; half-backs Peter Harris and Dennis Richards; and forwards D. Thomas, Jim Smith, Colin Stephens, L. Jenkins and Nigel Flowers. Players who came to

Match results place BFRFC scores first

the fore were second rows Clive Friend and Albert Gleaves, left wing Peter Brennan, centre Steve Smart, half-back Dean Hoare and John Thomas.

AGM

At the AGM, Roger Amphlett (next season's captain) presented outgoing captain Closs Jones with a coffee set as he was leaving the Ferry to work in Caerleon.

Roger Amphlett's 141 points just missed creating a new points scoring record. Re-elected were chairman Morgan Jones, vice chairman Llew Llewelyn, president Trevor Davies, secretary Roy Evans, assistant secretary Ted Richards (taking over from Hubert Adams who retired) and committeemen A.L. Llewelyn, J. Thomas, A. O'Shea, D. Mills, G. Richards and G. Jones.

The Morgan Jones Player of the Year Award was won by Malcolm Edwards, which was a popular choice.

> MALCOLM EDWARDS was featured in *Welsh Rugby* in August 1972, which said that this venerable forward had no intention of stepping out of the Briton Ferry spotlight and that he was looking forward to his fourteenth season with the club.

In the district

A new local competition was launched, the O.G. Davies Cup. The first final was contested between Crynant and Tonna at the Gnoll. Crynant edged it to become inaugural winners.

The Quins played in the local sevens at the beginning of the season and after beating both BP Llandarcy (12–6) and Gwernyfed in the local cup, they lost to Neath Athletic in the semi-final at Skewen. Both Peter Harris and J. Davies made the district squad, as did Briton Ferry Steel players J. Griffiths, J. O'Sullivan, D. Broad and D. Harding.

Briton Ferry Steel had a disappointing year but did manage an excellent 32–10 win over Glamorgan Wanderers Extras in September.

Cuan O'Shea was selected to play for Neath against St Luke's College in April.

9.5 1971/72

Back Row: P. Brennan; M. Edwards; L. Rees; T. Pollack; A. Hopkins; M. Williams; K. Harris; S. Smart; R. Amphlett; G. Thomas. Middle Row: L. Tregonning; B. Hill; H. Mills; E.C. Jones (captain); D. Hoare; J. Williams; J. Schmidt. Front Row: P. Kops; J. Thomas; P. Davies; R. Evans

1972/73

Ex-Welsh international Brian Thomas was now training the club, alongside Ron Trimnell.

9.6 Chat with Brian Thomas

Captain
Roger Amplett

The First XV started the season in September with an 8–7 win over Treherbert, Peter Bell grabbed a double. But followed it with defeats by Cwmavon, Laugharne, Brynmawr (16–25), Crynant in the O.G. Davies Cup (0–28, when both Peter Bell and John Morris were sent off – Neath coach Brian Thomas was also sent off in October), and Taibach (9–12, locks Dai Thomas and Cuan O'Shea were injured, but the good news was that front prop Gerald Lewis resumed playing after a gap of a couple of seasons).

Ferry got back to winning ways in October by defeating Ogmore Vale away. But injuries continued to mount and eight players were out. New prop Mike Howe was proving to be a good find and fullback Ken Harris was outstanding. But Ferry lost their next games to Mumbles and Resolven

(9–15, Smart and Amphlett 2 penalties each) but they did defeat BP Llandarcy 20–3, to end the month on a high (Smart kicked 2 goals).

Briton Ferry RFC 1972-73

Back row-Dave Herbert; Cyril Beasley; Roy Evans; Harry Melding; E.C.Jones; A. Hopkins; J. John; G. Lewis; Idris Jones; Gwynfryn Thomas; L.Tregonning; L. Jenkins; Ref. Lyn Thomas; D. Mills

Front Row-S. Forrester; D.L.Thomas; B. Hill; Peter Davies (Capt.); R. Amphlett; G. Jones; T. Woodland;

Seated on floor- Paul Kite; Dean Hoare; Eric Jones.

9.7 1972/73

November games were against Llandaff and then two against Dinas Powis. Ferry inflicted the double on Dinas Powis, 21–16 away and 12–0 at home. Dean Hoare 1 drop goal and John Thomas bagged 1 try that was converted by skipper Amphlett. New centre Phil Jones, hooker John Rue, centre Peter Brennan and flanker Clive Anthony were playing really well. Wings Peter Bell and Colin Watkins were looking particularly strong on the end of passes from centre Dai Lewis. Ferry then suffered a narrow 11–17 home defeat to previously unbeaten Newport Saracens; and to Aberavon Quins, 11–16 – John Thomas with a try.

The Ferry ended the year with a perfect month by defeating Llantwit Major (16–4, Watkins and 19-year-old flanker Dai Jones with tries, Smart converted 1), BP Llandarcy (4–3, Peter Bell with the game breaker), Skewen (10–0, B. Pill and young flanker Nigel Flowers with tries, Ken Harris converted 1), and finally Resolven (7–0, Anthony with a try and Smart kicking a penalty.

During December Neath RFC had started to invite local teams to come to the Gnoll to help with their training programme, and the first two clubs invited were the Ferry and BP Llandarcy!

Sadly, there was a complete reversal in January with defeats by Aberavon Quins 0–10, Llantwit Major (9–14, fielding their youngest team ever, averaging 20 years old, Jeff Williams 1 try, half-back Hoare denied 2 tries; skipper Amphlett led well and Mal Edwards damaged his ribs), then Mumbles, where Ferry conceded a double.

In February Ferry defeated Porthcawl 9–0 (John Thomas again on the try sheet and new wing Clive Williams showing promise), but they ended the month with a 4–20 defeat at the hands of Cilfynydd (Quins centre John Evans played well).

Then in March they lost narrowly to Abercynon, 4–3. Hooker Mal Edwards, scrum-half John Thomas and young flanker Kevin Bowring played really well.

> A future captain of the club, young SPENCER LEWIS, gained a place in the Welsh Secondary Schools squad to play the Welsh Youth. He was playing for the very successful Neath Grammar School, who had been coached by Ron Trimnell. During Trimnell's reign the school went unbeaten for five seasons and had only lost sixteen games out of 299. Twenty-five Neath Grammar School players won secretary school caps.

The Ferry did go on to defeat Barry 16–0, Bynea 20–4 and Nantymoel 30–0. Peter Brennan kicked a penalty against Barry, and Bowring, Thomas and Peter Davies bagged tries against Nantymoel, with Brennan converting. New centre Peter Kopp played very well in his first few games for the club.

During the last month of the season Ferry lost to Llandaff 6–13, but beat Ogmore Vale comprehensively, 64–3 – a new club record score. P. Davies (2), Colin Watkins and John Thomas were among the try scorers and skipper Amphlett converted 8 of the 12 tries.

Quins

The Quins also had a bad start and were knocked out of the Neath & District Cup by Bryncoch. They did get some wins in the autumn, including 10–4 over bitter rivals Skewen. They lost to Cimla, 23–4, with Reg Mundy bagging a try.

Youth rugby

There was a hope that the Youth XV would re-form during the season, helped by the council making pitches available. In fact, around twenty-four came to training and the first youth game since 1969 was played at home to Cimla on 2 April, although they lost narrowly 11–19. They also lost eventually to Morriston.

Tour

The Easter tour went to Birkenhead where they beat Wallasey 32–13 and lost to Caldy 12–7. John Johnson became the club's liaison officer and George Brown the entertainments organiser. New to the tour party were: backs K. Parris, P. Brennan, Clive Williams and Colin Watkins; and forwards Mike Howe, Courtney John, Clive Friend, Bernard Hardwick, Terry Keefe and Kevin Bowring.

> The manager of the Central Hotel in Birkenhead wrote to the WRU to praise the club's exemplary behaviour during their visit!

Briton Ferry RFC 1973 Tour to Southport-21st April vs. Wallesley won 32-13

Back Row– Terry Gregory, Cyril Beasley, Terry Woodland, Jim Smith, Albert Gleaves, Clive Williams, Mal Edwards, John Johnson, Allan Hopkins, Mike Howe, Terry Keefe, Roy Evans (Sec.) , John Selby, Morgan Jones (Chairman).
Front row– Peter Davies, Clive Friend, Ken Harris, Roger Amphlett (Capt.), Jeff Williams, Peter Brennan, Kevin Bowring
On Floor– John Thomas and Dean Hoare.

Briton Ferry RFC Tour to Southport 23rd April 1973-vs Caldy-lost 7-12
Back row– John Selby, Jim Smith, Kevin Bowring, Jeff Williams, Clive Friend, Roger Amphlett (Capt.), Ken Harris, Albert Gleaves, Allan Hopkins, Mike Howe, Terry Keefe, Bernard Hardwick..
Front row-Mal Edwards, Peter Davies, John Thomas, Roy Evans (Sec), Dean Hoare, Clive Williams, Peter Brennan, Terry Woodland.

9.8 1973 tour to Southport (top) v. Caldy, (bottom) v. Wallesley

Annual presentation

At the annual presentation scrum-half John Thomas was awarded the Player of the Year trophy for his 21 tries through the season. Thomas had also featured in *Welsh Rugby* during April, where they described him as a resilient, pint-size scrum worker, who had hardly missed a game all season and who could make an impact in first-class rugby with his all-out style of play. Roger Amphlett was chosen to lead the side again for the coming season. Chairman Morgan Jones surprised long-serving baggage man Idris Jones by presenting him with a tankard in recognition of his forty-five unbroken years at the club. He'd joined at twenty-four years old and had acted as dressing room attendant and assistant cellar man among the many other chores that kept the club going.

In the district

In November Briton Ferry Steel had been drawn to play Gwernyfed away in the Neath & District Cup, which they won, but then lost to Seven Sisters in the final, 10–8. A row was brewing with the Glamorgan Education Authority who had deemed that the Cwrt Sart pitch would not be available to Briton Ferry Steel for the rest of the season – with no official notice given to the home club. So Steel would now have to travel to Cwrt Herbert. Meanwhile, ex-Briton Ferry Steel boy John Budge made it on to the WRU referee list.

Dennis Hare was playing well for Ferry Steel. He'd started his rugby with Taibach Youth in 1948 and then had a long stint with the Ferry (1955–1965) before joining the Steel –where he is now called Grandad.

The O.G. Davies Cup was won by Crynant again, who beat Bryncoch in the final.

1973/74

Up to sixty players turned out for pre-season training. Ex-player Doug Jones attended these sessions, along with Ron Trimnell, and the coming season was looking positive. The club hoped to run three teams: First XV, Quins and Youth.

They got off to a good start by beating Tonna 14–7 in the first round, first leg of the O.G. Davies Cup. They lost the second leg (wing Peter Bell got 3 tries), but progressed on aggregate. Ferry lost to Seven Sisters in the WRU Cup, 20–26 (they also lost to them in their invitation sevens competition) and to Llandaff 14–16 (Dean Hoare, Allan Hopkins and Clive Williams bagged tries, prop Courtney John played well) and to BSC Port Talbot 9–11 (John Thomas and Albert Gleaves scored 1 try apiece, Amphlett and Smart kicked 1 goal apiece). Ferry did end the month with a win, beating Carmarthen Athletic 18–8.

October started with an away draw at Ynysybwl, they then defeated Felinfoel 13–12 (wing Roy Evans 1 try, Allan Hopkins converting, Phil Manning, Peter Davies and Hopkins playing well), but they then lost 0–7 to Resolven.

Ferry defeated Tonna again in November (9–6). Skipper Amphlett kicked 3 penalties and Doug Jones played on permit from Mumbles. They then defeated Gorseinon 4–0, in their first meeting for ten years, but the rest of the month was frozen off. The pack had improved considerably with Jones rejoining them, as his experience rubbed off on the younger players.

Results varied in December. They beat Ogmore Vale 38–0 (G. Llewelyn 1 try, Roger Amphlett 14 points, including 2 tries, Mal Edwards took 3 against the head).

Match results place BFRFC scores first

They then lost to Dinas Powis (P. Bell 1 try) and drew 0–0 with Tonna (Dennis Richards played well).

Also in December, Doug Jones was selected to play for a Central Glamorgan XV and Allan Hopkins was selected as reserve for the game against Mid-District on New Year's Day at Aberavon. Cuan O'Shea played for the Midlands UAU, who beat Southern Universities in a British Universities trial.

The new year started with a 7–23 defeat at home by Abercynon (Smart kicked a goal and hooker Mal Edwards broke his jaw). There were a lot of problems with the pitch, so an end of the month home game with Caldicot had to be switched at the last minute to Baglan. Ferry lost 6–14. Amphlett's boot again provided the points. Young second row Spencer Lewis was impressing with his performances.

Facing the Ferry for Caldicot was ex-Newport outside-half JOHN UZZELL who, a few years previously, had dropped a goal for Newport to defeat the All Blacks.

Unfortunately, in February the Youth XV was disbanded due to lack of numbers. The remainder of the squad then joined up with the Quins to see the season out. Two players went straight into the First XV, wing Ron Willis and outside-half Keith Roberts (son of Cyril). The pitch problems meant a lack of games during the month and training was switched to Sundays, with some of it spent painting the club. The O.G. Davies Cup semi-final against Cwmgrach was also called off because the pitch at Seven Sisters was waterlogged – when this game was eventually played in March, Ferry lost. They ended the month with a defeat to Llandaff.

A few more games were played in March (including that semi-final) and they suffered a heavy defeat to BSC Margam, 0–31. Ferry did manage a 6–6 draw at home to BSC Margam at the end of the month, and narrowly defeated BP Llandarcy, 7–6. Albert Gleaves scored a try and then broke his ankle. Skipper Amphlett added the extras. The youngsters were to the fore in these games, with Spencer Lewis, Ron Willis and Keith Roberts playing well alongside Peter Bell and Peter Davies.

Tour

During April, the club embarked on an Easter tour to Teignmouth in Devon. They played the home club, Newton Abbot and Torquay.

Presentation night

Wing Peter Bell claimed the Player of the Year Award, which was presented to him by ex-player, Chief Superintendent Vernon Friend. Plaques were also presented to retiring players Albert Gleaves and Malcolm Edwards, and wedding gifts to John Evans and Brian Wills.

In the district

Although the Youth team had disbanded they did hold a festival of rugby in April, which Crynant won.

The local O.G. Davies Cup was won by Seven Sisters, who defeated Cwmgrach in the final.

Match results place BFRFC scores first

1974/75

Peter Davies had previously captained local rivals Skewen. He was joined by player coach Kevin Bowring, who had offered to help out when home from university, along with fellow student Cuan O'Shea.

The season started with 3–19 away defeat at Tonna in a first leg match for the O.G. Davies Cup. Allan Hopkins kicked a penalty. Ferry did win the second leg 9–3, but it was not enough to take them through to the next round.

October was a struggle as they managed a 6–6 draw at home with Resolven, in which centre G. Llewelyn bagged a try, converted by Smart. Second rows Courtney John and John Morris showed up well, as did no.8 Spencer Lewis and fellow centre Allan Clifford. Ferry were then defeated at home, first by Gilfach Goch, 6–7 (Keith Roberts kicked the goals), and then Cilfynydd. They ended the month with an away fixture at BSC Margam.

> Hooker **BARTON WILLS** was back in the side after a holiday in Canada where he had played for Toronto Irish! But out injured went fly-half **DAI LEWIS**.

Ferry got off to a better start in November with a 6–3 win at home to Caldicot (Gareth Llewelyn try, converted by K. Roberts) and newcomers Les Thomas and Nigel Edwards did well. But the weather took care of the rest of the month and waterlogged pitches meant game after game was called off. One bright spot was the selection of Peter Bell, Courtney John and Spencer Lewis for O.G. Davies XV v. Penygraig this month.

Scrum-half Andrew Shufflebotham returned from injury in December, but this didn't prevent a 4–24 defeat away to Tonna (Ronnie Willis 1 try). But with Cuan O'Shea

Captain
Peter Davies

Coach
Kevin Bowring

Playing record
P 30
W 17

and Kevin Bowring returning for the Christmas period there was hope on the horizon. Although Ferry lost their next game 0–6 at home to Abercynon, they did end the year with home wins against Risca (7–0) and Carmarthen Athletic (10–0). New wing Andy Bell (brother of Peter) bagged 1 try in each game and Smart added the extras. Bowring also got 1 try in the latter match. New half-back combination of Roberts and Cimla scrum-half Cliff Morgan worked really well and there was a hope that Morgan might join on a regular basis.

The new year got off to a great start with a 15–0 win away at Resolven. More cancellations followed, before ending the month with a 6–4 home win over Tonna – Allan Hopkins kicked a 40-yard penalty to win the game. This gave the teams two wins each for the season, as they had each won a match in the O.G. Davies Cup.

The First XV were undefeated in February, with the double over Ogmore Vale, 14–0 at home and 32–10 away, and a 7–7 away draw with BP Llandarcy. Andy Bell was on the score sheet again with 2 at home to Ogmore. The versatile Mr Allan Hopkins played fullback (in fact, he played everywhere bar the front row for the club). Hooker John Rue took 12 heads in the away game at Ogmore, when flanker Robert Knight had a fine debut. Ferry scored 7 tries at Ogmore. A Smart penalty saved the game at BP Llandarcy.

KEVIN BOWRING was selected to play for Neath against Swansea in February and was also selected for the English Colleges XV against Berkshire, in which he scored a try in the 36–3 win. He had also been selected by Middlesex County XV for their semi-final against Warwickshire – drafted in to replace Andy Ripley, who was getting married in Austria.

CUAN O'SHEA had taken over the fitness training at the club, which was proving to be a good move.

A future Ferry player was getting his Under-16s Welsh Schoolboy cap against England in February, STEVE KNIGHT played in the second row in a 16–9 win.

March was a different story. Ferry lost 6–20 to Crynant (2 Smart penalties) and 3–6 to Pontycymmer.

Ferry lost two out of six games during April, away at Skewen and at home to Ystalyfera (17–22, C. O'Shea and Colin Watkins tries, Smart conversion), but defeated Cwmavon (9–6 Smart 3 penalties; Robert Knight, Peter Davies and Kevin Bowring were exceptional), a first win against Llandaff for ten years (13–6, A. Bell try; Alan Clifford was outstanding) and Skewen at home (scrum-half Cliff Morgan was outstanding).

Tour

For the annual Easter tour the club visited Lincolnshire and played Market Rasen and Grimsby RFCs.

The tour players were: Peter Bell, Ron Willis, Hugh Davies, Jeff Beaton, Keith Roberts, Steve Smart, John Rue, Cuan O'Shea, Gareth Llewelyn, David Jenkins, Lloyd Phillips, Geoff Whomes, Andy Bell, Alan Clifford, Hugh Ryall, Kevin Hawse, Keith "Tonto" Thomas, Les Thomas, Des Whitelock, Robert "Nitty" Knight, Steve "Buster" Morgan and Jeff "Olly" Davies. New committeemen this year were assistant secretary Lyn Jenkins, Second XV secretary P. Davies and fixture secretary Albert Gleaves.

Quins

in November the Quins managed an away game against Metal Box, which they won 10–7. Graham Davies and Jeff Beaton played well, and Roger Amphlett kicked two goals.

Presentation night

At the end of the season awards wing Peter Bell was top try scorer, with 19, and he received the Annual Player of the Year award having played in every game during the season. Top points scorer was prop Steve Smart, with 135 points. Kevin Bowring was presented with a travelling bag for representing the British Colleges. A wedding clock went to Spencer Lewis. A surprise award was made to Cuan O'Shea for his helping with the coaching, especially since they'd finished the season with the best playing record for a decade.

The club donated the W.S.D. Davies Cup to Cwrt Sart Comprehensive to be played for annually in memory of the ex-Ferry secretary. New vice president Terry Woodlands donated a new Player of the Year board to the club, which was unveiled by secretary Roy Evans.

In the district

In Neath, ex-player David Parker announced his retirement from the game and was presented with a plaque as thanks for his service.

Briton Ferry Steel RFC featured in *Welsh Rugby* in August as part of their tenth anniversary celebrations. They won the H.G. Lewis Cup, beating Crynant in the final, and then the Metal Box All Winners Cup against Bryncoch. This was the first time since 1968 that they had won both trophies.

9.9 Briton Ferry Steel in 1975, (top) v. Bryncoch; (bottom) v. Crynant

Match results place BFRFC scores first

1975/76

A landmark season, the club's seventy-five anniversary of full WRU status. BFRFC was one of the first junior clubs to gain that status.

Neath RFC came to the Ferry early in September to help celebrate and went away with a 34–10 win (Andy Bell bagged 1 try to go with Smart's 2 penalties).

> The club signed-up scrum-half **CLIFF MORGAN** in September, which was to have a great significance for them. He joined from Cimla RFC's junior side and made an instant impact.

In one of Cliff Morgan's first games he bagged a hat trick of tries and conversions (18 points) against a South Wales Police XV (a week after they'd knocked the Ferry out of the WRU Cup). Peter Bell also on the score sheet in that 42–0 win. Ferry then bagged their first Silver Ball win of the season against BP Llandarcy. Prop Courtney John got his third try in as many matches, flanker Clive Penharwood and centre Huw Davies played really well. But Ferry really struggled in their O.G. Davies Cup rounds and lost 0–75 on aggregate to a strong Seven Sisters side. They also lost their first game at home, 8–21 to Crynant.

Captain
Peter Davies

Peter Bell, Cliff Morgan and Spencer Lewis represented the club in an O.G. Davies XV.

Ferry had an excellent October, with wins over Tredegar Ironsides (35–12), Skewen (38–12) and BP Llandarcy (27–3) at home. Cliff Morgan amassed points, Peter Bell got 3 tries, and Clive Penharwood and the outstanding flanker Dave Jones got further tries. Then Ferry lost away to Abercynon.

In November Ferry were only defeated once, 10–14 at home to Abercynon (when Cliff Morgan reached 100 points in the season). They registered wins over BSC Margam (6–0, Morgan 2 penalties), Carmarthen at home (28–17), Ogmore Vale at home (38–0) and Taibach away (6–0, Courtney John 1 try, Morgan 1 conversion)., Ex-Neath players Norman Rees and Brian Thomas helped out in the BSC Margam game, when winning points came from the outstanding Cliff Morgan. Try getters against Carmarthen were Colin Watkins, Spencer Lewis and Clive Penharwood. Lewis was a try scorer in the rout of Ogmore.

9.10 1975/76

(back) Terry Gregory, Peter Davies, Ted, Richards, Hughie Watkins, Llew Llewellyn, Morgan Jones, Jack Thomas, Rod Morgan (WRU representative), Roy Evans, Harry Melding, Albert Gleaves, Jacky Bell, committeemen; (3rd row) John Selby, referee, Doc Beasley, Malcolm Edwards, Andy Bell, Clive Penharwood, Roger Amphlett, Spencer Lewis, Mike Curtis, Courtney John, Brian Thomas, Stuart Forester, Des Whitelock, Albert O'Shea, Alan Cliffor, Lyn Jenkins; (2nd row, sitting) John Rue, Hugh Davies, Allan Hopkins, Peter Davies, Peter Bell, Colin Watkins, Ron willis, Norman Rees, Ewart Adams;(front) Clifford Morgan, Keith ROberts, Hugh Ryall

On 6 December, the versatile Allan Hopkins reached his 500th game, another significant day in the history of the club. They played Tonna at home and Allan was captain for the day. He duly delivered by bagging a brace of tries in a 32–7 win. Peter Bell also made 2 tries, Penharwood 1 and Cliffy Morgan converted 3.

> The **HOPKINS FAMILY** were also involved with the Ferry. Both sons, Ceri and David, played youth rugby at the club. David captained the side and went on to play senior rugby. Allan's daughter Rhian joined his wife Frances on the ladies committee.

A model display by a model player ...

ALAN HOPKINS is the sort of player any club would like to possess, uncomplainingly turning out — and doing a good job — in whatever position in the side he is required for.

In a rugby-playing career with Briton Ferry spanning 17 years, model clubman Hopkins has at one time or another filled literally every position in the team, even taking over as hooker despite his lanky frame when another player was injured.

It was appropriate that the memorable milestone of Hopkins' 500th appearance in the Ferry colours should have been in a local derby clash, and it was Tonna who were on the receiving end as he marked the occasion with two splendid tries.

Our picture was taken before the Tonna match, but after the game, in which Ferry romped home 32-7, Hopkins was officially presented with a statuette by the club, presented on their behalf by Mr. Rod Morgan, one of the two representatives on the Welsh Rugby Union of the district which includes Briton Ferry.

He was also presented with a Tonna Rugby Club plaque, which he in turn presented to the Ferry Club for display in the clubhouse.

9.11 A model display: Allan Hopkins (19 December 1975)

In the following week at home, Ferry swamped Gorseinon 40–9. Morgan scored 24 points (a new individual club record). Morgan was selected to play for Neath against Penarth the week after and kicked 5 conversions in a 42–4 win. The following Monday he scored the 5 points he needed to break the Briton Ferry scoring record of 144 points held by Harold Roberts for 23 years! Morgan's total was now 146 points.

> On Boxing Day the Under-30s challenged the Over-30s to a game. Pencilled-in for the over-30s were Doug Jones, Ernie Jones, Roy Evans, John Simonson, Jack Shore, Hugh Watkins, Brian Thomas and Dai Parker. Rocky Ellis and his Gazoot combo were to provide the pre-match music and entertainment and the Mayor of North Kennington, Bryan Hire, was to kick-off the match.

Morgan started off the new year by bagging all the points in a 12–9 win against Aberavon Quins. Forwards Brian Thomas and Kevin Bowring and fullback Keith Roberts were outstanding. Ferry were now lying ninth in the Glamorgan Silver Ball competition and thirteenth in the Truman Cup (awarded for most tries).

> IAN BELL returned from a five-week home visit to Canada after stint. STEVE ROPER played for Aberavon and NORMAN REES helped out Llanelli.

Towards the end of January, Ferry defeated South Wales Police "A" away 9–0. This was Brian Thomas' fifteenth game for the season, and he had been on the winning side thirteen times.

> The tour venue was to be Bournemouth, to take part in their festival, and a sub-committee was formed to organise a tour to Canada in two years' time.

In February, a late penalty from Cliff Morgan gave Ferry a win over Tredegar Ironsides on their own patch and put him on 175 points. Great play came from veteran Colin Watkins, despite injuring his shoulder, and from centre David Williams (a local teacher) on his debut. Later that month another debutant was influential in an 18–11 home win over Llandaff, Ron Lilley scored 1 try, which Morgan converted, to go with a Bell Brothers contribution – Andy with 1 try and Peter with 2. Peter was also on target in the last match of the month and scored in the win over Ogmore Vale away – Dai Williams got a hat trick.

In March:

- Ferry boy David Pickering was selected to play for Welsh Schools against Italy
- Kevin Bowring was selected to play for Middlesex County on their tour to Sweden
- Peter Bell was selected to play for West Glamorgan
- The town of Briton Ferry played host to the French Television Service during the weekend of the Wales v. France match, as a certain Mr Brian Thomas was interpreter for the show.

The club had good wins over Skewen (doing the double, Williams 1 try, veteran Allan Hopkins 2 tries, Morgan kicked 8 points). They then defeated Pontardawe, 29–3 at home. "Twmas" got a hat trick of tries, Peter Bell added another (his nineteenth of the season and a club record), Keith Roberts added 1 to go with 1 conversion and 1 penalty. Ferry then defeated Resolven. Cliff Morgan was outstanding again and reached 194 points in 25 games. His form drew an invitation to go on tour with Neath to the West Indies at the end of the season. A draw with Taibach away from home ended a good month for the club.

KEVIN BOWRING was selected again for Neath against Cross Keys and "CLIFFY" was selected against Glamorgan Wanderers in April,.

In April, in the WRU Sevens at Porthcawl the Ferry defeated Kenfig Hill and Seven Sisters on their way to the semi-finals, where they lost to South Wales Police. Morgan, Williams and Norman Rees were outstanding in this tournament.

The First XV played Mumbles home and away. During the home game Morgan kicked 1 penalty, 1 conversion and 1 drop goal to add to 1 try from skipper Peter Davies. Ferry won 12–10. Prop Courtney John was Man of the

Match results place BFRFC scores first

Match. Welsh selector Jack Young watched the game and said afterwards that it was the best second-class game he'd seen all season.

Quins

The Quins ended March on a high by defeating Baglan 7–6, their third win in succession.

Presentation night

Cliff Morgan was selected as Player of the Year, he was top scorer with 223 points – a new club record. Peter Bell was top try scorer and Peter Davies was awarded Clubman of the Year.

In the district

At the end of January in the Neath & District league, the Quins were lying bottom but one (with 1 win and 1 draw from 11 games), while Briton Ferry Steel were eighth (with 4 wins and 1 draw). Seven Sisters claimed the title at the end of the season.

1976/77

Coach Brian Thomas was joined later in the year by Dai Parker. Quins captain Keith "Tonto" Thomas was an outstanding back rower.

> Early in the season BRIAN THOMAS and veteran DAI PARKER played in a benefit match at Neath for former player KEITH MORRIS who had broken his neck in a training incident.

The club got off to a good start with home wins over Pontycymmer (31–6) and Tredegar Ironsides (21–16). Morgan's previous season's form continued, and Roger Amphlett and Norman Rees got tries. Ferry then defeated Llantwit Major 32–13 at home. Rees, Steve Williams, Keith Roberts and Morgan were all on the try sheet, with Morgan adding the extras. They then completed an early season double by defeating Ironsides 15–10 – Kevin Bowring and young fullback Jeff Beaton played well.

> NORMAN REES was selected to train with the Welsh squad. He got married on Saturday and was at training on Aberavon Beach on Sunday.

Ferry played Tonna in a double header in the O.G. Davies Cup and, over two legs, lost on aggregate by 28–4. Ron Willis got the only try and Courtney John was sent off. They also lost in a midweek friendly.

> Once again SPENCER LEWIS and CLIFF MORGAN were selected to play for the O.G. Davies XV.

In October's first game, the First XV ended up kicking themselves as they let slip a half-time lead, to lose 20–21 at Resolven, despite Roberts adding 2 penalties. They lost two more games: 0–6 to Pyle in the WRU Cup; and 12–13 at home to Nantymoel, when Cliff Morgan got 4 penalties.

Captain
Peter Davies

Quins captain
Keith Thomas

Coach
Brian Thomas

Playing record
P 35
W 17
D 1
L 17

Match results place BFRFC scores first

Ferry then lost 4–8 to Mumbles in November, before defeating Cilfynydd 27–0 at home – with Morgan contributing 15 points and Clive Penharwood, John Rue and Roger Amphlett all back from injury. The month ended on a happy note by defeating South Wales police A 29–7, with Morgan on the score sheet again and Steve Williams bagging a try.

They ended the year with a 6–8 home defeat to Aberavon Quins. But they did win against Porthcawl (10–6, Clive Penharwood 1 try, Morgan 2 penalties), against Dunvant (20–0) and against Carmarthen Athletic (15–7). Dai Parker, playing in the centre, scored a try in a 20–0 home win against Bonymaen – Penharwood 2 and Cliff Morgan 1 and 1 conversion, Keith Roberts converted the other. Both Spencer Lewis and Peter Davies were sent off in this game.

The club played a Past v. Present game on Boxing Day.

The First XV started the new year seventh in the Truman Cup on 122 points and 21 tries.

In January they were defeated 6–23 at Maesteg Celtic (A. Hopkins try, Morgan conversion), and 6–26 at home to Resolven (Morgan 2 penalties).

Then in February they defeated Aberavon Quins 3–0 away (Roberts kicked a penalty and youth players Nigel Lovering and Ian James were on the bench. Then lost 9–12 at Llantwit Major (Morgan 3 penalties) and won 34–3 at home to Ogmore Vale, when Roberts got 3 tries, Steve Williams, Peter Bell and Mal Robertson got the others and Morgan kicked ten points.

Ferry also lost to Mumbles in March (0–6), and to Skewen (3–6, a Roberts penalty). They defeated Cwmgors away 21–3 (P. Bell 2 tries, Roberts 1, Morgan 1 and 1 penalty and 1 conversion) and ended the month with a midweek fixture against Borough Road College.

They played two fixtures in April against Bynea; Brian Thomas returned up front in the away match and Morgan bagged 5 points to go with 1 Keith Thomas try, but the match ended in a 9–9 draw. Ferry also played fixtures against Gowerton and Skewen.

Ferry finished fifteenth in the Truman Cup with 22 tries and 134 points.

Youth XV

The Youth XV was re-formed in October with players such as Richard Lawrence, Mike Curtis, Nigel Powell, Steve Richards, Ian James and Ian Matthews and with Albert Gleaves and Norman Rees as coaches. In their first game they drew with Tonna. They were defeated later in the season by both Dunvant

(4–16) and Neath Colts, then drew 3–3 with Abercrave and lost to Bridgend Athletic, Seven Sisters and Tonna.

Presentation evening

Top scorer was Cliff Morgan with 173 points. Keith Roberts had played in every game and scored 113 points. Player of the Year went to back rower Keith Thomas and Youth Player of the Year was second row Steven "Gonk" John. Most Promising Player of the Year went to fly-half Keith Roberts. Presentations were made to Malcolm Edwards as Clubman of the Year and Alan Clifford, Peter Davies, Cliff Morgan and Andy Bell received wedding clocks.

Mr W.L. Williams, ex-treasurer, was appointed as the new club president after forty-five years of service. Ted Richards took over as treasurer. Peter Davies and Colin Watkins were elected to the committee.

In the district

Seven Sisters defeated Crynant in the O.G. Davies Cup final to retain the title they had won the previous year against Tonna. Their Second XV made it to the Neath & District Cup final and became championship winners. The Quins had lost to Tonna in an earlier round (Courtney John scored 1 try, Alan Clifford 2 penalties and 1 conversion), and then disbanded before the end of the season.

At Briton Ferry Steel, Player of the Year and Most Promising Player awards both went to fullback Martin Williams, who joined the Ferry when the clubs merged. Colin Adams was Clubman of the Year. His brother Roland (vice chairman), Ron O'Rourke (treasurer), Graham Ellis and John Budge (secretary) were given an awared for ten years of service to the club by chairman Brian Allen at the Tudor Club.

> During the close season, the annual golf competition was held between Briton Ferry RFC and Resolven RFC. Trophy holders Ferry were narrowly defeated. Team members included captain John Selby, Peter Johns, Gwyn Morris, Dean Hoare, Alan Vaughan and Terry Gregory.

1977/78

Ferry held an invitation sevens tournament at the club in August and were defeated by Resolven, who beat Crynant in the final. Ferry were also invited to the Aberavon Green Stars Sevens in late August.

> COLIN WATKINS and PETER DAVIES announced their retirements and they both went on to serve on the committee.

September was a poor start to the season for the club and they went the whole month without a win. In the first full game of the new season Ferry were defeated at Gowerton (Peter Bell and Dai Williams with tries and Roberts 1 conversion).

> Skipper Bell was selected to make his debut for Neath in September in their home win against Welsh cup holders Newport (future coach Dai Lewis also played in this game). Bell's brother Andy and centre Dai Williams were selected to play for an O.G. Davies XV against Seven Sisters; while Spencer Lewis, Steve Williams and Peter Bell were selected for an O.G. Davies XV against Glamorgan B.

Ferry lost to Seven Sisters on aggregate 4–43 in the O.G. Davies Cup (the only try from Andy Bell), then to Nantymoel 6–10 in the WRU Cup, to Abercynon 9–32 (S. Williams try, Roberts kicked the other points), and to Llantwit Major 0–9. Scrum-half Cliff Morgan transferred back to Cimla RFC and Ferry eventually replaced him with Andrew Shufflebotham from Crynant (ex-captain of Neath Grammar School), who proved a good signing for the club. They were also having a bit of an injury crisis as forwards Peter Davies, Roger Amphlett, Courtney John and Allan Hopkins were all out.

Captain
Peter Bell

Coaches
Dai Parker
Brian Thomas

Playing record
P 28
W 11
D 1
L 16

In October, the First XV finally got a win and beat Cwmgrach 18–8 at home. Keith Roberts scored 14 points. But then lost at home to Maesteg Celtic. Spencer Lewis skippered a side that was missing forwards Norman Rees and Ron Lilley. Deputy hooker John Rue took five strikes against the head in this game. Roberts added the extras to Andrew Shufflebotham's try.

Bryncoch were their next opponents and they defeated them 14–6 at home. Roberts kicked 2 penalties and skipper Bell added 1 try. Coach Dai Parker was forced to play fullback in this match and young youth prospect centre Paul Woodland did well on his debut. They then drew 12–12 at Mumbles and ended the month with a 7–3 home win over Llantwit Major. Young Woodlands got his first try of many for the club. Dai Parker was filling in for Shufflebotham at scrum-half. The back row of Ron Lilley, "Tonto" and Clive "Bow" Penharwood were outstanding.

> KEVIN BOWRING had gone back to Borough Road College, and he was selected to play for London Welsh in October – and scored a try against Coventry.

Keith Roberts kicked two penalties in a 13–7 home win over Cefn Cribbwr in November.

> KEITH ROBERTS was selected to play for Crawshays Welsh XV against Aberavon later in the month. He'd played for them against Llanelli earlier in the season (lost 9–8). These games had been organised to raise money for the silver jubilee fund.

> Peter Bell was selected to play for Central Glamorgan against East District and Andrew Shufflebotham was selected for Neath against Bridgend.

Prop Peter Davies and veteran back rower Allan Hopkins came back from injury but were unable to prevent a 0–10 defeat against a Caldicot side containing ex-Welsh centre Dick Uzzell. The month continued in this vein with further defeats at Dunvant (3–17) and 9–14 at home to Resolven (Roberts bagged all the Ferry points with the boot), fullback Peter Davies came out of retirement to play in this game.

> December saw the debut of yet another youth player. Scrum-half RICHARD LAWRENCE would go on to have a long career with the club, on and off the field, as player, coach and youth coach.

Richard Lawrence's first game was against Nantymoel in a 20–7 home win (Andy Bell 1 try, Roberts 1 conversion). Ferry then lost 0–13 at home to Maesteg Celtic. They then defeated Brynmawr 17–0, before a double header with Aberavon Quins before and after Christmas. Ferry conceded the double,

3–32 away and 10–26 at home (Keith Thomas 1 try, Keith Roberts kicked the extras).

> Ferry also attempted to rejoin the West Wales Rugby Union league system, but failed to gain admission. So they immediately put their thoughts into joining the newly talked about Central Glamorgan League with fifteen other clubs. A ballot was held for this new ten-team division. The Ferry lost out by one vote – they got 27 votes, Resolven received 28 and Tonna 31. Along with Lampeter, Ferry also failed in a bid to join the new Section E. Lampeter lodged a complaint via the WRU on the grounds that they would fail to find fixtures and therefore suffer financially if they were not voted in. They hoped there was a slim chance that the section might be extended to 12 clubs. The WRU looked into it and went in favour of the Welsh Wales Rugby Union vote.

Ferry started the new year with a home fixture against Aberavon Quins. Then they took Bonymaen's home ground record, which had stood since December 1976, with a narrow 7–0 win (Spencer Lewis 1 try, Roberts 1 conversion). They lost narrowly at home to Abercynon (6–10), with the adaptable Allan Hopkins slipping up to prop for the game (Roberts kicked the points). Ferry then lost 0–14 at Carmarthen Athletic.

> Carmarthen Athletic proved to be the last game for hooker JOHN RUE after ten years at the club. He was moving to Leicester with his job at the Metal Box Company. He was to have captained the club at home to Brynmawr in February, but this was one of many games cancelled because of the big freeze.

In March, Ferry played Mumbles at home on the Sunday after the Wales v. Ireland game, and lost 3–21 (Roberts again kicked the points, prop Emrys Landeg played well). Pontardawe were the next opponents at home and Ferry lost the game 9–21. Andy Bell 1 try, Roberts added the rest. The back row of Thomas, Williams and Penharwood, and young centre Woodlands were outstanding in this game.

Ferry defeated Cleckheaton 8–6 on tour in April. The two Keith's got a try each. They then lost to Bramley (9–14, Roberts kicked three penalties) and to Kenfig Hill at Porthcawl in the WRU Sevens (4–12, Shufflebotham 1 try). Ferry then defeated Cwmgors 29–7, back rowers Steve Williams and Keith Thomas were among the try scorers, with Keith Roberts bagging the goals. They then gained revenge on Pontardawe by defeating them on their own patch.

Youth XV

The Youth XV struggled throughout the season. They lost 3–34 to Neath Colts in the Neath & District Cup in September. They then lost to Tonna, Skewen, Seven Sisters and Bryncoch. They had their first win for 16 months in April over Glynneath, 14–0, with tries from Gareth Davies, Chris Chappell and H. Davies, fullback D. Lewis converted 1. One of their centres that day was David Pickering who, along with fullback Lewis, was outstanding. Pickering had also kicked a couple of penalties in the defeat against Bryncoch.

9.12 Future Ferry player, second row Andrew Vaughan, was selected to play for the Welsh Schools against Australia

Tour

The Ferry's Easter's tour was a trip to Leeds to play Bramley and Headingley. Bramley were then to visit the Ferry in March.

Presentation evening

In the annual awards at the end of the season back rower Keith Thomas once again bagged the Player of the Year Award, presented to him by Welsh International Dai Morris. Fellow flanker Steve Williams picked up the Most Improved Player award, top scorer was fly-half Keith Roberts.

Chairman Morgan Jones praised the work of the club's voluntary helpers and he made Cyril Beesley, who had been with the club for twenty-six years, a life member. Terry Gregory won Clubman of the Year.

Jack Young of the WRU presented the Youth Player of the Year award to flanker Brian Davies and Most Promising Player to fullback David Lewis. Other presentations were made to Mr W.L. Williams, in recognition of his service to the club as treasurer, and to young David Pickering (the chairman said he looked like a future Welsh international) and a wedding clock to Ronnie Willis. The chairman also mentioned that ex-player Kevin Bowring had won Young Player of the Year at London Welsh – a magnificent personal achievement and a proud moment for the Ferry.

In the district

This year's O.G. Davies Cup final was between Seven Sisters and Skewen – Seven Sisters were victors again. In the newly introduced Neath Guardian trophy, Skewen became the inaugural winners, the Ferry finished seventh. Cimla took all the Neath & District honours.

Briton Ferry Steel were struggling, with a defeat by Aberavon Quins and a 0–0 draw with Tonna among the results. The Albion itself was starting to struggle and the company made the first redundancies the following June, with full closure in November.

In November, Neath & District Youth honoured Briton Ferry Youth founder Phil Griffiths by making him a life member. He was only the second person in history to be acclaimed in this manner.

9.13 Phil Griffiths and youth player Richard Lawrence; certificate of Life Membership

1978/79

Ferry had an excellent start by beating Taibach 26–6 at home. Steve Williams bagged 2 tries, Keith Roberts' boot dropped 1 goal and converted 1 try. They then defeated Tonna away (Williams again on the score sheet), and BP Llandarcy 13–12 at home in the preliminary round of the WRU Cup (Williams scored his fourth try in three games, Roberts pushed himself up to 37 points). Skipper Spencer Lewis was leading well from the front, ably assisted in the boiler house by young Andrew Vaughan, who was home on leave from Cardiff College (his father Alan was a club committeeman). Ferry lost their next game, at Nantyfyllon, before getting back to winning ways at home, 18–6 over Brecon (Andy Bell 2 tries double, Roberts converting). Unfortunately, Roberts got sent off and was subsequently banned for six games. A very young Steve Knight and newcomer in the front row David Becker made their debut in this game. But the First XV ended the month with a narrow 9–10 defeat at Nantymoel (Jeff Beaton 1 try, young Lawrence 1 conversion, 1 penalty) which put them out of the WRU Cup.

In October, youth coach Dean Hoare played for the First XV to help out while Roberts was banned, and starred alongside fellow half-back Andrew Shufflebotham in a 14–4 home win over Llantwit Major. But Ferry followed this with a heavy 0–43 defeat at Bridgend Sports, a narrow 12–15 home loss to a strong Swansea Athletic side, and a 7–15 defeat at Ogmore Vale 7–15 (despite good play by the youngsters; Woodlands scored a try, Lawrence kicked a penalty and hooker Gareth Chamberlain came off the bench for his debut).

Captain
Spencer Lewis

Coach
David Parker

Youth coach
Dean Hoare

Match results place BFRFC scores first

Young prospect **PAUL WOODLANDS** (who'd been selected for the O.G. Davies XV in September, along with Peter Bell) made his debut for Neath in November and then played a few more games through the season.

    SPENCER LEWIS played for the O.G. Davies XV against West Wales champions Hendy.

With players returning from injury – Robert Knight, Ron Lilley and Emrys Landeg up front – Ferry were hoping for a better November. They took Brynmawr's ground record in a 6–4 away win. Shufflebotham was captain for the day in the absence of skipper Lewis. Ferry then won at home against Pontycymmer, 12–3 (centre Davies 1 try, converted by the returning Roberts). Then they lost narrowly to Swansea Athletic at St Helens, 6–22 (Roberts kicked two goals) The foul November weather then improved and kept it up into December.

    There was a rumour that front rower **JOHN MORRIS** was transferring back to the club from a stint with Baglan.

By February the club lay in joint third place (with Seven Sisters) in the Guardian league and, after giving Aberavon Quins a 30–3 drubbing on 27 January, they were favourites to jump to second place. The return of outside-half Keith Roberts from suspension was a great help. He'd already notched up 100 points and had forged a good partnership with scrum-half Andrew Shufflebotham – they were both selected to play for Glamorgan against Cardigan later that month, along with no.8 Steve Williams.

9.14 Andrew Shufflebotham in action against Bryncoch 1978/79

Also in February Ferry defeated Ogmore Vale 17–3 at home. Roberts contributed 9 points with 1 try, 1 penalty and 1 conversion. Keith Thomas and Peter Bell each added a try. The month ended with their eleventh straight win, 13–3 at home to Brynmawr. Thomas and Shufflebotham scored tries, Roberts converted 1 and kicked a neat drop goal.

At the end of March, Ferry paid a visit to Pontardawe and came away with the spoils by 19–0. The scorers were Jeff Beaton and Shufflebotham with 1 try apiece, Roberts converted 1, and kicked 2 penalties and 1 drop goal. Centres Paul Woodland and Jeff Williams played superbly in defence and attack.

In April, Tonna knocked Ferry out of the O.G. Davies Cup in the quarter-finals, 4–7 in a tight away game – Shufflebotham scored the try.

Briton Ferry RFC 1978/79
Back row– R.Lilley; K. Thomas; A. Hopkins; A. Clifford; P. Woodland; S.Williams; M. Curtis
Middle row– G. Thomas (1st aid) ; P. Bell; D. Hoare; J. Williams; B. Mills; J. Beaton; K. Roberts, R. Knight; A. Vaughan; G. Preddy ;
Front row–R. Lawrence; A.Shufflebotham; R. Evans (sec); S. Lewis (Capt.); M. Jones (chairman); M. Price; E. Landeg

9.15 1978/79

Youth XV

The Youth XV had an excellent start to the season with wins over Abercrave, Cwmgrach and Ystalyfera. They reached the Neath & District Cup semi-finals by defeating Ystradgynlais. Lawrence bagged 11 points with his boot and Martin Gwynne scored a try. Flanker Nigel Lovering and skipper Nigel Powell had fine games.

Match results place BFRFC scores first

In April, they were knocked out of the local cup in the semi–finals by Neath Athletic, 9–18. Richard Lawrence played well and kicked 3 penalties – he had a good partner in scrum-half Courtney Lester. They also lost 12–18 to BSC Port Talbot in the National Sevens at Porthcawl.

Tour

The club toured Leeds at Easter and played West Leeds RFC. New names in the tour party were Richard Lawrence, Mark Price, Paul Woodland, vice captain Andrew Shufflebotham, Emrys Landeg, Mike Curtis, Spencer Lewis, Brian Davies, Ron Lilley, Steven "Gonk" John and Mark Best. The trainer was George Thomas. New on the tor committee were assistant secretary Colin Watkins and P.H. Davies, P. Davies, D. Hoare and Des Whitelock.

Presentation evening

Roy Evans was awarded Clubman of the Year and given Life Membership. The Morgan Jones Player of the Year award went to Spencer Lewis and Most Improved Player went to Keith Roberts. The Youth XV Player of the Year was Nigel Lovering, and Most Improved Youth Player was Carl Swales. There was also a special presentation to mark David Pickering's selection for the Welsh Secondary Schools U19s XV, with honoured guests Mr Brian Thomas of Neath RFC and WRU officials Mr Gwilym Treharne and Mr Rod Morgan.

Committeemen

- Terry Woodlands was brought to the Ferry by Graham Michael and started his career in 1955 against Kenfig Hill. He captained the club and was chairman of the social club. Terry was very instrumental in keeping the club's head above water during a slump in the mid-1980s.

- Roy Evans started his career with Neath YMCA straight from school and had a Welsh Boys trial. He joined the Ferry after leaving the army and played for the club for five years before being selected to play for Neath (along with Roy John, Rees Stephens, Courtney Meredith and Morlais Williams). A reporter once wrote that if pairs were to be chosen for Welsh trials why not select the Neath pair of Roy and Keith Evans! Roy ended his playing career at the Ferry, after 14 seasons. He then became secretary of the club.

- Morgan Jones' career started in the boxing ring in 1928 in a series of ten-round fights against "Tiger" Davies, Cyril Lewis and young Baglo, all for a ten-shilling prize. These fights usually took place at the Briton Ferry Public Hall. He moved to rugby around 1929, when he captained the Melyn Barbarians. Even then the feeling was that, as far as training was concerned, it was good to mix it up. But after playing against Neath Sports Club in front of quite a large crowd, rugby captured him. Morgan started by playing for Bridgend but soon moved to Briton Ferry, because it was nearer to home and because the fixture list was very strong. He took over the fullback role from Rowly Hill and scored the match-winning try in his debut against Skewen in 1930. It must be recorded that Morgan Jones trained for the Ferry when past his fiftieth birthday. In fact, many years after retiring he returned to play in the rain against Vardre and a clipping from the *News of The World* said that his rock-like defence was the mainstay of the team that day. He was chairman of the club for thirty-four years, a member of the Welsh National Opera for sixteen years and he was a life member of a local operatic society. Morgan once sang in *Tosca* with Bruce Dargavelle and Jean Hammond!

9.16 Committee 1978/79

(back) D. Mills, P.H. Davies, C. Watkins, J. Evans, N. Bowering; (middle) A. Gleaves, G. Jones, T. Gregory, D. Whitelock, H. Melding; (front) R. Evans (secretary), M. Jones (chairman), E. Richards, W. Williams

1979/80

In April 1980 Ferry played a Les Keen International XV to raise funds for Cwrt Sart School's minibus fund. They lost 8–36 – C. Morgan and S. Williams were the try scorers. Among the players in the International XV were A. Martin, G. Jenkins, D. Pickering, C. Shell, D. Morris, C. Williams, J. Richardson, E. Rees, B. James.

The Ferry XV also played a charity soccer match at the Ferry ground against a Ghurkha XI in November, which ended in an 8–8 draw. This was to raise money for Clive Nagle, a young player who had broken his neck playing against the Ferry Youth the previous season and who would be confined to a wheelchair for the rest of his life. They raised over £500 and a number of stars were guests of the Ferry on the day, such as Chico Hopkins, Alan Martin, Elgan Rees, John Bevan, Alan Phillips, Gareth Edwards, Dai Parker and Brian Thomas (who ended up in hospital with an Achilles injury after stubbing his foot!).

Captain
Spencer Lewis

Vice captain
Paul Woodland

Coach
David Parker

First XV playing record
P 28
W 14
D 2
L 12

Quins captain
Jeff Williams

Quins vice captain
Alan Clifford

Youth coach
Dean Hoare

Quins playing record
P 30
W 11
D 2
L 17

9.17 Charity game v. the Ghurkhas 1979

After the game, the Ghurkhas entertained the crowd with dancing and drumming. They also stayed on for an evening concert laid on by local amateur artists. Later in the year professional artists held another concert for this fund.

Skipper and second row Spencer Lewis was a former Secondary Schools cap for Wales. Centre Paul Woodland's father, Terry, had been prop for the club in the 1960s. Both coaches had been half-backs for the club. Quins skipper Jeff "Bonehead" Williams was an experienced centre and his vice captain was no.8.

PAUL WOODLAND played for Neath and scored a try against Dutch club Haagshe – KEITH ROBERTS and future Ferry player HYWEL GRIFFITHS also played.

Flanker Jonathan Roberts was skipper of the Youth XV, with promising fullback David Lewis as his vice captain.

The Ferry XV started the season off with a good 19–7 win over Amman United. Ron Lilley, Keith Thomas and Gareth Preddy made tries, Keith Roberts kicked 2 conversions and 1 penalty. Centre Gary Davies and David Welham (returning from Skewen) played well.

Back row –J.Beaton; P.Bell; D.Williams; R.Lilley; A. Vaughan; A. Hopkins; K.Thomas; R.Amphlett; A.Shufflebotham; S.Williams; ref. P.Squires
Front row– R.Lawrence;G.Davies;P.Woodland; S.Lewis (capt) ; E.Landeg;G.Preddy;K.Roberts

9.18 1979/80

There was then *that* terrific win over South Wales Police in the Welsh Cup. Outside-half Keith Roberts kicked the side to victory with 4 penalty goals. The

Match results place BFRFC scores first

pack were outstanding with a front row of Gerald Lewis, Gareth Preddy and Emrys Landeg, backed up by skipper Spencer Lewis and Roger Amphlett in the second row, and a back row of Ron Lilley, Keith Thomas and Steve Williams, and the substitute, veteran Allan Hopkins.

Ferry defeated Pontycymmer 12–7 in the Silver Ball competition, in Ponty. Keith Thomas scored the only try, which Keith Roberts converted, and he added a couple of fine penalties.

9.19 In action against Pontycymmer 1979/80
Mark Best, Spencer Lewis, Terry John, Roger Amphlett, Steve Williams and Keith Thomas in this lineout up against Barry Banner of Ponty.

Tredegar Ironsides were the visitors in October and Ferry defeated them 18–9, with tries from Chris Chappell (on his senior debut), Gary Davies and Keith Roberts, and 2 penalties kicked by Richard Lawrence kicking two. No.8 Hywel Griffiths made his first appearance on permit from Cimla in this match. The month ended in an 8–16 away defeat to a strong Swansea Athletic side at St. Helens. Two tries were disallowed: Allan Hopkins apparently dropped the ball in the act of scoring; and Keith Thomas was deemed to have grounded the ball before the line. The game perked up for the Ferry when Cliff Morgan replaced the injured fullback Jeff Beaton. Morgan had recently transferred to the club from Cimla and made an immediate break, which led to a Chris

Chappell try. Then Keith Roberts added a penalty. Quins hooker Martyn Bate made his First XV debut in this game.

During November's annual visit by Caldicot, the Ferry won comfortably 37–3. Tries came from prop Terry John, Cliff Morgan, Keith Roberts, Keith Thomas, David Williams and Paul Woodlands. Roberts converted 3 and adding 1 penalty. This was followed by a 7–14 defeat up in Cwmgrach – Hywel Griffiths scored 1 try and Cliff Morgan added 1 penalty in Roberts' absence.

In December Ferry made another big home win, this time against Ogmore Vale. Man of the match Cliff Morgan scored 22 points, with 3 tries and 5 conversions. He narrowly missed beating his own club record of 24 points in a match. Keith Thomas, Roger Amphlett, David Williams and Paul Woodlands also scored tries, and Ron Lilley got 2.

At the end of December Ferry drew 12–12 away at Tredegar Ironsides in which they drew. Three second-half tries went unconverted, 2 from no.8 Howell Griffiths and 1 from veteran fullback Peter "Sniffer" Davies. As usual, the back row of Griffiths, Keith "Tonto" Thomas and former Welsh Secretary schools cap Andrew Vaughan were outstanding.

First up in the new year was a local derby with Aberavon Quins which Ferry lost and thereby conceded the double by the slim margin of 3–7. Cliff Morgan kicked a penalty and wing Peter Bell was the standout player. The weather made the rest of January was a bit of a washout.

In February, Ferry made the long journey up to old friends at Caldicot and won the game 10–3. K. Thomas and D. Williams were the try scorers and K. Roberts added the extra two points. Steve Williams in the back row stood out, as did wing converted to fullback Andy Bell and Quins hooker Martyn Bate. The weather kicked back in until the end of the month, when Ferry played Nantymoel at home and hammered them 56–7. Doubles came from P. Woodland, H. Griffiths and C. Morgan, and further tries from Roger Amphlett, K. Thomas, D. Williams, Ron Willis and veteran Allan Hopkins. Youth fullback David Lewis, who was making his debut, kicked 6 out of 11 conversions.

On 8 March Ferry were the first 'second-class' club to defeat Abercynon, 15–12, with Hywel Griffiths again on the score sheet along with Spencer Lewis, and Richard Lawrence adding the extras. It was also pleasing to see two rising stars in 20-year-olds Rhys Thomas (second row) and Mark Best (prop) playing well.

Ferry followed this up with a 16–0 home win over Pontycymmer. K. Thomas, Ron Willis and C. Morgan were the try scorers, Morgan added 1 conversion and R. Lawrence another. Hooker Gareth Preddy was very prominent in this game. Ferry defeated Ogmore Vale 22–10. Among the try scorers were C. Morgan (2), P. Woodland and K. Thomas. R. Lawrence added the extras. Flanker Ron Lilley was outstanding.

Ferry lost out in the first round of the O.G. Davies Cup to Bryncoch over two legs for an aggregate score of 12–28: 6–9 at home with Gareth Preddy scoring a try and Keith Roberts converting from the touchline; and 6–19 away, with just 3 penalties from K. Roberts. But they were a little more successful in the Schweppes Cup with wins over South Wales Police at home by 12–7, then 7–0 away to Cefn Cribbwr (Paul Woodland 1 try, Roberts 1 penalty). Ferry then drew 6–6 away to Old Illtydians in Cardiff and lost on the try count.

Ferry ended the season eighth position in the Guardian merit table.

Youth

Quins scrum-half **KERRY JONES** received his Duke of Edinburgh Gold award while with the Royal Regiment of Wales.

Five times capped Welsh Secondary Schools player **STEVE KNIGHT** was home from the navy, as was Quins player **DAVID JAMES** from HMS Battleaxe.

The Youth had good wins over Bryncoch, Aberavon Green Stars, Skewen, Vadre, Brecon and Ystalyfera.

Peter Derrick and David Lewis both had trials for the District.

9.20 Welsh Secondary Schools caps: Steve Knight and David Pickering

Awards

Des Whitelock was awarded Clubman of the Year.

Presentation dinner

There was a special dinner to honour 50 years of service by club player, captain, committeeman, secretary and chairman Morgan Jones (who chaired the committee for 35 years, until 1990). He was presented with a silver tray and goblets by Mr Rod Morgan from the WRU.

9.21 Chairman Morgan Jones

In the district

Briton Ferry Steel did well during the season, and fullback Martin Williams was one of their star performers.

Cimla won the championship by beating Crynant 12–4.

Seven Sisters won the O.G. Davies Cup.

Scrum-half **ANDREW SHUFFLEBOTHAM** transferred to Maesteg and was very successful.

LONDON WELSH
Kevin Bowring

Ex-player and London Welsh captain Kevin Bowring (also of Middlesex County, Welsh Presidents XV, Wales B squad in 1978, and national team coach) was chosen to start the relay of a message from the Queen for the WRU's centenary year.

One of many senior players from Neath Grammar School, this 6ft 1ins 14-stone flanker played for Briton Ferry and then Neath before going to West London to study teaching at Borough Road College. He was captain of the College team before joining the London Welsh in 1978 and is enjoying both his rugby and his teaching in the English metropolis.

9.22 Kevin Bowring

PART 10: 1980–1990

10.1 Relay for WRU Centenary in Briton Ferry

1980 – WELSH RUGBY UNION CENTENARY

Ex-player and coach Kevin Bowring started the relay for the WRU centenary with a special rugby ball that contained a message of congratulations from the Queen. He accepted the ball on behalf of the WRU and London Welsh RFC at 9.45am on 15 July in Buckingham Palace, It then passed through the hands of every WRU member club from Coventry, Rugby and Birmingham Welsh, across the Shropshire border to the north Wales clubs and finally made its way down into south Wales.

10.2 Prince Charles handing the Queen's message to the WRU on their centenary celebrations to London Welsh captain Kevin Bowring

When the ball arrived in Briton Ferry on 22 July the club was represented by: First XV captain Spencer Lewis, accompanied by schoolboy Neil Gregory; Second XV captain Martyn Bate, accompanied by schoolboy Paul Watkins; and Allan Hopkins, accompanied by his son David Hopkins in the final leg.

They ran down to Aberavon Quins and the ball arrived at Cardiff Arms Park in time for the start of the WRU Centenary celebrations. It had been travelling for ten days and had covered more than 1,300 miles after leaving Buckingham Palace. The Queen's message read:

Rugby Football occupies a special place in the life of Wales and Welshmen have played a major part in spreading the game throughout the Commonwealth and beyond. I am delighted that the Welsh Rugby Union has decided to mark this with such a grand programme and wish you every success in the coming season.

1980/81

Captain
Spencer Lewis

Vice captain
Cliff Morgan

Coaches
Dean Hoare
Peter Davies

Quins captain
Martyn Bate

Youth captain
Andrew Jenkins

Youth vice captain
Peter Derrick

Second row Spencer Lewis captained the club for a third season.

During the season, the Ferry played an Argentine touring side, the Under-21s from Circulo Ex Cadetes Licen Motray Cenefal San Martin, Buenos Aires. Coach Carlos Villegas had visited the Ferry during the WRU centenary celebrations and was so impressed with the welcome he got that he promised to include a fixture with the club when his side came on tour. Ferry won 18–12. The Argentineans also played a Metropolitan Police XV and beat them 21–6!

The season started in the O.J. Davies Sevens, with wins over Tonna and Skewen (14–10 in the semi-final), but they were defeated 12–15 in the final by home team Crynant. Cliff Morgan was awarded Man of the Tournament. Ferry then lost 0–26 to Bedwas in the first round of the Richard Barry Sevens at Aberavon Green Stars. They also lost the services of coach Dai Parker, due to pressures of work, and of back rower Keith "Tonto" Thomas, who emigrated to Canada.

In September, Ferry were defeated at Abercynon. Vice captain Cliff Morgan kicked for Ferry's 3 points. This was Allan Hopkins 600th game for the club in this match, and he was part of a formidable back row alongside newcomer no.8 Hywel Griffiths and Steve Williams.

Ferry lost on aggregate (6–38) to Crynant in the O.G. Davies Cup.

In the first round of the Principality Cup, Ferry defeated Skewen 12–3 (D. Thomas scored a try and Roberts added 2 penalties and 1 conversion. They then lost 0–20 to Neath Athletic in the next round.

Match results place BFRFC scores first

10.3 Allan Hopkins painted by Dai Poley

Wins against Cwmavon, Cefn Cribbwr 24–7, with veteran hooker Norman Rees scoring a try along with A. Bell, Kevin Harris and K. Roberts who also added a penalty, and C. Morgan adding another along with one conversion,

Ferry away beat Nantymoel 19–0. Harris, H. Griffiths and Peter Bell were on the try sheet, Roberts added 2 conversions and 1 penalty. Hooker Preddy played well and took 5 against the head. After conceding 50 points Ferry had their first win in three games when they beat Pontycymmer, 12–6. Andy Bell made a rare drop goal and Howard Pitman scored 1 try, converted by Roberts, who also added 1 penalty. They followed this with a 24–19 win against Ogmore Vale (K. Roberts 2 penalties, 1 conversion and 1 try, tries from Hywel Griffiths and Paul Woodlands). Roberts' try was a 70-yards cracker that came from a strike against the head by hooker Martyn Bate in his own 25, which was taken 30 yards by centre Paul Woodlands, who passed to Roberts, who placed it under the posts.

Then Ferry went down to a heavy defeat at Maesteg Celtic, 0–44. The team was short of players and played the full game with thirteen men, which included old stalwart and committeeman Jeff "Olly " Davies in the front row. The scrums went so badly that they resorted to playing with only the front row.

Ferry then defeated Brynmawr 16–3 at home at the beginning of November. Lilley and H. Griffiths were the try scorers, Lawrence added a couple of penalties and Roberts took the extra two points. But they were defeated 0–18 at home by Swansea Athletic – prop Terry John shone. Ferry then finished November with a 17–10 win against old rivals Taibach at home. Griffiths scored another try, along with Ron Willis, Roberts added 2 penalties and C. Morgan 1 drop goal. New wing Steve Davies played well in this game as did Morgan, Griffiths and hooker Preddy.

The year ended in a 3–27 home defeat to Aberavon Quins.

Games were called off in the new year due to the weather, but they did have an early win at home to Trimsaran, 18–7. Returning wing Kevin Harris bagged 2 tries, Keith Roberts kicked 2 penalties and Andrew Vaughan added 1 try, Robert John played well at fullback. Ferry followed up with another home win, 18–0 over Blaengarw. Roberts bagged 10 points and Richard Lawrence and Paul Woodland added 1 try apiece. Wing Dominic Davies played well.

In February the First XV defeated Nantymoel 25–10, but lost to Kidwelly away, 0–42.

There were further disruptions to fixtures in March and April and two more defeats, 3–29 to Mumbles and 0–22 to Cwmavon.

Having struggled to maintain form and lacking a little bit of killer instinct, despite having a fairly hefty pack, Ferry ended the season third in the Guardian League.

Quins

The Quins ended their season with just three wins, over Pyle, over BP Llandarcy (20–6, N. Powell, R. Peale, vice captain J. Williams and Dom Davies were the try scorers and Robert John added 2 points), and over Skewen. They lost 10–16 to Banwen in the Neath & District Cup away, and 11–6 in the Neath & District quarter-finals to Briton Ferry Steel.

They finished second from bottom in the Neath & District League Division 2 table, having played 4, won 1, lost 3 and scoring just 5 tries. This was a building period for them though and no great disappointment was felt at the club.

Tour

Ferry toured to the Isle of Man on 27 March and came away with 1 win and 1 defeat. The First XV beat Douglas Vagabonds 9–7 (for whom prop David "Piggy" Powell, ex-England, Northampton, Lions and Barbarians, was playing). The Quins lost 8–14 to Douglas RFC.

10.4 Quins on Isle of Man tour 1980/81

(back) Andy Bell, Mike Curtis, Roger Amphlett, Rhys Thomas, Noigel Lovering, Allan Clifford, Chris Chappell, Ron Willis, Mike Beaton, Mike Simonson; (front) Dean Hoare, Emrys Landeg, Martyn Bate (captain), Jeff Williams, Dom Davies, Robert John, Mal Edwards

Youth XV

The Youth XV won 15–9 against Gorseinon (D. Evans and R. Gregory scored tries, D. Lewis added the extras) and 13–4 against Maesteg Celtic (when Lewis scored all the points, 1 try, 3 penalties), and then 7–4 against Tumble (scrum-half Richard Harris was the try scorer and Lewis added the extra; this was centre Keith Holifield's debut for the club.

They made it five wins out of seven by defeating Pontrhydyfen 9–4 (Lewis dropped 1 goal and added the extra 2 after centre Andrew Jenkins ran in for a 50-yard interception try) and then defeating Skewen 22–0 (P. Pibbard (2), A. Jenkins, S. Nicholls and I. Broad were the try scorers, Lewis 1 conversion).

The Youth XV also defeated Skewen 32–0 in the quarter-final of the Neath & District Cup. The scorers were skipper A. Jenkins, C. Swales, P. Evans, P. Pibbard, S. Nicholls and D. Lewis, who also added 3 conversions. They were then defeated in the semi-finals by Neath Colts. They also defeated Ystalyfera 10–0. Jenkins on the score sheet again, along with his future brother-in-law R. Parris, and Lewis added the extra 2.

Awards

Player of the Year was awarded to hard-working prop Terry John, and Most Improved Player to Ron Lilley. Rhys Thomas was Quins Player of the Year. D. Lewis was awarded Youth Player of the Year trophy and Holifield was Youth Most Improved Player. Life memberships were awarded to long-standing members D.J. Poley, Howie Thomas, Hughie Watkins and Llew Llewelyn.

Clubman of the Year award went to Quins skipper Martyn Bate.

Bryn Lewis and Terry Keefe came on to the committee.

In the district

Centre Gary Davies led the Police 'G' Division to a win in the final of the interdistrict sevens competition.

Briton Ferry Steel had two representatives in the Neath & District side that played Cardiff & District in the final of the Howells Cup, fullback Martin Williams and flanker Ian Edwards, while Kevin Gutteridge was on the bench (they lost by 4–20).

Spencer Lewis and Cliff Morgan had played for the O.G. Davies XV against cup holders Seven Sisters on New Year's Day; while new second row Howard Pitman had played for them against Neath in February.

1981/82

For the fourth season in a row Spencer Lewis was club captain.

The Ferry XV started with a tough away game at Bargoed, which they lost heavily. They then entered into a bout of cup games and defeated BP Llandarcy over two legs by an aggregate score of 21–15 in the O.G. Davies Cup (Paul Woodland and Ron Willis among the try scorers). They also defeated Nantyfyllon at home, 15–9 in the WRU Cup (young Jonathan Roberts really playing well in the back row, along with skipper Spencer Lewis in the second row and hooker Gareth Preddy).

The club got to the final of the O.G. Davies Sevens at Llandarcy by beating Tonna in the first round and Crynant in the semi-final (with tries from Dai Williams, Andy Jenkins and Chris White), but they faltered against Resolven in the final and lost 10–20 (Chalky White bagged 2 tries and Richard Lawrence converted 1).

In a couple of friendlies, the First XV drew 9–9 at home with Pontrhydyfen, before losing10–18 in Pontycymmer. They then went to Cefn Cribbwr for the next round of the WRU Cup and lost narrowly (12–16).

The Central Glamorgan Wistech league started this year and Ferry began with a 25–9 home win over Nantymoel, followed by wins over Taibach (8–7) and BSC (13–11, Peter Bell 1 try, C. White 3 penalties), and a draw with Maesteg Celtic (13–13). In between these league games they took a narrow away win, 6–4 at Gilfach Goch, then back home, lost 3–26 to Heol-Y-Cyw, drew 3–3 with Ogmore Vale (C. White penalty) and defeated Blaengarw 24–7 (tries from D. Lewis, S. Lewis, S. Williams and A.

Captain
Spencer Lewis

Vice captain
Dai Williams

Coaches
Dean Hoare
Tony Philpin

First XV playing record
P 30
W 11
D 4
L 15

Quins captain
Martyn Bate

Quins vice captain
Steve Davies

Youth captain
David Lewis

Youth vice captain
S. Shaw

Jenkins, D. Lewis added 2 conversions and 1 penalty; policemen and tough forwards Hywel Miles and Howard Pitman played well).

The new year started slowly, with the weather taking care of the first few league games. Ferry then ran into three straight league defeats, at Nantyfyllon (3–29), at home to Kenfig Hill (10–17, E. Landeg and J. Roberts tries, Lawrence converting), and away at Maesteg Celtic (10–32). A match against Ogmore Vale ended a repeat 3–3 draw and a repeat sole penalty from White.

At the end of February, Ferry were defeated by BSC, 3–20 at home in a league match.

In March, Ferry had two away league defeats against Nantymoel (6–14) and Taibach (6–16) and an excellent friendly win at Ystalyfera (12–9, Chris White kicked all the points; centres Paul Harris and Andrew Jenkins made outstanding play together).

In the final month of the season and Ferry were defeated by Nantyfyllon in the final league game at home (6–16, John Thomas 1 try, converted by C. White; youngsters P. Woodland, N. Lovering and Dom Davies played well, as did Robert Willis and Peter Bell).

Then came the O.G. Davies Cup semi-finals and Ferry lost on aggregate to Bryncoch, 5–26.

The Ferry XV lost their final game of the season 0–14 at home to Resolven.

The club finished fifth in the Guardian league with a 43.33% playing record.

Quins

The Quins lost 0–19 to Seven Sisters in the Neath & District Cup, and only managed wins over Banwen (twice), BP Llandarcy (9–7) and Briton Ferry Steel in the league. They lost 6–11 to Aberavon Quins in a friendly.

Quins finished fourth in the Neath & District League B.

Youth XV

The Youth XV had good wins over Maesteg Celtic, Resolven (9–4, Dom Davies 1 try, I. Broad converting) and Hirwaun, but they lost 8–14 to Ystradgynlais in the cup, had a 0–0 draw with Merthyr, and lost 7–12 at Neath Youth (a future Ferry player played well against them that day, Adrian Griffiths), 6–42 to Glynneath (K. Holifield 1 try, Broad converting) and 0–16 to Skewen (Alan King played well). They were then beaten by Maesteg Celtic, 8–9.

Fullback Dai Lewis featured in a Welsh Youth trial.

Tour

The club returned to the Isle of Man, where they defeated Ronaldsway 11–8.

Awards

Rhys Thomas completed a rare double by being awarded the Senior XV Player of the Year trophy after winning the Quins Player of the Year trophy in the previous year. Young Jonathan Roberts won the Most Improved Player award. Flanker and ex-naval man David James was Quins Player of the Year. The Youth Player of the Year went to flanker Richard G. Alderson, and Youth Most Improved Player to Duncan Beasley.

Clubman of the Year went to hard-working committeeman Terry Keefe. Ex-player Allan Hopkins came on to the committee.

Around the district

Crynant won the O.G. Davies Cup by beating Bryncoch 12–6.

Neath Athletic defeated Rhigos to win the Neath & District Cup, and Neath Colts won the Neath & District Youth Cup by defeating Glynneath in the final.

Abercrave took the league honours.

10.5 Briton Ferry RFC District Sevens Winners 1982
(back) Roy Evans (Secretary), John Thomas, Allan Clifford, David Hopkins, Keith Burt, Nigel Lovering, Allan Hopkins; (front) Mark Best, Richard Alderson, Keith Holifield, Richard Lawrence, Jonathan Roberts, Ian Chesterfield

In other news

Mention must be made of BP Baglan Bay with regard to players' welfare, as George Thomas, Dai "Lefty" Jones, Brian "Moose" Makinson and ex-player Gerald Lewis all played their part with the "magic sponge" during this period of the club's history.

Old-stager Arthur Lemon sadly passed away this year.

Ex-player Harold Powell took over the reins as chairman of Neath RFC for the third time (1961 and 1962). He'd been vice chairman for the previous seven years. Powell joined Neath in 1932 from the Ferry and had played for them and Swansea alternately up until the outbreak of the Second World War. He was Swansea's record try scorer during the 1937/38 season, with 39 tries from the wing. He'd joined the RAF and had played for them in the centre fourteen times, alongside the great Bleddyn Williams. He was stationed in Penarth at the time and also played two seasons for Cardiff. On completion of his RAF duties, Powell rejoined the Ferry and played until he was 38, a grand twenty-one seasons of rugby.

Former player Albert O'Shea, with Paul Thomas, had come second in a cross-channel yacht race for limbless ex-servicemen as part of a five-man crew on the Beli Esprite. The race, organised by BLESMA (The Limbless Veterans), went from Chichester to Cherbourg and back. Albert had lost a leg in the Second World War; Paul had lost both legs and an arm in an IRA bomb blast.

The clubhouse had started to struggle with its finances and announced that it would be closing down indefinitely, which happened on Saturday 24 April at 6 p.m. Both the rugby and the cricket sections feared that the loss of a clubhouse building could put them in danger of folding as they would lose the use of dressing rooms and showers. Neath Council were approached to help, as the heavy rates bill was crippling. After a week the club decided to experiment with opening for four nights a week and with being run by volunteer club members to save costs.

1982/83

Lewis, in his fifth season as skipper, also assisted Dean Hoare with the coaching.

The season started on a bright note with a 15–6 win at Cwmgrach, but the Ferry XV then suffered defeats at Cwmgors (13–18) and at home to Felinfoel (0–15), but then defeated Cefn Cribbwr 9–6 at home.

In October, Ferry defeated BSC Port Talbot 16–4, with tries from Andrew Jenkins and Andy Bell, 1 penalty from R. Lawrence and conversions and a penalty from fullback Dai Lewis. They then lost on aggregate, 12–25 to Tonna, in the first round of the O.G. Davies Cup. They also went out in the first round of the WRU Cup to Nantymoel away, 3–30.

Two friendlies were played before the commencement of the league, away to Kenfig Hill (lost 6–21) and at home to Pentyrch (lost 7–9).

Their league started poorly on 30 October with a 12–13 defeat at home by Taibach, then a heavy away defeat at Porthcawl (13–30). It was then back to friendlies. First, at home to a London Irish XV which ended in a 0–0 draw in conditions that were very bog-like – and with cold showers after as the boiler had packed in! Followed by another home defeat to Brynmawr (6–16) and an away defeat at Pentyrch (4–32).

League fixtures returned in December and Ferry defeated Nantymoel (20–9) and Blaengarw (15–0), both at home. The only other fixture played that month was a Boxing Day match between a Past XV and a Present XV, which the Present side won, 32–0.

Captain
Spencer Lewis

Vice captain
Peter Bell

Coach
Dean Hoare

First XV playing record
P 27
W 8
D 0
L 19

Quins captain
Steve Davies

Quins vice captain
Dai James

Youth captain
Ian Broad

More defeats followed in the new year. At Taibach, 6–15 (D. Lewis kicked 2 goals), and at Ogmore Vale 0–20, both in the league. They then managed a narrow defeat of Pontycymmer (7–6 at home), also in the league, but ended the month with an away league defeat, 7–15 at Blaengarw.

Only one game was played February, due to the weather. In a home league fixture against Porthcawl, Ferry lost 0–12

Matters didn't improve much in March as they lost a friendly to Caldicot, 7–14, then lost 0–17 to Nantymoel in a league match, 0–24 at BSC Port Talbot in a friendly, and 9–12 to Tonna in the O.G. Davies Cup (D. Lewis 3 penalties). Ferry's only win was against English tourists Chew Valley Old Boys, a magnificent 58–4.

Ex-Ferry player DAVID PICKERING, who was now with Llanelli, won his first full Welsh cap against England during this year's Five Nations.

In April, Ferry lost 6–19 at home to Ogmore Vale in the league, then defeated Pontycymmer 7–3 away in their final league game. Ferry then beat Kenfig Hill, 15–10 at home, in a friendly and lost their last two friendlies away at Pyle (3–28) and at Resolven (4–8).

Ferry ended the season ninth in the Guardian league, with a poor 29.63% win record.

Quins

The Quins, having lost 6–30 to Glynneath in the cup, failed to win any further games. After a 0–0 draw on 27 November against Llanelli Wanderers they were unable to raise a team for the rest of the season.

Youth

The Youth finished with wins over Maesteg Celtic and Seven Sisters. David Hopkins, son of Allan, was top scorer and won the Fred McPharlane Cup. Steve Hopkins was the Youth Player of the Year and Neil Richards was Most Improved Youth Player.

Awards

All-action flanker Mike Simonson won the Player of the Year trophy and his fellow back rower Ian Chesterfield picked up the Most Improved Player award. Popular committeeman Jeff "Olly" Davies was Clubman of the Year. Quins Player of the Year was back rower Nigel Lovering.

New to the committee this year were John Johnson, Jeff Davies and Leighton Friend. Committeemen John Selby and Dudley Mills were made life members of the club for their years of service on and off the field. The ladies committee was very busy off the field helping to "keep things on the straight and narrow and ensuring that there was always food after the games". They were mostly the wives of committeemen, Anne Evans, Mary Gregory, Dorothy Davies, Susan Whitelock, Pat Jones, Val Mills, Frances Hopkins, Jill Watkins and Myra Woodland – joined this year by Rhian Hopkins, Allan's daughter.

10.6 (left) Steve Hopkins getting his Youth player of the year trophy from David Pickering 1982-83; (right) Presentation night 1982-83 (back) Ian Chesterfield, Jeff Davies, Mike Simonson and Nigel Lovering (front) Steve Hopkins, Neil Richards and David Hopkins

In the district

Briton Ferry Steel were starting to find things a little tough, both on and off the field. They ended up fourth in Division B of the Neath & District league, having played twelve games, won six and lost five with one draw, scoring 177 points, conceding 138 and with 32 tries.

Seven Sisters were Neath & District champions. Ex-Ferry product Chris White scored all their points in the league final against Neath Athletic. They also won the H.G. Lewis Cup for the third time in four years.

This was the season of the first Briton Ferry Pram Race in memory of a young Ferry boy, **DAVID MAY**, who had lost his fight with cancer at 19. The race attracted 105 three-person teams and was a great success for many years.

10.7 Briton Ferry Pram Race memories

1983/84

The new coach, Mel Pugh, came from Tonmawr. Youth team captain David Hopkins was the son of Allan (and his vice captain was no relation).

The club played a fundraising match in memory of ex-player JOHN "TINY" MORRIS, who had died young.

Ferry combined with Baglan RFC on a Sunday in September to play against an International XV at the Ferry. The combined team lost 10–36 (1 penalty and 1 conversion from Ferry's Dai Lewis, 1 try from Ferry hooker Martyn Bate). Among the stars who turned out that day were David Pickering, Gareth Jenkins, Derek Quinell (Llanelli), Norman Rees, Dai Morris (Neath), John Richardson, Alan Martin, Les Keen (Aberavon), David Nicholas (Llanelli) and Barry Clegg (Swansea). Man of the Match went to Ferry's no.8, Spencer Lewis.

The First XV played two friendly trial matches to start the season and defeated Pontycymmer 25–9 (Lawrence 3 conversions, 1 penalty; tries from K. Burt, J. Beaton, A. Bell and J. Thomas) but lost 6–18 to Briton Ferry Steel.

The season got off to a good start with the club winning the O.G. Davies Sevens in Tonna. They beat Seven Sisters 27–4 in the final and Keith Holifield was Man of the Match.

They then lost 0–10 at Blaengarw in the WRU Cup, and at Tonna in the O.G. Davies Cup 6–12. Followed by a succession of defeats in friendlies, both at home against Maesteg Celtic (6–32, Lawrence 2 penalties, down to 14 men), Milford Haven (6–25), Glynneath (3–4), Mid Glamorgan champions Tylorstown (4–24, K. Burt try, which was second row Rhys Thomas' last game before joining Llanelli), and Llantrisant (4–22, Gareth Evans try),

Captain
Richard Lawrence

Vice captain
Mike Simonson

Coach
Mel Pugh

First XV playing record
P 31
W 12
D 0
L 19
Points for 300
Points against 450

Youth captain
David Hopkins

Youth vice captain
Steve Hopkins

369

and then away at Resolven (6–11), Felinfoel (3–15) and Tylorstown (0–30). The backs were all playing really well, including Gareth Evans, Keith Burt, Keith Holifield, Andrew Jenkins, Alan King and John Thomas.

Then it was into the league programme, starting with a tough away game at Aberavon Quins, which Ferry lost 18–30 (I. Chesterfield and A. Jenkins 1 try apiece, Lawrence 2 conversions and 2 penalties. They then took their first win at home, 12–11 against Ogmore Vale. Another away friendly defeat followed against Glynneath, 9–13, before returning to league action with two away defeats, at Pontycymmer 0–14 and Blaengarw 6–9 (M. Simonsen 1 try, Lawrence 1 conversion). Ferry then defeated Nantymoel, 13–6 at home. Lawrence kicked a penalty and converted a K. Burt try. The first try of this game was hailed as one of the best seen on the ground for many a year: Nanty kicked off and the ball fell to centre Andy Jenkins, he made ground from his 22-metre line to the halfway, where he passed the ball to fullback Gareth Evans, who linked up with wing Peter Bell on the opposition 22 and, when tackled, passed back inside to centre Jenkins, who was up in support to score the try. Centre Paul Woodland and second rows Simon Mogford and Chris Chappell all played well.

On 17 December Ferry took an away win at Pontyclun, 10–6, and on 30 December a home win over Cwmgrach, 23–7 (K. Burt 3 tries, D. Lewis 1 try, Lawrence 2 conversions, 1 penalty). So they ended the year on a high.

There was also an 18–10 win for the Present XV against the Past XV on Boxing Day.

It was back to league fixtures in the new year and Ferry lost 10–34 at Ogmore Vale. They then won the next five league matches. At home to Pontycymmer (12–10, Lawrence 4 penalties), to Cefn Cribbwr (12–6, S. Lewis 1 try, P. Bell 2 tries) and to Blaengarw (6–3, Lawrence 1 penalty, D. Lewis 1 penalty from 54 yards and on the touchline). Then away at Nantymoel (17–9, A. Jenkins, P. Bell and K. Burt tries, Lawrence 1 penalty and 1 conversion), and at Cefn Cribbwr (18–4).

> Throughout this period some players were stepping up to the mark and playing really well, such as, young prop Neil Richards, experienced fellow prop Ceri Davies, and their fellow front rower hooker Martyn Bate, along with back rowers Chesterfield, Simonson, Lovering and Alderson, and behind the scrum, wing Dom Davies, Peter Bell and Keith Burt.

The First XV lost momentum in the next couple of matches and were defeated at home by Caldicot (7–24) and Crynant (9–10). Their final league game was

Match results place BFRFC scores first

at home to already-crowned champions Aberavon Quins. A Peter Bell try, converted by Lawrence who also added a penalty, and a fine drop goal by young David Lewis (playing at 10) were not quite enough to upset the odds and the Quins managed to squeeze home by a point, 12–13. So Ferry finished the league with seven wins out of twelve matches.

They played two more friendlies before the end of the season. First, at home against Pontardulais (their first match for twenty years), which Ferry lost 14–27. Tries from P. Bell (2) and K. Burt, and Lawrence converted 1. Prominent in this game were hooker Martyn Bate and second row Simon Mogford. Second, at home to Resolven, which Ferry won 13–9.

RHYS THOMAS made his debut for Llanelli on 12 September against Gorseinon and played eight-four games for them up to the 1986/87 season, scoring 3 tries and touring Australia and Fiji with them (playing two games on tour).

At the end of the season the club played in a number of sevens tournaments. They lost to Cwmavon in the Nationals at Porthcawl, and lost to both Resolven and Bonymaen before beating a Presidents XV in the Tonna Sevens and then beating BP Llandarcy. But they lost to Seven Sisters in the Carl Hughes Memorial Sevens at Resolven.

Youth

The Youth team only played one game against Ystalyfera, which they won, before disbanding through lack of interest.

Awards

Top scorer for the season was outside-half and skipper Richard Lawrence with 120 points. Top try scorers were Keith Burt with 11, Peter Bell with 10 and Andrew Jenkins with 7.

Mike Simonson was again the recipient of the Player of the Year trophy, Keith Burt received the Most Improved Player trophy and treasurer Harry Melding the Clubman trophy, on the presentation night at the Jersey Beach Hotel. Among the guests were ex-players David Pickering (Llanelli) and Kevin Bowring, fresh from winning the Middlesex Sevens with London Welsh. Top try scorer was Peter Bell with 10 tries and top scorer was skipper Richard Lawrence with 120 points. Players who were married during the season and received a wall clock were Chris Chappell, Ron Lilley, Mike Simonson and Paul Woodland.

As former players and after involvement with the Youth XV, assistant secretary Peter Davies and vice chairman Colin Watkins played a vital role during this period of the club's history as important links in the chain that formed the committee.

Tour

The club got a 10–10 draw on their tour to Stockport, when they played Dukinfield RFC (Bredbury Hall) on 24 March 1984.

10.8 Stockport tour against Dukinfield 1983/84

(back) Simon Mogford, Neil Richards, Andy Jenkins, Emrys Landeg, Ian Chesterfield, Mike Curtis, M. Edwards, G. Evans, ?, G. Brown, B. Worth, N. Bowring, C. Davies, ?, D. Nicholls, T. Gregory; (front) M. Bate, R. Alderson, D. Lewis, P. Bell, R. Evans, J. Thomas, R. Lawrence (captain), R. Knight, ?, R. Lilley, J. Vaughan, ?, ?

Around the district

Seven Sisters won the O.G. Davies Cup, beating Bryncoch in the final.

Cimla won the H.G. Lewis Cup, but then lost to league champions Seven Sisters in the All Winners Cup.

Resolven were Youth champions.

Match results place BFRFC scores first

1984/85

Last year's captain and vice swapped roles and a new coach came on board. Disappointingly, the club had neither a Quins nor a Youth XV, so they had to rely on a single group of players to pull them through the season.

The season started in August with the local O.J. Davies Sevens being held in the Ferry.

Pontyclun were Ferry's first opponents at home and they got off to a good start with a 12–3 victory. Richard Lawrence scored the only try, which the outstanding Dai Lewis converted and then added a penalty and a drop goal. Forwards Spencer Lewis, Simon Mogford and skipper Simonson played magnificently.

Next up was a visit to the Gnoll to play Neath in a friendly. Ferry gave a good account of themselves but were eventually overhauled 10–29 by a strong Neath team. Dai Lewis bagged 1 try and kicked 2 penalties. It took a 21-point, Man of the Match performance by Paul Thorburn to quell the Ferry in the end. Props Ceri Davies and Simon Mogford gave a good account of themselves.

Another away trip awaited them in the first round of the WRU Cup. They came unstuck on their visit to Pyle and lost by 1 point (15–16). Dai Lewis dropped 1 goal, added 2 penalties and 1 conversion of Richard Lawrence's try.

During the match, loyal Ferry servant PETER BELL suffered a nasty injury and was forced to retire from the game with a ruptured spleen.

Ferry then had three tough local derbies in a row, all at home. The first ended in defeat to Resolven (lost 3–19); the second was in the O.G. Davies Cup, and they lost to Skewen, 12–19; and then lost narrowly to Cwmgrach,

Captain
Mike Simonson

Vice captain
Richard Lawrence

Coach
Tony Philpin

First XV playing record
P 31
W 11
D 1
L 19
Points for 392
Points against 481

9–11 (Lewis 2 penalties and 1 drop goal). In between they played a home friendly with Ogmore Vale and hammered them 41–0. Right wing Stuart Shaw (4), Paul Woodland (2), Keith Burt and Simonson were the try scorers. Dai Lewis converted 7 and adding 1 penalty. They ended September with a 22–10 away win at Trimsaran.

October began with a couple of away friendlies in Glais (lost 13–14) and Glynneath (lost 9–31) before completing the month with two home games against Tonna and Aberaman. In the Tonna game Ferry lost prop Neil Richards straight from the kick-off after hooker Martyn Bate took the ball but was hit heavy from behind, which resulted in his head clashing with Richards' nose as he came in to support. Along with the loss of flanker Jon Roberts due to injury and the unavailability of eight first-team players, it was no wonder Ferry were defeated 13–28. Tries came from Simonson and Shaw, who also kicked a penalty. Keith Holifield made 1 conversion. Ferry also lost to Aberaman (4–21).

The Wistech Central Glamorgan league programme started in November. First up were local rivals Aberavon Green Stars (away), Ferry lost 16–22. Andy Bell and Paul Woodland got the tries and Dai Lewis converted 1 and added 2 penalties, Ferry then lost their second game at Taibach, 9–32. Dai Lewis kicked 3 penalties. Forwards Chris Chappell and Spencer Lewis were to the fore, along with hooker Dai Evans. Ferry ended the month with a friendly home draw with BSC Port Talbot, 12–12. Jon Roberts got the only try, which Lewis converted and then added 2 penalties. New scrum-half Steve Preedy played well, as did flanker Ian Chesterfield and centre Dai Williams.

Six games were played in December, five in the league. They started with a really disappointing 9–10 home defeat to Ogmore Vale. Roberts again with the try, converted by Lewis, who also kicked a penalty. Prop Kevin Jones, wing Dom Davies and scrum-half John Thomas were all outstanding. Ferry then got back to winning ways at home to Nantymoel, beating them 22–9. Tries came from Roberts, again, Keith Burt and prop Martyn Bate. Lewis converted 2, dropped 1 goal and added a penalty. Ferry then lost their next game narrowly, at Pontycymmer 3–4. The weather caused the next match, at home to Cefn Cribbwr, to be abandoned while Ferry were losing 0–12. They also lost a return friendly at home to Trimsaran, 0–10, and then ended the year with a heavy 6–45 defeat at league leaders Tondu.

The weather got the better of the first couple of weeks of the new year before the league programme restarted, at home to Aberavon Green Stars. Ferry won the return match 24–6. New flanker Carl Jordan, from Cimla, was outstanding in open play, along with fellow back rowers Chesterfield and Roberts, both of whom made 1 try, as did Stuart Shaw. Scrum-half Spencer Pugh played well and his partner at half-back, Lewis, converted all three tries and added a couple of penalties. The new second row partnership of Ron Lilley and centre Paul Woodland worked really well and they supplied plenty of ball throughout the game.

February got off to a bad start with Ferry losing their next game at Ogmore Vale, 7–12. But they recovered to defeat Pontycymmer at home, 25–0 – with tries from Roberts (2) and hooker Martyn Bate, and 1 penalty try. Lewis made 3 conversions and added a penalty to end the month in style.

March was a poor month for results as they slipped to defeat at home to Tondu (9–44) and Taibach (12–15, Lewis kicked 1 drop goal and 3 penalties; the back row of Roberts, Jordan and Tyrone Herdman were outstanding), and lost an away friendly at Bridgend Athletic (9–21).

In the final month of the season a 20–3 away win against BP Llandarcy got things going. Both wings, Shaw and Burt, scored tries. Centre Andrew Jenkins made a 40-yard sprint after a fine break from his fellow centre Holifield. Richard Lawrence came back from a broken arm in October to kick 2 penalties and 1 conversion.

On their return from tour Ferry completed the double over BP Llandarcy, winning 10–6 at home.

The final fixture of the season was Cardigan at home. Playing well were Ron Lilley, Nigel Lovering and Tyrone Herdman in the back row, burly policeman Howard Pitman in the second row and the whole front row of Kevin Jones, Martyn Bate and Neil McPhee. Ferry won 18–10.

A cup had been donated by coach Tony Philpin, who hailed from Cardigan and had been their coach a few years previously. So this game was to be played alternately home and away, hopefully on an annual basis.

This was hooker Kevin Phillips' last appearance for Cardigan. He was presented with his kit (and kaboodle) after the game by Neath RFC, who were taking him on tour to Portugal.

Ferry were invited to the Carl Hughes Memorial Sevens in Resolven during May. They defeated Crynant and Seven Sisters, but lost to Glynneath in the final.

Tour

Ferry welcomed English touring side Staines in April, and defeated them 19–3, before going on tour to Plymouth, where they defeated Devonport HSOB 15–9.

Awards

Long-serving committeeman Terry Woodland received Clubman of the Year and was awarded Life Membership. Flanker Jonathan Roberts was Player of the Year and Stuart Shaw was Most Improved Player, these two were also presented with the top try scorers awards (9 each) and Dai Lewis with the top scorer award for 208 points (which included 9 drop goals). Former players David Pickering and Rhys Thomas of Llanelli and referee Denzil Lloyd presented the awards.

Around the district

Briton Ferry Steel were knocked out of the Welsh Brewers Cup by Baglan in the first round (6–46, Colin Hopkins 2 penalties) and struggled throughout the season to recapture their old form.

Former and future Ferry players Cliff Morgan, Dai Davies, Carl Jordan and Martyn Williams were starring for Neath & District while playing for the Cimla. Morgan was later chosen to play for the Welsh Districts against Belgium, along with another ex-player, now playing for Seven Sisters, outside-half Chris White.

Later in the season Morgan created a record in a match for Cimla against Tonna Second XV when he scored 7 tries and converted them all – a brilliant feat!

Crynant beat Seven Sisters in the O.G. Davies Cup final, 12–9

The Neath & District champions were Seven Sisters. Division 1 winners were Cimla and Division 2 winners were Banwen. Youth champions were Glynneath, who beat Abercrave in the final.

Future Ferry First XV players, Keith Holifield and Gary Davies, were both part of Neath College's sevens squad that won the Rosslyn Park Sevens. This was the first time in thirteen years that a Welsh team had won this prestigious Schools tournament.

In other news

During December, flats in the Saltings area of the Ferry were demolished in the first phase of much-needed improvements to the area.

1985/86

Mike Simonson continued as skipper and a new coach arrived from the Cimla, fireman Terry Herdman (father of Tyrone and Simonson's father -in-law).

Ferry started with a good run in the O.G. Davies Sevens at Crynant by beating Cwmgrach 22–10, but they lost to Crynant in the semi-final (14–18).

The season got underway with a 22–0 home win over Swansea Uplands. They were then defeated 3–16 at Caldicot in a midweek fixture, before coming back strongly to beat Trimsaran at home 14–0 (D. Lewis 1 penalty, 1 drop goal, wing S. Shaw 2 tries). Ferry narrowly lost in the first round of the WRU Cup, away at local rivals Skewen, 0–7. In a home midweek friendly they went down to Glais, 3–9. To end a very busy September, they bounced back and defeated Cwmbran 19–7 home.

Ferry then played three away fixtures in a row in October. They lost at Abercynon (10–54) and at Cwmbran (9–27), but beat Cwmgrach (21–18) in the O.G. Davies Cup. They ended the month with a 6–6 draw at home to Blaengarw.

Once again, the league competition stared in November and their first opponents were the Aberavon Green Stars, away. They reversed the previous season's result and defeated them 17–3. Ferry then completed the double over Cwmgrach in a friendly, winning 12–0 at home, before going up to Blaengarw for a league encounter. Ferry won 9–6 and came away with Blaengarw's long-standing home record (Dai Lewis 1 more drop goal, Richard Lawrence kicked 2 penalties). Prop Neil McPhee was outstanding in a front row that stood up well to the

Captain
Mike Simonson

Coach
Terry Herdman

First XV playing record
P 31
W 20
D 1
L 10
Points for 352
Points against 274

strong scrummaging of the opposition. In the dying seconds, with the score at 9–6 to the Ferry and a scrummage on the Ferry line under the posts, hooker Martyn Bate took a vital strike against the head for Lewis to clear at the final whistle. Also outstanding were the midfield duo of Holifield and Williams, who tackled non-stop throughout the game, and wing Peter Clifford who put in a try-saving tackle on the Blaengarw second row. This win took the club to the top of the table and a win at home to Ogmore Vale (12–0, Richard Lawrence 1 converted try and the extras to a Mike Simonson try) kept Ferry at the top by the month's end.

Ferry started December with a thumping 44–3 home win over Nantymoel, which not only maintained their 100% league record but also meant they were still in contention in the Silver Ball competition, with only one defeat so far this season. Try scorers against Nantymoel were Mike Simonson, Keith Burt, John Thomas, Spencer Lewis, Tyrone Herdman, Keith Holifield (with a 50-yard special) and Jonathan Roberts. Richard Lawrence kicked 2 penalties and 3 conversions. Again outstanding were the front five of Terry John, Martyn Bate, Neil McPhee, Spencer Lewis and young tyrant Simon Mogford. Then Ferry lost their unbeaten record in a tough encounter at Pontycymmer (0–6) before scraping a 3–0 win over Cefn Cribbwr to end the month.

● Briton Ferry RFC: Back row (left to right): K Burt, N McPhee, T John, R Lilley, S Lewis, J Roberts, R Woolford, D Williams. Middle: Terry Herdman (coach), S Shaw, P Bell, Tyrone Herdman, K Hollifield, I Edwards, P Woodland, M Edwards (committee), I Chesterfield, A Bell, T Keefe (committee). Front: K Collins, J Thomas, A Jenkins, R Lawrence, M Bate, D Lewis, E Landage.

10.9 1985/86 (in Western Mail)

Match results place BFRFC scores first

Sadly, December saw the demise of the **BRITON FERRY STEEL** rugby club. Their final fixture list included games with Nantyfyllon, Pontardawe, Tonna, Glynneath, Aberavon Naval Club, Resolven, BSC, Rhigos, Glyncorrwg, Cimla, Metal Box, Vardre, Taibach, Tonmawr and Baglan. Briton Ferry Steel had only been around for twenty years, but since January 1965 they'd been a significant presence in, and had made a huge contribution to, Neath & District. It was not an easy decision for their committee, but it was a necessary one. The remaining players and committee voted to join with the BFRFC, and they made a considerable contribution to the senior club, both on and off the field.

Bad weather delayed the start of matches in the new year. Finally, their first game was another narrow win at home, 9–6, to complete the double over Blaengarw, and then another double at home to Aberavon Green Stars, winning 30–6.

February's games were all totally wiped out by the inclement weather, so, with the Five Nations games also kicking in, their next game was not until 8 March, where they went down 6–9 at home to BSC Port Talbot in the league. They slipped up in their next game at home to Caldicot, losing 7–18, before doing the double away, over BSC Port Talbot, beating them by a point (7–6). Ferry ended the month with a home league win over Pontycymmer, 19–9. Tries from K. Burt and an Andrew Jenkins special (at least two windmills), Lawrence kicked 1 conversion and Dai Lewis dropped 1 goal and kicked 2 penalties. Jenkins and wing Kevin Collins were outstanding.

Back in the club, secretary Roy Evans presented Ponty scrum-half **ALAN "WALLY" WALTERS** with a club tie to honour his last-ever game at the Ferry.

Also during March, Ferry could claim a unique double as ex-players **DAI PICKERING** and **CLIFF MORGAN** both captained the national side; Pickering became the new Wales captain and Morgan captained the Welsh Districts against Belgium.

April was a really busy month as Ferry played seven games. First up were Abercrave, who were defeated 9–8 at home.

The following day, Westlands (Yeovil) RFC on tour beat a Briton Ferry XV 0–4 with a single try.

Ferry defeated Glynneath 6–3 at home in the O.G. Davies Cup, before going down 9–24 in a vital league match at Cefn Cribbwr. They scraped a 3–0 league win in torrential conditions at Nantymoel, which assured them of promotion. The whole pack were the heroes that day by totally outplaying the opposition.

A Richard Lawrence penalty was the only score, although there was a disputed disallowed try by J. Roberts for the Ferry.

They were then knocked out of the O.G. Davies Cup in the semi-finals by Bryncoch (3–10, Lawrence penalty) but Ferry did complete their league programme with an 18–9 away win at Ogmore Vale. Lawrence kicked both conversions and added 2 penalties to 2 tries from centre Dai Williams, both from open play. Outside-half Andrew Jarrett created a break, before passing to wing Kerry Frey, who passed back inside to Williams to score. This was followed by a brilliant breakout by Keith Burt from his own 25-yard line, he found hooker Martyn Bate on his shoulder, who was dragged down a yard or two before the line but managed to offload to Williams, who again went over for the score.

In May, Ferry paid a last-minute visit to Yeovil to play a return match with Westlands RFC, this time Ferry won 18–4. Ferry were also invited back to the Carl Hughes Memorial Sevens in Resolven. But they came unstuck in both games, 4–12 to Crynant and 4–13 to Cwmgrach.

Awards

Top scorers for the season were Richard Lawrence with 103 points and Dai Lewis with 79. Keith Holifield, Keith Burt and Mike Simonson all ended with 5 tries each. Veteran second row Spencer Lewis won the Player of the Year trophy and Nigel Lovering was Most Improved Player. Strongman Ian Edwards, who had joined the club with the Steel, won the Quins Player of the Year award. Barry Evans, again from the Steel, was Quins Most Improved Player. Gareth "Faggots" Davies was awarded the try of the season in a Quins match. Clubman of the Year was veteran player John Thomas. Club committeeman Terry Gregory received an award from the ladies committee for his help throughout the year. David Pickering was presented with a trophy in recognition of his international career. He then reciprocated by presenting the club with a French jersey worn by Jean Pierre Rives.

> In April 1986, the *Western Mail* said that the Ferry were on their way back after two decades in the doldrums and that promotion to Division 1 was a certainty. They also felt that the 1960s decision to opt out of the West Wales RU had been a fateful one, as the ambitious plans, which were fair at the time, had failed to materialise and had brought the club nothing but disappointment, debt and depression. They hoped that the fixture list could start to resemble that of the 1930s, with the likes of Aberavon, Bridgend, Maesteg and Neath. However, the battle was now being won on the field of play under new coach Terry Herdman (ex-Seven Sisters no.8) and his son-in-

law, captain Mike Simonsen. Results were starting to improve and players were showing more grit and determination. To date, the Ferry had only conceded 2 tries and 55 points in eleven league games. Morgan Jones, their 77-year-old chairman, was supervising the revival. He'd spent fifty-five years with the Ferry, thirty-four of them as chairman. They also stated that Briton Ferry had a tradition of producing quality players and captains, two good examples being Kevin Bowring for London Welsh and David Pickering for Wales.

Terry Ellis and Emrys Landeg came on to the committee this year and Mhenir Keefe joined the ladies committee. Mhenir's husband Terry took over as assistant secretary.

Around the district

Bryncoch beat Neath Athletic to win the O.G. Davies Cup.

Glynneath won both the Neath & District League and the sevens competition.

For the first time Gwernyfed beat Banwen to win the H.G. Lewis Cup and then they defeated Glynneath for the All Winners trophy.

1986/87

Captain
Spencer Lewis

Vice captain
Jonathan Roberts

Coaches
Terry Herdman

First XV playing record
P 30
W 15
D 0
L 15
Points for 366
Points against 458

Quins captain
Nigel Lovering

After a gap of three years Spencer Lewis became captain again.

The season started with a 20–6 win at Swansea Uplands, but they then went down badly to Cardigan in the Tony Philpin cup, 9–28. They got back to winning ways at home to Alltwen, 19–9, and continued with a fine Welsh Cup run. In a home win over Cwmavon, Keith Burt and Kevin Collins got tries, Lawrence kicked 3 penalties and 1 conversion and Dai Lewis dropped yet another goal. This was the first time for ten years that they had progressed past the first round. In a tough encounter at home with Tylorstown, the Ferry came through 15–7. Prop Steve Knight bagged 2 tries, Dai Williams 1 and Lewis added 1 penalty. The back row of Ian Edwards, Ian Chesterfield and Tyrone Herdman were outstanding.

October started with two away games in Swansea. The first at St. Helens, against a strong Swansea Athletic side containing British Lion prop forward Clive Williams and England international second row Maurice Colclough. Ferry lost 13–22 with a K. Burt try and penalty, an R. Lawrence conversion and the game's best try, scored after fine linking work by second rows Spencer Lewis and Steve Knight, carried on magnificently by scrum-half John Thomas and finished in style by centre Dai Williams. Welsh second row legend Geoff Wheel accompanied a sing-song in the bar afterwards. Ferry won the second away game, 20–19 at Swansea University (S. Shaw 2 tries, J. Roberts 1 try, Lawrence converting). Next up was a second-round cup match at home to Maesteg Quins. Ferry won 20–0, with tries from Jon Roberts, John Thomas, Herdman and

Match results place BFRFC scores first

Martyn Bate (who was outstanding in this game) with Lawrence adding the extras. Unfortunately, the return match with Cardigan for the Tony Philpin cup was postponed, and that trophy is still in Cardigan's clubhouse!

Ferry's Division 1 league campaign started in November with home defeats to Aberavon Quins (7–15) and Kenfig Hill (15–19). Then it was back to the cup with a home game against a strong Newport Saracens side.

> The Saracens were so confident of winning that they had already prepared themselves for the next round and printed posters and programmes for the draw pairing of a home fixture against mighty Pontypool!

But the Ferry were determined to land that game for themselves and they prevailed, winning 13–6 with tries from Paul Woodland and Jon Roberts. The outstanding Lawrence converted 1 and kicked 1 penalty. Scrum-half John Thomas was also outstanding. Second row Rhys Thomas was back from Llanelli for this game. Then they ended the month with a league defeat, 14–18 at Pyle.

In the final month of the year Ferry went down at home to league leaders Tondu, 3–15, despite the home pack coming off the best against the much-vaunted Tondu pack. The back row of Ian Edwards, Tyrone Herdman and Nigel Lovering were everywhere, and second rows skipper Spencer Lewis and Rhys Thomas did tremendous work in the lineouts. The front row of Steve "Meany" Jones, Martyn "Dubroca" Bate and Steve Knight were superb in the tight and in their loose play. The scorer was R. Lawrence, with 1 penalty.

Then Ferry were into their next WRU Cup match, the big one, at home to the might of Pontypool.

What a day in the great history of the Ferry! Two thousand tickets were printed. The team trained up on the Gnoll in the week preceding the game with Neath RFC. The build up was very tense. When the players stepped out on the field the reaction of the crowd was terrific. Every part of the ground was full and the clubhouse side must have been at least three or four people deep.

Pontypool had a reputation of being a big, hard, physical team who took no prisoners, but the Ferry manfully went about the task of trying to take their scalp. The Pontypool side contained Welsh internationals John Perkins, Mark Brown and Staff Jones and B international Steve Jones up front, not to mention a certain British Lion, Graham Price. They proved too strong in the end, despite a massive brave effort from the Ferry. Paul Woodland and Rob

10.10 Schweppes Challenge Cup, Briton Ferry v. Pontypool

Match results place BFRFC scores first

Woolford were powerful tacklers in midfield and kept the Pontypool back line in tag for the whole match, especially Roger Bidgood (who was being pushed very strongly in all quarters to play for Wales in the forthcoming Five Nations). The final score was 6–20 to Pontypool. The Ferry only managed 2 penalties from outside-half Richard Lawrence. Ponty were very gracious in their praise for the effort put in by the home side, both on and off the field. Coach Ray Prosser came into the home changing room after the final whistle to say, "You have done your town and club very proud, and the effort you put into this game was second to none." The Pontypool committee issued an invitation to watch a game later in the season, as a compliment to the club.

Ferry finished the year off with a 7–3 home league win over Pyle (Spencer Lewis 1 try, Lawrence 1 penalty).

The new year started with two tough away league games. Ferry won 19–17 against Porthcawl (Cliff Morgan and Paul Woodland tries, awarded 1 penalty try, D. Lewis converted 2 and 1 penalty). They lost 0–32 at Kenfig Hill. Then at home they defeated Cefn Cribbwr 9–6. J. Roberts got 1 try, Lawrence converted. Scrum-half Morgan 1 neat drop goal from a quick strike in the scrum by hooker Martyn Bate.

February began with an excellent 12–7 win at Aberavon Quins and then they went down fighting, 15–27, at league leaders Tondu (Lawrence kicked an early penalty; wings K. Collins and K. Burt were resolute in defence). Ferry ended the month with a narrow friendly defeat at Tonmawr, 10–13.

First up in March was Nantyfyllon at home, which Ferry won 10–9 with 2 penalties from R. Lawrence and 1 J. Roberts try. Nanty flanker and captain, Mark Arthur, was sent off during one of the many bouts of fighting during this game. Ferry then had a short respite from league action and played Crynant at home in the O.G. Davies Cup, and won 26–9. But ended the month with another league defeat, 6–16 at home to Porthcawl (Lawrence 2 penalties). Exciting new scrum-half Robert Buckley made his debut in this game.

April was another busy month. First up was a semi-final in the O.G. Davies Cup, away at Seven Sisters, which Ferry lost 7–27. They bounced back in the following game and won 21–0 in Cwmgrach. Three Quins players were in the side, second row Steve Hopkins was joined by two making their debut, prop Leighton John and flanker Mark Harris. Hopkins had a fine game in the tight and in the loose. Ian Edwards and Keith Burt made tries, Lawrence converted both and added two penalties. Buckley kicked a long-range penalty. Ferry then came unstuck in their final two league games at Cefn Cribbwr (3–13) and

Nantyfyllon (3–23). They then played home and away friendlies with Resolven to end the season – strangely, losing 3–47 at home but bouncing back to win 17–13 away.

Ferry had scored 42 tries in the league programme. The Ferry were also in two sevens tournaments at the end of the season. In the Pyle Invitation Sevens they beat Cimla but lost to Bridgend Sports. In Resolven for the Carl Hughes Sevens they lost to the hosts 0–22 and to Crynant 4–6.

10.11 1986/87

(back) T. Herdman (coach), M. Bate, K. Burt, S. Shaw, N. Lovering, S. Knight, R. Thomas, T. Herdman, I. Edwards, D. Williams, P. Woodlands, A. Jeffries, S. Mogford; (front) D. Lewis, G. Baker, R. Lawrence, S. Lewis (captain), J. Thomas, A. Jenkins, M. Best, M. Edwards (touch judge), E. Landeg (trainer)

Quins

The Quins lost out to Gwernyfed in the Neath & District cup, 3–19, but had wins over Skewen (twice), Pontrhydyfen, Neath Athletic, Porthcawl and Pontardawe (28–19, D. Evans, G. Baker, M. Harris and M. Williams with tries, Buckley 2 penalties and 2 conversions). They drew with Seven Sisters, Crynant, Cimla and Bryncoch. Quins also played host to Bedfordshire Prison Service XV, whom they defeated 52–0.

At the end of the season the club were struggling to stay afloat. The twenty-one-year lease on the ground (of £20 per annum) had expired three years previously and the council were proposing another twenty-one-year, but at £300 per annum. The club responded that these terms would cripple them financially and they wouldn't see the end of the following season. The council then offered a seven-year-lease on a nominal sum,

Match results place BFRFC scores first

but nothing had been agreed. It seemed that the council were deferring a decision, pending an investigation into the club's finances.

Awards

Strong man Steve Knight won the Player of the Year award and Tyrone Herdman the Most Improved Player award. Top scorer for the season was Richard Lawrence, with 145 points, and top try scorer was Jonathan Roberts with 7. Quins top scorer was Andrew Jarrett, and Quins top try scorer was Martin Williams. Steve Hopkins won Quins Player of the Year award, with Andrew Bowen getting Quins Most Improved Player award.

Allan Clifford, ex-Ferry Steel men Brian Evans, Kenny Moyle, Keith Samuel and Roland Adams came on to the committee. Roland also won the coveted award of Clubman of the Year in his first season with the Ferry.

Around the district

The district trophies were dominated by Banwen who not only won all three on offer but also added the trophy for the most tries.

In other news

In October, ex-player David Pickering unveiled a new honours board in Cwrt Sart School that would list all the internationals in all the sports produced by the school. He also opened a new restaurant in Neath, Legends, in conjunction with Ferry flanker Nigel Lovering.

1987/88

Before the season got underway, a fun game between West Glamorgan Health Authority East Unit and the Authority HQ was held on the ground to raise funds for Neath Hospital patient amenities. An all-female pack faced an an all-male pack and it ended in an 8–8 draw! They raised £172.30.

In the first month of the season proper Ferry defeated Swansea Uplands 14–8 at home. Jon Roberts scored the first try of the season, followed by tries from Gareth Baker and Nigel Lovering. Richard Lawrence converted 1. Powerful centre Paul Woodland and the three Martyns (fullback Williams, no.8 Williams and hooker Bate) were showing good early season form. They then lost their next home game to Pyle, 0–32, and also went down heavily at Bridgend Athletic in the WRU Cup, 3–41, and at home to Gilfach Goch, 21–32, before arresting the slide with a 15–15 draw at home to Cefn Cribbwr.

The first league match in October was at home to Kenfig Hill, but Ferry were defeated 6–13 –Dai Lewis' 2 penalties the only scores. Next up was an away game at Porthcawl and another defeat, 6–16 – Martyn Williams' 2 penalties their only score. In the next two friendly games Ferry notched up victories at home to Ogmore Vale (66–9, 14 tries, hat tricks from both Tyrone Herdman and Alan King, 2 each for Kevin Collins and John Thomas, 1 each for Andrew Jenkins, Rhys Thomas and Jon Roberts; fly-half Andrew Jarrett added 5 conversions) and then 14–6 at BSC Port Talbot. The month ended with yet another league defeat, 3–41 at Tondu.

Captain
Jonathan Roberts

Coach
Cliff Morgan

Quins captain
Nigel Lovering

Match results place BFRFC scores first

November was a far happier month as Ferry defeated Pontycymmer 9–6 away in a friendly, then drew 9–9 at home with Maesteg Celtic to claim their first league point of the campaign (skipper Roberts with the touchdown, Rob Buckley's boot adding the extras). Then they defeated Taibach at home for a first league win. Buckley's boot was again on form and notched up 10 points to add to tries from A. Jarret, John Thomas and a 75-yard scorcher from Andrew Jenkins.

10.12 Match in 1987/88

December was not a good month on the field as the club went down to three league defeats at home: to Porthcawl 12–18 (tries from A. Jenkins and K. Burt converted by Lawrence); to Aberavon Quins 6–34 (1 penalty each from M. Williams and A. Jarret); and away to Kenfig Hill 6–13 (Jenkins with yet another try, converted by Lawrence).

10.13 1987/88

January was a poor month weatherwise and only one game went ahead. Unfortunately for the Ferry it was another league defeat, this time at Maesteg Celtic 4–22, which put them at the bottom of the table going into February.

Three heavy defeats in the league followed, two at home (Nantyfyllon 0–51 and Tondu 0–63) and at Aberavon Quins 3–39 (a sole penalty from Paul Woodland. In between they had another home defeat in a friendly with Blaengarw, 9–13.

In their final league game in March, Ferry were away at Nantyfyllon and their 3–50 defeat confirmed their relegation to Division 2 of the Central Glamorgan League. To rub salt into their wounds their next opponents were a strong Swansea Athletic side, away at St. Helens. As expected, Ferry were defeated 6–51. In a home date for the O.G. Davies Cup with local rivals Tonna, Ferry were narrowly defeated 13–18. Now they were out of contention in the league and for both cups, all that was left to try to salvage such a poor season were a few friendlies and a tour! Ferry started with two good away wins, at Resolven 29–15 and at Cwmgrach 10–0, but they lost 6–18 at Trimsaran.

Ferry toured to Weymouth in April and defeated the local side 44–0. They met up with former prop Alun Hargest, who was landlord of a pub in the area. Back home they defeated Resolven again, 18–0, with tries from K. Burt and P. Woodland and extras added by Lawrence. They also won away at Morriston, 46–9.

At the end of the season Ferry were bottom of the Guardian merit table with a 31.82% playing record. Not a good omen for the season ahead, when the club would celebrate its centenary.

> CHRIS BOWRING, brother of former player and coach Kevin and son of committeeman Norman, transferred to the club from the Metal Box.

Quins

Quins had defeated Cross Keys Hotel XV 18–12 in the first round of the Neath & District Cup, but lost 6–18 to Resolven in the next round.

They'd also achieved wins over Aberavon Naval Club, Cross Keys Hotel, Seven Sisters, Crynant, Resolven, Cwmavon (twice), Metal Box, Baglan, Taibach, Skewen, BSC and Pontrhydyfen, and draws with Crynant and Resolven (0–0).

Awards

Top try scorer was Andrew Jarret, and top scorer was Richard Lawrence who, strangely enough, was also top scorer for the Quins XV. Top try scorer for the Quins was Gareth Baker. Player of the year was Martin Williams and prop Leighton John was Most Improved Player. Quins Player of the Year was dynamic flanker Mark Harris with Ian Michael as Quins Most Improved Player. Clubman of the Year award went to Keith Samuel. Robert Knight came on to the committee.

> BILLY WILLIAMS made a substantial contribution to the club's history and had served on the committee for a number of years. As press officer he'd made sure that the club was always represented well in the media. He'd produced many reports over the years, many of which helped in the making of this book. His father, Mr W.L. Williams (or Billy Golf Ball, as he was known) was a long-serving life member of the club. His son-in-law and grandson, David and Joe Evans, both played for the club in the front row.

In the district

Seven Sisters won the O.G. Davies Cup.

Ex-player David Pickering joined Neath RFC from Llanelli.

A future Ferry captain was heading out to Italy with the Welsh Schools Under-15s XV, scrum-half Mike Moran.

Other news

Local councillor Fred Kingdom received the CBE for services to the local council.

Local councillor Huw James called for the redevelopment of the town.

The town of Briton Ferry was in an ongoing struggle against the Gypsies' camp, which they lost the following April.

1988/89 – CENTENARY

Centenary celebrations

A special centenary dinner took place on 26 August 1988 in the Gwyn Hall, Neath. Distinguished guests were Mr Brian Thomas, Councillor John Warman (Mayor of Neath), David Pickering, Mr Russell Jenkins (honourable secretary Crawshays RFC), Mal Langford (Glamorgan County RFC), John Knight (South Wales Police), Mr Ron Jones (WRU representative for Central Glamorgan), Mr Clive Rowlands (Lions tour manager), Myrddin Jones (president of the WRU), Rod Morgan (WRU), Elgan Rees, and ex-internationals Mr Viv Evans and Cyril Roberts. This was followed with a live studio interview at Swansea Sound, when chairman Mr Morgan Jones, press officer Bill Williams and captain Martyn Bate talked about the club's history and upcoming events.

Mr Cedric Edwards of Manor Way was commissioned to bake a centenary cake, iced in club colours and with the club badge, that would provide about 280 pieces for members and guests.

Captain
Martyn Bate

Vice captain
Paul Woodland

Coach
Cliff Morgan

First XV playing record
P 36
W 17
D 1
L 18

Quins captain
Stuart Shaw

Quins playing record
P 29
W 21
D 1
L 7

10.14 Cedric Edwards and centenary cake

The club was invited to a reception in the Mayor's parlour, where captain Martyn Bate presented the Mayor, Councillor John Warman, with a centenary plaque.

The club held a successful reunion buffet in March and, to top the season off nicely, Mr Douglas Symmons, managing director of the club's main sponsor, OCS (Wales) Ltd, presented the chairman Mr Morgan Jones with the keys to a new minibus and his firm's good wishes for a long friendship.

BRITON FERRY Rugby Club completed their centenary season on a high when OCS (Wales) presented th club with a new minibus. The managing director of the company, Mr. Douglas Symmons, said his compan were delighted to help a second class club and he hoped their association with the club would continue for man years. Club chairman Mr. Moryon Jones said the minibus had put the seal on a very successful centenar season. Mr. Jones is pictured receiving the keys of the vehicle from Mr. Symmons.

10.15 Presentation of new minibus from Douglas Symmons (MD of OCS Wales) to Morgan Jones (BFRFC chairman)

On the field

Hooker Martyn Bate captained the team in its centenary year, with centre Paul Woodland as vice captain. Stuart Shaw led the Quins. Cliff Morgan continued as coach.

In August, Ferry played in the Aberavon Green Stars Sevens against Pyle and in the O.J. Davies Sevens in Skewen, where they beat the hosts 10–0 but then lost to Crynant 10–12.

The club also played a special double centenary game against old friend Cefn Cribbwr RFC, who were also celebrating their centenary. On 4 March, Ferry triumphed by 21–10 in the return match to complete a hat trick of wins over Cefn. The scorers were Wayne Cook, Robert Kemeys and Stuart Shaw with tries, Richard Lawrence converted them all. The double celebrations went on into the night and both sets of players were presented with double centenary engraved mirrors. Ferry won the game 21–10.

10.16 Centenary First XV, 1988/89
(back) Keith Burt, Andrew Jarrett, Chris Chappell, Dai Boast, Keith Hollifield, Dai Evans, Leighton John, Wayne Cook, Robert Pritchard, Cliff Morgan (coach); (front) Martin Williams, Stuart Shaw, Chris White, Robert Broome, Martyn Bate (captain), Andrew Jenkins, Mike Simonson, John Thomas, Steven Knight

The season kicked off with a visit on Thursday 1 September by Schweppes cupholders Llanelli. A large crowd watched the Scarlets take a 27–0 half-time lead. The Ferry stuck gamely to their task and continuously disrupted and harassed the senior side, which included Tony Copsey, Colin Stephens, Steve Bowling and Carwyn Davies, but the match ended in a 6–37 defeat. The Ferry's scores came from a Richard Lawrence penalty kick and a snap drop goal from wing Adrian Griffiths. The front row of Leighton John, Martyn Bate and Steve Knight gave their opposite numbers a torrid time in the scrums, and back row forwards Ian Edwards and Tyrone Herdman were outstanding.

The next game was also a celebration game and on Tuesday 6 September a large crowd came to see the losing cup finalists of 1987/88, Neath. Huw Richards, Colin Laity and Alan Edmunds were in a Neath side captained by Rowland Phillips. The Ferry took the lead midway through the first half with an interception try from Andrew Jarrett, which was converted by outside-half Gary Owen. There were quiet hopes of a shock on the cards, but tries from the All Blacks in the second half led Neath to a 42–6 win.

10.17 Match in 1988/89

Ferry then won a friendly away at Aberavon Green Stars, 6–3, before the third celebration game on Tuesday 13 September against Maesteg, who included Alan Bateman, Jeff Bird and Mervyn Owen in their ranks. Maesteg triumphed 35–4 against a much-changed Ferry side. In came Dai Evans at hooker, Rob Pritchard at lock, Nigel Lovering and Martin Williams in the back row, and Chris Bowring into the centre, led this time by vice captain Paul Woodland. The scorer was Andrew Jarrett with a try.

10.18 Match in 1988/89

In the first round of the WRU Schweppes Cup, Ferry were defeated 7–14 at home by St. Peters of Cardiff. Jarrett again scored a try and Owen added a penalty.

Nantymoel were defeated 24–7 in the next home friendly fixture.

The first game of the season in the Central Glamorgan League Division 2 was played in October, at home to Porthcawl, who were captained by ex-Ferry skipper and second row Spencer Lewis. Ferry lost 6–9, with only 2 penalties from G. Owen. Then they lost 9–22 at Bridgend Athletic. It was back to a friendly for the next game and a 48–10 away win at Ogmore Vale, before resuming the league campaign with a 12–9 home win over Tonmawr (R. Lawrence 4 penalties). Then it was three away league games on the trot. First at BSC Port Talbot, where they literally slugged out a 9–6 win (Lawrence kicked three penalties). Paul Woodland and home skipper Mark Morgan were sent off with ten minutes to go, despite not being anywhere near the punch-up that had broken out. They were followed a couple of minutes later by home hooker Owen who, in dispute with the referee, walked off the pitch. The second set of opponents were Cefn Cribbwr and, in a close game, the Ferry triumphed 23–20. Andrew Jenkins, Mike Simonson and Rob Buckley were the try scorers, Buckley added 1 conversion and Lawrence added 2 penalties. The third league game was another defeat by Porthcawl, 6–8.

10.19 Match in 1988/89

Two more friendlies were next on the card, and first up was Pontardulais at home, who won by 17–27 (C. White, W. Cook and A. Jarrett were the try scorers, White converted 1 and K. Pollifield kicked a late penalty goal). Second was a 22–18 home win over Aberavon Green Stars. Then it was back to league action, at home against Bridgend Athletic, which Ferry lost 3–12 (R. Buckley 1 penalty). This was followed by a 21–21 draw with Tonmawr (try scorers were A. Jarret 2, A. Jenkins and Ian Michael, 1 penalty and 1

Match results place BFRFC scores first

conversion from R. Lawrence), and a 27–15 home win over BSC Port Talbot (C. Bowring, M. Williams, M. Simonson and A. Jarret the try scorers, Lawrence with 2 conversions and 1 penalty, Buckley with 2 conversions).

Ferry won a Christmas home friendly with Taibach, 30–10. K. Pollifield 2, R. Buckley, R. Broom and J. Thomas were the try scorers and Buckley converted 3.

The new year started with a 22–9 home league win over Cefn Cribbwr in the final game of the league season, which put Ferry in third position. On a trip to Pontycymmer, Ferry triumphed 16–12. Two home wins followed. The highlight of Nantymoel 24–0 was a superb individual effort by A. Jarret. Against Aberavon Green Stars, Martin Williams was among the try scorers in a 29–10 victory.

Only two games were played in February. One against Blaengarw away, which Ferry lost 7–27, despite Rhys Thomas and Steve Hopkins dominating the lineouts and taking almost every ball (Rob Kemeys 1 try, R. Lawrence 1 penalty. At home to Tonna, Ferry won 9–0. Stuart Shaw scored the try, converted by Lawrence, and C. White kicked a 50-yard penalty.

They also held a successful players reunion where many players from the past attended and relived old times. A 6–9 away defeat at Ammanford was followed with a 7–24 away defeat by Crynant in the first round of the O.G. Davies Cup.

10.20 Team photo 1988/89

The final month of the centenary season was very busy, with seven games to play. First up was a home defeat, 18–28 to Caldicot (R. Kemeys try, Lawrence 1 conversion, 3 penalties). Then came the visit of Swansea on Wednesday 5 April in another celebratory fixture, which Ferry lost 9–64. Mark Titley was in scintillating form for the All Whites, along with Paul Arnold and

Alan "Santa" Reynolds. Titley scored two amazing tries, from 65 metres and from 75 metres. A. Jeffries scored the Ferry try, Lawrence added 1 conversion and 1 penalty. Ferry bounced back in their next game at home to Ogmore Vale, winning by 52–10. The 10 tries came from K. Collins 2, K. Burt 2, Mark Harris, Rob Broom and Tyrone Herdman 4. Lawrence kicked 6 conversions. On Monday 10 April, Ferry hosted a Crawshays Welsh XV containing ex-Ferry player now with London Welsh Kevin Bowring, Pontypridd hooker Phil John, Steve Powell of Neath, Byron Hayward of Abertillery and captained by Ferry boy David Pickering. Crawshays triumphed 16–44, but the Ferry fought hard under the captainship of long-serving Ron Lilley. K. Collins and Chris Bowring scored tries, C. White converted 1 and added 1 penalty, S. Shaw also added 1 penalty.

Glamorgan Wanderers A were the next visitors and in a highly entertaining game they defeated the Ferry 18–32. The final celebratory game of the season was on Wednesday 19 April. Players for visitors Aberavon included Martin Thomas, Neville Roberts and lock Ian Brown. Once again the Ferry put up a brave battle, but a long hard season had started to take effect and, after conceding three late tries, they were eclipsed 6–50. Shaw scored the try, converted by Lawrence. Sadly, Ferry then lost their last home game of the season 3–12 to Resolven.

Ferry finished third in Division 2 of the Wistech League, on 11 points with 5 wins and 1 draw from 10 games, scoring 138 points, with 131 against, and bagging 14 tries.

Quins

The Quins, despite losing 19–23 at home in the cup, went on to become champions of Neath & District Division 2, beating Tonna (24–9) and Metal Box (53–0) on their way.

They also played a couple of special centenary games against a Welsh Districts XV, lost 3–54,which contained future first-class players in Owen Reed (Bridgend) and Arwel parry (Ebbw Vale) and Neath & District XV lost 4–12. They had been unbeaten until the end of October and had scored almost 300 points in 10 games, one of which was a 24–3 win over old rivals Skewen with tries from J. Thomas, Wayne Preece, Kevin Collins and Martyn Bate with Gary Owen adding 2 conversions and 1 penalty., they also beat Baglan in November by 22–3 away from home, but were defeated by 8–3 up in Glynneath in December, in the New Year they defeated Aberavon Quins by 27–20 with T. Herdman 2, Barry Evans the try scorers and Owen converting them all and adding a drop goal, and Morriston by 20–0, Ian Chesterfield, Steve Knight, Tyrone Herdman and Kerry Frey the try scorers.

10.21 Briton Ferry Quins 1988/89

Back row L-R:-Kevin Collins, John (rat) Thomas, Wayne Cook, Ian (Ned) Edwards, Wayne Preece, Nigel (thommo) Lovering, Ian Chesterfield, Dai Evans, Gareth (faggots) Davies, Steve Hopkins, Malcolm (buller) Edwards –touch judge. Front row –L-R:- Neil (Nelly) Richards, Gareth Baker, Stuart Shaw (Captain), Andrew (stumpy) Bowen, Leighton (pebbles) John, Robert (Norster) Howells

Tour

The tour returned to the Isle of Man, where Ferry played and beat Ramsey 21–12. Captain Martyn Bate scored an opportunist try. The tour party consisted of: backs S. Shaw, K. Collins, A. Jeffries, W. Cook, C. Bowring, A. Jenkins, K. Frey, R. Kemeys, R. Lawrence (vice captain) and J. Thomas; forwards I. Michael, N. Richards, R. Lilley, C. Chappell, I. Chesterfield, N. Lovering, M. Parris, C. Poward, W. Preece, D. Evans, R. "Boyo" Clifford and skipper and hooker Martyn Bate.

10.22 Ferry's return to the Isle of Man 1989

Awards

Richard Lawrence finished as top scorer, with Andrew Jeffries as top try scorer. Once again Martin Williams was Player of the Year. Most improved Player of the Year was Andrew Jeffries (formerly Jarret). Quins top scorer was skipper Stuart Shaw, who also won Quins Player of the Year award. Quins top try scorer was Kevin Collins, who won Quins Most Improved Player award.

Brian Evans received the Clubman of the Year Award. Two special awards were made to Kerry Frey and Ron Lilley for their dedication in getting to both training and matches throughout the season. Press Officer Bill Williams received a presentation for his hard work towards the season. Players and officials were presented with centenary blazer badges.

In the district

Neath Athletic won the O.G. Davies Cup against Seven Sisters, and they also topped the Guardian Merit table – Ferry were third.

Bryncoch won the O.G. Davies Sevens for the second year running.

Seven Sisters won the H.G. Lewis Cup, beating Glynneath.

Cimla won the league.

Table 10.1 Team line-ups against major centenary opponents

	Llanelli	Neath	Maesteg
15	S. Shaw	S. Shaw	R. Lawrence
14	A. Jeffries	A. Jeffries	K. Burt
13	P. Woodlands	P. Woodlands	P. Woodlands (C)
12	A. Griffiths	A. Jenkins	Chris Bowring
11	K. Burt	K. Burt	A. Jarrett
10	R. Lawrence	G. Owen	G. Owen
9	J. Thomas	C. White	C. White
1	L. John	S. Jones	L. John
2	Martyn Bate (C)	M. Bate (C)	Dai Evans
3	S. Knight	S. Knight	S. Knight
4	Chris Chappell		C. Chappell
5	Ron Lilley	Kevin Gregory	Rob Pritchard
6	Ian Edwards	I. Edwards	M. Simonson
7	Mike Simonsen	M. Simonson	N. Lovering
8	Tyrone Herdman	T. Herdman	M. Williams

	Swansea	Crawshays
15	Rob Broom	S. Shaw
14	K. Collins	C. Bowring
13	A. Jeffries	A. Griffiths
12	A. Jeffries	A. Jeffries
11	R. Kemeys	K. Collins
10	R. Buckley	C. White
9	R. Lawrence	J. Thomas
1	I. Michael	L. John
2	M. Bate (C)	Dai Evans
3	S. Knight	Neil Richards
4	Rhys Thomas	Ron Lilley (C)
5	Steve Hopkins	S. Knight
6	I. Chesterfield	I. Chesterfield
7	C. White	Mark Harris
8	M. Williams	Nigel Lovering

Other news

The club requested financial assistance from Neath Council in the form of sponsorship towards extra costs during this special year, as Tonna had done the previous year.

Plans were made to build a new railway station in Briton Ferry.

Brian Thomas quit his post as team manager as he was disillusioned with what was going on in the game, he later returned as a management consultant after a brief time in the same role with Penarth.

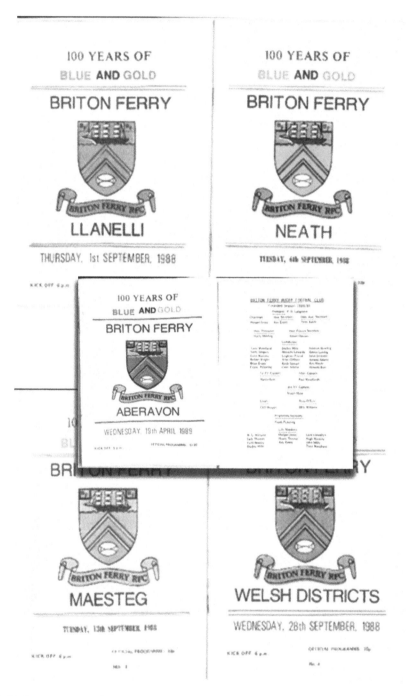

10.23 Centenary matches programmes

Match results place BFRFC scores first

1989/90

Flanker Chris White was the new captain for the end of the decade.

The month of September produced wins over both Caldicot and BSC Port Talbot away and over Ogmore Vale and BSC Port Talbot at home, all in friendlies. Ferry lost at home to Skewen and were defeated once again in the first round of both the WRU Cup (16–39 away to Llantrisant) and the O.G. Davies Cup (3–35 away to Neath Athletic).

This was the final season for the old Central Glamorgan League, which had lasted for just nine years.

Ferry had a good start to October with away wins over Tonmawr and Maesteg Quins, and at home to Taibach.

November presented a mixed bag of results, with a home league win over Blaengarw sandwiched between a defeat at Porthcawl and a draw at home with Neath Athletic.

Ferry ended 1989 with wins over Cefn Cribbwr and Tonmawr at home, and defeats at Maesteg Celtic and at home to Maesteg Quins.

But the new year got off to a bad start with away defeats at both Taibach and Blaengarw, before winning a friendly at Aberavon Green Stars. Outside-half Andrew Jenkins was outstanding in this game and made at least two 50-yard breaks, resulting in tries for Robert Miles and Andrew Jeffries. Miles, Mark Stephens, Chris White and Kerry Frey made further tries, White and Jeffries added a conversion each.

By February Ferry were lying fifth in the local Guardian merit table and had slipped to twelfth in the Silver Ball.

Captain
Chris White

Coach
Cliff Morgan

Playing record
P 31
W 17
D 1
L 13

Quins captain
Stuart Shaw

Ferry were lying third in the Wistech League, but slipped down after an away defeat at Cefn Cribbwr. They also lost at home in a friendly to Caldicot.

Ferry played a series of friendlies against West Walian opponents throughout March. At home to Furnace United (won 18–3, R. Miles 2 tries, R. Lawrence 1 conversion;a front row of Miles, Couchman and Michael were outstanding), and away to Cefneithin (won 30–10, Mark Newton 1 try, skipper White 1 try and 2 conversions, 2 tries from outstanding flanker Mark Harris). They completed the month with a fixture against Penclawdd.

In the final month, Ferry completed their league season with a 3–22 defeat at home by Maesteg Celtic. Chris White kicked a penalty. Busy and brave flanker Ian Chesterfield and backs Adrian Griffiths and Chris Bowring all played well. This put them in fourth place, with a 50% record. They also played, and lost, further friendly matches against Ammanford (7–14) and Croesyceiliog (14–30).

Tour

During May, Ferry travelled up to Newcastle on tour and defeated Newton Aycliffe, 26–6. Chris White scored 2 tries and 1 penalty, Wayne Cook, Rob Couchman and Ian Chesterfield each scored a try.

Quins

The Quins once again won the the Neath & District Division 2 championship and they also won the cup for scoring the most tries in the competition. They had double wins over Skewen, Bryncoch and Crynant, and a win and a draw with Tonna, with further wins over Gowerton, Bonymaen and Metal Box RFC.

Awards

Top scorer was Richard Lawrence once again, with Wayne Cook the top try scorer. Player of the Year was new hooker Robert Miles, with Wayne Cook as Most Improved Player. Quins top scorer was Stuart Shaw for the second consecutive year, and Quins top try scorer was wing Robert Kemeys. Quins Player of the Year was veteran scrum-half John Thomas. Flanker Mark Harris was Quins Most Improved Player.

At the end of the season three presentations were made for loyalty to the club to: ex-player and committeeman Dudley Mills; field officer Gareth Blight; Terry Gregory; and a special loyalty award to Roy Evans. Long-serving committeeman Norman Bowring was Clubman of the Year. Mark Stephens received a Merit Award. Ex-player and fixture secretary Albert Gleaves was honoured with a Life Membership for his service to the club. New to the committee this year was Bill Watkins, who won the ladies award.

The decade had seen many ups and downs, and many players and committeemen come and go, but with 100 years of history behind them Briton Ferry RFC were preparing the way for their next chapter.

PHIL LANGSTONE was club president throughout this decade. He was a successful businessman who, as a Ferry boy, had supported the club immensely over the years, and his contribution was not lost on the club.

Chairman throughout was Morgan Jones, supported by vice chairmen Llew Llewelyn and Colin Watkins and secretary Roy Evans. Throughout the decade many assistants had learnt from Morgan Jones, such as Dean Hoare, P.H. Davies, Allan Hopkins (also youth secretary) and Terry Keefe, who had acted as Quins secretary. Treasurers were Ted Richards and Harry Melding. Albert Gleaves was fixture secretary. Other committeemen who served during the decade were J. Selby, D. Poley, D. Mills, T. Gregory, M. Edwards, G. Jones, P. Davies, T. Woodland, N. Bowring, J. Evans, B. Lewis, H. Watkins, J. Johnson, J. Davies, L. Friend, T. Ellis, E. Landeg, R. Adams, C. Adams, A. Clifford, W. Watkins, H. Burt, R. Knight, B. Evans, K. Samuel, F. Pickering and K. Moyle.

Warm welcome for Irish visitors

OFFICIALS and members of Niwagh Ormond RFC, Southern Ireland, paid a courtesy visit to Briton Ferry RFC, during their recent to Wales for the Wales-Ireland international fixture at Cardiff.

The visit culminated with an exchange of plaques to commemorate 30 years friendship. The chairman of Briton Ferry Community Council was invited to take part in this year's event.

10.24 Visit in paper

PART 11: 1990–2000

- Nedd Under-21s played a few games on the Ferry's ground against Afan and against Llynfi in the 1990s

- Neath Ladies RFC played at the Ferry for two seasons in the early 1990s, once against Amsterdam Athletic

- 1991/92–to date, try increased to five points

1990/91

Chris White continued as captain for a second season, while long-serving scrum-half John Thomas took over as Quins captain. Former players Nigel Flowers and Peter Davies became the new coaches.

Hopes had been high at the start of the season as Ferry secured two wins out of three friendly matches: defeating Caldicot and Ogmore Vale (54–3) but losing narrowly to Tonna. Then fortunes turned and Ferry lost in the first round of both the WRU and O.G. Davies Cups – to Cwmbran away and Tonmawr at home, respectively.

There were league wins over Taibach (21–13), Cefn Cribbwr (14–0) and a double win over Blaengarw. Then Ferry suffered defeats in the return matches with Taibach and Cefn Cribbwr (7–27) and double defeats to Bridgend Sports and Neath Athletic.

In friendlies at home they lost 15–24 to Tumble, but won against Abercrave. They played friendlies away at BSC (lost), at Cwmavon (won 10–9), at Pontycymmer (won) and at Resolven, Crynant, BP and Bryncoch.

Quins

The Quins struggled from the start of the season and only recorded one win over Skewen. They were defeated heavily at home in the Neath & District Cup first round by Cross Keys Hotel RFC.

They ended up cancelling nearly all their fixtures for the rest of the season.

Captain
Chris White

Coaches
Nigel Flowers
Peter Davies

Quins captain
John Thomas

Match results place BFRFC scores first

Awards

Top scorer for the season was Paul Watkins (son of ex-player and committeeman Colin Watkins) and top try scorer was skipper Chris White.

At the end of season presentation the senior Player of the Year award was awarded to second row Mark Stephens, with Most Improved Player going to front rower Ian Michael. A loyalty award was presented to long-serving player Ron Lilley. Clubman of the Year award went to Rowly Adams.

Significant changes happened to the committee with the retirement of long-standing officers Morgan Jones, Roy Evans and Harry Melding. They were replaced with Roger Amphlett, Terry Keefe and Kerry Frey for the start of the 1991/92 season. Terry Griffiths took over as assistant secretary. Former skipper and wing Peter Bell, Leighton Rees, Chris Chappell and Jim Adams joined the general committee.

Members of the Briton Ferry RFC team pictured with members of the NORFC at the clubhouse on Sunday last prior to their departure home after a week-end in Nenagh.

11.1 With members of the Nenagh Ormond RFC at the clubhouse

11.2a Under-13s 1990/91

(back) Carl Casey, Geraint Griffiths, Gavin Puckett, Stuart Jenkins, Graig Wyatt, Gary Jones (captain), Lloyd Griffiths, Gavin Mort, Steven Lambert, Ceri Wyatt, Simon Rees; (front) William Carroll, Aaron Norman, Darryl Gillard, Ceri Williams, Neil Rees, Greg Tregonning, Lee Elwell

11.2b Under-13s 1990/91

(back) James Morgan, Stuart Jenkins, Steven Lambert, Graig Wyatt, Lloyd Griffiths, Gary Jones (captain), Dai Watkins, Simon Rees, Neil Rees, Ceri Wyatt, Carl Casey; (front) Neil Wood, Lee Elwell, Tony Davies, Aaron Norman, Darryl Gillard, Ceri Williams, Greg Tregonning, Gavin Puckett, Carl Wood

11.2c Briton Ferry Juniors 1990, Craig Wyatt clears the ball, his twin brother Ceri is watching his back

Match results place BFRFC scores first

1991/92

Chris White continued as captain and the Quins reins were taken up by returning hooker Martyn Bate, who had spent two seasons as player coach with Cross Keys Hotel RFC. Coach was ex-prop Steve Knight. The club engaged physiotherapist Stewart Dickson and dentist Alun James for the players to use when needed.

Nigel Flowers took over the re-formed Youth XV, captained by back rower Paul Jones. Other junior teams formed for the season were an Under-15s, captained by Gary Jones, and an Under-12s. Gary Norman, Keith Pyles, Alun Rees, Paul Tregonning (Under-15s) George and Jonny Jones (Under-12) took on coaching the juniors.

Yet again, the club was defeated in the first rounds of both the WRU and O.G. Davies competitions. The first, 3–12 away at Newport Saracens (Steve Jeynes 1 penalty); the second, 6–25 at Skewen (R. Lawrence 2 penalties).

The season had started badly with a 6–31 away defeat at Caldicot (R. Lawrence and R. Buckley 1 penalty each), but Ferry bounced back with an 18–6 home win over Baglan (skipper White scored all the points with 1 converted try and 4 penalties).

Ferry only had one win in the Wistech Central Glamorgan League Divison 2, over Aberavon Green Stars.

The first game in the league was a home fixture with Taibach, which Ferry narrowly lost, 12–13 (tries from no.8 Martin Williams, scrum-half John Thomas and wing Adrian Griffiths). A 3–28 defeat followed, away at Blaengarw (Steve Jeynes 1 penalty). Cwmgrach beat Ferry at home, 19–24 (Steve Jeynes 2 tries and 3 penalties, R. Buckley 1

Captain
Chris White

Coach
Steve Knight

First XV playing record
P 27
W 2
D 1
L 24
Points for 238
Points against 568

Quins captain
Martyn Bate

Youth XV captain
Paul Jones

Youth XV coach
Nigel Flowers

Under-15s playing record
P 33
W 35
Points for 715
Tries 157

conversion). A 6–21 away loss at BSC (Buckley 2 penalties) took Ferry to the end of October still looking for their first league win.

On the day the First XV were losing to Cwmgrach, the Quins were away, losing 9–14 to Crynant (P. Hughes 3 penalties) and the Youth XV lost 9–44 to Rhigos (prop Leighton Sly the only try scorer).

November brought four more defeats: 21–22 at home to Nantymoel (Ron Lilley, Mark Harris and Steve Jeynes the try scorers, Jeynes added 1 conversion and 1 penalty, R. Buckley 2 conversions); 7– 9 in a friendly away at Baglan (A. Griffiths 1 try, R. Buckley 1 penalty); away at Tonmawr by 16–18 (Gareth Baker 1 try, R. Lawrence 4 penalties); and finally, 10–16 at home to Ogmore Vale (tries from Jeynes and no.8 Martin Williams, 1 conversion from R. Lawrence).

The only league win, over Aberavon Green Stars, came in December, away 7–6 (Wayne Cook 1 try, R. Lawrence 1 penalty). But it was accompanied by another defeat, 3–27 to Cwmavon (R. Lawrence 1 penalty).

The new year brought two further defeats. The away match at Taibach was a remarkable repetition of the home match, same score, same scorers (12–13, tries from no.8 Martin Williams, scrum-half John Thomas and wing Adrian Griffiths). Blaengarw was 10–22 (M. Williams 1 try, S. Jeynes 2 penalties.)

February got no better with four further defeats: away at Nantymoel (0–29); away at Ogmore Vale (12–19, R. Lawrence 4 penalties); at home to Tonmawr (7–31, A. Griffiths 1try, R. Lawrence 1penalty); and against Aberavon Green Stars (10–12, A. Griffiths 1 try, R. Lawrence 2 penalties).

After cancellations and internationals there was only one game in March. It also ended in defeat, 16–22 to Cwmavon, with 4 penalties from R. Lawrence and a try by hooker Robert Miles.

Quins

The Quins picked up two wins over Tonna (Jason Jones and Alan King were among the try scorers) and wins over Skewen and Nantymoel, which featured some great play from Adrian Griffiths, Steve Hopkins, Jason Jones, Ian Michael, and two youth front rowers, Lee Marshall and Leighton Sly. Tries came from Michael, Griffiths and Bate; Robert Washington added 2 conversions and 2 penalties. The try of the match involved some great back and support play from the forwards from the halfway line for inspirational skipper Martyn Bate to score the try. Quins then drew with Metal Box RFC. The highlight was a fine solo effort by Martin Edwards in the centre. They then lost 4–20 to Bridgend

Sports (prop D. Evans try), but won 14–12 away at Aberavon Green Stars (Gareth Baker, M. Williams and A. Williams tries, Stuart Shaw 1 conversion).

Youth teams

The Youth XV had good wins over Resolven, Glynneath, Bryncoch, Rhigos, and Maesteg Celtic, but lost 14–20 to Seven Sisters (P. Evans 2 penalties and 1 try, A. Holmes 1 try). They defeated Tonna in the first round of the Neath & District Cup, but lost to Abercrave in the next round (hooker Lee Marshall showed up well).

The good news in November was that the Under-15s were continuing their winning streak by defeating Neath Athletic 17–14. Tries came from Neil Rees, Chris Pyles and Gavin Puckett, Pyles added a conversion, and fullback Carl Casey kicked a late drop goal to win the game. The Under-12s were also in winning form and defeated Ogmore Vale by 20–4. Andrew Caan (2), Chris Jones, Matthew Amphlett and Christian Ellis were the try scorers.

The Under-15s finished with wins over Dunvant, Tonna, Hendy, Swansea Uplands, Waunarlwydd, and double wins over Bryncoch, Morriston and Aberavon Green Stars. Players who shone throughout the season were Craig Wyatt, Geraint Griffiths, Aaron Norman, Ian Jones and Carl Casey. The Under-15s narrowly lost in the final of the Swansea and District League cup final at St. Helens, 9–11 to Ystradgynlais. They went 9–0 up after a try from Gavin Puckett was converted by outstanding fullback Carl Casey, who then added a penalty. But Ystrad came back with two tries. One in the last few seconds of extra time was hotly disputed as the Ystrad player appeared to have been tackled into touch at the corner flag before grounding the ball; but the try stood and the game was lost. The front row of Steve Lambert, Aled Evans (grandson of Viv Evans, ex-Neath, Wales and Briton Ferry) and Simon Rees (son of ex-player Leighton) were outstanding was. They also finished as semi-finalists in the cup competition.

The Under-12s had good wins over Llanelli Wanderers and Maesteg Welsh. They had a new recruit back from Australia, flanker Ross Jones. Also showing up well were scrum-half Leigh George, fly-half Andrew Caan, and centres Ricky Green and Mark Lewis.

Awards

Top scorer was Richard Lawrence with 71 points, while Steve Jeynes and Adrian Griffiths were joint top try scorers with 4 each. Senior Player of the Year was skipper Chris White and Most Improved Player went to centre Martin

"Pobyl-Y-Cwm" Edwards. Jason Jones was Quins Player of the Year. Clubman of the Year went to former wing Brian Evans.

Tour

The club returned to old friends Nenagh in Ireland for their tour at the end of the season. and drew 12–12.

'Welsh rugby visitors enjoy our pub culture

Members of Nenagh Ormond RFC and Briton Ferry RFC, Wales at a gathering in the Dapp Inn last weekend. Briton Ferry have been visiting Nenagh on a bi-annual basis since 1988 prior to the Six Nations Ireland v. Wales rugby fixture.

(Picture: B. Delaney)

11.3 Irish papers fete the Welsh visitors

11.4 BFRFC at Nenagh 2 May 1992

(back) Colin Watkins, Kerry Frey, Martyn Bate, Paul Hughes, Mark Harris, Ian Michael, Martin Williams, Robert Miles, Ron Lilley, Rob Couchman, Anthony Eaton, Mal Edwards; (front) Chris White (captain), John Thomas, Richard Lawrence, Adrian Griffiths, Jason Jones, Mark Broom, Mervyn Mayers

Match results place BFRFC scores first

1992/93

Gareth "Faggots" Davies came on to the committee as Quins XV secretary. Mark Davies took over the reins of the Youth team. Ex-skipper Spencer Lewis and assistant Keith Burt took over the senior coaching roles.

> In a move to improve training Keith Burt sent out a fitness programme to all the First XV for pre-season training, which did boost the fitness of the squad.

However, once again they tasted defeat in the first round of both the WRU and O.G. Davies Cups: to Pontardulais away (3–37, Paul Hughes penalty); and to Seven Sisters at home (16–27, A. Griffiths 1 try, Robert Washington 3 penalties, 1 conversion). After finishing bottom of the league the previous season, there were hopes of an improvement for this year, but they struggled again in the Wistech Central Glamorgan League Divison 2. First, an opening defeat at Taibach (8–32 away, C. White 1 try, R. Lawrence 1 penalty), then a series of double defeats: to Nantymoel, 6–32 away (P. Hughes 2 penalties) and 5–22 at home (R. Lawrence try); to Cwmavon, 9–10 at home (Paul Evans 3 penalties) and 13–25 away (K. Burt 1 try, R. Lawrence 1 conversion, R. Broom 2 penalties); to Tonmawr, 10–12 at home (P. Hughes 1 try and 1 conversion, A. King 1 drop goal) and 0–19 away. In a further defeat by Blaengarw, 6–7, R. Broom kicked 2 penalties.

Ferry then had two draws with Maesteg Quins, 15–15 at home (N. Hopkins and A. King tries, R. Lawrence 1 conversion and 1 penalty) and 14–14 away (R. Couchman 1 try, R. Broom 3 penalties).

Then a series of wins: over Blaengarw (24–23, tries from R. Miles, G. Baker, K. Collins and Steve Hopkins, R.

Captain
Chris White

Coaches
Spencer Lewis
Keith Burtt

First XV playing record
P 32
W 14
D 2
L 16
Points for 412
Points against 604

Quins captain
Martyn Bate

Youth XV captain
Mark Davies

Youth XV coach
Nigel Flowers

Under-16s captain
Ceri Wyatt

Under-12s captain
Chris Jones

Lawrence 2 conversions); over Aberavon Green Stars, both away (13–10, C. White and A. Griffiths tries, R. Broom 1 penalty) and at home (30–15, A. Griffiths (2), J. Hughes, A. Jenkins tries, R. Broom 2 conversions and 2 penalties); and a double against Ogmore Vale, 13–10 away (A. Griffiths 1 try, R. Lawrence 1 conversion, 1 penalty), when talented three-quarter Paul Hughes broke his leg, and 13–6 at home (Mark Harris 1 try, R. Broom 1 conversion, 2 penalties; and finally, 12–0 over Taibach (4 penalties from fullback Robert Broom).

> The club introduced a Player of the Month award and the first two recipients were First XV wing ADRIAN GRIFFITHS and Second XV flanker PAUL JONES. Prop forwards Anthony Eaton and Jonathan Hughes and second row pairing Wayne Preece and Mark Stephens also played well throughout the season.

The First XV played quite a few friendlies through the season. They began by beating Crynant away, 8–5. Nigel Hopkins was the try scorer and R. Lawrence added a penalty. However, with weakened teams they went down heavily in the next two away games, 8–61 at Cefn Cribbwr (C. White 1 try, R. Lawrence 1 penalty), and 7–67 at Tenby United (A. Griffiths 1 try, R. Lawrence 1 conversion). They did manage to win the last game of a bad month, 29–10 at Baglan (tries from Jonathan Hughes, Martin Edwards and Robert Washington, who also converted it, Paul Hughes added 2 conversions and 1 penalty). A further friendly at Brynamman was arranged for October, but Ferry were defeated 15–25 (tries from R. Broom and R. Miles, R. Lawrence 1 conversion and 1 penalty).

In November they entertained Llantwit Fardre and beat them 13–10 (C. White 1 try, R. Lawrence 1 conversion, 1 penalty).

In December, Baglan came to the Ferry for a return match and were defeated 13–12 by tries from G. Baker and R. Broom and a Paul Evans penalty.

> In March, young AIMEE LEWIS, daughter of Spencer, led out the Welsh team against Ireland as official mascot.

There were further friendlies in the new year. The first was a poor home game against Crynant, which Ferry lost 5–15, their only score a K. Burt try. The second was a 19–10 home win over Glais (tries from K. Burt, M. Simonson and C. White, R. Broom converted 2). They followed this with another home win, 30–24 over Abercrave (M. Stephens, A. Griffiths, I. Michael and G. Baker tries, R. Broom 2 conversions and 2 penalties). Only to end with two away defeats: 5–15 at Caldicot (1 try from K. Burt), and 5–30 at Tonna (again, Burt the only scorer).

Match results place BFRFC scores first

Future player **PAUL JACKSON** played for Neath and Aberavon during this period; as did future player coach **ALUN BEVAN**.

Quins

The Quins only managed four wins: 11–7 away at Baglan (Paul Jones 1 try and J. Thomas 2 penalties); 13–0 at home to Baglan (try from Lee Marshall converted by Paul Woodlands, who also added 2 penalties); 8–6 against Metal Box RFC (J. Thomas try, P. Woodlands penalty); and against Porthcawl.

Third XV

For the first time in their history the club fielded a Third XV. Their first game ended in an 11–30 defeat by Bridgend Sports in November – with 2 penalties from Craig Evans (brother of Paul) and a try from scrum-half Mark Llewelyn.

Youth teams

11.5 Boys Clubs Caps: (top) Carl Casey, Aled Evans, Aaron Norman; (bottom) Carl Winters, Neil Rees

Unfortunately, the Youth XV, coached by Nigel Flowers, abandoned their season after a defeat to Glynneath due to lack of players.

Under coaches Gary Norman, Paul Tregonning, Alun Rees and Keith Pyles the Under-16s had good wins over Blaina (64–0, tries from Aled Evans 2, C. Casey 2, G. Tregonning, I. Jones, N. Rees and A. Norman, and a hat trick from C. Pyles, there was also 1 penalty try), over Ystradgynlais, over Waunarlwydd (61–0) and over Pontardawe. Seven of the side got into the BCW Under-16s squad of twenty-five for the international season. Not only did all seven players get their caps in one game against Gloucestershire, but also all the points scored on the day came from Ferry players (Neil Rees 2 tries, Anuerin Davies 1 try, and Carl Casey 2 penalties, 2 conversions). After being 10–0 down at half-time, they came back to win 25–10. Other players to earn their caps were hooker Aled Evans, centre Chris Pyles, scrum-half Aaron Norman and prop Carl Winters.

11.6 Under-16s 1992-93, including Ferry's seven WBC caps: Carl Winters, Neil Rees, Chris Pyles, Anuerin Davies, Aaron Norman, Carl Casey and Aled Evans

The Under-14s were coached by Chris Chappell and Roger Amphlett, and the Under-13s by John and George Jones.

Tours

For the first time Nenagh visited the Ferry, but were beaten 52–22 (tries from C. White 2, K Burt, K. Collins 2, M. Stephens, A. Griffiths and M. Edwards, and 6 conversions from P. Evans).

Ferry toured to Glasgow, where they played Strathclyde Police RFC and won by 20–5 (tries from M. Edwards, R. Miles, A. Griffiths, and N. Lovering).

Awards

The season's top scorers were R. Broom with 76 points and R. Lawrence on 42. Top try scorer was A. Griffiths with 9, closely followed by C. White and K. Burt, both on 7. The Senior Player of the Year award went to fullback Robert Broom. Second row Wayne Preece received the Most Improved Player award. Neil Jones took the Quins Player of the Year award. Clubman of the Year was awarded to Peter Bell. Long-serving member Malcolm Edwards was awarded Life Membership.

1993/94

Nigel Flowers took over as fixture secretary, Terry Griffiths as youth secretary and new general committeemen were Martyn Bate, Chris Chappell, Alan Rees and Gary Norman.

After a 26–0 defeat at Tonmawr in the first round of the O.G. Davies Cup, the First XV took a first round win in the WRU Cup 18–14 at Cefneithin (J. Hughes and G. Baker tries, R. Broom 2 penalties and 1 conversion) and then a 26–24 home win over Llanybydder in the next round (C. White, Mark Davies and M. Stephens tries, S. Jeynes penalty. But then conceded defeat at home to Pyle in the third round, 3–35 (S. Jeynes penalty).

In friendly matches, Ferry defeated Crynant at home (30–11, tries from R. Lawrence, R. Miles and K. Burt, R. Broom kicked 2 penalties and 2 conversions), won at Baglan (19–5, the only try from C. White, R. Broom again on form with 4 penalties and 1 conversion), then lost at Porthcawl (27–12, R. Broom 4 penalties). At Friday night friendly, Llanharan proved a little too strong for the Ferry and they won 0–62. This was followed by three more defeats in friendlies, at home to Nantymoel (0–31) and to Caldicot (0–3) and away at Abercrave (3–49).

In the Wistech Central Glamorgan League Divison 2, Ferry suffered a 9–14 defeat in their first game against Taibach at home (2 penalties from R. Lawrence, 1 from R. Broom) and also lost the return match, 14–6 (2 penalties R.L Lawrence). They then lost a whole series of doubles: to Pontycymmer, away 0–33 and at home 8–27 (M. Stephens try, R. Lawrence penalty); to Cwmavon, 12–13 at home (tries from K. Burt and J. Hughes, R. Broom 1 conversion) and 10–16 away (C. White try, S. Jeynes conversion and

Captain
Chris White

Coaches
Spencer Lewis
Keith Burtt

First XV playing record
P 26
W 7
D 1
L 18
Points for 284
Points against 546

Quins captain
Nigel Lovering

Youth XV captain
Ceri Wyatt

Youth XV Coaches
Gary Norman
Keith Pyles

Under-14s captain
Ross Jones

Under-14s Coaches
Martyn Bate
John Jones
George Jones

Under-13s Coaches
Kerry Frey
Ray Williams

penalty); to Blaengarw, away 10–16 (P. Jones try, R. Broom conversion and penalty) and 6–12 at home (2 penalties R. Lawrence); to Maesteg Quins, 10–11 at home (scrum-half Andy Bowen try, S. Jeynes conversion and 1 penalty) and away 15–18; and to Aberavon Green Stars, at home by 3–31 (R. Lawrence penalty) and 10–32 away (tries from C. White and Alan King). Ferry only took two wins, both over Ogmore Vale (8–0 away with an A. Griffiths try and a penalty from R. Lawrence, and 11–8 at home, Griffiths again the try scorer with 2 penalties from Lawrence. Ferry finished seventh in the league with 2 wins and 12 defeats in 14 matches, scoring 117 points against 246 with only 10 tries.

The club also hosted Strathclyde Police and defeated them 26–7 (A. Griffiths 2, P. Evans and P. Jones the try scorers, 1 conversion by Evans, 2 by Broom).

Quins

The Quins failed to improve on things as they also lost in the first round of the Neath & District Cup, 3–17 to Tonna, and then went on to concede double defeats to CMB (Metal Box), Glynneath, Resolven, Crynant and Tonna, and a single defeat to Cwmgrach. But Quins did have a good 34–10 win over Cardiff Prison Service XV.

Third XV

Another fillip was the formation of a Third XV (commonly known as the Warblers), who played a few games, all captained by Martyn Bate. One match was against the Cardiff Prison Service, where Keith Burt was a prison officer. Rob 'Boyo' Clifford was the connection for a match against the Neath and Welsh Territorials. They also played BP Baglan Bay XV.

Youth teams

The Youth XV had three good wins over Cefn Cribbwr and also beat Aberdare, Skewen and Waunarlwydd.

The Under-14s had good wins over Mumbles and Skewen.

They're dressed for success

BRITON Ferry RFC under-14s were presented with new kit by Neath firm, George Jones Artexing Specialists.
The squad, pictured left, include Mr George Jones and team coaches Martyn Bate and John Jones.

11.7 New kit for Under-14s sponsored by George Jones Artexing Specialists

11.8 Briton Ferry Warblers 1993/94

11.9 Juniors 1993/94

Tour

The club toured again to Nenagh (Ireland), where they drew, 40–40, and were joined by the Youth XV.

11.10 Youth team tour to Nenagh, April 1994

(back) Gary Norman (coach), Iam Mort, Gavin Jones, Paul Evans, Carl Winters, Leyton Sly, Lloyd Griffiths, Paul Jones, Alun Rees (coach); (front) Tony Moore, Kevin, Craig Wyatt, Neil Rees, Mark Longman, Geraint Griffiths, Aaron Norman, Jason

Awards

First XV Player of the Year was Adrian Griffiths and Youth XV Clubman Award went to Mark Longman. The season's top try scorer was A. Griffiths with 5, and top points scorer was R. Broom with 66 points, Lawrence on 33 points came second. Quins Player of the Year was Martyn Bate.

11.11 Under-13s, 1993/94

1994/95

Captain
Chris White

Coach
Spencer Lewis

Quins captain
Robert Broome

Youth XV captain
Lloyd Griffiths

Youth XV coach
Gary Norman

Under-15s captain
Ross Jones

Under-15s coaches
Martyn Bate
George Jones
Jonny Jones

Under 13s coaches
Kerry Frey
Ray Williams

Chris White captained the club for the sixth year on the trot. Fullback Robert Broome became Quins skipper. Gary Norman continued to coach the Youth XV, with Lloyd Griiffiths as their new skipper. Martyn Bate coached the Under-15s, skippered by Ross Jones.

Leyton Sly and Robert "Boyo" Clifford joined the committee.

Ferry lost in the first rounds of the O.G. Davies and WRU Cups, both were away matches. In the former, an 8–24 defeat by Crynant (Steve Davies try, Mike Evans conversion) and in the latter to Morriston, 6–44 (M. Evans and P. Evans 1 penalty each).

> A new trophy was introduced, the CENTRAL GLAMORGAN CUP, to be played for by teams in the Central Glamorgan League.

Ferry were defeated, away at Nantyfyllon 10–25.

> The league was now national and the Ferry was placed in Division 8 Central B, where they finished in eleventh position.

Ferry's league season started poorly with a one-point defeat in the opening game at home to Tonna, 9–10 (wing Mike Evans 3 penalties) – and they lost the return match by one point. The First XV also conceded doubles: to Aberaman, 6–48 away (M. Evans 2 penalties) and 11–32 at home; to Bryncoch, 10–55 away (P. Hughes try, M. Evans 1 conversion, 1 penalty) and 3–30 at home; to Pontycymmer, 6–26 away and 13–25 at home; to Bargoed, 3–60 away and 10–36 at home; to BSC, 8–11 at home and 10–13 away; to Cefn Coed, 0–15 away and 3–40 at home; to Penygraig, 3–28 at home and away 91–0 (an unwelcome record); and Cefn Cribbwr, 7–17 at home (Jason Jones try, R. Lawrence conversion) and 10–36 away. Ferry did win the double against Ogmore Vale, 13–6 away and 33–3 home.

The First XV won friendlies in September – 18–14 at home against Bridgend Sports – and in November – 18–13 at home to Gowerton. Then lost away to Porthcawl, 15–28, in the last friendly of the season.

> Long-serving press officer BILL WILLIAMS was still going strong. His son-in-law, prop DAVID EVANS, was to play for the club – along with David's son JOE, also in the front row.

Awards

Nigel Flowers was awarded Clubman of the Year.

Quins

The Quins won their matches against Taibach, Tonna, CMB, Aberavon Green Stars and Baglan, and drew with Porthcawl.

Youth XV

The Youth XV ended with good double wins over Cwmgrach, Cwmavon, Crynant and Abercrave. They won single matches against Ystalyfera, Bryncoch, Cefn Cribbwr, Glynneath and Seven Sisters.

Outside half Craig Wyatt (Ceri's twin brother) was capped for Wales Youth against Japan, against Scotland (landing two conversions), against Ireland, when he kicked the winning conversion in a 17–15 win, and against New Zealand alongside Vernon Cooper and Ian Gough (the opposition winger that day was Doug Howlett).

11.12 Craig Wyatt, Welsh Youth Cap Presentation, 1995

11.13 Youth Swansea & District Challenge Cup runners up 1994/95

Tour

The club hosted Nenagh for the second time, and defeated them 55–7.

The successful **NEATH LADIES XV** made the Ferry their base for the first of two seasons. They hosted sides from all over the country and from Amsterdam.

Neath Women's Rugby Football club would like to extend a warm welcome to Amsterdam Athletic on their Welsh Tour. We would like to thank Briton Ferry R.F.C. for the use of their faclities and the support they give us. We hope that Amsterdam enjoy their stay in Neath and we would like to thank them for coming

NEATH SQUAD	AMSTERDAM SQUAD
Sian Thomas	Anja Stoffels
Nicola Gwynne	Annelies Ijseldijk
Cath Taylor	Caroline Chossen
Lorraine Curry	Charlotte t Wey
Dahne Gammon	Fransje de Warrd
Lisa Lewis	Gaby Ouwens
Caroline Williams	Klaarke Krakau
Heather Rees	Marlies Veltmen
Christina Maher	Martine Mees
Sarah Williams	Monique Dijkers
Dawn Stoneman	Odillia Legierse
Jayne Bamford	Petra Van Lance
Alaine Francis	Petra Houthuijzen
Emma Jones	Ploni Veenendaal
Melonie Moore	Sandra Lodewiks
Tracey Hillier	Sanne Veltcamp
Anne Marie Jones	Suzan Norton
Cheryl Thomas	Wilma Zandbergen
Janine Thomas	Ilonke Berentzen
Cath Harries	Mariette
Charlotte Griffiths	Elke
Carol Roach	Jacqie
Jessica Wood	Yvonne

11.14 Neath and Amsterdam Women's Squads

Match results place BFRFC scores first

1995/96

Hooker Robert Miles took over as club skipper. Spencer Lewis brought in Ian Williams as assistant coach. Martyn Bate skippered the Quins. Nigel Flowers took over Youth coaching duties, along with David Puckett, and Jason Landers was their skipper.

Leyton Sly and Robert Clifford left the general committee and Ray Williams joined. Field attendant for the season was Gareth Blight.

> JOHANN PRETORIOUS arrived from Western Province in South Africa for a Welsh rugby experience. His pace and ability were exceptional and he became a popular member of the squad. He'll never forget an away match in Pontycymmer on a freezing cold, windy day in January. He was so cold he asked to be excused from the field at half-time as hypothermia was setting in!

11.15 Johann Pretorious

The Ferry's first game of the season was a friendly against Bridgend Sports in August, which they lost narrowly, 14–21 (Paul Hughes and Steve Hopkins were the try scorers, Hughes converted both. In further friendlies, Ferry lost 15–21 at Gowerton (D. Puckett and A. Griffiths tries, Evans 1 conversion and 1 penalty) and then 0–35 away to Pontycymmer. They did get a 26–0 home win over

Captain
Robert Miles

Coaches
Spencer Lewis
Ian Williams

First XV playing record
P 30
W 18
D 1
L 11
Points for 713
Points against 462

Quins captain
Martyn Bate

Youth XV captain
Jason Landers

Youth XV Coaches
Nigel Flowers
David Puckett

Neath Athletic (Gavin Puckett, D. Puckett, W. Cook and J. John tries, C. Wyatt 3 conversions), but then a midweek home defeat by Resolven (D. Puckett, A. Griffiths and Martyn Bate tries, with 2 conversions from P. Evans).

Ferry lost heavily in a midweek first round Central Glamorgan Cup game at home (0–93) to a very strong Tondu XV. They suffered a similar fate in the WRU Cup, 7–21 away at Waunarlwydd (D. Puckett try, K. Rue conversion). They did reach the semi-final of the O.G. Davies Cup after away wins over Neath Athletic (28–7, J. Whitefoot, A. Griffiths, M. Moran, K. Rue tries, Craig Wyatt penalty), and Bryncoch (32–13, Griffiths 2, G. Baker, S. Popkins tries, Evans 3 conversions, 1 penalty). However, they lost by one point in an exciting game against Glynneath in Crynant (35–36, M. Moran 2, A. Griffiths and Lloyd Griffiths tries, Evans 3 conversions, 3 penalties).

At last, the First XV managed a turnaround in the league and finished third in Division 8 Central B, behind champions Banwen and runners-up Tylorstown.

Ferry started with a 3–14 defeat at home to Banwen (P. Hughes penalty), but went on to record twelve wins:

- Single matches: over Bangor, 20–6 at home (M. Moran, P. Jackson and M. Williams tries, J. Whitefoot 1 conversion, 2 penalties); over Tylorstown, 18–0 at home (D. Puckett, J. Pretorius tries, Whitefoot 2 penalties, 1 conversion); over Banwen, 8–6 away (P. Evans try, A. Jeffries penalty).

- Then victory doubles: over Gwernyfed, 55–13 away (Paul Jackson 2, Steven "Tudor" John, R. Couchman, A. Jeffries, J. Whitefoot, M. Stephens, Alan King and Paul Hughes the try scorers, Kristian Rue converted 5) and 20–8 at home (J. Pretorius, R. Couchman and Gareth Baker the try scorers, Paul Evans 1 conversion, 1 penalty); over Welshpool, 33–10 away (D. Puckett 2, M. Stephens, K. Collins and Mark Davies tries, J. Whitefoot 4 conversions) and 34–8 at home (J. Whitefoot 3, Adrian Griffiths 2 and K. Collins tries, P. Evans 2 conversions; Welshpool's only try was also scored by a Ferryman, M. Bate was helping out by playing for them); over Bryncoch, 23–10 away (D. Puckett, P. Jackson and P. Jones tries, Whitefoot 1 conversion, 2 penalties) and 37–8 at home (M. Moran, P. Hughes, S. John, J. Whitefoot, M. Stephens, W. Cook and A. Jeffries tries, Jeffries 1 conversion); over Brecon, 14–3 away (K. Rue try, Jeffries 3 penalties) and 68–19 at home (N. Rees 3, S. John 2, D. Puckett 2, G. Puckett, A. Griffiths, A. Jeffries, M. Stephens and K. Rue tries, conversions from Rue, Whitefoot, Jeffries and R. Miles). Against

Crynant Ferry won 41–7 away (J. Pretorius 3, Jackson, D. Puckett, L. Griffiths tries, Evans 4 conversions, 1 penalty) but drew 8–8 at home (Whitefoot 1 try, Jeffries 1 penalty).

Ferry did suffer a double defeat to Ystalyfera, 16–19 at home (Jackson and Griffiths tries, Whitefoot and Rue penalty each) and 0–13 away. They were also defeated away by Bangor (28–31, Mike Moran, A. Jeffries, P. Jackson, Jeremy John tries, P. Evans 4 conversions) and by Tylorstown (7–30, M. Stephens try, the fiftieth of the season, P. Evans conversion).

Ferry hosted Strathclyde Police for a second time, and won 30–25 (M. Moran, K. Collins, J. Pretorius, R. Brettle and J. Whitefoot tries, P. Evans 1 conversion, 1 penalty).

Tour

The club returned to Nenagh on tour and came home victorious, 40–14.

A Youth XV joined the tour, but lost to Nenagh.

Quins

The Quins fared a little better this season, with wins over Skewen, Tonna, BP Llandarcy, CMB, Bridgend Sports, Maesteg Quins, Bryncoch, Crynant, Baglan and Pontrhydyfen. They beat Pontrhydyfen again in the first round of the Neath & District Cup, then lost 20–52 to Resolven in the quarter-final.

Players for the Quins included Jason Jones, Phil Jones, Adrian Sambrook and Kelvin Smith.

Youth XV

The Youth XV only suffered seven defeats all season and lost to Rhigos in the semi-final of the Neath & District Cup.

They also entered the Esso Welsh Cup but were defeated at home by a strong Newport side that contained a few future Welsh internationals, including second row Ian Gough. They recorded wins over Tondu, Abercrave, Trebanos, Llanelli, Pyle, Bridgend Athletic, Penclawydd, Maesteg Celtic, Rhigos, BSC and South Gower; and doubles over Seven Sisters, Crynant and Resolven.

Cwrt Sart Schoolboy MARC DAVIES won an Under-16s Welsh Schools cap as a replacement in a match against Portugal.

LLOYD GRIFFITHS was selected to play in the Wales Under-18 FIRA squad at an international youth tournament in Italy. He went on to represent both Neath and Aberavon with distinction.

11.16 Lloyd Griffiths and his Welsh jersey

Awards

At the end of season top try scorer was D. Puckett with 12, closely followed by Jeffries on 11. Top points scorer was Whitefoot with 83, then P. Evans on 73.

Wayne Curtis was awarded Most Improved Player, while Clubman of the Year went to hard-working Rowly Adams for the second time.

The club were still in the red to the tune of some £900 and would take a while to get back on their feet.

The club was one try short of a century for the season!

1996/97

Captain for the season was ex-Neath player Paul Jackson, and the coaches were ex-players Cliff Morgan and Dave Puckett. Steve Hopkins captained the Quins. Ex-player Richard Lawrence coached the Youth, whose new skipper was Lee Hopkins.

In the first round of the O.G. Davies Cup Crynant defeated the Ferry 10–22.

It was a different story in the WRU Cup. In the first round Ferry took a 22–5 home win over Milford Haven (R. Miles, D. Puckett, R. Davies and P. Evans a try apiece, Evans 1 conversion) and followed it in the second round with another home win, over local rivals Cwmavon (1 penalty try, Steve Hopkins 1 try, Evans 1 conversion and 4 penalties). In the third round, they were pitted against Whitland, a strong Pembrokeshire unit who were a couple of divisions above the Ferry. A titanic struggle on the Ferry gound went into extra time, when Whitland scored the decisive winning points. the 13–21 result was disappointing for the Ferry and their supporters but Whitland were gracious in victory.

In the Central Glamorgan Cup, Ferry were defeated by Cwmavon, 0–24 at home.

In the Heineken League Division 8B Central, Ferry finished fourth. A 46–10 victory over Porthcawl at home was a good start. They also won the return game 25–13. Ferry followed this with doubles over Baglan (37–11 and 18–10), Cilfynydd (22–12 and 18–16), Bryncoch (48–42 and 33–11) and Gwernyfed (48–26). After a 68–9 win at home over Welshpool, they were defeated 15–17 in the

Captain
Paul Jackson

Coaches
Cliff Morgan
Dave Puckett

Quins captain
Steve Hopkins

Quins vice-captain
Martyn Bate

Youth XV captain
Lee Hopkins

Youth XV coach
Richard Lawrence

away game. They also fell to double defeats by Brecon (12–29 and 10–18), by Bridgend Sports (19–28) and Bangor (10–64 and 0–32).

The First XV played friendlies early in the season with Cwmgors, Cimla (won 26–16) and Pontrhydyfen (lost 25–28) and at the end of the season at Taibach (won 26–10) and Abercrave (lost 24–28).

Tour

Ferry hosted Nenagh again and won 46–17.

Quins

The Quins were also defeated by Crynant in the Neath & District Cup, 10–15 at home in a sour match. They ended the season with wins over Cefn Cribbwr, BP Llandarcy and doubles over Tonna and CMB.

The Quins finished third in Division 2 of the Neath & District League, having scored 336 points (51 tries) for and with 380 against.

Youth XV

The Youth XV also lost in the Neath & District Cup, 29–10 at home to Resolven. They did have wins over Ogmore Vale, Taibach, Rhigos, Hirwaun and Bryncoch, and a double over Skewen.

No.8 Luke Williams and prop Mark Anthony were included in the Wales Youth squad.

Awards

On awards night wing Adrian Griffiths took the Senior Player of the Year trophy, and Quins Player of the Year was hooker Martyn Bate, who'd played in 17 out of 19 games. Quins top try scorer was Kevin Collins with 13, who also finished top scorer with 116 points, by adding 15 conversions and 7 penalties.

Importantly, the club broke even for the first time in a number of seasons.

Local school CWRT SART made the final of the Neath–Port Talbot Schools Year 10 Cup and played Maesydderwen. Fifteen of that squad of twenty went on to play for Ferry's First XV, one went to Maesteg and one for the Ferry Quins – an excellent record.

They were: Geraint Morgan, Karl Lewis, Andrew Crook, Matthew Fleming, Jon Low, Steve Griffin, Gavin Jones, Leonne Daniel, Andrew Kreischer, Luke Williams, Neil Hampton, Nigel Anthony, Owain Anthony and Jonny Knight; along with Gareth Goodridge and Matthew Kingdom.

1997/98

Scrum-half Mike Moran took over as captain. Martyn Bate took over duties as team manager and liaison officer for the club. Centre Wayne Cook took over as Quins captain.

New transfers to the club were: Chris Morgan (a local boy) from Bonymaen, Jason Massey from Bryncoch, Owen Jones from Cardiff Youth and no.8 Gareth Rice from Vardre.

> To help retain players and ensure their loyalty the new idea was to put them on a written contract – which included a payments system for attending training, to be spent in the club!

Undoubtedly, this First XV season was their best performance for many years. They reached the semi-final of the O.G. Davies Cup, after defeating Cwmgrach, 22–18 at home, then Crynant, 15–10 away, before succumbing to Tonmawr 0–24 in the semi-final.

In the WRU Cup the First XV had a bye in the first round after Cwmgrach scratched. They then defeated Nantyglo 49–10 at home. Disappointingly, they had to scratch themselves in the third round against Penygraig at home because they were unable to put out a recognised front row.

Their cup success didn't end there as they finished in the top four in the Silver Ball competition and were involved in the play-offs. They defeated Pentyrch 51–34 at Waterton Cross in a really exciting game with a hat trick of tries from speed merchant wing Owen Jones, a brace from the other wing, Adrian Griffiths, and a try from fullback Gavin Puckett. Outside-half Paul Evans weighed in with 21 points, made up of 1 try, 2 penalties and 5

Captain
Mike Moran

Coaches
Cliff Morgan
Dave Puckett

First XV playing record
P 16
W 16
D 0
L 0
Points for 421
Points against 184

Scores
Tries 62 for 55 points
Bonus points 7

Quins captain
Wayne Cooke

Youth XV captain
Ross Jones

Youth XV Coach
Richard Lawrence

conversions. In the semi-final they were pitched against BSC Port Talbot at Pisgah Street, Kenfig. BSC were a couple of divisions above them and, after a brave fight, Ferry lost 11–17.

In the Central Glamorgan Division 7B, Ferry were unstoppable. They completed doubles over Blaengarw, Aberavon Green Stars, Bryncoch, Taibach, Porthcawl, Crynant, Nantymoel and over Bridgend Sports in the last game of the season with a narrow 14–12 win (Mark Stephens 1 try, Paul Evans 1 conversion and 2 penalties, one in the last minute to win the game). The Ferry First XV ended the campaign as unbeaten champions.

11.17 Unbeaten in the league, 1997/98

Ferry also hosted tours from Strathclyde Police (won 41–12) and Beverley RFC from North Yorkshire, who defeated the Ferry XV (27–31).

On 3 May 1998 the club held a dinner at Blanco's to celebrate their glorious season. They also attended a championship dinner in Cardiff as guests of the WRU.

11.18 National League 1997/98 Presentation Evening

Table 11.1 Championship victories in 1997/98

Opponents	Away	Home
Blaengarw	22–17	38–19
Aberavon Green Stars	23–9	24–18
Bryncoch	43–0	17–5
Taibach	42–20	66–5
Porthcawl	22–20	24–8
Crynant	15–12	20–10
Nantymoel	20–9	24–20
Bridgend Sports	8–0	14–12

Quins

The Quins had a memorable season under the captaincy of centre Wayne Cook. After losing 5–40 to the Neath & District XV, they went on to win against Bryn Wanderers (28–10), CMB (43–7), Crynant (17–10), Seven Sisters (19–10), Resolven and twice against BP Llandarcy (27–5 and 21–3). This put them into the semi-finals of the league play-offs, where they were matched up with Rhigos in a hard-fought battle. The Quins eventually lost 7–39 to Resolven up in Vaughan Field. In the Neath & District Cup, Quins defeated Crynant 21–18 at home. In the second round they defeated CMB 10–6, which put them into the semi-finals, where they were pitched against BP Llandarcy, again on the Vaughan Field. This time they were victorious, 20–10. This put them into the final for the first time for years. Their opponents were Cwmgrach and the game was played on the Gnoll at Neath. After a tough, tight encounter they emerged as joint champions. Quins were winning 3–0, after a rare penalty kick from no.8 Martin Williams, but in the seventh minute of injury time referee Martin Grimes awarded Cwmgrach a penalty, which they duly converted. This was the first time that the trophy had been shared.

The Quins team that day were:

15. Nigel Hopkins	10. Paul Hughes	4. Wayne Davies
14. Wayne Cook (C)	9. Kevin Collins	5. Wayne Preece
13. Terry White	1. Robert Couchman	6. Paul Jones
12. Martin Edwards	2. Martyn Bate	7. Mark Davies
11. Neil Baggeridge	3. Phil Jones	8. Martin Williams

Subs: Steven John, Mike Moran, Steve Hopkins, Tony Moore, Simon Rees, Gareth Baker and Jason Jones

Youth teams

The Youth XV played Nenagh away (0–0) and then lost narrowly at home. They also lost to Tonna in the Neath & District Cup, but went on to post wins over

Tonna, Bryncoch, Skewen and Glynneath (away 10–8, Paul Hughes 2 tries, 1 conversion).

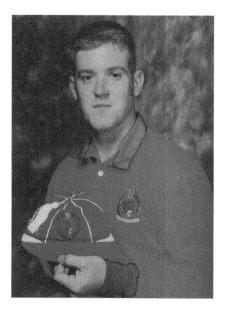

11.19 Fullback Geraint Morgan gained his Under-16s BCW cap.

In the junior section, the Under-14s beat Mumbles 14–10 in the quarter-final of the Swansea and District Cup to reach the semi-finals.

1998/99

Outside-half Paul Hughes became Quins captain. Ex-centre Steve Davies joined the general committee.

The club had to scratch from both the Central Glamorgan and O.G. Davies Cups as they had difficulty raising sides for midweek fixtures. Also, they were knocked out by Vardre in the first round of the WRU Cup, 10–44 away.

In March, the chairman's car was stolen along with the First XV's kit. Despite offering a £50 reward for information leading to its return, the kit was never recovered. Sponsors had then to be sought to help with the purchase of new kit.

Captain
Mike Moran

Coaches
Cliff Morgan
Dave Puckett

Quins captain
Paul Hughes

Youth XV captain
Martin Edwards

Youth XV coach
Richard Lawrence

11.20 Kit theft

In the Central National League Division 6, Ferry finished fourth. They started with a 16–16 draw away at Pontycymmer and then defeated them at home later in the season. The First XV completed doubles over Bargoed, Aberavon Green Stars (they achieved their highest league

Left to right: Dai Puckett, Gareth Rice, Chris White, Mike Moran, and Wayne Curtis

Chris White, Wayne Davies, Gareth Rice and Steven John (Tudor) combining well to supply ball to scrum-half Jonathan Hoskins

Mike Moran box kicking, with Craig Baggeridge in the background, and touch judge Roger Amphlett

Second row Mark Stephens climbing high

Centre Gareth Rice offloading in a tackle

Centres Jason Massey and Martin Edwards combine to snuff out an attack

11.21 Action from Ferry away at Cwmavon 1998

score ever in the 80–5 home win), BP Llandarcy, Alltwen and Maesteg Quins. They took home wins over Ogmore Vale and Abercrave, but suffered double defeats to Cwmavon, Bridgend Sports and Cefn Cribbwr. They finished with a league record of 22 played, 13 won, 1 drawn, 8 lost.

Quins

The Quins had good wins over Bryn Wanderers, Tonna, Seven Sisters, Resolven, Taibach and Baglan (twice). They also finished with a 0–0 draw with Baglan. In the H.G. Lewis Cup the Quins defeated Tonna in the first round, 15–3, but lost in the quarter-final to Banwen (3–9 away). Bobby Davies and Paul Jones were selected for the Neath & District XV against Cardiff & District at Glamorgan Wanderers ground in March.

Youth XV

The Youth XV also enjoyed wins over Bryncoch, South Cornelly, Glynneath, Hirwaun, and Cwmgrach, and twice each over Skewen and Baglan. They toured to Scotland in March and were narrowly defeated 7–12 by Kelso RFC. They hosted a Clifton College side in September, coached by Alan Sullivan an ex-youth player, but narrowly lost to them.

Awards

During the end of season awards night, no.8 Gareth Rice picked up the Senior Player of the Year award and Chris Jones the Most Improved Award. Ryan Davies was Quins Player of the Year. Chairman Roger Amphlett was Clubman of the Year.

1998/99

BRITON FERRY RFC: (Pictured below)Divisi
A highly creditable season for the Ferry, who finished fourth after being promoted as unbeaten division seven champ After losing three early games, Ferry were always strugg with the promotion chasers but their young side played so and reached the quarter finals of the Glamorgan Silver even had to contend with the loss of their kit after it was s club chairman's car following a defea

11.22 1998/99

1999/2000

Captain
Mike Moran

Coach
Chris White

Quins captain
Martyn Bate

Youth XV captain
Martin Edwards

Youth XV coach
Richard Lawrence

Under-15s captain
Lee Irvine

Under-15s coach
Martyn Bate

A change in the coaching staff took place at the end of the decade as ex-captain Chris White took over from Cliff Morgan and Dave Puckett, but Richard Lawrence continued as Youth coach. Mike Moran remained as club captain for his third term. The Quins were again led by old stalwart Martyn Bate, while the Youth XV kept Martin Edwards as skipper. The club also ran an Under-15s side, coached by Martyn Bate and skippered by Lee Irvine. Phil Thomas and Paul Woodland joined the General Committee.

The First XV had a good run in the O.G. Davies Cup as they had a walkover win away at Cwmgrach in the first round, and then a narrow home win over Neath Athletic in the quarter-finals, 24–20, which put them into the semi-finals against Division 2 Seven Sisters. Unfortunately, the Sisters were on fire and defeated Ferry 70–19.

In the WRU Cup the First XV had a bye in the first round, and were drawn at home in the second round to West Wales club Llanidloes. This time it was the Ferry who were on fire and they blitzed the away team 86–0 (Ferry's highest-scoring cup win). They were then given a stern challenge in the third round with an away match at Penygraig. In a hard-fought game the Rhondda side came out on top, 10–17, which ended Ferry's cup run for another season.

In the Central Glamorgan Cup they started off with a good win at home over Ystrad Rhondda, 27–19, but they came unstuck at Maesteg in the second round, where they lost to the Quins, 47–17.

In Central Division 6, they finished eighth (the champions were Pontycymmer). Ferry had a good start with a 35–20 home win over Blaengarw, but they lost the return match 10–41 up in the Garw valley. Other wins followed: twice against Cwmgrach (29–7 away, tries from Gavin Puckett, Adrian Griffiths, Ross Jones, Ryan Davies and Dai Puckett and 1 conversion each from Chris Jones and Paul Evans; and 30–8 at home); against Cefn Cribbwr (21–15); against Bargoed (25–12); and against Alltwen(74–0). Ferry drew with Bridgend Sports (27–27) and Alltwen (18–18). They were defeated in the return matches with Cefn Cribbwr (19–24), Bargoed (19–23), Bridgend Sports (22–24) and suffered double defeats to Banwen (17–18 away and home), to Abercrave (10–16 at home and 10–20 away), to Pontycymmer (16–19 home and 15–21 away), to Nantymoel (20–24 away and 21–22 home) and to Maesteg Quins (17–47 away and 8–20 home). It was a poor league season for the club.

No friendlies were played this season as league matches were spread throughout.

Awards

Martyn Bate was awarded Clubman of the Year.

Quins

The Quins lost 7–52 away to Resolven in the H.G. Lewis Cup (Cimla defeated Bryncoch in the final).

They did take league wins over Aberavon Naval Club (43–17), BP Llandarcy (19–13), Bryncoch (29–10), Tonmawr (37–27) and a 7–3 win and 5–5 draw with Crynant. The Quins were defeated by Resolven, Seven Sisters, Bryncoch, Glynneath, Tonmawr, Cimla and Cwmgrach. Cimla became league champions.

Youth XV

The Youth XV had a very good season. They defeated Baglan, Hirwaun and Cwmgrach and they inflicted double defeats over Bryncoch, Seven Sisters, Tonna and Skewen. They lost to Crynant in the semi-finals of the Neath & District League play-offs, but won the Neath & District Cup after defeating Ystradgynlais in the final. This put them into the Champion of Champions Cup against Crynant, who defeated them narrowly.

The Youth XV also went on tour to old friends Nenagh, where they won 35–17.

Other news

A future Ferry First XVer Andrew Kriescher scored a try at no.8 for Neath Port Talbot College against Llanharri.

Ex-player Dai Williams coached Dwr-a-Felin school to an unbeaten, six-match tour of South Africa.

Future club coach Steve Martin received a cap for playing 100 games for Neath (he'd also played a few games for Llanelli).

In April, the NPT Cancer Challenge five-mile run was held in the Ferry, starting in Ynysymaerdy Road and ending at the rugby club.

PART 12: 2000–2014

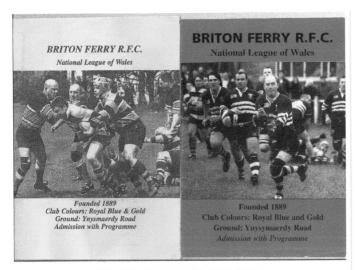

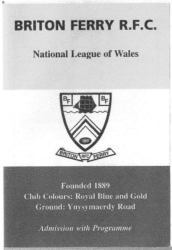

12.1 Programme covers from the 2000s

2000/01

Second row Wayne Davies became captain for the first season of the new century; and there was a new team of senior coaches D. Puckett, C. White and A. Griffiths. The Quins also had a new skipper in hooker Steve "Tank" Jones.

The Ferry had no pre-season success in Tonmawr and lost heavily to Resolven in the O.G. Davies Sevens tournament. After friendly wins over Baglan (26–12) and Glyncorrwg (36–9) it was thought that maybe this season would pan out to be reasonably successful. Although they defeated BP Llandarcy in the preliminary round of the O.G. Davies Cup, they were defeated 20–47 away by Skewen in the first round.

In the Principality WRU Cup, Ferry defeated Gwernyfed 30–6 away and drew Penarth at home in the second round. Ferry defeated 48–16, with scores from Aaron Norman (2), Paul Evans, Gareth Baker, Terry White and Adrian Griffiths (3). Chris Jones kicked 4 conversions. But in the next round, Ferry lost 15–31 away at Bargoed.

In the National League Central Division 6 the First XV finished ninth. They had a good start by inflicting a double defeat on Banwen, first at home by one point, 18–17, then 44–15 away. They also took the double over Ogmore Vale, and then had wins over Bridgend Sports (11–10), Crynant (16–10), Nantymoel (15–5) and Cefn Cribbwr.

> The return match was abandoned after the referee retired injured.

They also suffered double defeats, from Aberdare, Abercwmboi, Abercrave, Maesteg Quins and Bryncoch (10–20 in the away match, when the Ferry's points came

Captain
Wayne Davies

Coaches
David Puckett
Chris White
A. Griffiths

Quins captain
Steve Jones

Youth XV captain
Luke Williams

Youth XV coach
Richard Lawrence

Under-16s captain
Lee Irvine

Under-16s coach
Martyn Bate

from a Martyn Bate try and Gavin Puckett conversion and penalty); and defeats by Cefn Cribbwr, Nantymoel, Crynant (at home 21–31) and Bridgend Sports. In fact, the club was almost relegated after conceding 521 points.

The deciding match was on an early evening in May at Briton Ferry, the last game of the season and the replay against Cefn Cribbwr. Two penalties in the last ten minutes by Youth player Karl Lewis pushed the score to 19–13 to the Ferry and kept them up for another year.

Quins

The Quins were struggling to keep interest going and only managed to play two games throughout the season. They defeated Aberavon Naval Club but lost to Banwen.

Youth teams

The Youth XV went from strength to strength with wins over Upper Afan (3), Brynamman (2), Bryncoch (2), Tonna (2), Cefn Cribbwr, Tumble, Seven Sisters, Pontrhydyfen and Skewen.

12.2 Under-16s 2000/01

After a 13–13 draw at Baglan (as the away team they won) in the first round of the Neath & District Cup, they defeated Taibach 26–19 in the next round, but lost in the final 10–37 to Aberavon.

They also had a run in the Welsh Cup, defeating Ammanford 48–0 and Pentyrch 18–11, before losing 3–29 at home to a strong Newport side that contained a certain Ian Gough.

Match results place BFRFC scores first

The Youth XV also reached the play-off stage in the Dragons Trust League and defeated a strong Penarth outfit 15–7, before losing in the quarter-finals, 18–24 at home to Merthyr.

The Under-16s only managed wins over Bryncoch and Ystalyfera (twice) but they did reach the semi-finals of both the Neath & District (lost to Aberavon) and the Interdistrict Plate (lost to Penclawydd) competitions.

Awards

During the club awards night chairman Roger Amphlett was granted Life Membership for his tireless work for the club. Long-standing player Adrian Griffiths was awarded Clubman of the Year.

Around the district

Seven Sisters beat Glynneath in the H.G. Lewis final.

Other news

Ex-player and club secretary Roy Evans passed away while on holiday with his wife, Anne. Apparently, he was singing his favourite song "Till" at the time.

12.3 Roy Evans in 1999, at the start of the World Cup in Cardiff

Future coach Steve Martin was playing for Neath and ran a regular spot in the press, 'News from the Gnoll'.

Ferry boy and paramedic Robert Edwards came tenth in the Ferry five-kilometre run, with a time of 27.6 minutes. He went on to take part in the London Marathon.

In a shock move, Wales' team manager Dai Pickering resigned in April 2001 – he'd been in the position since July 1998. David Pickering had received full school honours, had captained Wales and been team manager at Llanelli. He was first capped in 1986 and had logged 19 caps, 3 tries and 12 points. He was chairman of the WRU general committee (2003–2014), became head of the Six Nations in 2008 and joined the World Cup board in 2012.

12.4 Newspaper feature on David Pickering

2001/02

Hooker Lee Hopkins led the side, and the senior coaches were Chris White and Richard Lawrence. Steve Jones led the Quins again. Martyn Bate continued to coach the Youth team led by Julian Knight. Chairman Roger Amphlett stepped down from the committee and, in an unusual move, the new secretary Kerry Frey also took on the role, Phil Thomas took over as treasurer from Kerry, and ex-prop Mark Best took his place on the general committee.

> The O.G. DAVIES CUP was no more, a sign of the times and of how the leagues were taking over.

The First XV started the season with two trial matches at home and won against Tonna (19–19) and against Glyncorrwg (12–7). Once again, the club lost out in the first round of the WRU Cup, 17–26 up in Rhigos.

In the WRU National League Division 6 Central the club ended up in eleventh position and were relegated. However, after changes were made to the leagues the following season they retained their position in Division 6 Central for 2002/03. This season began with a 7–26 loss at home to Taibach, Ferry conceded the double to them later by losing 14–20. The First XV were also doubled by Abercrave, 9–26 away and 14–20 at home; by Abercwmboi, 16–27 at home and 10–28 away; by Banwen, 0–66 away and 11–68 at home; by Nantyfyllon, 0–50 away and 16–23 at home; by Bridgend Sports, 9–19 at home and 6–19 away; by Aberdare, 20–45 away and 8–71 at home; by Cefn Cribbwr, 15–18 away and 6–20 at home. The First XV were also defeated by Crynant (13–14 away) and by Nantymoel (17–36) at home. The First XV

Captain
Lee Hopkins

Coaches
Chris White
Richard Lawrence

Quins captain
Steve Jones

Youth XV captain
Julian Knight

Youth XV coach
Martyn Bate

did take wins at Nantymoel, 17–6 away, and over Crynant 15–6, and two wins over Maesteg Celtic, 18–13 away and 28–21 at home.

Quins

The Quins also struggled and only played eight games. They managed three wins (over Baglan 26–18, Tonna 16–5 and Cwmgrach 21–0), but lost to Neath Athletic 10–18, to Bryncoch 8–21, to Seven Sisters 0–45 and to Glynneath 12–35. The Quins stopped playing after October due to players' lack of interest. Although they did manage one more home game at the end of February, against Glyncorrwg, which they lost 7–10.

Youth XV

The Youth XV defeated Tonna, Bryncoch and Trebanos, but were knocked out of the Neath & District Cup by Resolven, 27–14 at home.

After a poor season overall, they played in the Premier 2A Division of the National Youth League and finished second in the table, with just 5 points – having played 3, won 1 and lost 2 – among other teams: Baglan, Tonmawr, Cwmgrach, Trebanos, Bryncoch and Seven Sisters.

Youth players such as Brett Thomas, Andrew Chappell, Craig Jewell, Jonathan Davies, Kelvin Davies, Scott Cole, Chris Burgess, Lee Irvine, Chris Holloway and Kevin Richards would all feature in the First XV, two as captains.

12.5 Under-12s 2002

Awards

Stephen Griffiths, Jonathan Davies (top try scorer with 11 and top points scorer with 62 points), Joel Daniels and Andrew Chappell were prominent players and skipper Julian Knight was awarded Youth Player of the Year (he also received the BT Dragons Player of the Year award). Andrew Chappell was Youth Most Improved Player and Brett Thomas Youth Clubman of the Year.

Andrew James was awarded Clubman of the Year and David Parker was given Life Membership.

2002/03

The Youth were initially skippered by David Ball, but Scott Cole took over after David left the club. An Under-12s got up and running under coaches Andrew James and Gareth Baker.

After losing 0–26 at Cwmgrach and winning 34–12 at home to Taibach in pre-season friendlies, the First XV had a bit of a run in the WRU Principality Cup. They beat Fishguard 19–16 at home in the preliminary round and then had an outstanding victory over Machen, 32–0 at home. The next match ended in a 26–26 tie at home against Tredegar Ironsides. It was a thrilling game that went into extra time. Since Ferry had the highest try count, they were declared the winners. This gave them an away match at Bridgend Athletic, but they had to scratch due to front row unavailability.

In the National League Division 6 Central Ferry ended the season seventh. Their campaign started with a 36–3 away win at Cilfynydd. The team that day was:

backs	forwards	
G. Morgan,	L. Morris,	L. Williams and R. Davies;
J. Knight, K. Lewis, C. Hendy,	L. Hopkins (captain), W.	subs S. Rees, M. Fleming,
G. Puckett,	Curtis, J. Knight,	J. Low and S.
C. Jones and	W. Davies,	Griffiths.
A. Griffiths;	L. Daniels,	

The First XV also beat Cilfynydd at home later in the season. They managed doubles over Dowlais (39–7 at home, Karl Lewis 3 tries) and Bridgend Sports.

The First XV both beat and were beaten by Alltwen, Taibach and Neath Athletic. They managed a win and a

Captain
Lee Hopkins

Coaches
Chris White
Richard Lawrence

Quins captain
Steve Jones

Youth XV captain
David Ball/Scott Cole

Youth XV coach
Martyn Bate

Under-16s coach
Steve Jones

Under-12s Coaches
Andrew James
Gareth Baker

First XV league record
P 22
W 11
L 11

draw with Maesteg Celtic and suffered double defeats against Abercwmboi, Rhigos and Aberdare.

The First XV also played a home friendly against Neath Under-21s and lost 10–57, Gavin Puckett was among the try scorers.

Quins

The Quins only played eight games and won just one match against Pyle (21–17).

12.6 Under-16s 2002/03

Under-16s (back) Martyn Bate (coach), Ashley Davies, Andrew Ball, Ashley Williams, Lee Irvine, Scott Cole (captain), Daniel James, Nicky Dawkes, Johnny Lewis, Carl Jenkins, Robert Franklyn; (front) Brett Thomas, Darren Richards, Andrew Chappell, Gavin Pugh, Carl Griffiths, Gavin Jefford

Youth XV

The Youth also struggled a bit and only played ten games, with just the one win over Crynant.

> There was a nasty incident during a match against Nantyfyllon, which they were losing 10–19, when second row **RICHARD EDWARDS** went down in a tackle and received a nasty neck injury. He was airlifted off the field and the match was immediately abandoned – luckily, he wasn't hurt too seriously.

The Youth XV also played a combined junior match with the Under-16s against the touring Nenagh juniors, which they won.

Awards

At the awards night skipper Lee Hopkins was Senior Player of the Year and Jon Low the Most Improved Player. Clubman of the Year was awarded to Hazel Amphlett of the ladies committee. There were no Youth awards this season.

Other news

Future player/coach Chris Hunt was playing for Neath Under-21s.

The club had an official invite to the Mayor's Parlour in Neath and officials and skipper Lee Hopkins were photographed with Mayor Colin Morgan.

12.7 Visit to Mayor's Parlour in Neath 2002/03

The first Junior Schools Festival of Rugby was successfully held at the Ferry in October 2002 (see Figure 12.7).

The Courier, Wednesday, October 16, 2002   49

ORT EXTRA . . .SPORT EXTRA . . .

Tournament popular with boys and girls

KICK-OFF: Welsh Rugby Union Dragon Trust development officer Aled Thomas, Briton Ferry youth coach Martyn Bate and junior school pupils mark the first Briton Ferry Rugby Festival, in conjunction with Neath Port Talbot Sports Development Unit.

New junior schools event proves a big hit

THE inaugural Briton Ferry junior schools rugby tournament proved a big hit with both boys and girls.

Six local schools — Tyle'r Ynn, Gnoll, ryndyn, Llansawel, Ynysmaerdy and St oseph's — competed on a round robin asis. No winners were declared but that idn't stop the day from providing budding rugby stars with new skills.

The competition was staged at Briton Ferry RFC's headquarters in Ynysmaerdy Road and club officers, along with students from Neath Tertiary College, helped in making it a memorable day for the children.

"The tournament was organised as a celebration of rugby and it proved so popular that two more competitions are pencilled in this season," said tournament organiser

Martyn Bate, who is also youth team coach at Briton Ferry RFC.

Meanwhile, Briton Ferry RFC play at under-12 and under-16 age groups and games have also commenced at youth level.

☎ Further details from Martin Bate on 01639 769408 or the Briton Ferry RFC clubhouse 01639 812227.

● More pictures in next week's Courier.

52   The Courier, Wednesday, October 23, 2002   WW

Junior school teams enjoy inaugural tournament

BUDDING STARS: Following our feature last week, the remaining four schools which took part in the inaugural Briton Ferry junior schools rugby tournament are pictured here. Clockwise (from top left) are: Ynysmaerdy, Llansawel, St Joseph's and Gnoll. The teams competed on a round robin basis and although no winners were declared, it didn't stop the day from providing budding rugby stars with new skills. The competition was staged at Briton Ferry RFC's headquarters in Ynysmaerdy Road and club officers, along with students from Neath Tertiary College, helped make it a memorable day for the children. The tournament was organised by Briton Ferry RFC youth coach Martyn Bate. Picture: Gayle Marsh.

12.8 First Junior Schools Festival of Rugby 2002 (The Courier 16 and 23 October 2003)

2003/04

Outstanding hooker Lee Hopkins captained the side for the third season in a row. New coaches were Dai Lewis and Rob Locke. Flanker Andrew Thomas led the Quins.

The club defeated Monmouth 35–22 in the first round of the WRU Konica Minolta Cup, then disappointingly lost 14–23 at home to Glais in the next round. After yet more changes in the league system they found themselves in National League Division 4 South West, where they finished fourth.

The First XV started the season with a home friendly against Crynant and defeated them 39–10. The following week they were into league action with an away game at Cwmgors, which they lost 17–29. They also lost their next game, 17–22 away at Alltwen.

The first home league game produced a comfortable 53–6 win against Rhigos. This was followed by two wins on the trot, away to Morriston 21–5 and at home to Glais 37–18. They then slipped to a narrow 27–35 defeat at Pyle.

By now they were into November and Abercrave provided the opposition for a tight game on a chilly day at the Ferry, which the Ferry won 33–26. In their next game at Taibach they lost narrowly, 16–19. They did finish the month with a flourish and won both home games, against Amman United 30–13 and against Maesteg Celtic 28–23.

Inclement weather put paid to most of December and they only played one game, a one-point defeat at Cefn Cribbwr, 10–11.

In the new year, the Ferry XV produced an unbeaten run of five matches, starting with an away win at Rhigos (21–7), then home to Morriston (19–14), away at Glais (20–

Match results place BFRFC scores first

13), home to Pyle (63–5) and away at Abercrave (33–0). The run was broken by a defeat at home to Cwmgors (20–32) then a 10–10 draw in a table-topping clash with Taibach in February (Gavin Puckett scored the only try and Chris Jones converted and added a penalty; Taibach's try was scored by ex-Ferry juniors player Neil Wood).

In two away games in March they won 34–13 at Maesteg Celtic, but lost 15–27 at Amman United.

They ended the season with three home games: one win, 34–8 against Cefn Cribbwr; and two losses, 10–25 to Alltwen and 20–32 to Cwmgors.

12.9 2003/4

Quins

The Quins defeated Bryncoch in the Neath & District Cup and lost in the semi-finals to Cimla.

They played very little rugby during the season and ended with defeats by Tonna (twice), Neath Athletic (twice) and Pontrhydyfen.

Youth XV

The Youth XV played the most games in the whole district but only managed wins over Tonna and Trebanos and two high-scoring draws with Crynant at home – one of which was in the Neath & District Cup, which meant the away team qualified for the next round.

Youth XV players included hooker Gavin Jenkins, who was top try scorer, with 9 tries, and top scorer with 104 points. Other young players who featured strongly were Lee Irvine, Thomas Probert, Matthew Williams and Martin Jenkins.

Tour

A joint Youth and First XV toured to Nenagh. On 1 May, the Youth XV lost 7–24. The First XV won 45–30, the team included scrum-half Richard Lawrence and veteran front rowers Ron Lilley and Martyn Bate.

12.10 Tour to Nenagh 2004

Match results place BFRFC scores first

12.11 BFRC First XV, Nenagh 2004

12.12 BFRC Youth team, Nenagh 2004
(back) Martyn Bate (coach), Matthew Williams, Scott Cole, Kevin Richards, Simon Williams, Lee Irvine, Dean Kreischer, Martin Jenkins, Steven John; (front) Brett Thomas, Neil Hampton, Phil Knight, Gavin Jenkins, Michael Arnold, Gareth Jones, Ashley Davies

Awards

Ross Jones was the outstanding choice for Senior Player of the Year. Gavin Jenkins was Youth Most Improved Player. Forward Jonny Lewis received

Youth Clubman of the Year. Outstanding wing Ashley Davies secured Youth Player of the Year.

The club finished the season in the black again, which was a credit to the discipline of the hard-working committee – and perhaps to the calendar featuring the players and committee in risqué poses!

12.13 Risqué calendar 2004

2004/05

No.8 Luke Williams (son of fixture secretary Ray) became First XV captain.

Although Andrew Thomas was announced as Quins XV captain, they never managed to muster a team during the season. They did play a friendly against Porthcawl's First XV, losing gallantly 15–30, and a couple of games each against Pontrhydyfen and Cwmgrach, with one win and one defeat in both cases.

The Youth XV suffered a similar fate. Kevin Richards became skipper, but they only played one league game – losing at Crynant – before folding. They did take part in the District tens, winning one and losing two.

After this disappointment within the club the First XV set down an early marker by defeating Loughor 35–14 in a pre-season friendly, before taking on Burry Port in the WRU Cup preliminary round and beating them 21–19. In the next round they were drawn away to Division 2 side Tondu and produced a shock 13–10 win. In the next round they went down fighting against Division 1 side Whitland, who won 43–0.

Captain
Luke Williams

Coaches
Dai Lewis
Rob Locke

Quins captain
Andrew Thomas

Youth XV captain
Kevin Richards

Youth XV coach
Martyn Bate

Welsh Cup
preliminary round
28/08/04

at Ynysymaerdy Road
Kick off 3PM

Briton Ferry RFC.

vs

Burry Port RFC

12.14 Programme v. Burry Port RFC

463

The Ferry had won a prize the previous season in a WRU draw, which was a training session from new Welsh coaches Mike Ruddock and Scott Johnson. They came down to the club in late September and all available senior and youth squad members took part, along with their coaches Dai Lewis, Rob Locke and Martyn Bate. There were more than forty players on the field for a very interesting and demanding session. Although it still didn't help to drum up enough players for a Quins or a Youth team! A sign of the times?

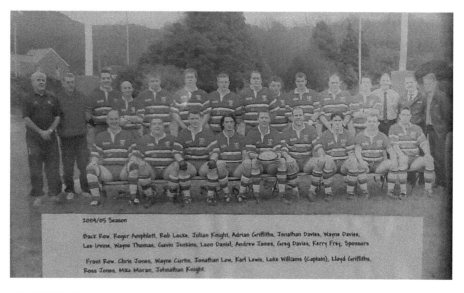

2004/05 Season

Back Row. Roger Amphlett, Rob Locke, Julian Knight, Adrian Griffiths, Jonathan Davies, Wayne Davies, Lee Irvine, Wayne Thomas, Gavin Jenkins, Leon Daniel, Andrew James, Greg Davies, Kerry Frey, Sponsors

Front Row. Chris Jones, Wayne Curtis, Jonathan Low, Karl Lewis, Luke Williams (Captain), Lloyd Griffiths, Ross Jones, Mike Moran, Johnathan Knight.

12.15 2004/05

Ruddock at the Ferry

WALES coach Mike Ruddock and his assistant Scott Johnson will be taking division four south west side Briton Ferry for a training session next Wednesday at their Ynysmaerdy ground.

The session came about because Briton Ferry won a competition last year. Spectators are welcome to go along to watch Ruddock and Johnson in action, starting at 6.30pm.

Wales coach Mike Ruddock, who will be taking a training session at Briton Ferry this Wednesday with his assistant Scott Johnson

Ruddock and Johnson coaching at the Ferry

WALES coach Mike Ruddock and his assistant Scott Johnson will be taking division four south west side Briton Ferry for a training session this Wednesday at their Ynysmaerdy ground.

The session came about because Briton Ferry won a competition last year. Spectators are welcome to go along to watch Ruddock and Johnson in action, starting at 6.30pm.

12.16 Ruddock at the Ferry

In the league the First XV finished fifth in Division 4 South West. They were unbeaten in September for an excellent start. They saw off Aberavon Green Stars and Trebanos at home, 23–15 and 40–7 respectively, and Ystradgynlais away, 19–17.

12.17 Lineout

Ferry continued the run into October, defeating Heol-Y-Cyw 26–25 at home and Pyle 34–20 away, before going down to Resolven, 15–31 at home. Scorers were the outstanding flanker Ross Jones, 2 tries, Chris Jones converted 1 and added a penalty. Also outstanding in this game was second row Wayne Davies.

This defeat seemed to disjoint the team slightly as they went into November drawing 15–15 in Morriston before losing again at home, 13–15 to Glais.

In December they picked themselves back up and defeated both Maesteg Celtic and Aberavon Green Stars away from home, 38–13 and 25–20 respectively, and Ystradgynlais at home 31–5.

The club started the new year with a disappointing narrow defeat, 19–20 away to Trebanos. Once again they found it difficult to regain momentum and lost both of their other games, at Heol-y-Cyw 6–20, and at Resolven 6–38.

There was only one game in February – a disappointing loss to local rivals Tonna, 13–20 at home. But they got back to winning ways in March with league wins over both Taibach away 35–11 and Morriston at home 21–10. Fluctuating performances in the final month delivered wins over both Maesteg Celtic (34–3) and Taibach (37–14) at home, but defeats at Glais (13–16) and Tonna (10–37).

Youth teams

The Under-12s defeated Vardre 36–12 in the Neath & District Cup, with tries from future First XV players Jonathan Field and Calum Surman, with others from Ryan Griffiths and Thomas Redman (3), Surman converted three.

Midfield player Jason Massey was part of the Wales Student's Rugby League team that won the Four Nations tournament.

12.18 Shirt and photo donated by Jason Massey

Awards

During the annual awards night tricky wing Johnny Knight was Player of the Year.

12.19 Plymouth tour v. Devonport HSOB, 2005

2005/06

Scrum-half Mike Moran was the new senior captain. Cliff Morgan and Lloyd Griffiths were to be the new coaches but, unfortunately, they both both stood down, so Mike Barnett was brought in. New faces on the committee were former players Wayne Curtis and Mark Davies alongside Rob Woodhouse and David. M. Parker.

In three pre-season friendlies the First XV were defeated by Loughor, 12–24 away, and by Aberavon Quins, 10–17 at home, but they did make it a 57–10 home win over Glyncorrwg. In the WRU Konica Minolta cup the Ferry beat Cefn Cribbwr 38–22 at home in the first round by, but then lost 15–34 in the next round, at home to New Tredegar.

The Ferry's league run started really badly by losing 0–13 away at Birchgrove, followed by three home defeats: 22–29 to Glynneath; 10–34 to Pontycymmer; and 17–34 to Glais.

The First XV's first league win was at Maesteg Celtic 26–24, only to slip up 5–27 away at Morriston.

The only game played in November was a 23–20 win over Taibach in the Ferry.

December started with a good 28–0 away win at Aberavon Green Stars, but that was followed with a 9–14 home defeat by Birchgrove.

The new year got no better, with four defeats in January. The first was 18–33 at home to Heol-Y-Cyw and the rest were all away: to Glynneath 7–46; to Pontycymmer 6–19; and to Glais 10–15.

In February, the First XV got back to winning ways over Maesteg Celtic, 29–12 at home, and over Abercrave 31–

Captain
Mike Moran

Coach
Mike Barnett

Quins captain
Andrew Thomas

Match results place BFRFC scores first

24 away (Jonny Knight 2 tries, Gavin Puckett, Karl Lewis and Steve Williams a try apiece, Gavin Jenkins 3 conversions; first-choice kickers for both teams were their hookers, Jenkins for Ferry and J. Stevens for Abercrave) and over Trebanos 46–14.

12.20 Barney (Mike Barnett) rallying the troops

The Ferry's unbeaten run continued right into April with home wins over Morriston, 35–19, Trebanos, 58–5 and Aberavon Green Stars, 27–13 and a 3– 3 draw away at Taibach. The run was broken by a 15–23 defeat at Heol-Y-Cyw. The First XV won their final league game 45–28 at home to Abercrave and finished seventh in Division 4 South West.

Tour

The club returned yet again to visit their friends in Nenagh and won 31–29.

12.21 Nenagh 2006

(standing) Ray Williams, Kelvin Hawes, James Watkins, Terry Saunders, Ron Lilley, Peter Bell, Mike Moran, Stephen Hare, Phil Knight, Chris Jones, Stephen Griffiths, Karl Lewis, Andrew Crook, Lee Hopkins, Leon Daniels, Mark Best, Andrew James, Mark Davies, Rob Woodhouse, Geraint Morgan, Wayne Curtis, Wayne Davies, Greg Davies, Gavin Puckett, Martyn Bate, Andrew Thomas, Steve Williams, Brian Evans, Andrew Caan, Johnny Jones, Martin Jenkins, Andrew Williams, Jeff Whitefoot, Roger Amphlett, Scott Cole, Kerry Frey, Steven John, Richard Lawrence; (crouching) David Parker, Johnny Knight, Julian Knight, Malcolm Edwards, Jonathan Davies

Quins

The Quins played fourteen games and won five, all away from home: Baglan, 48–15; Tonna, 16–15; Aberavon Naval Club, 52–5; Aberavon Green Stars, 61–24; and Bryncoch, 47–10. They lost at home to Aberavon Quins, Bryncoch, Pontrhydyfen and Cimla, and away to Aberavon Green Stars twice, Aberavon Quins, Crynant.

The Quins heaviest defeat was in the cup, 82–8 away to BP Llandarcy. They did score 40 tries during the season and Quins top try scorer was Paul Jones with 7, Chris Burgess was close with 5. Quins top scorer was Kevin Collins with 59 points.

Youth teams

Mark Davies applied to the committee to form mini and junior sections, including Under-9s. Such was the initial interest that playing numbers increased from six to fifty in weeks!

Awards

The First XV Player of the Year was outstanding back rower Ross Jones. Quins Player of the Year was Wayne Thomas. Clubman of the Year was young Lee Irvine.

2006/07

Prop Wayne Curtis became captain. At the end of a successful season they finished as league runners-up and were promoted to Division 3 South West.

The First XV were invited to enter the Richard Barry Sevens in August. They reached the semi-finals and lost 12–29 to Aberavon.

In September, the First XV put up a good fight on a visit to Division 2 Seven Sisters in the Konica Welsh Cup, before losing 27–39 (Wayne Curtis, Scott Cole and Steve Williams the try scorers, Adam John 3 conversions, 2 penalties). Next up was a 22–11 away win at Llantwit Major, then a 34–12 home win in a friendly against a spirited Glyncoch side. In a league fixture against Alltwen, Ferry secured a 27–3 win (Scott Cole, Chris Burgess and Adam John the try scorers, John 3 conversions and 2 penalties). They lost in the dying minutes of a match at Abercrave (Ross Jones, Gavin Puckett and Karl Lewis the try scorers, Chris Jones 2 conversions.

In October, Ferry took a thumping home victory over Ystalyfera, with 7 tries from Ross Jones, Greg Davies, Mike Collier, Carl Hendy, Scott Cole and Karl Lewis (2, who also added 2 conversions). In a tight-fought home game Ferry defeated Pontycymmer 10–3 (Greg Davies 1 try, Chris Jones 1 conversion, 1 penalty. Next up was a top of the table clash at home with BP Llandarcy, which they won 10–3 with tries by Wayne Davies and Chris Jones.

Four wins in December followed, at home against Birchgrove (48–0) and Taibach (22–10), then away against Trebanos (25–3) and Glynneath (25–17).

Captain
Wayne Curtis

Coach
Mike Barnett

Quins captain
Wayne Thomas

The new year started rolling with home doubles over both Llantwit Major (15–3) and Pontycymmer (12–3) things, followed by a revenge home win over Abercrave, 26–21. They suffered a narrow 19–21 defeat on a return visit to Ystalyfera (Johnny Knight, Gavin Puckett and Adam John tries, John 2 conversions). BP Llandarcy beat them 13–21 in another tight game.

Then came a resounding away victory at Resolven, with Ross Jones, Gavin Puckett, Chris Jones, Greg Davies and Karl Lewis the try scorers and Adam John adding 3 conversions and 1 penalty. Ferry also scored highly in the return home match to take the double over Resolven (try scorers were Carl Hendy, Chris Jones, Lee Morris, Chris Burgess (2) and Adam John, who also added 4 conversions and 1 penalty).

Birchgrove away was the next fixture and the First XV took a tremendous 67–7 victory. Chris Jones scored a hat trick of tries, with other tries from Steven John, Adam John, Scott Cole, Karl Lewis, Chris Burgess and Mike Collier. Adam John added 22 points with 7 conversions and 1 penalty.

Another record was made in a runaway 88–20 victory over Trebanos at home, as Chris Jones scored 48 points with 5 tries, 10 conversions and 1 penalty. Karl Lewis added 4 tries. Steve Williams, Ross Jones, Chris Burgess and Johnny Knight were also on the try list.

> **CHRIS JONES** performance in the game against Trebanos broke a host of Ferry records: by scoring the first try within nine seconds; by scoring 5 tries in one game; by notching up 48 points in one game. Also, the First XV were unbeaten at home.

The biggest crowd of the season saw the Ferry beat promotion rivals Glynneath by 33–27 in an exciting game. The Ferry back row of Ross Jones, Scott Cole and Chris Burgess were outstanding. Greg Davies, Gavin Puckett, Scott Cole and Adrian Mainwaring were the try scorers and Chris Jones added 3 penalties and 2 conversions.

Taibach away were next up and again Ferry came out on top in an exciting 34–21 game (Ross Jones, Karl Lewis, Gavin Puckett and Adam John the try scorers, John 4 conversions, 1 penalty and 1 drop goal. Ferry made the final game of the season another fine away win, 47–17 at Alltwen, to finish with a league playing record of 24 played, 20 won, 4 lost, 0 draws, with 688 points for and 262 points against, scoring 97 tries and conceding just 29 to end on 57 points.

Quins

The Quins started really badly with a 14–71 home defeat by Tonna. They dusted themselves down and came back with a 40–10 home win against Bryncoch. A tight away game to Aberavon Naval ended in a 19–19 draw, before yet another heavy defeat, 74–0 away at Cimla. Then came two more away defeats. to BP Llandarcy (35–15) and Aberavon Quins (45–3). Unfortunately, a game at Seven Sisters in between these two defeats was abandoned after five minutes play, due to a really bad injury to Ferry player Neil Baggeridge.

12.22 Quins 2006/7

(back) Richard Jones (kit supplier/sponsor), David Parker (sponsor DKB Locksmith), David Parker and Martyn Bate (commiteemen), Lee Hopkins, Julian Knight, Ceri Wyatt, Matthew Williams, Wayne Thomas, Lee Irvine, Andrew James, Kevin Collins, Craig Baggeridge, Andrew Thomas (captain), Kris Pemberton, Steven Thomas, Dean Hoare (sponsor) and sponsor DKB Locksmith; (front) Ceri Low, Paul Hughes, Jordan Davies, Terry White, Kelvin Davies, Gavin Jenkins, Steve Jones, Andy Bettamey, Paul Jones

The Quins won their next game 21–5, a first-round cup match against Seven Sisters. However, four away defeats in a row followed: to Tonna twice (17–29 and 10–29); Crynant (0–50); and Neath Athletic 27–7. At this point the team was struggling to raise a team each week and sometimes had to play one or two players down, hence the manner of the defeats. In the new year they bounced back by defeating BP Llandarcy 62–5. Sadly, that was to be their last win in a very difficult season as they went down to Pontardulais away (24–26), Cimla at home by (7–34), Tonna 26–40 at home in the cup semi-final, away at Aberavon Green Stars (30–39) and at Seven Sisters 0–46. Quins finished fourth in the Neath & District table.

That twenty-four different players scored tries, showed the type of rugby Quins were trying to play.

Youth teams

The juniors did well. The Under-14s hosted a festival of rugby in April and the Under-16s reached the final of the Osprey's Shield by beating Aberavon Quins 24–7 (Sam Baker 1 try, 2 conversions, Jonny Gwynne 2 tries, Ashley Roberts 1 try).

12.23 Under-16s Boys Club of Wales caps Ashley Roberts and Rhys Thomas

Tour

Nenagh were the touring visitors this year and they were defeated 26–15.

Awards

Presentation night was held in Blanco's. Clubman of the Year was awarded to young Mark Davies for his efforts with the minis.

Quins' Craig Baggeridge was top try scorer, with 7, and Kris Pemberton was Quins top scorer with 48 points (2 tries, 16 conversions and 2 penalties). Kevin Collins bagged 30 points (2 tries, 7 conversions and 2 penalties).

Other news

A BFRFC team in the national golf competition for rugby clubs won the regional group at the Manor House course and went on to represent the region in the national finals at Walton Heath on 26 October. Team members were Andrew Jacobs (5), Chris Jones (18, 43 points), Craig Evans (9) and Lloyd Griffiths (17, 46 points).

Future Ferry prop Steven 'Tudor' John was capped for Welsh Districts XV against Denmark while playing for Cimla RFC.

2007/08

Once again Ferry were invited to the Richard Barry Sevens in August. They lost 0–47 to the Welsh Wizards in the first game, but won the next game against Glynneath 34–21, which put them into the semi-final. They beat Cwmavon 38–12, but sadly the Canterbury VII were too strong for them in the final and they lost 48–0.

They also played a game in August at home to Heol-Y-Cyw – a delayed match from the previous season for a place in the final of the Central Glamorgan cup. Ferry won the game 27–17, but were outclassed in the final at the Talbot Athletic ground in November by a good Pencoed side, to the tune of 8–72.

Captain
Wayne Curtis

Quins captain
Adrian Griffiths

12.24 Match in 2007/8

Ferry's run in Division 3 South West started with an away defeat, 30–39 at Kenfig Hill, swiftly followed by their first win, 29–21 in the home game against Skewen (Chris

Match results place BFRFC scores first

Jones produced 19 points with 4 penalties, 2 conversions and 1 drop goal). Next up was an away game at Maesteg Quins, and the First XV came away with the spoils, 19–16.

12.25 Match in 2007/8

There was a little break from the league in October when they played a club game against Division 2 Tumble at home on a Friday evening; they won this game comfortably by 41–27.

12.26 Match in 2007/8

Back to league action next and Ferry lost a tight home fixture with Seven Sisters, 10–13. This was the start of a bad run of league results as they went on to lose to Aberavon Quins (15–31, Jonny Knight and Gavin Puckett tries, fly-half Chris Jones 1 conversion, 1 penalty) then 18–23 away to Tonna, and 13–21 at home to Tondu.

In between the league games they defeated Senghenydd in the WRU Cup, away 13–3 (S. Williams and M. Collier tries, C. Jones converted 1), then lost 21–37 at Mountain Ash in the next round.

December brought them back into league action with yet another defeat, 0–22 at Banwen. In the last game of the year Ferry went to BP Llandarcy and took their unbeaten two-year home record with a 13–12 score line. Chris Jones was Man of the Match after kicking 1 penalty, converting 1 penalty try and then kicking 1 drop goal to win the game for the Ferry.

12.27 Match in 2007/8

Ferry also played a friendly at home in December against Senghenydd, they won again, 38–17, to complete the double.

The new year started off well with a revenge home win over Kenfig Hill, 27–25 (Bobby Davies, Gavin Puckett and Ross Jones were the try scorers, Chris Jones 1 try and 2 conversions, hooker Gavin Jenkins 1 penalty). But

January came to an end with a 0–8 defeat at Skewen and a 20–30 home defeat by Maesteg Quins.

Due to the Six Nations only one game was played in February, a 3–21 away defeat at Seven Sisters in which second row Wayne Davies was sent off.

The First XV had mixed fortunes in March. They lost 6–15 at home to Aberavon Quins, then hammered Tonna 35–6, also at home, and gained a creditable 13–13 draw away at Tondu.

In a flurry of matches in April, two home wins, over Banwen 56–0 and Vardre 27–12, lifted them out of the danger zone in the league. Then came a narrow away defeat at Nantyfyllon, 22–27, in which no.8 Craig Kelly dropped the ball in the act of scoring on the stroke of full time. Followed by a 5–20 home defeat to the eventual champions, BP Llandarcy.

The First XV finished the season in style with a revenge home win over Nantyfyllon, 23–10, and an away win at Vardre, 33–24, with tries from Chris Jenkins, Ross Jones, Gavin Puckett, Julian Knight and Chris Jones (who also added 4 conversions).

Ferry end of season league stats read: P20 W8 D1 L11; scoring 358 points for and 391 against; tries for 45 against 46; to end on 42 points. The league had introduced the bonus point system and Ferry acquired 5 for scoring 4 tries or more, and 3 for coming within 7 points while losing).

Quins

As a development squad Quins were going along nicely with home wins over Maesteg Quins (18–14, A. Probert 1 try, 2 penalties, 1 conversion, C. Baggeridge 1 try) and Bryncoch (24–17, T. White, J. Davies, J. Low and C. Burgess tries, K. Collins 2 conversions) and a home draw with Tonna (26–26, A. Davies, J. Davies and C. Baggeridge tries, G. Jenkins 1 try, 3 conversions, 1 penalty), and an away win at Seven Sisters (31–5, T. White (2), C. Baggeridge, A. Davies and A. Griffiths tries, G. Jenkins 3 conversions). But they did lose away to Tumble in their first game (5–29, Ryan Davies try), and at home to Aberavon Quins by (16–25, A. Thomas 1 try, Jenkins 2 penalties and 1 conversion, Probert 1 penalty goal). They ended the year with a narrow defeat at Gowerton (22–24, J. Davies (2), M. Williams and G. Jenkins tries, Michael Arnold 1 conversion) followed by a 17–0 home win over BP Llandarcy (first tries for Chris Jenkins, younger brother of Gavin, and for Gavin Jefford, plus a C. Baggeridge try, converted by T. White).

The new year began with a 13–10 away win at Bryncoch (Wayne Thomas 2 tries, Jenkins 1 penalty, but they were brought back down to earth with a heavy 7–41 defeat at Kenfig Hill (K. Richards 1 try, converted by skipper Paul Hughes). Next up was a quarter-final Neath & District Cup match, away to Crynant, which they won narrowly, 13–10 (scrum-half Jamie Nicholls scored the only try, converted by T. White, who also kicked a couple of penalties).

local rugbylcwales.co.uk   Thursday, March 27, 2008

CHAMPIONS! Briton Ferry celebrate winning the celebrate after winning the Neath and District Merit Table title

Pictures: Glyn Davies

Quins are the conquerors

Briton Ferry Quins 13
Cimla 3

BRITON Ferry Quins were crowned champions of Neath and District Merit Table after beating Cimla in the title decider.

A large crowd witnessed an entertaining game between two determined sides.

Ferry opened the scoring with a penalty kick from outside half Michael Arnold.

Cimla soon found themselves reduced to 14 men after centre Chris Piles saw red.

To their credit Cimla managed to pull level with a penalty by fly-half Phil Williams, making the half time score 3-3.

In the second half again the Ferry were on top and the back row of Lres, John and Burgess were outstanding in attack and defence.

Arnold kicked another penalty – this time after Cimla were further reduced to 13 men when prop Daz Boost was sent off.

It was a feisty game with several yellow cards also brandished, but referee Phil Rees managed to keep things under control.

Late in the game sub Craig Kelly steamed over after breaking several tackles for the only try of the game, converted by Arnold.

There were some anxious moments for Ferry in injury time but a determined defence held on the win and brought the championship trophy to Ynysymaerdy Road.

TROUBLE BREWING: Ferry's Adrian Griffiths and Cimla's Scott Kelly square up

ON THE BURST: Adrian Griffiths breaks through the Cimla defence

FULL STRETCH: Cimla's David at a lineout

12.28 Quins are the conquerors (27 March 2008)

A double over Seven Sisters was the only game in February. They won 36–0, with tries by A. Davies, C. Baggeridge, D. Jefford, S. Williams (2) and J. Low, who converted his own try, P. Hughes converted another two. This put

Match results place BFRFC scores first

the team third in the league and in March they had a tough encounter with Tonna at home in the semi-final of the league play-off. They were victorious by a narrow margin of 8–5 (Chris Jenkins the try scorer, T. White 1 penalty). They then played Cimla in the final of the league play-offs in Glynneath. The game was marred by sending offs, two for Cimla and one for the Ferry, and a flurry of yellow cards. But Ferry won through to finish 13–3, with Craig Kelly scoring the only try of the game and Michael Arnold converting and adding two penalties.

But Quins went down to two heavy defeats after this game, at Tonna 12–41 (C. Baggeridge try, K. Collins try and T. White conversion) and at Glynneath 10–50 (J. Davies and veteran Martyn Bate the try scorers).

12.29 Quins are the conquerors

In a cloud of controversy over dates for games, the H.G. Lewis Cup semi-final game at home to Tonna was called off and the Ferry were told they were to be ousted from the competition. They launched an appeal and Tonna announced that they were handing the game to the Ferry. So they found themselves in another final, this time at Seven Sisters to face Cimla once again. The game was a great spectacle, although Ferry lost 15–22 (C. Davies and A. Griffiths the try scorers, T. White kicked 1 conversion and 1 penalty). This defeat meant they had to face Cimla one more time in another final, the Champion of Champions play-off in Cwmgrach. Unfortunately, they were bettered on the night by 19–29, despite tries from Chris Jones, Steve Williams and Craig Kelly, two converted by Terry White.

Once again Craig Baggeridge ended up as top try scorer, with 6. Terry White was top scorer with 39 points (3 tries, 6 conversions and 4 penalties).

12.30 Match in 2007/8

12.31 Quins 2007/08, Neath & District Cup Finalists
(back) Steven John, Paul Hughes, Matthew Williams, Jon Low, Jonathan Davies, Carl Griffiths, Kevin Richards, Craig Baggeridge, Ceri Wyatt, Andrew Chappell, Terry White, Phil Knight, Brett Thomas; (front) James Wybron, Ceri Low, Chris Jenkins, Aled Lloyd, Andrew Thomas, Adrian Griffiths, Julian Knight, Gavin Jefford, Jamie Nicholls, Ashley Davies, Martyn Bate (coach/secretary)

Match results place BFRFC scores first

Tour

This year's tour was a trip to old friends Nenagh in County Tipperary, Ireland, a celebration of a 50-year friendship between the clubs. The welcome was as warm as ever. Ferry lost 7–19 (Michael Arnold scored the only try and converted it himself).

12.32 Briton Ferry RFC and Nenagh RFC on the 50th anniversary of the friendship between the clubs, this time in Nenagh 2009

On 3 May 2008, the *Nenagh Guardian* printed:

Welsh visitors return for friendly

With the competitive part of the club season now ended, there is one fixture left to fulfil and it is a friendly against our long-standing visitors from Wales, Briton Ferry, on Saturday next at Lissatunny. It is now almost fifty years since then club secretary Ger Lewis got a letter from Bill Davies, his opposite number at Briton Ferry requesting a fixture on their tour of Ireland for the next long Easter weekend. The request was accepted and indeed a second fixture on the

Bank Holiday Monday was also arranged with the Thurles club, and so began a relationship that still exists today. It did die out for a while in the mid-sixties, probably as much down to economic circumstances in the Ireland of the fifties and sixties as any lack of enthusiasm for its continuation. Then one international weekend in the eighties, on a visit to watch a Tony Ward-led Greystones play the locals (Neath RFC) on the Friday Night, a trio of former players

from the historic first meeting spotted a sign for Briton Ferry RFC.
The Nenagh trio Joe Gleeson, Frank Flannery and Ger Lewis made
their way to the club and as Ger remembers it, a bit of luck fell their
way as who should they bump into on entering the club, but Roy
Evans, Captain of the first Ferry visitors to Nenagh.

The red carpet was immediately rolled
out, and from that day on the links have
been strengthened with visits of full sides
and youth sides travelling in both
directions. There is of course the social
side of it too and both clubs now leave
very few stones unturned in welcoming
the visitors to their respective shores. The
Ireland of the fifties was an austere and
claustrophobic place as Ger and indeed history remember it and
when this visit was mooted by the rugby club it was quickly seen as
an opportunity to show off a bit of what we had here for tourists
and the toastal committee, then in charge of such promotional
things in that area of endeavour, took up the running and organised
a bus tour for the visitors that took them through Portroe, the look-
out and on to Killaloe on Easter Monday.

Next weekend, it is hoped to relive a little
of that historic first visit when the surviving
members return for another visit along
with a sizeable contingent of the younger
generation that of course includes a team.
Just like fifty years ago, there will be a rugby
match too. The arrival of that first team was
though, a unique event in its day, and their
arrival at the railway station was greeted
by a large contingent from the club and
the civic authorities. The brass band led
the whole mass of people up through the
town to the Hibernian Inn where they were
accommodated for the duration of their stay.
A formal dinner was hosted by the Ormond club in the then new
Ormond Hotel that night. Once again, some of that will be relived
with a formal dinner for the survivors who are still in the area and
the surviving Welshmen too on Friday night at the Peppermill and
a civic reception at the municipal buildings on Saturday at 11am,

later on in the day comes the match to be followed by an evening of music and song in the clubhouse. By the time of their departure on the Tuesday after the long weekend, the crowd that sent them off had grown to much larger proportions than the one that greeted their arrival. They had won both hearts and minds. A few things catch the eye when reading contemporary Guardian reports of the events of that moment in time. The first was the special plaque presented to Nenagh Captain Denis Connolly, crafted by one of the Welsh players D.J. Poley, featuring Welsh dragon, shamrock and the Prince of Wales feathers. Another was the fact that they had chartered a plane to fly to Dublin and travelled down by train. The visitors were entertained in the Ormond Hotel on the night of the dinner by some Irish dancers and the names are worth recalling, they were Marie Ryan-Gortlandroe, Nuala Maguire-Knockonpierce, Catherine Fitzgerald-Tyone, and Sarah Walsh–Gortlandroe. There is certainly the personnel and talent available at the present time to reprise that particular event, so let's hope that doesn't slip through the list of to dos (it didn't the club were entertained by a couple of young Irish dancers in the club before the game).

Again as Ger Lewis says, there was also a game, won by the Ferry 19–12, and wouldn't you know it? They had a brilliant fly-half, 19-year-old Terry Dowrick, who dazzled all who saw him play with his amazing range of skills, that's when they had the manufacturing plant down in the collieries that ran out number tens on a conveyor belt for club and country, at least that's the Max Boyce version of it anyway. Another item of note that would raise an eyebrow or two nowadays, was the programme produced for the match, price of 3d. Now to those of you who think New Pence was old money that really was old money, secondly the members of the committee included yes, wait for it, shock horror players, Ger Lewis the aforementioned secretary was an active player at that time and of the others, most were only recently retired or still playing the odd game. So now, almost fifty years on, they return once more, perhaps it will be some of the grandchildren of those who joined in celebrating their first visit that will do so now once more and, hopefully many of those who have arrived in Nenagh in the interim will get to see something special take place within the community. But the granddads and grannies won't be found wanting either, nor indeed the in-between generation, The visitors won't be found wanting for sure and no doubt before they leave this May weekend, will once more have won hearts and minds of people they have never met before. As we said at the outset it's not about rugby, it's what rugby is all about. Won't it be great to have it back if only for a few fleeting moments? For the record, the teams that took the field that day long ago were as follows:

Nenagh Ormond :Jimmy O'Brien, Donie Morrissey, Noel Hasset, Denis Connolly (captain), Teddy Morgan (vice captain), Sean Sheedy, Seymour Kenny, Sean Morrissey, Gerard Lewis, Joe Gleeson, Frank Flannery, Pat Duggan, Charlie Powell, Pat McMahon and Matt McGrath.

Briton Ferry: Algi Baker, Lawrence Morgan, Haydn Walters, Roy Evans (captain), John Simonson, Terry Dowrick, Granville Pugh, Hugh Watkins, Douglas James, Terry Woodland, Gareth Burns,

Bryan Hire (vice captain), Brian Donovan, Gordon Matthews and Ernie Jones, and the substitutes were Charlie Hanford, Ken Smith, Max Keer, D.J. Poley. Trainer was Cyril Beasley, touch judges were W.J. Fitzgerald and W.S. Davies, and the game was refereed by Frank Lewis.

NENAGH ORMOND HONOURS VISITING BRITON FERRY RFC -Nenagh Ormond RFC President Ger O'Gorman makes a presentation to Briton Ferry RFC Chairman Kerry Frey. Also present are Denis Butler, Ger Lewis and Milo Gleeson at New Ormond Park Nenagh on Saturday last. Photograph: Bridget Delaney.

12.34–38 Tour to Nenagh

Youth teams

The Under-15s were winning against previously unbeaten opposition. Thomas Redmond, Thomas Jones, Calum Surman, Jamie Hopkins, Jon Doyle and Cory Phillips were all to the fore in a 15–12 win at home to Pontardulais in the Ospreys Cup.

Also in the Under-15s was fullback Jonathan Field. He scored 1,004 points across three seasons, in all games, including 155 tries and 112 conversions. He was a member of the Afan Nedd district team for the previous two years. He also represented Neath schoolboys, along with him in that squad were 15 other Briton Ferry boys, surely a record – forwards Jon Doyle, Marcus Boobier, Danny Stevens, Gavin Jones, Liam Willis, Taylor Morgan, Thomas Redmond and Cori Phillips; backs Gareth Davies, Thomas Jones, Calum Surman, Luke Williams, Jamie Williams, Conor Williams and Thomas Crowther.

Field, Doyle and Boobier also attended the Ospreys summer school. Field and Boobier made the Ospreys Under-16s squad for the 2008/09 season.

12.39 Under 14s, 2007 in Kenfig Hill

Junior's playing records 2007/08

In all 161 junior matches played, this surely looks good for the future of this great club.

	Played	Won	Drew	Lost
Under-7s	28	4	1	23
Under-8s	30	28	2	O
Under-9s	23	16	4	3
Under-10s	5	2	2	1
Under-11s	28	7	3	18
Under-13s	16	2	0	14
Under-15s	31	21	2	8

Awards

Player of the Year award went to Johnny Knight and Most Promising Player to Wayne Thomas. The player's Player of the Year was Ross Jones. The Quins player's Player of the Year award went to promising young hooker Chris Jenkins. Youth Player of the Year went to fullback Phil Knight. Clubman of the Year was Under-15s coach Lee Irvine, who also became the youngest coach in Wales to gain a level three coaching award.

The club were also by far the best supported team in the division, and the supporters earned plaudits from many of the opposition for their staying power! The Aberavon Quins website even said:

> *After the home game the Quins were entertained by the superb Briton Ferry supporters and any club hosting these fans will be in for a rare treat. In this age of professionalism and semi-amateurism the memories of days gone by came flooding back with a warm glow.*

2008/09 – 120TH

In the club's 120th year the First XV appointed flanker Ross Jones as their new captain. The Quins captain was outside-half Paul Hughes; Youth captain was Daniel Morgan. Mike Barnett made it a third season as senior coach, with Wayne Curtis, Lee Irvine and Adrian Griffiths as youth coaches.

Before the season started the club hosted a challenge from the British Army to raise funds for the newly formed charity, Help for Heroes, for our injured service men and women. The aim was to kick a goal on every rugby ground in a set time.

12.40 Help for Heroes challenge

The 120th year started with a trial match at home to Division 5 side Pontardawe. Ferry were outscored by 3 tries to 2 in wintry conditions, despite it being 12 August!

Development hooker Chris Jenkins and wing Chris Davies scored the Ferry tries. A visit to Tumble (who had been relegated from Division 2) yielded 43 points for the Ferry in a great 43–5 win (S. Williams and captain R. Jones 2 tries each, L. Moran, L. Morris and G. Puckett tries, M. Arnold converted 4).

Ferry had dropped out of the Aberavon Green Stars Sevens and instead faced a final friendly away to Division 5 West side Aberaeron. In a free-flowing match the First XV were victorious 39–5. Tries came from K. Lewis (3), Liam Moran (2) and Jonny Knight, M. Arnold converted 2.

Ex-coach **MIKE BARNETT**, who had only stood down from his role a few weeks previously, collapsed right at the end of a match against Morriston at home in October. He passed away that night. He had been coaching rugby for over twenty years with various clubs and, indeed, with the Neath district. He'd helped many young players on their way, such as James Hook and Adam Jones, and was Neath Port Talbot Sports Council Coach of the Year in 2003. Friends described Mike as a true legend within the grassroots game, who never sought the trappings, publicity or fame that the game can provide. They said he had coached, influenced and guided many a player in the Welsh game and that he was always frank and able to convert a youngster to the game. One youth player said, "Everything I do in rugby from now on is for Mike." You cannot underestimate the power of those words!

The Ferry's league campaign started with a 17–12 home win over old rivals Maesteg Quins, which was then followed by a heavy 7–30 away defeat at Skewen. Then another home win, 33–22 over Nantyfyllon, but they then failed to win the next four games: at home, 3–9 to Aberavon Quins and 6–17 Morriston, and away, 7–44 to Glynneath and 13–28 to Tondu.

In their only league match in November Ferry defeated fellow strugglers Tonna by one point, 28–27 away. They then lost their next two matches, 0–5 at home to Kenfig Hill and 10–21 away to Maesteg Celtic.

Ferry had a bye in the first round of the Welsh Cup and were drawn away to Divison 1 North side Ruthin in the second round, where they won 15–10. They were drawn away again in the third round, to Division 3 East side Aberdare and once again came away with the spoils, 25–23. However, in another away draw in the fourth round Ferry were defeated 5–40 by Division 2 East side Ynysybwl.

Adverse weather conditions made it a slow start to the new year as a number of games were called off. Their first two games ended in defeat, away to Nantyfyllon 15–10 and at home to Skewen 10–26. But Ferry ended the month with a very good, if narrow, 7–0 home win against division leaders

2008/09 – 120th Season

Tondu. A number of youth players were blooded into the team and did really well.

February's one game was an away defeat to Aberavon Quins, 38–5.

Just two games were played in March and Ferry lost both, defeated at home by Glynneath 0–19 and away by Morriston 12–29.

This meant April was the crunch month if the club were to stay in Division 3 South West. The First XV started with a bonus point win at home to Tonna, 34–24; went on to a heavy away defeat at Kenfig Hill, 13–55; then a good 32–20 home win over fellow strugglers Maesteg Celtic, and a bonus point; before succumbing to three defeats in a row, first 13–16 at home to Seven Sisters, then 10–32 away at Maesteg Quins, ending with a cracking game against Seven Sisters, 35–43. They had done just enough to survive and were now ready to rebuild and regroup for the coming season, once again in Division 3. Ferry ended the league campaign having won just 6 out of 22 games, scoring 300 points against 541, and netting 35 tries against 64; with bonus points for 3 tries and 4 losing, to end on 31 points.

Quins

The development squad started with a bang away to Swansea Uplands, winning 76–0, with 12 tries, including a hat trick from flanker, and Youth XV coach, Mark Davies. They continued with wins over Cwmavon (29–22) and Gowerton (59–13), before suffering their first defeat at Aberavon Quins (8–44), but they were soon back to normal with a quarter-final Neath District Cup win over Neath Athletic by 59–0. Further wins over Cwmgrach (34–10), Bryncoch (34–0) and Tonna (35–19) saw them through to November. Two defeats then brought them back to earth, Bryncoch (3–59) and Glynneath (0–8).

They began December with another defeat, 3–42 at Cwmavon, but they completed the month with a double over Gowerton, 29–11. After a four-week gap, they suffered a surprise 7–10 defeat at Crynant and then comprehensively beat Bryncoch at home, 27–14, before meeting Seven Sisters in the semi-final of the H.G. Lewis Cup at Cefn Saeson. It was a nail-biting game that went to the wire. It was 19–19 at the end of normal time, then a penalty goal kicked by Michael Arnold in extra time divided the teams. Extraordinarily, the game was stopped as the officials realised that, as the Ferry had outscored Seven Sisters by two tries to one, they should have been declared winners at the end of normal time. So, once again, the Ferry were heading for a cup final, thanks to a try double from Phillip Knight and 3 penalties from Michael Arnold. It was a long wait into February for their next game, which turned into a complete whitewash as a weakened team lost 0–70 to Aberavon Quins – and lost their home record.

No games were played in March. Despite this, due to their earlier results they were declared top of the Neath & District League and started April with a league final at Resolven against Tonna, in which they were defending the title that they had won the previous year (beating Cimla 13–3). The game was a humdinger and the Ferry took charge from the start with a 10–0 lead after a try from centre Steve Williams was converted by Michael Arnold, who also kicked a penalty. Then back came Tonna to take the lead 17–10, but the Ferry were made of sterner stuff and they bounced back with a cracking try in the corner from wing Ryan Locke, which went unconverted. Then hero of the day, substitute hooker Gavin Jenkins (who had replaced his younger brother Chris Jenkins) stepped up to kick the winning penalty from 40 metres with less than five minutes to go. So Ferry retained their trophy and title of Neath & District League champions. Second row Jonathan Low was Man of the Match.

12.41 Presentation night: (left) Jonathan Low, Man of the Match; (right) Paul Hughes lifting the cup

Sadly, a weakened side then suffered yet another home defeat, 0–34 to Pyle, before they faced Glynneath in the H.G. Lewis Cup final at Glynneath, despite protests from Ferry officials. So the heat was on from the kick-off, and a ding-dong battle took place in dreadful conditions. All the Ferry had to show from a tough first half was a solitary penalty from Gavin Jenkins, so the half-time score was 3–7. To add to their woes Glynneath added another try to increase their lead to 3–12. Then, with some really good work by the whole team, they stormed back with tries from Jonny Low, converted by Michael

Arnold. The winning try from outside-half Paul Hughes went unconverted and at the final whistle Ferry were out on their feet after some 10–15 minutes of intense pressure on their line, but for the first time in the club's history Ferry lifted the cup, and therefore the Champion of Champions cup for a unique treble.

It would be nice if the season had ended there but they had one more game to play. Weakened by first team call ups and player unavailability they suffered a 15–38 away defeat at Seven Sisters.

Top try scorers for the season were Steve Williams and Craig Baggeridge, with 8 apiece. Top Quins scorer was Michael Arnold with 49 points, consisting of 2 tries, 12 conversions and 5 penalties. Top appearances went to scrum-half Jamie "Pickles" Nicholls, with 18, even though he had spent some time on the touchline due to a couple of knee injuries.

Awards

First XV Player of the Year was Andrew Chappell, player's Player of the Year was Jonathan Knight and Clubman of the Year was Mark Davies. Quins Player of the Year was Craig Baggeridge, and Quins player's Player of the Year was Andrew Pope.

The First XV received 6 try bonus points and 3 losing bonus points for a total of 47 points.

Youth rugby

There had been discussions between the club and Corus about amalgamating teams as neither squad had enough players to compete. An agreement was made, with the WRU's blessing, and the Ferry Steelers were born, to play in Division B of the Ospreys region. They were captained by Daniel Morgan and kicked off their new journey by winning the Neath & District ten-a-side tournament at Tonna. They beat Tonna, Resolven, Trebanos and finally Glynneath in the group games, and then defeated Abercrave 19–7 in the final. They scored 19 tries in the process. They then defeated Cwmavon 34–15 in their first full game, which they followed with wins over Maesteg, Baglan, Morriston and Vardre, and a draw with Abercrave. They were beaten in the Welsh Cup by Burry Port and also lost against Merthyr, Tonmawr and Trebanos.

Young scrum-half John Baptiste Bruzulier was selected to play in the Four Nations Schools tournament. He would go on to play for the Ferry Youth and in a few games for the First XV, before playing for Worcester and then for Clermont in France.

Youngster Andrew Collins netted the unique achievement of three Schoolboy Welsh caps, all at different sports – rugby, soccer and cricket.

12.42 2008/09

2009/10

As became the norm, a couple of friendlies were played in August at home, against an Aberavon Development XV (which Ferry lost heavily) and Pontardawe (a good win, 29–7). They were then invited for the Bank Holiday weekend to the annual Aberavon Green Stars sevens tournament at the Little Warren. Ferry managed to reach the quarter-finals before being knocked out.

The season began with a run of eight games in a very competitive National Division 3 SW:

- at home to Nantyfyllon with a 7–23 defeat
- a similar score line away in Seven Sisters, 3–23
- finally breaking the duck by beating Brynamman at home, 44–24
- only one more win in the next five games, at home to Cwmavon, 34–20
- they lost to Tondu (0–24) and Kenfig Hill (5–17) away
- to Skewen 13–20 at home
- and Bryncoch 23–28 in Ynysymaerdy Road.

They then faced local rivals Glynneath in Abernant Park in the National Plate competition, losing narrowly 8–19. Ironically, after a postponed away game at Ystalyfera, their next game was again in Abernant Park, but the weather took its toll and the game had to be abandoned with the home side leading 3–6.

The weather really affected the season as the next four league games all had to be postponed and only one game was played before the end of the year – a friendly club game against Tonmawr at home, which Ferry lost 8–11.

Captain
Andrew Chappell

Vice captain
Jonathan Knight

Coaches
Wayne Curtis
Mark Davies

Quins captain
Ryan Davies

Quins vice captain
Steve Williams

Seniors team manager
Phil McGuire

Youth captain
Ben Jones

First XV playing record
P 26
W 6
D 0
L 20
Points for 337
Points against 595

Quins playing record
P 14
W 5
D 1
L 8
Points for 203
Points against 284

It was well into January when league action recommenced at Ystalyfera, where the Ferry shipped 19 points without reply. They then lost the next two games: at home to Tondu (7–31); away at Tennant Park, 0–34 to Skewen.

Ferry ended February with a win, beating Kenfig Hill at home 25–11, and a loss, at home to Glynneath 3–29.

Out of four matches played in March, three away all ended in defeat (Cwmavon 5–30, Brynamman 5–19 and Bryncoch 15–17), the only win was at home against Maesteg Quins (14–13).

April was a busy month with league games: home to Ystalyfera (won 30–5) and Seven Sisters (lost 14–19) and away at Glynneath (lost 10–27), up the Llynfi valley against Nantyfyllon (lost 14–26) and at Maesteg Quins (lost 18–27)

The First XV gained 3 try bonus points and 3 losing bonus points, to end at 26 points – tries for 34, against 59. These results sadly meant that an eleventh league place relegated them to Division 4 SW.

Top scorer was Terry White with 39 points and Craig Baggeridge was top try scorer.

12.43 First XV 2009/10

Quins

The Quins competed in the newly formed Neath and Aberavon Combined Merit Table, but with nearly all of the area's second teams struggling for players they only managed to play nine games, winning only two at home (Seven Sisters 19–9 and Cwmgrach 14–12). They drew away at Cwmavon (17–17) and lost away at Aberavon Quins 3–26, Swansea Medicals 10–23, Bryncoch 7–17 and Glynneath 5–46, and at home to Tonna 5–31 and Skewen 0–22.

Quins did reach the semi–final of the H.G. Lewis Cup by beating Crynant 64–5 at home, only to lose 0–44 away at Seven Sisters in the semi.

They also squeezed in three friendlies, winning away at Tumble 44–5 and at home to Bryncoch 15–0, and losing away at Ystradgynlais 0–27.

Two players played in every Quins game, Phil McGuire and Gavin Jefford. Top scorer was Michael Arnold with 46 points in 6 games for 2 tries, 15 conversions, 1 penalty, 1 drop goal; Terry White also bagged 43 points with 4 tries, 10 conversions, 1 penalty; White was top try scorer, just behind were Nick Thomas and Julian Knight both on 3 each. The Ferry used a staggering sixty-four players through the season, fourteen on permit, and three from the youth! The team scored 39 tries through the season and ended fifth in the league with 23 tries and 14 points.

12.44 Quins 2010/11

Youth XV

The Ferry Steelers had a mixed bag of results. In the pre-season games they lost away at Tonmawr but won away at Neath Colts. They lost the first three games at home to Dunvant, Pontyclun and Bridgend Athletic, then won away at Vardre, before a six-match losing streak – at home to Trebanos, Morriston and Gorseinon, and away at Ystradgynlais, Gorseinon and Dunvant. They defeated Vardre again, this time at home 27-0, and also Skewen at home.

A hard-fought loss at home to Ystradgynlais was followed by a tight one at Taibach 9-10 and a heavy defeat at Kenfig Hill. They ended with a home league and cup double win over Tonmawr 17–10, before losing away at Ystradgynlais again, in an exciting 28-53 game.

These Youth players were learning and developing and becoming part of the club. Many would grace the First XV in a few years, such as dynamic centre Thomas Jones (who picked up a Boy's Clubs of Wales Under-16s cap this season), and young Ben Jones, who would also go on to play for Aberavon and Bridgend.

12.45 (left) Thomas Jones, Under-16s Boys Clubs of Wales cap; (right) Kieran Brennan, Under-11s WRU Schools cap

Mini section

The club's mini section did really well. The Under-7s, Under-9s and Under-10s all won their district tournaments. The Under-8s were runners up in the plate final. The Under-10s also won a regional invitational tournament in the South of England and the Under-8s were runners up in their group and the Under-7s and Under-9s were both third in their groups. The Under-9s were in their first season of tackling rugby and they started off with a bang by scoring 44 tries and only conceding 3 in their first three games. In celebration, sponsors Kiwi Sports presented them with new kit, which was handed over to them during a training session by rugby legend Jonah Lomu. They also played a game of tag rugby at half-time in the Liberty Stadium during a match between Ospreys and Harlequins, which they won. In fact, they maintained a 13-month unbeaten tag rugby record.

Three Ospreys players, Marty Holah, Jamie Nutbrown and Filo Tiatia, came along to coach the Under-7s, the Under-9s and the Under-10s.

The Under-10s were crowned Afan Nedd Champions after beating Neath Athletic in the semis and Bryncoch in the final. They were presented with a new kit by Shane Williams. During the juniors presentation night Callum Evans (prop) and Jake Hopson (flanker) of the Under-12s won the Player of the Year and player's Player of the Year respectively, a unique feat as they'd won the same awards for their soccer team, Neath Boys Club.

12.46 Under-12s 'The Pirates' 2010

FIRE: the club had to suspend its junior games during November as arsonists set fire to a portable storage unit containing the post pads and more. The unit burnt to the ground, causing about £1,500 of damage. A big effort had to be made to garner more sponsorship so that the club could purchase more equipment to be able to function again. A lot of hard work was put in by many former and current players, headed by Junior chairman Mark Davies, Paul Hughes, Adrian Griffiths, Andrew James, Lee Irvine, Leonne Daniels, Chris Jones, Gareth Baker and Wayne Curtis.

KEIRAN BRENNAN was capped for West Wales against East Wales Under-11s and was on the bench for the game against North Wales.

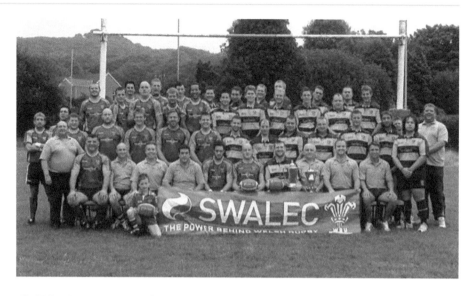

12.47 Senior squads 2009/10

12.48 Briton Ferry Rugby Club aerial view

Tour

The Club went over to Ireland again, but due to a lack of available players for the home team, the tour game against old friends Nenagh was cancelled.

2010/11

Wolfestone Translation, a leading language service, agree to sponsor a set of club jerseys and to contribute to the younger teams.

The new captain, fullback Gavin Puckett, had been with the club from a tender age. He took up the reins with a couple of friendlies: away at Alltwen (19–19) and at home to Aberavon Quins, losing 14–31.

A new league challenge in Division 4 SW began with home wins over Birchgrove (15–10) and Glyncorrwg (23–19) and an away win at Pontardawe (23–6). This was a reasonable start, but they did taste defeat in two away games in this sequence: at Vardre 27–38 and at Maesteg Quins 10–17.

In the first round of the National Bowl competition Ferry faced Crynant at home full of confidence, but came up short with a 25–30 defeat (Greg Davies, Aled Thomas and Dan Jones bagged 1 try each, Chris Jones kicked 10 points). So it was back to concentrating on the league for the rest of the season, starting with a couple of wins in October: over Pyle 27–12 at home; and at Ystradgynlais.

The weather took care of a couple of friendlies that had been organised as a break from the league, so only two games were played in November – both ending in defeat: at home to Maesteg Celtic 9–13; away at Porthcawl 12–19.

The bad weather continued to play havoc with fixtures throughout December and January. The only game that happened was away at Birchgrove. The conditions were horrendous, and resulted a Ferry defeat, 5–31.

Captain
Gavin Puckett

First XV playing record
P 25
W 11
D 1
L 13
Points for 612
Points against 560

Quins captain
Ryan Davies

Quins playing record
P 11
W 6
D 1
L 4
Points for 257
Points against 293

Youth coaches
Adrian Griffiths
Lee Irvine

February didn't fare much better. Again, only one game was played, away at Glyncorrwg, once more in dire conditions and ending in another defeat, 3–20. Bad weather did not suit the Ferry's style of play, which was a bit worrying for the club as their losing streak had lasted since 23 October.

After another defeat at Pyle (15–41) at the beginning of March, spring arrived and things started to pick up. There were two home wins, Pontardawe 32–29 and Ystradgynlais 42–6, and just one further defeat, at home to Vardre 10–29.

The Ferry went into the final period of the season with a bit more confidence, but this took a little knock when they lost 13–29 at Maesteg Celtic. A run of two wins at home, to Bridgend Sports 32–26 and Porthcawl 28–9, brought a smile back to everyone's faces. Smiles slipped after the return game at the Sports (22–29), then returned after a thrilling home and away double over Abercrave (35–22 and 33–30). Ferry concluded the season with an away defeat at Maesteg Quins (20–35) to finish fifth for the season.

12.49 Quins 2010/11 Neath & District Champions and Cup Winners and All-Winners Trophy holders

(back) Martyn Bate (coach/secretary), Adrian Kemeys, Dean Herman, Luke Williams, Michael Arnold, John Doyle, Danny Stephens, Julian Knight, Thomas Redmond, Liam Willis, Gavin Jenkins; (front) Jamie Hopkins, Calum Surman, Ashley Rosser, Jamie Nicholls, Gavin Jefford (captain), Andrew Chappell, Phil Knight, Chris Holloway, Greg Davies

But to see youth players (such as Callum Surman, Jamie Hopkins, Jonny Field, Thomas Jones, Thomas Redmond, Nathan Morgan, Cory Phillips,

Michael Owen, Jonny Doyle, Ben Jones, Liam Puckett, and Marcus and Scott Boobier) mixing in well with the senior players (such as Karl Lewis, Chris Jones, Ross Jones, Wayne Davies, Ryan Davies and skipper Puckett) was very encouraging for the Ferry's long-term future.

Quins

Under captain Ryan Davies the Quins continued to have mixed fortunes in the Neath and Aberavon Merit Table:

- losing away at Cwmgrach 17–27, Crynant 15–29 and Aberavon Green Stars 3–62
- drawing 19–19 at Bryncoch
- winning at home to Aberavon Green Stars 27–24, Neath Athletic 62–7, Cwmgrach 20–17 and Bryncoch 7–5.

They had a 57–0 away win at Neath Athletic, played as a double header. To fit in the H.G. Lewis Cup game and the final league game the district agreed to allow both games to hinge on the one result. Therefore Quins found themselves pitched into a semi-final the following week up in Seven Sisters. Sadly, they really struggled for players and took to the field with only thirteen men, which at one point dropped to eleven following injuries. Even first-aider and coach Martyn Bate went on the field, at 55-years-old. Inevitably, Quins lost heavily (5–78). But there was a twist to this tale.

Following a disagreement over player registration between the other semi-finalists, Cwmgrach and Glynneath, both clubs were expelled from the season's competition, meaning the Quins had to face Seven Sisters again in the final at Tonna. This time they were back to full strength and a cracking game ended at 25–25. The Ferry were deemed the winners as they headed the try count. What a turnaround.

There was also a bit of a story in the Merit Table. Quins ended up in the play-offs with Taibach. But Taibach failed to agree a date and then failed to fulfil the fixture, so the competition committee decided to award the title to the Ferry.

Quins took the treble after winning the Champions of Champions trophy outright.

Quins Player of the Year trophy was awarded to centre Terry White, Player's Player of the Year went to Gavin Jefford and Most Improved to Phil McGuire.

12.50 Quins, H.G. Lewis cup winners 2010/11

Youth

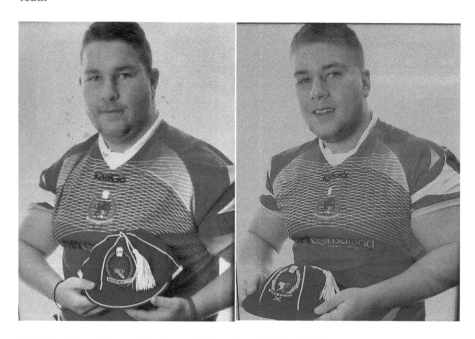

12.51 Scott and Marcus Boobier with their Boys Clubs of Wales caps

Under coaches Adrian Griffiths and Lee Irvine the Youth team competed in the Ospreys League Division B. They acquitted themselves well with home wins over South Wales Police, Kenfig Hill, Gorseinon and Morriston, and away wins at Dunvant, Taibach, Baglan, Kenfig Hill and Gorseinon. They drew at Morriston and only lost at home to fierce rivals Baglan.

Two games had to be abandoned due to a serious injury to an opposition player, one at Taibach and one at home to Kenfig Hill.

In cup competitions they beat Cwmavon away by 55–5, then Kenfig Hill away 28–9, before losing at home to Bonymaen. In the District Cup they lost away at Neath Athletic by 17–22.

Scott and Marcus Boobier made their family, and the club, proud by both gaining a Boys Clubs of Wales cap at Under-19s level.

Minis and Juniors

The Under-7s, Under-9s and Under-10s all won their District Tournament trophies. The Under-8s were runners-up in the plate competition.

In their age groups in the South of England regional invitational tournament the Under-10s won, the Under-8s were runners-up and the Under-7s and Under-9s were both third.

Former club prop forward CERI LOW succeeded in climbing Mount Kilimanjaro on Christmas day 2010 and he placed a Briton Ferry RFC tie at the summit. He also went to Mount Everest base camp in 2013.

12.52 Ceri Low at the top of Mount Kilimanjaro

2011/12

Captains
Daniel Jones
Aled Thomas

Vice captain
Jason Massey

Coaches
Craig Williams
Mark Morgan

Quins captain
Ryan Davies

Youth captain
Marcus Boobier

First XV playing record
P 26
W 8
D 0
L 18
Points for 349
Points against 707

Quins playing record
P 6
W 5
D 0
L 1
Points for 167
Points against 44

There was a great sense of anticipation at the beginning of the season as many of the previous season's youth players were now in the senior ranks, led by flanker Dan Jones, brother of Ben, but two pre-season defeats at home – to Bryncoch 12–21 and Aberdare 0–21 – showed there was work to do.

This was reinforced by a bad start to the league programme with four defeats in September: at home to Neath Athletic, 10–18; away to Trebanos (0–17), Maesteg Celtic (8–25) and Nantyfyllon (7–25).

Things did pick up a bit in October with wins over Birchgrove (26–19) and Resolven (28–21) at home. But away wins were still proving elusive, with loses at Pyle (27–34) and Cwmavon (5–55).

The Ferry did triumph in the SWALEC National Bowl competition by winning a thriller in round 1 against Baglan (36–35). But they lost to Glyncorrwg in the next round, at home 9–28.

Back to the league and further defeats up to the year end (at home to Trebanos 0–29 and away at Glyncorrwg 0–24). A 20–20 draw at home to Abercrave 20 was followed by a solitary win, 25–23 over Pontardawe.

January's results didn't improve as another two defeats (away at Neath Athletic 12–70 and at home to Maesteg Celtic 0–40) were followed by an 18–18 draw at home to Nantyfyllon.

Only one game was played in February, another loss, away at Birchgrove 7–20. Things were tough, and skipper Dan Jones, having had some injury issues, decided to join his local club Kenfig Hill. So fellow flanker Aled "Beany" Thomas took on the captaincy for the rest of the season.

Only two games were played in March, both at home. The first was a defeat to Pyle, 17–27. In the second they beat Cwmavon 24–20.

The run in to the end of the season was difficult. In the only home game they lost to Glyncorrwg, 3–15. After beating Pontardawe up in the Rec by 29–22, they lost the other games (Abercrave 12–20 and Resolven 14–40) to end the campaign tenth in the league.

Quins

This struggle had a knock-on effect on the Quins, who only managed to play five games all season under skipper Ryan Davies. It was strange times all around the district as many Second XVs were in a similar situation. A few teams agreed to help each other out, as with the Ferry, Bryncoch and Tonna.

The Neath and Aberavon Combined Merit Table failed and reverted back to the original districts.

Only two league games were played, both ending in good wins for the Ferry, First, they beat Neath Athletic away 67–5. Greg Sorokin and Jamie Hopkins (son of former second row/no.8 Steve) both got a hat trick of tries, Chris Burgess bagged a brace and Terry White, Gavin Jefford and Lee Hopkins added 1 a piece; Michael Arnold kicked 8 conversions. The second win was 44–10 against Tonna at home, in which youth players Sean Ford and Tom Williams each got two tries, while fellow youth players Thomas Redmond, Danny Stephens and Josh Mugford were also on the scoresheet, along with Terry White, while Mark Davies and Dean Herman added the extras.

The only other fixture played in 2011 was a friendly at home to Abercrave, which Quins won 26–0. Youth skipper Rhys Humphries was made captain for the day and celebrated with 2 tries, a further 2 were added by youth centre Thomas Jones (son of former prop Phil) and Gavin Jefford. Arnold converted three.

With the struggle to complete games, the district committee decided to abandon the league for the year, which meant the Champion of Champion's cup was not played. So the only action left in the new year was the H.G. Lewis Cup competition. This also turned into a strange old campaign.

Tonna failed to raise a side against Quins in the first round, so they were thrust yet again into the semi-finals without playing a game. They defeated

Cwmgrach 17–5 to reach the final in Seven Sisters against a strong Glynneath side and lost 13–24.

With there not being any league champions this year the Champion of Champions Cup was not played.

Youth

The youth side, led by flanker Rhys Humphries, only managed to play five league games. They beat Gorseinon, Morriston and Mumbles at home and lost away at Aberavon Green Stars and Mumbles. The away game at Gorseinon had to be abandoned due to injury.

In the local district cup, they reached the semi-finals by beating both local rivals, Skewen 35–7 and Bryncoch 26–10, and then lost to Pontardawe.

In the Welsh cup they were knocked out in the first round by a strong Kidwelly side, 10–21.

But they did manage a couple of friendlies, which resulted in wins over Nantyfyllon 45–10 and Bryntawe 17–5.

12.53 Under-9s 2011

2012/13

To steady the ship, stalwart outside-half Chris Jones took over as skipper, and former player Ceri Wyatt and ex-Neath captain Steve Martin as coaches. Tony Pickerell came on to the committee; he had played for the Ferry and Metal Box and was one of the club's qualified referees.

Ferry kicked off the pre-season with games at Swansea Uplands (lost 12–19) and at home to Aberavon Green Stars (also lost, 0–29). So the new coaches had some work to do.

The league campaign started with a great 33–17 win at Abercrave, before two heavy defeats to newly promoted sides. First, at home to Bryncethin 10–49. Then away at Penlan 5–54, when injury put them down to thirteen men. But they gritted their teeth and ended the first month with a 27–7 home win over Pyle.

In between the league games they were knocked out of the National Bowl competition, 14–22 at Birchgrove.

It was a sobering October, with three defeats in a row: away at Nantyfyllon 20–31 and Bridgend Sports 10–15; at home to Pontardawe 26–44.

November was also a grey month, with just two league games played and both lost: away at Cefn Cribbwr 18–22; at home to Cwmavon 6–12. The month ended with a friendly at home under lights, as hosts to a Fall Bay XV for the first time. It was an exciting game and Ferry won, 36–24.

Miserable weather kicked in again and only one game was played in December, in terrible conditions. Ferry were defeated, 0–31.

Captain
Chris Jones

Coaches
Ceri Wyatt
Steve Martin

First XV playing record
P 26
W 7
D 0
L 19
Points for 485
Points against 719

Quins captain
Gavin Jefford

Quins playing record
P 5
W 1
D 0
L 4
Points for 83
Points against 132

Youth captain
Ben Jones

In January, Ferry beat Abercrave at home 41–7 to complete a double and lost narrowly at Pyle, 20–21.

Results didn't improvement in February – with three defeats, at home to Birchgrove (6–42) and Nantyfyllon (8–13), and in an away thriller at Bryncethin (26–36).

March was a better month all round and Ferry managed wins out of two, both at home, over Bridgend Sports (17–12) and Cefn Cribbwr (46–19).

But the season ended badly in April with four defeats in five games. They lost at home to Glyncorrwg (5–14) and Penlan (14–57) and away at Cwmavon (29–57) and Pontardawe (10–33). The massive plus was a great 45–32 win at Birchgrove, which put them ninth in the league – a small improvement on the previous season.

Player of the year award went to outstanding centre Johnny Field.

Quins

The Quins were led by second row Gavin Jefford but they only managed to play four games as the district woes continued.

Quins lost away at Tonna (22–24) and Bryncoch (22–67), and at home to Glyncorrwg (15–22). They beat Neath Athletic at home, 24–19.

The Merit Table was cancelled for another season, so clubs who could regularly field a side looked at joining the Swansea and district leagues. This left the H.G. Lewis Cup as the only competition. Just four teams entered and the Ferry were drawn against their previous year's final opponents Glynneath, with Bryncoch pitted against Cimla in the other semi-final. Sadly, neither Ferry nor Cimla could field a side on the day, so the competition went to a straight shoot-out between Glynneath and Bryncoch, ironically played in the Ferry. Glynneath retained the cup for another year.

Youth, mini and juniors

Due to a lack of eligible players in the Youth age group, they disbanded – and weren't to recommence until 2016/17. But happily, the mini and junior sections were thriving under their excellent coaches and committee, headed up by Andrew James, Paul Hughes and chairman Mark Davies.

12.54 Under-14s 2013

2013/14 – 125TH

Captain
Andrew Chappell

Coaches
Ceri Wyatt
Steve Martin

Team manager
Gavin Puckett

First XV playing record
P 26
W 9
D 0
L 17
Points for 481
Points against 629

League playing record
P 22
W 8
L 14
Points for 354
Tries 48
Points against 534
Tries against 73

Youth skipper
Ben Jones

To begin celebrations for the club's 125th season, home games were arranged with Neath, Maesteg and Glynneath, who were also celebrating anniversaries. But, due to bad weather, all the games were cancelled. Even the rearranged matches couldn't take place. This was a great disappointment for the club, who wanted to celebrate in style.

Prop Andrew Chappell took over for his second stint as skipper.

In the pre-season friendlies Ferry were defeated away at Alltwen (17–29) and at home to Neath Athletic (17–34).

In the National Bowl competition they were given a bye in the first round and then lost 24–28 at home to a lively Cowbridge side. Ashleigh Rosser, Kevin Richards and John Doyle took 1 try apiece, Arnold converted all 3 and added 1 penalty.

The league campaign got under way in September with a 29–26 away win at Cefn Cribbwr (who were also celebrating 125 years). Jonathan Field scored the first try of the new season, Thomas Williams and Stephen Griffiths made 1 try each, Arnold converted 1 and kicked 4 penalties. This was followed by a 14–24 defeat at home to Pyle (Chris Burgess 1 try, Arnold 3 penalties) and a 22–26 away loss at Pontardawe (1 try each from Ashleigh Rosser, Bobby Davies and Jamie Hopkins, Arnold kicked 2 conversions and 1 penalty). The month ended with a 25–10 home win over promoted Cwmtwrch. Michael Arnold scored all the points with 1 try, 1 conversion and 6 penalties.

They had a short break from league action when Ferry faced a home fixture with Tredegar Ironsides and won 25–8 (J. Doyle, T. Williams, L. Morris, Andrew Thomas and A. Rosser scored tries, Chris Jones converted 2).

The club was featured in the new magazine, *The Rugby Club*.

Back in the league, away at Cwmavon, the Ferry lost 12–36 (C. Surman and A. Rosser 1 try each, Jones 1 conversion.) There were then two wins on the trot, followed by a 27–3 home win over promoted Betws (Ammanford) – G. Jefford, J. Hopkins, A. Rosser and Julian Knight tries, Arnold converted 2 and added 1 penalty – and away at Bridgend Sports (18–16). A red card for prop Wayne Curtis put them down to fourteen men, but Scott Boobier and Leigh Morris scored 1 try each, Michael Arnold converted 1 and added 2 penalties. Arnold's last penalty was from 30 metres out on the right-hand touchline against a powerful wind. Nobody at the ground thought he'd put it over to win the game in the very last play, except for Arnie. This gave the Ferry some hope for the season, but they couldn't back it up.

The First XV then lost the last three games of 2013: at home to Cwmgors (13–33, S. Boobier and J. Massey tries, Arnold 1 penalty); away at Nantyfyllon (10–52, A.Rosser 1 try, Arnold 1 penalty, J. Field 1 conversion); and away at Vardre (3–17, M. Arnold 1 penalty).

The Cwmgors game was the first use of the Ferry's new changing facilities, which had taken nearly ten years to design, to agree on the shared use with cricket, bowls and soccer (but Ferry Athletic dropped out prior to the build), to raise funds and to build. The three groups involved formed an association, with John Edwards as chair, David Hill as treasurer and Martyn Bate as secretary. Over £300,000 was raised and the building was opened by Briton Ferry Town Council members and dignitaries.

Two games were played in January: at home to Aberavon Green Stars (0–6) and away at Pyle (5–15, Aled Thomas try).

The club was invited to take part in the Scrum V studio audience in January. They were represented by coaches Ceri Wyatt and Steve Martin, skipper Andrew Chappell, long-serving player Gavin Puckett, cameraman Phil McGuire and long-standing committeemen Roger Amphlett, Kerry Frey and Martyn Bate.

12.55 Guests at the Scrum V studios
back row: Steve Martin, Roger Amphlett, Phil McGuire, Andrew Chappell; front row: Ceri Wyatt, Gavin Puckett, Kerry Frey and Martyn Bate

The one game in February was away at Cwmtwrch, which brought a welcome 30–25. Chris Jones, A. Field, G. Pryse, J. Hopkins and A. Rosser scored tries, Arnold added 1 conversion and 1 penalty in difficult conditions.

The Ferry struggled for results in March and only won two games out of five. They beat Pontardawe 26–10 at home (Bobby Davies, T. Williams, M. Boobier and C. Surman tries, Arnold 3 conversions) and Betws 25–10 away (tries by L. Morris, C. Surman and Arnold, who also kicked 2 conversions and 2 penalties). They lost at home to Cwmavon 12–17 (A. Chappell and Julian Knight tries, Arnold 1 conversion), to Cefn Cribbwr (13–20, A. Rosser and M. Boobier tries, Arnold 1 penalty) and to Bridgend Sports (17–43, C. Surman and Bobby Davies tries, Arnold 2 conversions, 1 penalty).

The season ended with mixed fortunes. In a 25–17 home win over Nantyfyllon, Andrew Kreischer, A. Rosser and Andrew Thomas all scored 1 try, and Arnold kicked 1 penalty and added 1 neat drop goal. This was followed by three straight defeats: at home to Vardre (12–57, Ross Jones 1 try, Shane Williams 1 try, Arnold 1 conversion); a midweek game away at Cwmgors (0–37); and away at Aberavon Green Stars (20–29, A. Chappell, J. Griffiths and A. Rosser tries, C. Jones 1 conversion, 1 penalty).

The Ferry ended the season in a familiar ninth position in the league.

Quins, youth

Disappointingly, there were no Quins or Youth games during the season due to a lack of age-grade players and a lack of player commitment at senior level, which was a sad way to mark 125 years of playing history.

Tour

The club nominated to tour Ireland and visit old friends Nenagh again, but they failed to raise a side and no game was played.

125th dinner

The celebratory dinner in honour of this milestone took place at the Tower Hotel on Friday 4 April 2014. A lavish spread, catered by former player and long-time sponsor Mr Clive Hopkins, was enjoyed by over 200 guests. The top table included WRU representatives David Pickering, Dennis Gethin and A.K Jones, Welsh international David Morris, club president of 36 years Mr. Phil Langstone, chairman Mr David Parker (who was also MC for the night), secretary Mr Kerry Frey and treasurer Mr Phil Thomas (both in their twelfth year in these roles), former chairman and life member Mr Roger Amphlett, Quins and fixture secretary Mr Martyn Bate. Guest of honour was the great Gareth Edwards CBE.!

12.56 Top table at the 125th anniversary dinner, Tower Hotel

The message to all was that the club would stick out its chin, take whatever comes and would come back stronger for the next 125 years, given the support of the likes of long-standing and loyal committeemen Malcolm Edwards, Brian Evans, Roger Amphlett, Kerry Frey and Martyn Bate, and of relative new boys Rob Woodhouse, Wayne Curtis, Phil Thomas and Jonny and Jason Jones.

12.57 Opening of the new changing facility at Ynysymaerdy Road complex 22 November 2013
Martyn Bate (secretary BFTSA). Michael Hiorns (M. Hiorns Building Contractor Ltd). Michael Dean (Dean and Thomas Ltd civil engineers)

12.58 Three future first teamers: Taran Jones, Morgan Jones and Kealan Jones in 2010

Past, present and future players, coaches and committee will all help in their own way to make BRITON FERRY RUGBY FOOTBALL CLUB **great again.**

Lightning Source UK Ltd.
Milton Keynes UK
UKHW022008121220
374981UK00001B/2